P9-AOP-383

Who Will Benefit from Psychotherapy?

Who Will Benefit from Psychotherapy?

Predicting Therapeutic Outcomes

LESTER LUBORSKY, Ph.D.
PAUL CRITS-CHRISTOPH, Ph.D.
JIM MINTZ, Ph.D.
ARTHUR AUERBACH, M.D.

Basic Books, Inc., Publishers   *New York*

Excerpts from the article: Crits-Christoph, P., & Luborsky, L. The CCRT as a measure of outcome in psychoanalytic psychotherapy. In Ghannam, J. (Ed.), *Psychoanalytic Research Methods*, New York: Guilford Press, (in press). With permission of Guilford Press.

Excerpts from the article: Luborsky, L., McLellan, A. T., Woody, G. E., O'Brien, C. P., & Auerbach, A. (1985). Therapist success and its determinants. *Archives of General Psychiatry, 42,* 602–611. With permission of the journal.

Excerpts from Table 2 in an article by Jim Mintz, "The role of the therapist in assessing psychotherapy outcome." In Gurman, A., & Razin, A., (Eds.), Effective psychotherapy: A handbook of research (1977), Elmsford, N.Y.: Pergamon Press, Inc. With permission of Pergamon Press.

Excerpts from the article: Luborsky, L., & McLellan, A. T. (1980–81). A sound mind in a sound body: To what extent do they go together before and after psychotherapy? *International Journal of Psychiatry in Medicine, 10,* 121–131. With permission of the journal.

Excerpts from the article: Mintz, J., Luborsky, L., & Christoph, P. (1979). Measuring the outcomes of psychotherapy: Findings of the Penn psychotherapy project. *Journal of Consulting and Clinical Psychology, 47,* 319–334. With permission of the American Psychological Association, Inc.

Excerpts from the article: Mintz, J., What is "success" in psychotherapy? *Journal of Abnormal Psychology,* (1972) *80,* 11–19. With permission of the American Psychological Association, Inc.

Excerpts from the article: Auerbach, A. H., Luborsky, L., & Johnson, M. (1972). Clinicians' predictions of psychotherapy outcome: A trial of a prognostic index. *American Journal of Psychiatry, 128,* 830–835. Copyright 1972 by the American Psychiatric Association, Inc. Reprinted by permission.

Library of Congress Cataloging-in-Publication Data

Who will benefit from psychotherapy?

   Bibliography: p.
   Includes index.
   1. Psychotherapy— Evaluation.   2. Penn Psychotherapy
Project.   3. Mental illness—Prognosis.   I. Luborsky,
Lester, 1920–   .   [DNLM: 1. Penn Psychotherapy
Project.   2. Outcome and Assessment (Health
Care)—methods   3. Prognosis.   4. Psychotherapy.
WM 420 W628]
RC480.5.W416   1988   616.89'14   88–47762
ISBN   0–465–09189–X

Copyright © 1988 by Lester Luborsky, Ph.D.
Printed in the United States of America
Designed by Vincent Torre
88 89 90 91 RRD 9 8 7 6 5 4 3 2 1

CONTENTS

CONCLUSIONS

How the Penn Psychotherapy Project Measures Up

PENN PSYCHOTHERAPY
PROJECT STAFF

Keith J. Alexander, M.A. Temple University

Leslie Alexander, Ph.D. Bryn Mawr College

Arthur Auerbach, M.D.* University of Pennsylvania

Henry Bachrach, Ph.D.* St. Vincent Hospital, New York City

Jacques Barber, Ph.D. University of Pennsylvania

John Cacciola, M.A. University of Pennsylvania

Marjorie Cohen, M.A.* University of Pennsylvania

Andrew Cooper, Ph.D. Temple University

Paul Crits-Christoph, Ph.D.* University of Pennsylvania

Amy Demorest, Ph.D. Swarthmore College

Deborah Fried, M.D. Yale University

Scott Friedman, Ph.D. Hahnemann University

Marilyn Johnson, Ph.D.* Rush University

Lester Luborsky, Ph.D.* University of Pennsylvania

David Mark, Ph.D. Philadelphia VA Medical Center

A. Thomas McLellan, Ph.D. University of Pennsylvania and Philadelphia VA Medical Center

James Mellon, B.A. University of Pennsylvania

Jim Mintz, Ph.D.* University of California at Los Angeles

Charles O'Brien, M.D., Ph.D. University of Pennsylvania and Philadelphia VA Medical Center

Carol Popp, M.D., Ph.D. University of Pennsylvania

Martin E. P. Seligman, Ph.D. University of Pennsylvania

Barton Singer, Ph.D. Rutgers Medical School

Robert Toborowsky, M.D. University of Pennsylvania

Thomas Todd, Ph.D.* Illinois School of Professional Psychology

George Woody, M.D. University of Pennsylvania and Philadelphia VA Medical Center

*Senior full-time project staff

THE CLINICAL VIEW

Otto Kernberg

THIS BOOK marks a crucial moment in the history of empirical research on psychoanalytic psychotherapy. The carefully designed and logically connected studies of the psychotherapeutic process so elegantly integrated here represent the culmination of a "third generation" of psychotherapy research.

The first generation, perhaps best represented by the long-term psychotherapy research project of the Menninger Foundation (to which Lester Luborsky himself contributed so importantly), was a major effort to capture the essential attributes of the patient, the therapist and his technique, the psychosocial environment surrounding the treatment, and the treatment process itself. The objective was to study the isolated and combined influence of all these features on treatment outcome. In part because of the enormous methodological complications uncovered by that particular study—and by other naturalistic studies of long-term psychotherapy—the field of psychotherapy research veered, in a "second generation," into the direction of empirical research on brief rather than long-term psychotherapy. This research was often carried out under conditions and with designs that varied significantly from the ordinary psychotherapeutic practice of the experienced psychotherapist and psychoanalyst. For a time, it seemed as if little of true importance for a next generation of studies of long-term psychotherapy would emerge from these early empirical efforts in studying short-term psychotherapy.

Against this background, it was Lester Luborsky's first great achievement to demonstrate that outcome measures (that is, degrees of improvement) were a relatively easy problem to solve: his health-sickness rating scale proved to be of impressive practical usefulness in evaluating outcome of long-term psychotherapy during which complex intrapsychic change was attempted. Later, together with the other members of the Penn Psychotherapy Project, he was able to carry out the most essential and urgent

Associate Chairman and Medical Director, The New York Hospital-Cornell Medical Center, Westchester Division; Professor of Psychiatry, Cornell University Medical College; Training and Supervising Analyst, Columbia University Center for Psychoanalytic Training and Research.

current task of psychotherapy research: to study the psychotherapeutic process itself.

In changing the focus from outcome to process, Luborsky and his co-workers not only influenced the field of psychotherapy research generally, but managed to operationalize the central psychoanalytic concepts of transference, transference interpretation, and insight, and to relate measures of these variables to outcome. These operational measures start from the clinical assumption that, regardless of the type of psychopathology, the effectiveness of psychoanalytic psychotherapy would depend on the patient's and the therapist's capacity to establish a working relationship within which the patient's transference could unfold, be understood and interpreted, and his insight increase. Luborsky and his co-workers have been able to design and successfully test a measure of the therapeutic alliance, and of the transference.

The extent to which the therapist is able to establish and maintain a therapeutic alliance in the context of his consistent effort to highlight, diagnose, and interpret the patient's transferences would seem an important, process-based predictor of a positive treatment outcome. One theoretical problem, however, as Luborsky himself points out, is the difficulty in sorting out the therapeutic alliance from the positive transference. To put it differently, the capacity to establish a therapeutic alliance is itself based on the availability of the patient's capacity for basic trust derived from very early experiences, experiences that constitute the precondition for the capacity to establish a positive transference as well. To talk about a realistic, positive therapeutic alliance or working relationship without considering its unconscious (transferential) roots would be naive.

A related problem is the practical one of differentiating the therapeutic alliance from the positive transference. Luborsky has dealt with this problem by distinguishing between two types of helping alliance: "type one" is characterized by the patient who expects the therapist to be supportive and helpful; "type two," by the patient who understands that he and the therapist working together are aiming to help him achieve a better understanding and resolution of his conflicts. This "type two" would reflect the therapeutic alliance in a more narrow sense.

In practice, the two types of helping alliances were found to be intimately related, and it may well be that the practical problem of sorting out the therapeutic alliance from the positive transference is still unresolved. What is interesting, however, is the consistent finding of the predictive value of a positive helping relationship for the outcome of psychotherapy, a finding that may be related to Robert Wallerstein's recent emphasis on the importance of the supportive elements in all psychoanalytically based psychotherapies, including psychoanalysis. It is possible, however, that another, still open, relevant issue here is the nature of the patient's psychopathology, particularly the severity of his personality disorder and its implications for the development of both transference and therapeutic alliance.

I have found the early interpretation of a predominantly negative transference of patients with borderline personality organization is a crucial precondition for the development of the therapeutic alliance. Thus, perhaps in contrast to what might be observed in better-functioning patients, consistent interpretation of negative transference may overshadow the development of a helping alliance, which would emerge only in later stages of the treatment, following rather than serving as a precondition for interpreting and resolving the negative transference. The Luborsky team's findings that the type two helping alliance increases late in the treatment in patients with better outcome, in contrast to a lack of increase in the type one helping alliance in patients with better outcome, may reflect this gradual increase in the specific aspects of the therapeutic alliance that can be differentiated from the positive transference.

The development of the concept of the core conflictual relationship theme (CCRT) is perhaps the most original and far-reaching contribution that Luborsky has made to the field of psychotherapy research. Fully aware of the relatively general and nonspecific nature of the helping alliance as a relationship factor, he moved on to clarify the specific transference developments in psychoanalytic psychotherapy. Luborsky developed an empirical frame that permits testing individualized transferences, and evaluating the therapist's capacity to become aware of these and to formulate them correctly in his interpretive interventions. The core conflictual relationship theme method is, in the authors' words, "a system to guide clinical judgments of the content of the central relationship patterns in psychotherapy sessions."

This book presents a comprehensive and clear description of this methodology, one that is, in my view, the most sophisticated empirical approach now available to diagnose dominant transferences in individual psychotherapy sessions. Implicit in this methodology is the assumption that the transference is the reactivation in the here-and-now of past internalized object relations.

Within this contemporary approach to the transference, which, as I see it, combines an ego psychology with an object relations theory framework, unconscious intrapsychic conflicts always involve the relationship of an aspect of the self relating to a significant object. Unconscious intrapsychic conflicts are never simply between impulse and defense; rather, the drive derivative finds expression through a certain internalized object relation, and the defense, too, is reflected by a certain internalized object relation. The analysis of past internalized object relations in the transference constitutes, at the same time, the analysis of the constituent structures of ego, superego, and id and their intra- and interstructural conflicts. The major task in psychoanalysis and psychoanalytic psychotherapy is to bring the unconscious transference meanings in the here-and-now into full consciousness by means of interpretation. This is the first stage in analyzing the relation between the unconscious present and the unconscious past.

Luborsky's methodology permits rating the patient's narrative episodes about relationships that include (a) the patient's principal wishes, needs, or intentions toward another person, (b) the responses of another person, and (c) the responses to that other person. This interactional frame for the definition of each relationship episode within the patient's narrative, carefully designed and successfully tested in a number of interconnected research efforts summarized and integrated in this book, provided Luborsky and his team with a powerful instrument to diagnose dominant themes in the transference. By the same token, their method permits them to evaluate the therapist's skills in diagnosing central transference patterns as they emerge in these core conflictual relationship themes in his interpretive interventions.

In their summary of the reliability and validity of their methodology, the authors report that the congruence of the core conflictual relationship theme-pattern and the content of interpretations correlates significantly with outcome of psychotherapy. In addition, changes during psychotherapy in the pervasiveness of relationship conflicts as measured by this method correlated significantly with changes in psychotherapy outcome. And the team convincingly shows how the characteristics of core conflictual relationship themes, their consistency throughout the treatment, their appearance in the relationship of the patient with the therapist, their becoming the content of the therapist's interpretive work, and their change throughout time as a predictor of outcome all fit with Freud's definition of the transference. Here, at last, we have an elegant and reliable measure that permits an empirical validation of the subtle and complex concepts of transference, its resolution, and its implication for treatment outcome.

A few other questions: How important are the characteristics of the patient before entering psychotherapy in determining the outcome of the treatment? How important are the therapist's experience, skill, personal characteristics, and his application of a specific technique in contrast to his general emotional availability? How powerful are the pretreatment predictors in contrast to the importance of process variables, and to what extent may the predictive value of process variables be differentiated from the potential contamination of such predictions by early manifestations of outcome (improvement)? The reader will here find not only a comprehensive review of the predictive value of all these features of the psychotherapeutic process, and of the currently available empirical evidence to respond to these questions, but a critical analysis of what we now know on the basis of Luborsky and his team's research and their objective and fair assessment of their findings in the light of other available evidence.

While it would be incorrect to assume that Luborsky's contributions have definitely closed the gap between clinical approaches to psychoanalysis and psychotherapy, on the one hand, and empirical research on psychotherapy on the other, with this work a point has been reached at which the findings of the researcher meaningfully resonate with the theoretical assumptions and clinical experience of the sophisticated therapist engaged in long-term psychoanalytic psychotherapy. The authors have dared to approach central and complex concepts and issues in evaluating the psychotherapeutic process, and their success may well inaugurate an entirely new phase of psychotherapy research, one in which clinicians and researchers may finally be able to collaborate in accelerating significantly the development of knowledge in psychoanalytic psychotherapy and clinical psychoanalysis. I need hardly add that clinicians will find this work most useful. It provides solid evidence of the value of the prognostic indicators established in the therapist's initial evaluation of the patient, as well as during the treatment itself.

THE RESEARCH PERSPECTIVE

Morris Parloff

AS a self-professed student of the field of psychotherapy research and as a self-confessed admirer of the work of each of the authors, I was quite familiar with the individual studies they had published earlier. When I was invited to write this foreword I frankly anticipated that much of the content of the volume would be familiar. I thought that it would consist of a medley of the authors' previous articles—their "golden oldies"—strung together by a lively patter leading to the repetitive transition phrase: "And then we wrote . . ."

I accepted this honorific chore long in advance of seeing the book itself. I was, therefore, delighted, upon the arrival of the manuscript, to find that the opus was far broader than I had expected. Directed to both the researcher and the practitioner, the book includes an integrated and updated review of the authors' own psychodynamically oriented research program and places it firmly in the context of the larger body of evidence developed by other investigators.

The specific questions addressed, concerning the essential elements of psychotherapy, were stimulated and provoked not only by the authors' own findings but by those of independent researchers. In addition, the volume contains a review and analysis of pertinent research that can only be described as majestic in scope.

The special value of a programmatic research report, in contrast to the merits of a publication based on a single study, becomes clearly evident. The investigators had the rare luxury of time and opportunity to follow up and explore the major clinical questions that inevitably were raised by their own previous research. Thus, the book permits the reader to glimpse the evolution of the authors' conceptualizations and interest in various issues as they modified their formulations and questions over the span of two decades.

With the luminosity of hindsight, this retrospective overview of a research program was able not only to discern its own "history" more clearly

Professor of Psychiatry, Georgetown University Medical School and Adjunct Professor of Psychology, American University but also to reanalyze some of its own data and those of other investigators. Reanalyses and new syntheses of old research evidence were made in the context of new evidence and new methods of statistical analysis that had become available since the publication of the original papers. Such a strategy permits one to stand on one's own shoulders while getting a "leg up" from others.

I wish to linger a moment over the unique benefits of the program review. Most psychotherapy investigators have conceded that despite stringency of research design and meticulousness of implementation, no individual study has ever been credited with fully answering any clinically interesting question. Similarly, single studies have not convincingly differentiated promising avenues from blind alleys.

For a variety of logically supportable reasons, it is highly unlikely that a single study can ever provide evidence that will be accepted as definitive, powerful, or even unambiguous. From the researchers' vantage point, our best single efforts fail either to open new doors or to close old ones. In contrast, this report of cumulative research findings does provide a compelling consensus of converging evidence.

Luborsky and his colleagues, being good researchers, have adhered to sound evidentiary approaches that will be congenial to fellow investigators. The researcher will be attracted by such features as the discussion of the authors' development of reliable measures of key concepts of psychotherapy and the critical reviews of evidence regarding the independent and interactive roles of patients, therapists, patient-therapist matches, and therapeutic alliances. The authors also suggest directions for future research.

I recognize that evidence based on statistics derived from rigorously designed research does not automatically impress the practitioner. The observation that the findings of experimental research impact but modestly, if at all, on the psychodynamically oriented therapist is by now commonplace. I believe, however, that the clinical questions addressed here and the pragmatic answers given may make the book credible and useful to the clinician-practitioner as well as to the researcher.

I also believe that the practitioner will be particularly interested in the confirmatory evidence regarding psychodynamic conceptions of basic curative factors, the description of process measures that practitioners can easily use in their practice, and the presentation of findings concerning clinical factors that influence the outcomes of psychotherapy. Should my prediction of clinicians' interest be fulfilled—even in part—then the authors' contribution will be truly unique.

The work of these clinician-researchers should help dispel the long-standing and carefully nurtured myth that the value and belief systems of experimental researchers and practitioners are separated by an unbridgeable chasm. Adherents of the two professions have been characterized as relentlessly and differentially advocating such counterposed values as: symbols versus facts, freedom versus determinism, meaning versus events, intuition versus logic, spontaneity versus standardization, and understanding versus measurement. This volume demonstrates that both sets of values can be worked with by the sophisticated researcher-clinician, even though complete reconciliation remains difficult.

Finally, I dimly recall that at some point during my youth (a number of weeks ago) I brashly advised researchers that their continued efforts to mine old research in the hope of finding some overlooked nuggets of information would be nugatory. More specifically, I suggested that in view of flagrant flaws and limitations old psychotherapy research studies, unlike old wines, did not improve with age. In the light of what the Luborsky group has now presented, however, I am willing to modify my statement. Clearly, they have demonstrated that old research, like old wine, can add much to the flavor of the ragout.

PREFACE

WHEN a patient and therapist meet for psychotherapy, how predictable are the patient's ultimate benefits? Most therapists are certain that psychotherapy is not just an unpredictable adventure. Yet after 75 years of formal psychotherapy practice, the tested knowledge when we began the Penn Psychotherapy Project was still unable to affect clinical practice (Luborsky, 1969). Little was known about the pretreatment qualities of the patients who are most likely to benefit, the therapists who are most facilitating, and the best matches of patients and therapists. Little was known of the during-treatment qualities of the patient-therapist interactions that are most helpful. Although the guidelines clinical wisdom offered therapists contained useful observations, not many had been adequately tested. It is the purpose of the Penn project and of this book to review the tested knowledge about these topics and to add more. This work should make it more necessary for practicing psychotherapists to learn more from the offerings of psychotherapy research (Cohen, Sargent, & Sechrest, 1982).

We hoped in the Penn project to identify the factors that influence the outcomes of psychotherapy, to evaluate the success of our predictions, and ultimately to use the knowledge of the predictive measures to better understand the nature of psychodynamic psychotherapy.

We were most interested in the form of treatment called most broadly psychodynamic psychotherapy—also called in this book psychoanalytic or psychoanalytically oriented psychotherapy—because it was and still is the most common type of outpatient psychotherapy provided in private practice and clinic settings (Feldman et al., 1958); in Henry, Sims, and Spray (1973) the therapists surveyed included not only psychiatrists but psychoanalysts, clinical psychologists, and social workers. Seventy-one percent of the 3,400 therapists considered themselves to have some form of psychoanalytic orientation as their main mode of treatment.

Despite rumors of its demise, evidence is plentiful that the preference for the psychodynamic orientation not only survives but prospers. A more recent report from a national survey of clinical psychologists (Norcross, Prochaska, & Gallager, 1987) found that 21% of the sample preferred the "psychodynamic orientation"—a term reflecting a spectrum of orientations that have been influenced mostly by the psychoanalytic one. Second most popular to eclecticism, this psychodynamic orientation among clinical psychologists actually increased from 16% to 30% in the 8 years preceding the survey. These researchers also noted that the preference for the psychodynamic approach is found to be even larger among clinical practitioners, as opposed to academician-researchers.

At least among private psychiatric practitioners, individual psychotherapy is the most prevalent form of treatment offered to patients. Marmor's (1975) study of a national sample of psychiatrists who spent more than 15 hours a week in direct patient contact in their private offices showed that individual psychotherapy is the preferred mode, the "cornerstone of practice." But despite the prevalence of the forms of psychoanalytically oriented psychotherapy, a commensurate amount of research has not been devoted to it (Luborsky & Spence, 1978). In contrast, a huge amount of research has been provided for the various behavior therapies.

Goals of the Research

One purpose of our research was to determine the *pretreatment* predictive factors in the patient and therapist (Project A of this book). Anyone who tries to rely on the large assortment of clinical and quantitative evaluation studies risks getting misled by a maze of diverse directions, often displayed as if they were the only signposts. Through our project we have reexamined these directions in order to tell how much can be predicted and therefore which qualities of the patient and therapist are important to consider in doing the prediction. We also hope that our studies will lead to better bases for matching patients with therapists and patients with treatments. Our other purpose was to determine the predictive factors *within the treatment,* especially in the early sessions (Project B of the book). Finding predictive factors within the treatment is not as difficult as finding the pretreatment predictive factors. After all, once the treatment is launched it may be easier to make predictions about its outcome because predictions can be based on samples of the actual interaction of the patient and therapist and not just on the anticipated interaction. The within-treatment predictive factors, once located, should help provide a better understanding of the curative factors in psychotherapy.

The Plan of the Book

This book will interest three types of readers: those who are practitioners of psychotherapy, those with a research interest in the topic, and those with both clinical and research interests. Most of the book should be understandable to clinical readers; only a few sections on the quantitative results might be less relevant to their interests.

The first part of the book, known as "Project A," is largely devoted to the Penn Psychotherapy Project as it was first conceived. Chapter 1 lays out the plan for the project; chapter 3 reports on how much the patients benefited in comparison with those in similar studies, and chapter 8 discusses how and how well these benefits could be predicted.

The second part of the book reports on "Project B," which is aimed at locating predictive factors within the early sessions of the treatment. It begins with a chapter (9) on our attempts to predict outcomes from the early sessions by conventional types of ratings, and it ends with a set of chapters on new directions for the study of the predictive factors within the treatment. Each of these chapters takes up a new operational method for measuring a curative factor within the treatment that is predictive of its outcome. Project B, therefore, offers a set of measures of the key concepts of psychoanalytic psychotherapy. This part of the book is the most recent line of development of the Penn Psychotherapy Project and will be most novel to most readers.

The book winds up with a massive chapter summarizing all the findings in the Penn study and comparing them with the findings of most other predictive studies of the outcomes of psychotherapy.

ACKNOWLEDGMENTS: THE BASICS OF THIS BOOK'S BEING

MY 13 Kansas years were fat years, the last 7 even more than the first ones. By the end of my stay at the Menninger Foundation in 1959, I had benefited from it with the best kinds of outcomes: I had come through psychoanalytic training and had become professionally formed by both the "free" and the colleagial associations.

Yet my parting from the foundation was premature in one important way: My 7-year participation in a major study of the outcomes of psychotherapy was interrupted. The Menninger Foundation Psychotherapy Research Project was then in midcourse, and I had wanted to see it through to completion. As compensation, though, I had learned the strengths and shortcomings of that project, and I had become determined that when I had an opportunity, I would try in a new project to preserve the strengths and to remedy the weaknesses of the Menninger Foundation project.

In 1968 the main chance to carry forward the Menninger Foundation Psychotherapy Research Project's type of research came through a 5-year National Institute of Mental Health research grant. It enabled our research team to assemble a major psychotherapy database that, after years of data analyses, led to this book and seems likely to continue to lead to many more analyses by us and others.

The research opportunity began to grow into a feasible design after I was transplanted into an environment at the University of Pennsylvania's Department of Psychiatry that was rich in people with interest and experience in psychotherapy research. Some of them made up the necessary "critical mass" of collaborating and contributing investigators that constitutes one of the preconditions to the planning and carrying out of a large-scale project. As the new project was being planned, the Fiske, Cartwright, and Kirtner (1964) report from the University of Chicago Psychotherapy Research Project appeared with its news of what they presented as largely unsuccessful results in the prediction of psychotherapy outcomes. The Chicago results seemed to fly in the face of my clinical and research experiences. I concluded that they had not done the project in the same way I would have and their data needed to be reanalyzed in other terms.

Since our past presages our present, I want to retrace the Penn Psychotherapy Research Project's oldest roots. These drew on the supportive associations with Robert Wallerstein, Lewis Robbins, Gardner Murphy, and Helen Sargent, with whom I shared from 1954 to 1960 the beginnings and middle stages of the Menninger Foundation's Psychotherapy Research Project. That project, first comprehensively reported by Kernberg et al. (1972), became the impetus, model, and foil in shaping the Penn Psychotherapy Research Project.

The Menninger Psychotherapy Project itself, in turn, had grown out of a research group that flourished from 1949 to 1953. This earlier group was assembled by Paul Bergman and headed by Benjamin Rubinstein. It also included Gerald Aronson, Michelina Fabian, Robert Holt, Helmuth Kaiser, Gardner Murphy, Donald Watterson, and myself. The group's most lasting achievement was the construction of the Health-Sickness Rating Scale (Luborsky, 1962a), which played a helpful role in the Menninger Psychotherapy Project as well as in the Penn Psychotherapy Project and others.

Even earlier, beginning in 1947 at the Menninger Foundation, Robert Holt and I were engaged in a study on the selection of physicians for training in psychiatry, a project begun by David Rapaport when he was head of the research department at the Menninger Foundation (Holt & Luborsky, 1958a, 1958b). Our aim was to find ways to predict which physicians would make good psychiatrists. (Predictive studies appear to possess a potent addictive potential!) In that setting and in that era it was virtually the same question as "Who will make a good psychoanalytic psychotherapist?" In that study we had to cope with some of the same prediction and criterion problems as in the later Menninger and Penn psychotherapy projects.

Psychoanalytic psychotherapy was a consistent interest in my research and practice for most of my career. That treatment was selected for the research in the Menninger Foundation Psychotherapy Research Project (Kernberg et al., 1972; Horwitz, 1974; Appelbaum, 1977; Wallerstein, 1986). Psychoanalytic psychotherapy was also the form that the Penn Psychotherapy Research Group as well as the Penn Department of Psychiatry's Outpatient Clinic staff was most at home with; the clinic was selected as the obvious main site for the research. The particular designation "supportive-expressive psychotherapy" and many of its techniques were the basis for my manual (Luborsky, 1984) and were derived from this prominent form of psychotherapy practiced at the Menninger Foundation from the 1940s onward.

The Penn Psychotherapy Research Project has profited from the participation of many persistent psychotherapy researchers who have gone on to illustrious careers in this field. The initial 5-year grant was awarded to me with Arthur Auerbach as co-principal investigator. The first research team assembled to collect the data stayed together well beyond the 5 data-collecting years. Some are still with me at the University of Pennsylvania, and others, now elsewhere, have remained collaborative. First Jim Mintz and later Thomas C. Todd, Jr., joined us; both had recently completed the New York University clinical psychology Ph.D. program, where they had the good fortune to work with Jacob Cohen and Robert Holt. Then Henry Bachrach joined us after completing a thesis in psychotherapy research at the University of Chicago. The early group was completed by the addition of Paul Crits-Christoph and Marjorie Cohen.

In the past decade our ongoing collaboration with members of the Drug Dependence Treatment Unit of the Philadelphia VA, A. Thomas McLellan and George Woody, has produced a fount of publications. A few examples of the topics of the collaborations were: a manual-guided comparison of the relative benefits of supportive-expressive psychotherapy versus cognitive-behavioral psychotherapy versus drug counseling, a study of the recognizability of different forms of psychotherapy, studies of conformity to the treatment recommendations in manuals, and studies of the relative success of different therapists with their patients. In the past decade another mutually generative collaboration has sprung up with Martin E. P. Seligman and his group in the Department of Psychology at the University of Pennsylvania. Its contributions relate explanatory style to helplessness in depressed psychotherapy-treated and untreated patients and subjects.

Since 1983 a collaboration has flourished with the research group on conscious and unconscious mental processes directed by Mardi Horowitz at the University of California, San Francisco (sponsored by the John D. and Catherine T. MacArthur Foundation). The research that has been stimulated and supported was on the development of relationship pattern measures (involving the Core Conflictual Relationship and Relationship Anecdotes Paradigms measures) and methods of identifying degrees of awareness within these patterns. Since 1980 an active exchange and collaboration has been under way with the Department of Psychotherapy at the University of Ulm with Horst Kachele and Helmut Thomae.

Over the long course of the project there were many others who helped it on its way. Jacob Cohen, our first research consultant, was catalytic in crystallizing the design and statistical methods. Robert Rosenthal has been statistical adviser and good luck charm in grant-getting. Andrew Baggaley helped in the middle phases of the data analysis. Martin Orne provided stimulation with his ideas for psychotherapy research. Marilyn Johnson was our overall organizer and collector of project data. Ellen Luborsky provided over the years a variety of presentational ideas for the book. Lise Luborsky has been legal adviser and research collaborator; Peter Luborsky has been in charge of translation. Jo Ann Miller, senior editor at Basic

Books, has overseen the production of this (and my earlier) book with her superb organizational and editorial talents. Laura Dahl's editorial skill has benefited the book. Nola Lynch has guided the overall editorial work by expert ministrations to the text. Many other co-workers over the years carried out the work of the main project and its offshoots: Barton Singer, Robert Toborowsky, Carol Popp, Deborah Fried, Frederic J. Levine, David Mark, Scott Friedman, Henry Markman, Andrew Cooper, Anita V. Hole, Kenneth D. Cohen, Paul Van Ravenswaay, Leslie Alexander, Anna Rose Childress, Roberta Harvey, Freda Greene, Donald Phoenix, Fred Fletcher, Katherine Crits-Christoph, Linda Levy, Beth Mintz, Ann Todd, Bruce Horowitz, Keith Alexander, Jim Mellon, Pam Schaffler, and Stephanie Ming.

After a few years Jim Mintz inherited the design and statistical role from Jacob Cohen and contributed his own solutions to the measurement of treatment outcomes and to the understanding of how judges evaluate success in psychotherapy. Arthur Auerbach was the primary developer of the Prognostic Index for Psychotherapy which became so central in our evaluation of patients for psychotherapy. In more recent years Paul Crits-Christoph in turn has taken charge of design and data analysis and has become an all-purpose consultant and a prime contributor.

Other members of the Department of Psychiatry of the University of Pennsylvania helped us with the project's administrative and scientific problems: Mark Hollender, Philip Mechanick, Albert Stunkard, John Paul Brady, and Peter Whybrow. Albert Stunkard was one of the chief backers of the project through most of its duration, a role assumed in the last four years by Peter Whybrow.

Support was provided in part by the U.S. Public Health Service, National Institute of Mental Health Grants MH-15442, K3MH-22648, MH-08686, and Research Scientist Award MH-47010 (to Luborsky); Research Scientist Development Award MH-22648 (to Auerbach); Post Doctoral Fellowship Grant 5 FO 2 MH-37854 (to Todd); a grant for the Core Conflictual Relationship Theme Method, MH-39673, and from the Fund for Psychoanalytic Research of the American Psychoanalytic Association (to Luborsky), and for the Accuracy of Interpretation Method, MH-40472 (to Crits-Christoph). Some tiding-over-fallow-periods support came from the Luborsky Biopsychosocial Foundation.

Several officials of the National Institute of Mental Health were remarkably nurturant during the project's initial stages. Particularly important among these dedicated mental health professionals, many of whom were also outstanding psychotherapy researchers, were Morris Parloff, A. H. Tuma, Julian Lasky, Louis Wienckowski, and, more recently, Gary VandenBos, Leonard Lash, Nancy Miller, Irene Elkin, Barry E. Wolfe,

Alice Lowery, Suzanne Hadley, Jack Blaine, Tracey Shea, and John Docherty.

We thank the patients and therapists who took part in the research, not only for their patience and participation but also for their trust that we would preserve and deserve their confidence after they had allowed us access to what is ordinarily very private information about their personal and occupational lives. Of course, we cannot thank the patients or their therapists by name.

As a remembrance of things not yet past, I wish to remember also among the factors influencing the completion of this book, the tranquilizing and prose-facilitating retreat at Martha's Vineyard, inhabited by me for annual Augusts along with the three generally patient generations of Luborskys. Certainly, significant contributions were also made by its restful grove of warbler-flitting locust trees and its ready telephone access to Marjorie Cohen, Paul Crits-Christoph, Keith Alexander, Jim Mellon, Nona Sach-deva, and Yvonne Medley (who presided over the book's last year of prodigious computer printouts).

A special spot is reserved here for Ruth Samson Luborsky, who has sustained the project and the book in all ways and for always.

Lester Luborsky
Philadelphia
April 1988

PROJECT A

Who Will Benefit from Psychotherapy? Predictions from Pretreatment

1

The Structure of the
Penn Psychotherapy Project

RIGHT ON SCHEDULE, exactly in the month our 5-year grant was funded—July 1968—we launched our study. Several months before the end of this 5-year period we completed data collection on 73 patients and 42 therapists. We present here the structural details of the Penn Psychotherapy Project, or Penn study: the design, the evaluations, the patients, the therapists, the observers, the treatments, and the proposed data analyses.

Research Design and Timing of Evaluations

The facets of the design of the study are based on Sanford's (1962) categories (figure 1-1), which are applicable to any "social change system" intended to change the person who goes through it. The patients received an intensive initial evaluation, which was to have taken place just before the first session of psychotherapy; for practical reasons of scheduling, the assessment was most often made right after the first session at "P-1." The patient–therapist interaction refers to the number of sessions—generally over a period of 8 to 9 months. The patients were intensively evaluated again at the termination of treatment ("P-2"), and a sample of them was reassessed five years later ("P-3"). The therapists provided some information about the patients initially ("T-1") and then much more at termina-

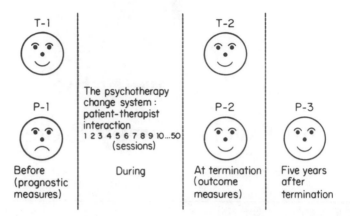

FIGURE 1-1.   Plan for Assessment of the Patient (P) and the Therapist (T) Before, During, and After the Psychotherapy Change System. (Based on Sanford, 1962, p. 155.)

tion ("T-2"). The therapists themselves were evaluated on a battery of special tests at some point during the course of treatment.

The Patients

All of the 73 patients in our sample had voluntarily applied for treatment for their problems, were generally thought to be suitable for psychotherapy, and were usually well motivated for treatment. The majority of them (60%) were treated at the Outpatient Psychiatric Clinic of the Hospital of the University of Pennsylvania, 33% were patients of private practitioners, and 7% ($N = 5$) were treated in New York City by therapists at the Lincoln Institute of Psychotherapy. Most of the patients were from the greater Philadelphia area; many were from the area around the university—"catchment area number 3," popularly known as University City.

Table 1-1 displays the patients' demographic profile. They ranged in age from 18 to 55, with a median age of 24. Of the 73, 44 were female and 29

TABLE 1-1

Patient Demographic Characteristics
$(N = 73)$

Age	
Range	18–55 years
Median	24.25 years
Mode	24 years
Mean	26.33 years
Sex	
Male	29
Female	44
Race	
Black	5
Oriental	1
White	67
Religion	
None	21
Jewish	25
Christian	27
Education	
Less than high school	1
High school graduate	7
Some college	30
College graduate	8
Some graduate school	17
Graduate degree	10
Marital Status	
Married	15
Divorced, separated, widowed	10
Remarried	4
Single	44

male. Most were single and white. The educational range was broad—the majority had at least some schooling after high school. The social class range (not shown on the table) also was broad. Many of the patients were students ($N = 29$, 40%) or employees of local colleges, hospitals, or businesses.

For those who were patients at the Outpatient Service, the fee scale was graduated—from $1 to $15 per session (the fee sounds small now, but this was before double-digit inflation). Those who were patients of staff members or of private practitioners paid the usual higher rate for private treatment; in those years it was $25 to $35 per session.

The clinic patients ($N = 44$, not including the 5 at Lincoln Institute) and the private practice patients ($N = 24$) differed in other ways, as table 1-2 shows. Those in the private practice group had a higher percentage of women and were treated by more experienced therapists who were more often Freudian.

TABLE 1-2

Demographic Characteristics of the Clinic versus Private Practice Subsamples

	Clinic (N = 42)	Private Practice (N = 24)
Age (Mean)	24.8 years	29.0 years
Sex		
Male	19 (45%)	7 (29%)
Female	23 (55%)	17 (71%)
Married		
Yes	14 (33%)	12 (50%)
No	28 (67%)	12 (50%)
Race		
White	37 (88%)	23 (96%)
Nonwhite	5 (12%)	1 (4%)
Religion		
Christian	19 (45%)	7 (29%)
Jewish	11 (26%)	13 (54%)
Other	12 (29%)	4 (17%)
Education		
Not high school graduate	0	0
High school graduate	6 (14%)	0
Some college	17 (40%)	11 (46%)
College graduate	4 (10%)	4 (17%)
Some graduate school	10 (24%)	5 (21%)
Graduate degree	5 (12%)	4 (17%)

NOTE: The total $N = 66$. Seven patients of the original 73 were not classified as clinic or private practice (5 were seen in an institute setting and 2 transferred from the clinic to private practice during the study).

TABLE 1-3

Patients Screened for the Study

	Number
Dropped out after pretests	3
Dropped out after 1 to 7 sessions	15
Refused tape recording	1
Did not complete post tests	3
Still in therapy at cut-off point	16
Completed therapy and pre and post tests	73
Total number of patients screened	111

BASES FOR INCLUSION

We planned to include all patients who had attended eight or more therapy sessions, had completed our pretreatment and posttreatment tests and interviews, and had had their therapy sessions tape recorded. Our minimum of eight sessions gave us a sample of patients who had continued in treatment. Compared with other clinic samples, our median length of treatment was substantial. According to one review (Garfield, 1978) of typical clinic data on length of psychotherapy, the median was about six sessions and about two-thirds of the patients had fewer than ten sessions.

There was some attrition of subjects in our study. Among the subjects dropped from the study (table 1-3) were 3 who took the initial tests but discontinued participation even before a therapist was assigned and 15 who had had from one to seven sessions before dropping out. One subject was not included because he requested that the taping of his sessions be discontinued. Three were not included because no posttreatment tests and interviews could be obtained. An additional 16—although they had been given our pretreatment tests and interviews and their sessions had been recorded—could not be included because the therapy was not over by the cut-off point of the project in 1973. In summary, the patients in the study represent 73 out of a sample of 111 who had been considered by the clinical intake evaluators as appropriate patients for psychotherapy. (There was an additional group who came to the clinic for initial evaluation sessions by the clinic staff but who decided not to proceed with psychotherapy. This group was never considered part of the project. It is not possible to know the exact size of this population, but from the usual experience in the clinic and from the work of Levinson [1962] on the steps toward "patienthood," it must number between two and three dozen.)

DIAGNOSES AND PSYCHIATRIC SEVERITY

Almost all patients were nonpsychotic. According to the American Psychiatric Association's *Diagnostic and Statistical Manual* (DSM-II) classification they included 30 neurotic, 18 personality disorder, 20 mixed neuroses, 3 "latent" psychotic, 1 situational maladjustment, and 1 psychophysiological disorder. The DSM-II diagnoses had been based especially on the tape-recorded Prognostic Index interviews (chapter 7). After the DSM-III appeared the diagnoses were reevaluated and converted to DSM-III equivalents (table 1-4). In DSM-III terms, by far the most frequent diagnoses were dysthymic and anxiety disorders.

The diagnoses in table 1-4 show the same preponderance of non-

TABLE 1-4

Patient Diagnoses

DSM III Category	Number
Dysthymic disorder	22
Generalized anxiety disorder	21
Schizoid personality disorder	10
Compulsive personality disorder	7
Inhibited sexual excitement	2
Passive aggressive personality disorder	5
Atypical personality disorder	1
Psychological factors affecting physical condition	2
Histrionic personality disorder	5
Mixed personality disorder	2
Schizotypal personality disorder	4
Ego-dystonic homosexuality	2
Adjustment disorder with academic inhibition	1
Obsessive-compulsive disorder	3
Narcissistic personality disorder	1
Paranoid personality disorder	2
Marital problem	2
Borderline personality disorder	1
Stuttering	1
Atypical eating disorder	1

NOTE: Numbers total more than 73 because many patients had more than one diagnosis.

psychotic diagnoses, with most being either mood or anxiety disorders. Diagnostic categories are best presented along with a measure of their psychiatric severity, since each diagnosis can cover a broad range of severity (Luborsky, 1962a; Luborsky & Bachrach, 1974). The Health-Sickness Rating Scale (HSRS) provides such a shorthand summary of psychological health-sickness (chapter 6); a simplified form of it is suggested as a supplement to the diagnoses in DSM-IIIR. The mean of the global HSRS rating was 59.5, which indicates that this patient group was capable of functioning moderately well and without hospital support (see comparisons with the other groups in chapter 3).

The Therapists

A demographic profile of the therapists is provided in table 1-5. The age range of the 38 male and 4 female therapists was broad: from 26 to 56 years, with a median of 32. Twenty-two of the 42 therapists were supervised second- or third-year psychiatric residents assigned to the Outpatient Services of the Hospital of the University of Pennsylvania. Most of the experienced therapists were also affiliated with the Department of Psychiatry, either as staff members of the Outpatient Clinic or as psychiatrists who were affiliated with the department but were in private practice. Of those twenty who were not residents, ten had more than ten years of experience.

In terms of their stated orientation, twelve out of the forty-two therapists were Freudian or neo-Freudian, and thirty were eclectic. However, for the treatments included in our sample, the primary influence even for many of those residents who described themselves as eclectic was dynamic or psychoanalytic orientation, since most of the forty-two were supervised by psychoanalytically oriented supervisors.

Thirty-six of the therapists had one or two of their patients in the study; three had three patients, two had four patients, and one had five patients in the study.

TABLE 1-5

Therapist Demographic Characteristics
(N = 42)

Age	
Range	26–55 years
Median	33 years
Mode	28 years
Mean	36.7 years
Sex	
Male	38
Female	4
Religion	
None	9
Jewish	22
Christian	11
Marital Status	
Married	35
Single	7
Professional Degrees	
M.D.	37
Ph.D.	2
M.S.W.	2
M.S.S.	1
Experience	
Resident	22
Less than 10 years	10
More than 10 years	10
Orientation	
Freudian and Neo-Freudian	12
Eclectic	30

The Independent Clinical Observers

In order to broaden our perspective on the participants in the psychotherapy, we also relied upon independent clinical observers as evaluators of the treatments. These independent observers were experienced clinicians (Arthur Auerbach, Henry Bachrach, Marilyn Johnson, Lester Luborsky, Jim Mintz, and Thomas Todd). Five were psychologists and one was a psychiatrist; all had had previous experience with the evaluation of psychotherapies. They conducted the pretreatment and posttreatment Prognostic Index interviews and based on that interview, made both ratings of patients' status and predictions of outcomes. They also evaluated 4-minute segments of sessions and whole sessions.

The Treatments

The aim of most of the treatments was both "symptom relief" and "personality change," with personality change predominating (table 1-6), according to our therapists' questionnaire responses. In two-thirds of the treatments no medications were prescribed. The treatment length ranged from a minimum of 8 to a maximum of 264 sessions, with a median of 32 sessions during a median of 34 weeks. Sessions were conducted once or twice a week, and all were tape recorded. The treatment features—the psychodynamic orientation, the frequency of sessions, therapists' orientation, and, to some extent, the length of treatment—are common in many outpatient clinics (Feldman, Lorr & Russell, 1958; Hollingshead & Redlich, 1958; Marmor, 1975; Norcross & Prochaska, 1982a, 1982b).

The Penn study was carried out in the era before it was considered necessary to guide therapists with a formal manual. This state of affairs was dramatically changed by the "small revolution" in practice that occurred with the advent of manuals. The Luborsky manual for psychoanalytic psychotherapy was first used for teaching in the Penn Department of Psychiatry in 1976 and then more generally in the United States and elsewhere after it was published in 1984. However, we have recently examined a sample of the therapy transcripts in the Penn study, and it is our impression that they generally are consistent with the main tenets of the manual. The mean ratings (table 1-7) are generally at about the middle of the five-point conformity scales. This degree of conformity to the man-

TABLE 1-6

Characteristics of Therapy

Goal of Therapy	
1. Symptom relief	6 (8%)
2. Mostly symptom relief	11 (15%)
3. Both	29 (40%)
4. Mostly personality change	20 (27%)
5. Personality change	7 (10%)
Use of Drugs	
None	47 (64%)
Some	26 (36%)
Length	
Range	5–149 weeks
Median	34 weeks
Mode	21 weeks
Mean	41.06 weeks

ual's techniques, even though the manual was not yet written at the time the therapy was done, should not be a great surprise because the therapists' supervisors were psychoanalysts and the manual was intended to be a formal statement of the local and general practice of psychoanalytic psychotherapy. In fact, the mean conformity rating for the Penn study therapists was only slightly less than that of the VA-Penn study therapists (table 1-7; Luborsky, Woody, et al., 1982), who had been trained to follow the manual. Other studies have found similar levels of conformity (Luborsky & DeRubeis, 1984).

The manual describes and exemplifies two main classes of techniques:

TABLE 1-7

*Ratings of Penn Psychotherapy Project Sessions versus VA Study
for Conformity to Luborsky's (1984) Manual[a]*

		Mean Ratings on 1–5 Conformity Scale	
	Pooled Judge Reliability	Penn[b] Study ($\pm$SD)	VA[c] Study
Giving support	.62	2.25 (.8)	2.5
Facilitating self-expression	.42	2.46 (.6)	2.7
Understanding relationship with therapist	.63	1.77 (.7)	2.2
Overall fit with manual	.43	2.51 (.7)	2.8
Treatment is supportive	.47	2.97 (.7)	
How well therapist conducted SE	.60	2.39 (.7)	

[a]Mean rating for 2 early sessions.
[b]$N = 43$
[c]$N = 37$

the supportive and the expressive. The former involves those aspects that the patient experiences as providing support; the latter includes those conditions that permit the patient to be expressive and then to review what has been expressed in order to gain understanding and other modes of overcoming the main problems presented.

ASSIGNING PATIENTS TO THERAPISTS

We compared two ways of assigning patients in the Penn study. We tried a random assignment condition for about half of the patients of the psychiatric residents: the therapists were given only a list of their patients' names with no other identifying information. In the therapists'-choice condition, the psychiatric residents were offered patients approximately in the order in which they appeared on the waiting list but were given full information based on the initial evaluations. The therapists were also given the option of refusing patients when they were not thought to be suitable in terms of the therapist's preference. The therapists on the staff and the private practitioners also had the same type of full information based on initial evaluation. For every patient assignment we obtained a therapist's questionnaire response to verify how much choice the therapist had exerted in the assignment of the patient. The results on the relation of type of choice to outcome are reported in chapter 11.

ENLISTING PARTICIPATION

The patients and therapists participated voluntarily in the study. All of the psychiatric residents who were working at the Outpatient Psychiatric Clinic in July 1968 volunteered to participate, as did virtually all of the residents in each succeeding year. Many were interested in the project and eager to learn what its findings would be.

Albert J. Stunkard, then chairman of the Department of Psychiatry at Penn, urged all staff members to consider participating. We then discussed the project individually with the more senior members of the department. The experienced psychiatrists did not all agree to participate, and patients of theirs included in our study began treatment somewhat later than the patients of the residents. When it became apparent that less than a half of our sample of therapists would be beyond residency training, Luborsky requested and got the participation of his fellow therapists in the Analytic Research Group of the Institute of the Pennsylvania Hospital; all agreed to enlist one or two of their next psychotherapy patients in the study.

To help get the patient's cooperation and to provide orientation, it was each therapist's responsibility in the first interview with the patient to discuss his or her participation in the project. The patient was asked to agree to have the sessions tape recorded and to participate in an initial and termination evaluation. The therapist explained that the treatment provided was not experimental and that the patient would receive the usual therapy she or he was to receive. The therapist then expressed the wish to participate and the hope that the patient would feel comfortable enough to do so also. The patient was assured that all precautions would be taken to ensure confidentiality and that the data would not be utilized for published reports until long after the psychotherapy was completed. (The dates of this and other publications show we have fulfilled this promise.) Virtually all the patients we approached readily agreed to participate. A high level of participation by patients tends to occur in psychotherapy research projects; moreover, as we rediscovered, the participation of patients is usually higher than that of experienced therapists. We can only speculate that therapists may be charier of consuming their time, and they may be more reluctant to reveal themselves than are patients. Patients may feel they have less to lose and more to gain by being cooperative; they typically expect and receive gains from the treatment.

The Proposed Data and Analyses

Three goals guided our planning for data analysis. (1) We wanted to describe each of the treatments comprehensively by selecting measures from several domains: (a) patient qualities, including demographic information and psychological tests as well as observer-rated patient attributes; (b) therapist qualities, including demographic information and psychological tests; (c) description of early sessions; (d) matches between patient and therapist; and (e) qualities of the treatment setting. (2) We intended to describe the posttreatment status of the cases comprehensively by selecting measures from patients and therapists, as well as from clinical observers who were not involved in the treatments. (3) We hoped to assess the extent to which the pretreatment data gave information that would be predictive of the patients' change.

PRETHERAPY MEASURES

An intention of this research was to compare the efficacy of measures from the different domains in predicting outcome. Within each of these domains we proposed to use a factor analysis to reduce the many, undoubtedly redundant, measures to a relatively small number of independent dimensions. Since the proportion of patients to predictors is important, Nunnally (1967) recommended having at least 5 subjects for each predictor variable. Our analyses of patient and treatment variables were to be based on 73 cases, a number we thought was adequate for examining 10 to 15 variables in each domain. Unique variables not loading on main factors would also be retained for use as predictors.

POSTTHERAPY MEASURES

Posttreatment measures were provided by the patient, therapist, and clinical observer. These measured the posttreatment status of the patient as well as the success (amount of benefit or improvement) of the treatment.

As it was for the pretreatment data, a factor analysis of posttreatment measures was necessary to reduce the number of variables to manageable proportions. The goal of this analysis of posttreatment data was to measure the outcome of therapy for each patient, a task that has presented a challenge for all psychotherapy researchers. On the one hand, it is known that simply taking the difference between a posttreatment status measure and the same pretreatment status measure (raw gain score) leads to problems related to unreliability of change scores and initial level effects. One solution offered by Manning and DuBois (1962) was to use the method of "residualizing" posttreatment data on the basis of pretherapy status (as a way to correct for initial differences among patients, as in chapter 11). On the other hand, we had reason to believe that the clinical meaning of "success" in psychotherapy may be more intimately tied to the patient's final status than to a simply defined change (chapter 2). Our solution to these problems, we decided, would be guided by the underlying factor structure of our posttreatment measures.

THE MODEL FOR DATA ANALYSIS

Multiple regression analyses were to be the mainstay of the statistical treatment of the data. For each type of outcome measure we planned to evaluate the set of pretreatment measures as predictors. Because we intended to factor within domains, we could evaluate the relative predictive efficacy of measures from each domain. It was obvious, however, that a rigorous analysis of each factor would be possible only if all other factors were held constant, i.e., analyses of interactions between factors would be highly exploratory.

The reasons for this should be evident. We anticipated having about 15 measures of pretreatment status within each domain. Although a multiple regression analysis of 15 predictors based on 73 cases would be possible, it would entail exploring 105 two-way interactions and 455 three-way interactions. Obviously, then, we simply would not be in a position to explore complex interrelationships among our predictors. In our view, the fact that variables from several domains would be simultaneously evaluated as predictors of various outcome criteria was sufficient. Not only were we in a position to cross-validate findings from our review of previous studies, but we were also able to compare systematically measures from different areas in a manner not previously attempted.

The proposed data analyses were (1) factor analyses of pretherapy measures to be done within each domain separately; (2) factor analyses of posttherapy measures; and (3) multiple regression analyses on each of the outcome criteria, using pretreatment factors as independent variables, assessing the relative contributions of variables from each of the domains.

These plans seemed both methodologically sound and communicable to those most likely to be interested in the results.

Summary

At this point, the following broad characterizations of the study emerge. The subjects were a varied group of nonpsychotic patients considered suitable for psychotherapy. They were treated by therapists with a broad range of experience. The treatment was mainly medium-length time-unlimited psychoanalytically oriented psychotherapy. The setting for most patients was the outpatient clinic of a university hospital. The data analyses were to be factor analyses of pre- and posttreatment predictors and multiple regression analyses on each outcome measure.

2

Measuring the Outcome
of Therapy

THIS CHAPTER BEGINS a four-chapter unit on the benefits of psychotherapy; the unit covers the outcome measures for assessing the benefits,
the magnitude of the benefits, the long-term maintenance of the benefits,
and the unanticipated physical benefits that go along with the psychological ones. This chapter lists the outcome measures and derives the principles
for making composites of them.

The Outcome Measures

Because the outcome of a patient's treatment might differ depending on
who judges it, we decided to sample measures of outcomes from three
viewpoints: the patient's, the therapist's and the clinical observer's. Within
each viewpoint, outcomes might differ depending on the type of measure
being used. We therefore collected, within each viewpoint, (1) ratings of
improvement and (2) measures of the patient's status before and after
treatment.

Our outcome measures included some that were specific to the patient's
goals. The specific patient and therapist measures are best represented by
the Target Complaints procedure (Battle et al., 1966), which provides a
way of measuring the outcomes that are specific to each patient's individual targets.

TABLE 2-1

Outcome Measures

Clinical Observer's Ratings
Prognostic Index Interview (chapter 7; Auerbach & Luborsky, 1979)
Health-Sickness Rating Scale (Luborsky, 1962a; Luborsky & Bachrach, 1974; Luborsky, 1975b)
Klein Adjustment Scales (Klein, 1960)

Patients' Self-Report
Target complaints (Battle et al., 1966)
Patient's rating of "satisfaction" on Termination Outcome Rating Scales (Rogers & Dymond, 1954)
Phipps Psychiatric Clinic Symptom Checklist (Uhlenhuth & Duncan, 1968)
MMPI Scales: Hs, Hy (Hathaway and Meehl, 1951), Ego Strength (Es), (Barron, 1953a)
Inventory for Social and Personality Functioning (ISPF) (Auerbach & Johnson, 1978)

Therapists' Ratings
Therapist's Termination Outcome Rating Scales: Therapist's rating of "success" (Rogers & Dymond, 1954), "satisfaction" (Rogers & Dymond, 1954), "improvement" (Luborsky, p. 233, in Waskow & Parloff, 1975)
Inventory for Social and Personality Functioning (ISPF) (short form called Brief Adjustment Rating Scale [BARS])
Target complaints (Battle et al., 1966)
Reason Patient terminated.
Therapist's rating of attractiveness of patient for psychotherapy.
Liking of patient (by therapist)

All measures are listed in table 2-1, where the name of each measure is followed by a reference that more fully describes it. Only the Prognostic Index interview, which was administered at the beginning and end of treatment, is fully described in this book (in chapter 7), since no detailed account has been published elsewhere.

The Principles for Creating Composites

Despite the multitude of studies attempting to predict outcomes of psychotherapy (chapter 19), only a handful of multivariate studies have tried to delineate the types of changes that take place in psychotherapy (e.g., Berzins, Bednar & Severy, 1975; Kernberg et al., 1972; Mitchell, Bozarth & Krauft, 1977). Measures of psychotherapy outcome may be usefully classified as to viewpoints (sources), content areas, and measurement methodology. The commonly available viewpoints for outcome information are the patient, the therapist, clinical observers, and relevant others, such as relatives. Areas of content include mood, behavior, personality, and similar rubrics. Common measurement methods include global change or success ratings, final status measures, pre–post differences, and complex functions such as the residual gain scores (Manning & DuBois, 1962). This chapter takes up questions in each of these areas as they impinged on and were dealt with in the Penn Psychotherapy Project.

SOURCES OF OUTCOME INFORMATION

The problem of choosing sources recalls the poor rabbi who was confronted at his door one day by a quarreling couple. Both of them started to pour out accounts of their convincing positions. Unfortunately, these were not easily reconcilable. The rabbi began by listening to the woman; at the end of her story he proclaimed, "You certainly have a point." Then he listened to the man and at the end proclaimed, "You certainly have a point." The sexton overheard these comments and protested, "Rabbi, they can't both be right." The rabbi considered for a moment, then announced, "You certainly have a point."

Much like the rabbi's conclusion, the consensus in the psychotherapy research community seems to be that representation of diverse sources is desirable and that agreement among viewpoints as to psychotherapy outcome is at times poor. Large-scale reviews of the psychotherapy outcome literature (e.g., Luborsky et al., 1971; Meltzoff & Kornreich, 1970; Strupp & Bergin, 1969) concur in the judgment that diverse sources represent sufficiently distinct viewpoints that measures of each should ideally be included in treatment studies. Fiske (1975) has presented this view strongly. The same line of thought is reflected in Waskow and Parloff's (1975) compilation of a core battery for assessing psychotherapy outcomes. The emphasis in their volume is on the source and content of the battery, and they pay little attention to methodological issues.

The acceptance of the concept of distinct viewpoints is widespread, as has been noted elsewhere (Luborsky, 1971; Mintz, 1977). Green et al. (1975) usefully summarized the evidence on this issue of agreement among sources; they suggested that its validity depends on the particular methodology of measurement used, as well as on the degree of inference required in the particular content area.

Berzins, Bednar, and Severy (1975) reported a sophisticated multivariate study of relationships among multisource measures of psychotherapy outcome. They concluded that methodological strategies, particularly the use of factor analysis, have obscured meaningful consensus in past studies. Mintz (1977) has also suggested that the discreteness of viewpoints may have been exaggerated in past studies.

CONTENT OF OUTCOME MEASURES

Areas of content to be measured are guided by researchers' clinical interests and the goals of the treatment (Waskow & Parloff, 1975). The well-known factor-analytic study of Cartwright, Kirtner, and Fiske (1963) stressed the importance of so-called method factors. Their analysis documents the existence of a large common factor (a global outcome measure) for each viewpoint. The analyses of Berzins, Bednar, and Severy (1975), using residual gain scores, also demonstrated broadly defined adjustment change factors.

MEASUREMENT METHODOLOGY

Measurement methodology has been a somewhat neglected area. For example, Waskow's (Waskow & Parloff, 1975) imaginary dialogue between a clinical researcher and a research consultant is almost entirely devoted to ensuring broad representation of measures concerning content and source. Practically no attention is given to the methodology of measurement. Excellent statistical papers on problems in measuring change (e.g., Cronbach & Furby, 1970; Manning & DuBois, 1962) are difficult for readers lacking statistical expertise.

What methodologies are available? Most obvious, perhaps, is the simple gain or change score, calculated by subtracting the pretreatment score from the posttreatment score. Although intuitively appealing, this method brings with it several serious statistical headaches. For one, change scores tend to be unreliable. Also, they usually correlate with initial level, to some degree spuriously because of measurement error. Ceiling effects distort interpretation of change at high levels. Regression to the mean is another expectable effect when extreme groups are selected for study, as is the case in most treatment studies, and this phenomenon increases in importance as reliability decreases. These considerations have led to widespread recommendations (Fiske, Hunt & Luborsky, 1970; Manning & DuBois, 1962) in favor of the residual gain score.

The residual gain score takes into account the extent to which the amount of raw gain is linked to initial level. Table 2-2 gives a simplified illustration of the process of calculating residual gain scores. Note that Subjects 1-3 all have initial levels of 1, whereas Subjects 4-6 all begin at 6 on our hypothetical measure. Further, the mean gain for Subjects 1-3 is greater ($M = 2$) than that for Subjects 4-6 ($M = 0$). In this simple example, the residual gain score, shown at the far right, rescales the gain score for each subject relative to the mean gain for subjects with the same initial level. This principle applies in more complex situations as well.

TABLE 2-2

Hypothetical Illustration of Residual Gain Scores

Subject	Pretherapy Score	Posttherapy Score	Mean Gain	Actual Gain	Predicted Gain	Residual Gain
1	1	0		−1	2	−3
2	1	4	2	3	2	+1
3	1	5		4	2	+2
4	6	5		−1	0	−1
5	6	6	0	0	0	0
6	6	7		1	0	+1

A closely related method is the analysis of covariance, using initial level as the covariate and posttreatment status as the dependent variable. This is the generally recommended method for analyzing change in experimental designs appropriate for the analysis of variance.

It is important to remember that the residual gain score removes the differential gains made by the two initial status groups in our hypothetical example. The mean residual gain for both the group with a high initial score and the group with a low initial score is zero, although raw gains obtained by the two groups differs. Similarly, if treatment groups differ in initial level, the analysis of covariance will "remove" some of the variance associated with treatment. In many studies, however, the systematic differences in outcome associated with differing initial levels should probably be carefully examined in their own right. Simply to dismiss the correlation of pretreatment status and gain as a measurement artifact may be to overlook meaningful results.

A possible drawback of these methods lies in their relative complexity. The dependent variables analyzed are derived statistically, and they often differ substantially from the raw data because of the "adjustments" for initial level. Interpretation of such analyses is therefore relatively difficult.

Another measurement strategy is to use final adjustment status alone as a criterion. Several writers (e.g., Green et al., 1975; Mintz, 1972) have noted that global ratings of outcome appear to be primarily influenced by final level. Green et al. (1975) have argued that final status is an appropriate measure of the extent to which therapeutic goals have been realized. The argument seems most cogent, however, when initial differences are minimal. Surely, a patient who achieves a given final level as a result of large positive change should be seen as benefiting more from treatment than one at the same posttreatment level who began at that level and has not changed.

A method of measuring treatment outcome in wide use is the direct rating of benefit or change. In the form of an overall rating of success or improvement on a simple scale, this has been reported as the most frequent outcome measure in studies of traditional psychotherapy (Luborsky et al., 1971; Mintz, 1977). The advantages of these measures include their obvious face validity, their flexibility in terms of unique evaluation of each case, and the ease with which they can be obtained. However, they are particularly open to criticism on the grounds of bias or distortion by the committed participants—the patient and therapist—who usually make them. Also, their very flexibility for evaluation of the individual case often leaves in question exactly what they measure.

An Analysis of Outcome Measures: The Penn and Chicago Studies Compared

This section explores the relationships among diverse psychotherapy outcome measures. We expand on prior presentations (Green et al., 1975) by including measures from patients, therapists, and independent clinical observers, by covering an extremely broad spectrum of measures, and by studying several distinct psychotherapy populations. We are able to present data from two separate, large, predictive psychotherapy studies: the Penn Psychotherapy Project (Luborsky, Mintz, et al., 1980) and the reanalyzed outcome data from the Chicago Psychotherapy Project (Cartwright, Kirtner & Fiske, 1963; Fiske, Cartwright & Kirtner, 1964), an often cited basis for the multisource outcome view accepted today.

AIMS

The basic questions, in terms of our schematic outline for classifying outcome measures, were the following.

Sources. How much overlap is there among sources? Can a useful common view of outcome be developed, or must we consider each source a wholly independent entity?

Content. How many distinct and useful domains of content can we identify in the area of treatment assessment? At the least, is a concept of "overall adjustment" a useful and scientifically meaningful one? How much change in overall adjustment occurred?

Statistical methods. What can we learn from the relationships among final adjustment, pre–post differences, and direct change ratings? How should our measures be used statistically to best represent what we actually mean by "success" in psychotherapy?

PROCEDURE AND ANALYSES

In the Penn Psychotherapy Project the measures of current adjustment were obtained both pretreatment and posttreatment. Measures of change or benefit were obtained posttreatment (chapter 6).

The Chicago study (Cartwright, Kirtner & Fiske, 1963; Fiske, Cartwright & Kirtner, 1964) included 93 outpatients, measured before and after therapy on a variety of tests and scales completed by patients, therapists, and clinical observers. Cartwright, Kirtner, and Fiske (1963) described the results of a factor analysis performed on raw difference scores. The method factors found were each defined almost entirely by measures from a single viewpoint, and thus they were taken to indicate a basic lack of agreement among patient, therapist, and diagnostician. That finding has had tremendous impact since its publication, providing a part of the empirical basis for the view that little or no consensus among sources exists (Fiske, 1975; see also Berzins, Bednar & Severy, 1975, and Mintz, 1977, for discussion of this issue). Fiske, Cartwright, and Kirtner (1964) subsequently reported on the negative results of attempts to predict those outcome factors on the basis of pretreatment data.

For the Penn Psychotherapy Project data, all analyses of criterion structure were calculated separately within the clinic and the private practice groups as well as for the pooled sample. Differences were small, so results for the pooled sample only are presented below.

Maximizing Reliabilities

We have noted elsewhere (Mintz, 1977) the problems caused by unreliability in some previous analyses of the structure of outcome measures in psychotherapy. To some degree, the appearance of method factors (Cartwright, Kirtner & Fiske, 1963) can be attributed to the effects of shared measurement error within each individual's ratings. As reliability of measures decreases, the relative importance of measurement error increases, making it particularly desirable to work with maximally reliable measures in analyses of agreement among sources.

There were many single-item ratings and multi-item tests gathered from the patient, therapist, and observer before and after treatment. Our first goal was to maximize the reliabilities of our measures of treatment effects. In general, composites made up of measures that intercorrelate positively will be more reliable than the components used singly (Nunnally, 1967). For most of the multi-item tests we first examined, by calculating the internal consistency reliability coefficient, whether simply summing the items would be a reasonable measure. Missing data on individual items were estimated by using the mean for the sample for each item. In the initial decision concerning whether a simple sum of items would be used, we adopted an arbitrary reliability criterion of .85. If a test failed to reach that level, an attempt was made to construct a more homogeneous test by selecting a subset of the items. Dropped items were included in later analyses as separate variables.

Tests of borderline acceptability, however, would have no clear interpretation if items were dropped or scored separately. In the case of the Minnesota Multiphasic Personality Inventory (MMPI) scales, we simply used the standard keys for scoring. We felt that by changing these well-known scales on the basis of item analyses in our relatively small sample we would lose comparability with other studies. In view of the relatively large number of measures obtained for each patient, our item-selection decisions might not be replicated by another investigator. However, our interest was not in the replicability of tests but in the broad underlying constructs tapped by those tests.

Two-stage Component Analyses

Our initial analyses were aimed at building measures that were as reliable as possible. The next steps were to find and eliminate redundancies among these measures and to assess agreement across viewpoints. Berzins, Bednar, and Severy (1975) and Mintz (1977) have discussed the reasons that conventional factor analysis is not a good method for exploring the structure of multisource data. Our procedure was similar to the two-step procedure described and recommended by Berzins, Bednar, and Severy (1975). Component analyses were first performed within each source (patients, therapists, clinical observers). Only then were the relationships among the components from different sources assessed.

Decisions concerning the number of components to retain for rotation and interpretation, and ultimately for use in defining composite measures, were based on consideration of the size of the components and their reliability coefficients and on an examination of the zero-order correlations among the salient measures summed to form the composite. We did not attempt measurement of any dimension unless the composite suggested by the component analysis was actually based on measures with substantial positive intercorrelations.

Our reanalysis of the data from the Chicago study proceeded along the same lines as our analysis of the Penn Psychotherapy Project data. Working within viewpoints initially, we reduced the measures by first, testing a priori hypotheses about which items could reasonably be formed into a composite by calculating internal consistency reliability coefficients; second, looking at principal-components analyses on the resulting composite measures within viewpoints; and then intercorrelating components from all viewpoints.

Exploring Different Kinds of Change Scores

Finally, we explored several alternative methods of measuring outcomes. One interest was to determine whether global posttreatment assessments are better understood as measures of change or of final status. More generally, we were interested in examining the relationships among raw change, initial and final adjustment status, residual gain, and global ratings of success or improvement obtained after treatment.

To find the best-fitting function we followed the strategy proposed by Cronbach and Furby (1970) of computing the multiple correlation between global posttreatment outcome ratings and pretreatment measures of adjustment status. That function was compared with other functions of pretreatment and posttreatment adjustment, such as raw gain (post minus pre), residual gain, and final status alone, to see how closely each of those approximated the best fit in predicting global ratings of benefits.

RESULTS

Analyses of Pretreatment Measures

Pretherapy information on each patient was obtained from the patient and from the clinical observer. A large first principal component appeared within each viewpoint. Estimated internal consistency reliabilities for these components, scored by summing salient standardized variables, were .86 for the patient measure and .82 for the clinical observer measure. These were interpreted as the overall psychological health of the patient or pretherapy adjustment status in each case.

The correlation between the patient and the clinical observer pretreatment adjustment composite was .59. We concluded that there was sufficient agreement between the two viewpoints to justify combining them to form a conjoint measure. The individual tests and scales making up the observer component were each standardized, to weight them equally, and then summed. The resulting composite was restandardized. The same procedure was followed for the salient patient measures. The two standardized composites were then summed to yield a conjoint pretreatment adjustment score, in which the patient and observer were weighted equally. The reliability of this conjoint measure was .88, using the formula for reliability of sums (Nunnally, 1967).

Analyses of Posttreatment Measures within Sources

Therapist measures. Although two components were retained in the analysis of therapist data, only one was of major interest. This large component obviously represented the therapist's posttreatment rating of the amount of change or benefits from treatment. The second component was based on a particularly high correlation between two ratings made by the therapist at the end of treatment. One was a rating of the patient's "attractiveness for treatment," and the other was a rating of how much the therapist liked the patient. This high correlation might, at least in part, have been an artifact produced by halo effects in rating, as they had appeared as adjacent items on a rating form.

The correlation between the two components, scored by summing salient items, was .45. Accordingly, we chose to score the therapist's overall evaluation in the most general manner. The decision to include all items in this composite minimized effects of chance selection, and appeared quite justified in light of the loadings on the first principal component and evaluations of reliability of such a composite. (We noted that selection of a subset of items did not appreciably improve estimated reliability of measurement of this criterion.) The estimated reliability of the final composite therapist rating of treatment benefits was .84.

Patient measures. Although three components were retained for rotation (due largely to statistical considerations), only the first two were of interest. Although highly correlated ($r = .56$ when these components were measured by summing salient variables), the first two components were interpreted as (a) posttreatment ratings of amount of change or benefit from treatment and (b) self-reported posttreatment adjustment status or overall psychological health at the end of treatment. The third component was the doublet of Hysteria (Hy) and Hypochondriasis (Hs) scales from the MMPI. We viewed this "component" as largely artifactual since many of the items on these scales overlap. A two-component rotation (and examination of reliability coefficients) convinced us that the Hs-Hy component could be pooled with the posttreatment adjustment status component. The estimated reliability of the patient-rated benefits measure was

.79; reliability of the patient-rated posttreatment adjustment measure was .86.

Clinical observer measures. Analysis of items rated by the clinical observers was relatively straightforward. Only one principal component appeared large enough to warrant interpretation. It clearly represented the clinician's overall assessment of the posttreatment adjustment status of the patient. Although there was substantial overlap among the HSRS, the Prognostic Index, and several of the ratings of the Klein Adjustment Scales, the items that had been dropped from the Prognostic Index in the initial test construction step remained essentially specific. We decided to measure this posttreatment adjustment status criterion using only the highly reliable composite tests, that is, the HSRS and the Prognostic Index. Reliability coefficients were, in fact, slightly lower when the Klein scales were included. The estimated reliability of the final clinical observer-rated posttreatment adjustment composite was .91.

Agreement among Viewpoints

To what extent were the therapist, patient, and observer views of outcome providing unique perspectives? Was there a commonly perceived outcome of treatment, or would we find substantial independence among our three perspectives? To assess this, we analyzed the basic measures from each of the three viewpoints together. The results of this component analysis are summarized in table 2-3. Two large components were rotated and interpreted. The first principal component is presented in the table as well and demonstrates the sizable common element.

The two major components are readily interpretable. They are clearly defined by content rather than viewpoint. In essence, there are agreements across viewpoints. We interpret them as (a) posttreatment adjustment and (b) rated benefits. The measures that defined the posttreatment adjustment status components from both patient and observer now appear on a conjoint posttreatment adjustment dimension; those that defined rated benefits for both patient and therapist now appear on a conjoint rated benefits dimension.

We felt that all participants in the evaluation process should be weighted equally in measuring the posttreatment adjustment and rated benefits criteria. Thus, the observer posttreatment adjustment dimension was scored by summing standardized tests, and the resultant composite was itself standardized. The patient posttreatment adjustment component was similarly generated. The two resulting standardized variables were then summed to provide the overall conjoint posttreatment adjustment criterion. (The correlation between these two view-

TABLE 2-3

Across-Views Analysis of Posttreatment Data:
Penn Psychotherapy Project

	Principal Components Analysis (Varimax Rotation)				
		Rotated Factors		Correlations of Items with Scored Criteria	
Variable	First Principal Component	I: Adjustment	II: Benefits	I: Adjustment ($r_{xx} = .93$)	II: Benefits ($r_{xx} = .88$)
Adjustment Measures					
Patient-Rated					
ISPF adjustment	.79	.64	.50	.82	.59
Symptom checklist[a]	−.80	−.68	−.48	−.83	−.59
Minnesota Multiphasic Personality Inventory:					
Hypochondriasis	−.58	−.73	−.16	−.67	−.32
Hysteria	−.47	−.51	−.20	−.51	−.29
Ego strength	.52	.75	.07	.69	.23
Observer-Rated					
HSRS	.72	.63	.42	.82	.48
PI adjustment	.83	.70	.50	.89	.59
Rated-Benefits Measures					
Patient-Rated					
ISPF change	.55	.09	.63	.35	.68
Satisfaction with therapy	.75	.29	.68	.55	.78
TC 1	.64	.32	.56	.52	.67
TC 2	.59	.22	.58	.46	.68
Therapist-Rated					
BARS change	.62	−.08	.86	.33	.80
SSI	.66	.07	.78	.40	.77
TC 1	.57	−.01	.73	.31	.70
TC 2	.60	.01	.76	.40	.73
Attractiveness of patient for therapy	.50	.13	.54	.35	.50
Liking for patient	.45	.03	.55	.28	.52
Reason for termination[b]	−.45	−.16	−.45	−.32	−.49

NOTE: ISPF = Inventory of Social and Psychological Functioning
HSRS = Health-Sickness Rating Scale
PI = Prognostic Index (Auerbach, Luborsky & Johnson, 1972)
TC = Target complaints change rating (Battle et al., 1966)
BARS = Brief Adjustment Rating Scale (Auerbach & Johnson, 1978)
SSI = Sum of therapist's ratings of patient satisfaction, success of therapy, and improvement
[a]Modified from the Hopkins Symptom Checklist (Derogatis et al., 1970).
[b]High = unnatural.

points was .60.) Similar operations for therapist- and patient-rated benefits measures produced two standardized subscores, which were then summed for the overall conjoint rated benefits criterion. (The correlation between the patient and therapist subscores was .60.) As might be expected in view of the large first principal component, the two composite dimensions, rated benefits and posttreatment adjustment, correlated substantially ($r = .60$).

Reliabilities of these multisource composites were estimated using the formula for reliability of sums (Nunnally, 1967) and are included in table 2-3. The reliability coefficients based on sums reflect Fiske's (1975) view that different sources are appropriately viewed not as alternate forms but rather as distinct entities. However, it should be kept in mind that combinations of reliable tests will also be highly reliable, even if the tests are totally unrelated. In such analyses, the resulting composite, although reliable, lacks construct validity, since the same score may reflect one dimension in one case and another dimension in a second case.

Accordingly, we also calculated by the Spearman-Brown formula the reliability coefficients obtained when the two sources combined for each composite are considered alternative measures. In both cases, the value obtained was .75. Although obviously lower, this level of reliability is still high enough to justify confidence in using the composite in research applications.

The very high correlations and high estimated reliabilities were, at least in part, spuriously elevated because the selection of measures for each composite was based on the factor analysis and thus capitalized on chance associations. However, it turned out that little selection of items was necessary for building reliable multi-item tests. Also, only the four single-item Klein Adjustment Scales were omitted in scoring composite criteria because of the scales' effect on estimated reliability of the composite measures. Accordingly, the role of chance factors in inflating these reliability estimates is probably relatively small. Of course, the study design did not include retesting. Therefore, these reliabilities are not estimates of stability of these measures within patients over time.

We are aware that at each step from the initial measures toward a more general criterion, some valid but relatively specific discrimination among cases made by some of the more reliable items is lost. The loss is, however, more than compensated for by the increased scope and generality of the resulting criteria, not only in clinical interest but in psychometric robustness as well, as indicated by the satisfying estimated reliabilities. The final structuring of the posttreatment analyses of Penn Project data is summarized in table 2-4.

TABLE 2-4

Correlations among Posttreatment Clusters:
Penn Psychotherapy Project

| | Rated Benefits | | Adjustment | |
Measure	Patient	Therapist	Patient	Clinical Observer
Rated Benefits				
Patient	1.00	.60	.53	.54
Therapist		1.00	.38	.46
Adjustment				
Patient			1.00	.60
Clinical Observer				1.00

NOTE: All correlations are statistically significant ($N = 73$).

A New Look at the Method Factors Data

Our initial within-viewpoint reanalyses of the University of Chicago data (Cartwright, Kirtner & Fiske, 1963; Fiske, Cartwright & Kirtner, 1964) demonstrated clearly that composites reflecting the same dimensions found in the Penn Psychotherapy Project could be measured with high reliability. Correlations among pretherapy adjustment measures derived from ratings by the patient, therapist, and interview diagnostician were all statistically significant. They were not high, however, ranging from .34 (between patient and diagnostician) to .46 (between patient and therapist).

Table 2-5 summarizes the analysis of agreement among the posttherapy

TABLE 2-5

Correlations among Posttreatment Clusters:
Reanalysis of University of Chicago Data

| | Rated Benefits | | Adjustment | | |
Measures	Client	Therapist	Client	Interview Diagnostician	Therapist
Rated Benefits					
Client	1.00	.60	.42	.49	.52
Therapist		1.00	.26	.52	.79
Adjustment					
Client			1.00	.39	.40
Interview Diagnostician				1.00	.59
Therapist					1.00

NOTE: Data from Cartwright, Kirtner, and Fiske (1963). All correlations are statistically significant ($N = 93$).

composites. As shown, measures drawn from the different sources correlated substantially. In fact, it was more difficult to make a case for distinct adjustment and benefits factors in the Chicago data than it had been in the Penn data. Results in the Chicago data were close to those obtained in the Penn Project analyses. Although the correlations obtained with the Chicago data were slightly lower, all differences between comparable correlations in the two analyses were nonsignificant.

Overall, the similarities are much more striking than the differences. In general, composite measures in the Penn Psychotherapy Project were based on many more component tests and scales than were available in the Chicago data. Accordingly, the Penn Project composites were somewhat more reliable and thus permitted higher intercorrelations among them to be obtained.

Are Ratings of Benefits Based on Changes in Adjustment?

Table 2-6 presents the correlations of the conjoint rated benefits measure with several functions of the conjoint pretreatment and posttreatment adjustment status measures. In the case of the best-fitting function, the correlation is a multiple correlation, finding the function of pretreatment and posttreatment adjustment that yields the best prediction of the level of rated benefits.

The results in table 2-6 include data from the Penn and Chicago studies, as well as some statistics from another study (Strupp, Wallach & Wogan, 1964), reported previously (Mintz, 1977). The best fitting function for

TABLE 2-6

Squared Correlations between Rated Benefits and Several
Functions of Pre- and Posttreatment Adjustment
in Three Studies

		\multicolumn{4}{c}{Study}
	Function	Penn	Chicago	Strupp	Mean
A.	Best Fit	.58	.58	.53	.56
B.	Residual Gain	.58	.50	.52	.54
C.	Raw Gain	.46	.30	.40	.39
D.	Final Level	.36	.49	.44	.43
	r_{AB}	.99	.93	.97	

NOTE: Penn   = Mintz, Luborsky, and Christoph (1979)
      Chicago = Cartwright, Kirtner, and Fiske (1963)
      Strupp = Strupp, Wallach, and Wogan (1964)
      r_{AB} = Correlation between best fit function and
                residual gain function

prediction of the global benefits measures was clearly most similar to the residual gain scores. This result has been discussed elsewhere (Mintz, 1977) and has been found in reanalyses of several studies.

Not only does the residual gain score appear to represent that component of change which is not confounded with or affected by initial adjustment level but it also appears to represent an important component of overall perception of benefits from treatment. Indeed, to the extent to which the global benefits measure can be interpreted as a pre–post change measure, it is best viewed as a measure of change relative to initial level—in short, a residual gain score.

Figure 2-1 shows the structure of the criteria in the Penn and Chicago data. As can be seen, results in the two studies were remarkably similar. Raw gain was calculated as the simple difference between pre- and posttreatment adjustment, each measured by the conjoint composites. Rated benefits was the conjoint patient–therapist measure, based on posttreatment ratings of change and benefits.

In figure 2-1, the raw gain measure has been partitioned into two independent components—one predictable on the basis of initial level of adjustment and the other independent of initial level (i.e., the residual gain score). The percentage of variance in the raw gain measure accounted for by each component is shown. Pretreatment adjustment accounted for about 15% of the variance in raw gain in both studies.

Similarly, the conjoint rated benefits measure has been partitioned into two components—one predictable from pretreatment and posttreatment adjustment levels and the other independent of those measures. These results are based on multiple regression analyses, using rated gain as the criterion and pretreatment and posttreatment adjustment as predictors. Again, proportions of variance accounted for by each component are shown. Results in both studies were almost identical, with pre–post changes in adjustment accounting for 58% of the variance in rated benefits.

Finally, these components were themselves intercorrelated. In both studies, the component of rated benefits predictable from pretreatment and posttreatment adjustment was very highly correlated with the residual gain score. In fact, in the Penn Psychotherapy Project data, the relationship was virtually perfect ($r = .99$). In the Chicago data, the relationship was lower, but still very substantial ($r = .93$).

DISCUSSION AND CONCLUSIONS

Two major points have emerged from our analysis of the Penn and Chicago data: (a) different viewpoints can agree to a substantial extent and (b) outcome as measured by ratings of improvement agrees substantially

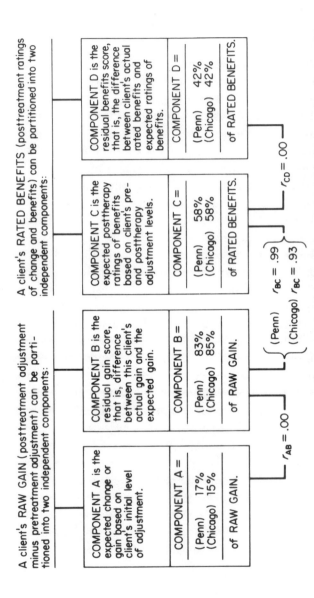

FIGURE 2-1. Some Components of Raw Gain and Rated Benefits Measures and Their Interrelationships

with residual gain scores calculated from pretherapy and posttherapy adjustment scores. In our own data, these criteria correlated .76; in the Cartwright, Kirtner, and Fiske (1963) data, .71. In both studies, the correlation between rated benefits and the residual gain score computed from pretreatment and posttreatment adjustment was very close to the best possible fit, based on multiple regression analyses. The slight differences in the results obtained in the two studies may, in part, reflect the inclusion of multi-item questionnaires in the adjustment composites in our own study, whereas in Cartwright, Kirtner, and Fiske (1963) only single-item ratings of adjustment (the 14 Behavioral Adequacy scales) were used to build composites.

We can now return to the basic questions posed at the outset about sources, content, and methodology. Several major conclusions stem from our analyses.

Sources: Agreement among Viewpoints

Substantial agreement among sources concerning therapy outcome was observed in both the Penn Psychotherapy Project and the University of Chicago data. The large correlations obtained among sources in the reanalysis of the Chicago data is a particularly striking finding in view of the fact that these same data were the basis for one of the most influential papers in the field (Cartwright, Kirtner & Fiske, 1963). In that paper, the overlap among sources was completely obscured.

Similarly, in Green et al.'s (1975) presentation, the correlations between patient and therapist measures are quite substantial, particularly when subscales of the measures are pooled to yield more reliable composites. In that study, when the five patient Symptom Checklist scales are standardized and summed and the five therapist adjustment measures are similarly standardized and summed, the correlation between the resulting adjustment composites, estimated from the formula for correlations of sums of standardized variables (Nunnally, 1967), is .64 pretherapy and .84 posttherapy. Correlations between the therapist rating of success and patient global ratings are apparently all significant and in several cases higher than those between two client-derived measures. In fact, the correlation between the single-item therapist benefit scale (probably of relatively low reliability) and a composite patient benefits scale, computed by standardizing and summing the patient ratings of symptom change and change in general, is .45. This is almost identical to the correlation between the two patient success ratings ($r = .46$).

This point has been discussed previously (Mintz, 1977) but needs to be repeated loudly and clearly. These findings deserve particular emphasis because they are in obvious contradiction to the common opinion. Relationships among similarly defined and highly reliable measures of outcome across different sources of evaluation ("viewpoints") were substantial, and conceptually meaningful composites with high reliability could be constructed.

In our view, there are several reasons for the now widespread acceptance of the idea that sources do not agree substantially. First, the factor-analytic methodology used in several studies making this point (e.g., Cartwright, Kirtner & Fiske, 1963) maximizes the importance of so-called method factors. Second, as noted by Gurman and Razin (1977), there is a strong conservative tendency in the field; once reported, conclusions tend to be believed indefinitely, even when subsequent data do not support them. Frequently, outcome measures are single-item ratings or change scores with poor reliabilities, both of which attenuate correlations (see Luborsky, 1971).

Finally, it should be said that distinct viewpoints *do* exist. Even in our data, correlations between sources did not approach the reliabilities. The correlations found in both the Penn Psychotherapy Project and the Chicago data were in the area of .5 to .6. Surely this represents substantial and important commonality of judgment concerning status and outcome. Berzins, Bednar, and Severy (1975) have stressed the importance of this consensus for establishing a foundation on which to base scientific evaluation of treatment outcome as well as ethical accountability of practitioners.

Content: Value of Adjustment and Treatment Benefits as Dimensions of Change

Our analyses provide strong support for the notion that broadly defined constructs of adjustment and benefits from treatment can be meaningfully measured. Although they obviously did not account for all of the information available in the many original measures, they did appear to represent the major common dimensions of outcome.

We began our data reduction analyses with hundreds of measures drawn from many domains of content. Reviewing the results of these analyses, the clinical reader may feel that reductionism has, to some degree, carried the day. In response to that criticism, we note that these broadly defined measures make clinical sense, and that in our analyses they related meaningfully across viewpoints and had very acceptable reliabilities.

We note with some post hoc regret that type of measure was confounded with viewpoint. Therapist measures were obtained posttreatment and were virtually all ratings of perceived benefits, success, or amount of change and improvement in the patient. Clinical observers interviewed the patient before and after treatment. Virtually all of the ratings obtained from that viewpoint were measures of current adjustment status. Only patients were asked to provide both kinds of ratings. In future studies, we believe, both adjustment status measures and ratings of benefits or change should be obtained from each viewpoint.

Measurement Methodology: Agreement of Outcome Ratings with Corrected Difference Score

We have learned that global ratings of gain or success made after treatment have a substantial and meaningful connection with change as measured by separate pretreatment and posttreatment assessments. In our data, the best predictor of success ratings was the residual gain score. This finding appears to have some generality, judging from other studies.

Green et al. (1975) presented correlations between three global success ratings and 10 pre and post dimensions (5 drawn from the patient and 5 from the therapist). For 28 of the 30 variables, correlations between global success ratings and residual gain scores were greater than the correlations with simple change scores. The authors commented on the superiority of the residual gain score to the simple difference score in accounting for global success ratings. What they did not state was that a similar result is obtained when residual gain is compared with final level alone. In 19 out of 28 cases (for two variables, results were the same), residual gain correlated more highly with success ratings than did posttreatment level of adjustment alone.

In this light, the frequent finding that global success ratings correlate more highly with final status than they do with difference scores takes on new meaning. The residual gain function does weight final status more heavily than pretreatment status. Indeed, when pre–post correlations are low, the difference between residual gain and final status is negligible. On this basis, we can agree with the recommendation of Green et al. (1975) to use final status as an outcome measure *when pre–post correlation is low.* But this rarely occurs; pretreatment status is often highly relevant to understanding the global evaluation of outcome. To the extent that global evaluations are based on change as measured by pre–post differences, they often appear to rescale change relative to the initial level. The degree to which this alters the scale of global ratings depends on the level of the pre–post correlation. The frequent recommendation to use the residual gain score as an outcome measure (Fiske et al., 1964; Manning & DuBois, 1962) is strongly supported by our data. In each block of data we analyzed, the residual gain score had the highest average correlation with other criteria (i.e., had more common variance). To be sure, this is to some degree a statistical artifact since the residual gain is a mathematical function of pretreatment and posttreatment scores. Nevertheless, it is the single measure that overlaps most with the total set of possible indexes.

An equally important implication of this finding is that a substantial and reliable portion of the variation in global success ratings is *not* simply related to gains as measured by pretreatment and posttreatment adjustment status. The determinants of this portion are largely unknown. It remains to be discovered to what degree it is best conceptualized in negative terms (such as bias or halo effect), in positive terms (such as insight), as process aspects of change not tapped by the pretreatment and posttreatment adjustment measures, as a unique weighting of elements of change in each case, or by some combinations of these elements.

Summary

We listed at the beginning of this chapter the broad range of outcome measures from three points of view: patients, therapists, and clinical observers. In the next section we presented the principles we evolved for combining outcome measures derived from the patient's, the therapist's, and the clinical observer's points of view (Mintz, Luborsky & Christoph, 1979). The core of the chapter is our comparison of our data with our reanalysis of the influential "method factors" outcome data from the Chicago study (Cartwright, Kirtner & Fiske, 1963). Results in the two studies were very similar: We found substantial agreement among viewpoints about broadly defined treatment outcomes, although distinct viewpoints did clearly also exist. Contrary to a common opinion, consensus measures of psychotherapy outcome could be meaningfully defined. A strong relationship was found between (1) posttreatment ratings of benefits from therapy (e.g., "rated benefits") and (2) measures of adjustment obtained before and after treatment (e.g., "residual gain"), suggesting that posttreatment ratings of outcome effectively take account of the fact that the amount of change to be expected depends on the initial level of functioning.

3

How Much Did
the Patients Benefit?

WE URGENTLY NEEDED to know early in our study how much benefit the patients achieved from their psychotherapy. If the benefits were slight, it would be unfortunate not only for the patients but also for the research-ers: it would not be worth persisting in the research effort just to predict slight benefits.

Before we present quantitative measures of the patients' benefits, we will give brief clinical outcome sketches of patients in the Penn Psycho-therapy Project. We offer these case descriptions because we believe that the richness of such clinical data taken together with the quantitative data will be more informative than either account alone.

Clinical Outcome Sketches

Six patients were chosen for these sketches because they represented extremes in terms of the outcome measures described in the preceding chapter: 3 of these patients ended treatment among the 10 most im-proved and 3 among the 10 least improved. Each of these sketches was provided by a research evaluator as part of the initial and termination evaluations.

MORE IMPROVED PATIENTS

Ms. Samuelson (#49)

Initial. Ms. Samuelson's initial symptoms were depression, suicidal thoughts, and phobias. She was a divorced woman who had custody of her two children and held a full-time job as a dress designer for a big firm. She considered herself talented at her work, and from time to time she was angry at her employers for not giving her commensurate recognition. She had been having a long-term affair with a married man; just before she came to treatment she realized that the man's wife would be unwilling to give him up and that she therefore should end the affair. That realization had a demoralizing and depressing effect upon her. However, one of her goals was still to give him up.

Termination. During the time she was in psychotherapy (about 28 months) she developed a style of life that largely satisfied her. She attributed most of the changes to the therapy without having much of an idea of how the therapy had resulted in these changes. The therapy appears not to have been very insight-oriented. Not that the therapist did not try at first to provide insight—to a large extent the patient did not seem interested in self-understanding.

Toward the end of treatment she resigned from the dress firm and began successfully to manage her own business. After therapy she was not depressed, did not have suicidal thoughts, and seemed to be much less phobic. Although she did not have any immediate prospects for remarriage, she had a number of friends of both sexes. There did seem to be a significant lack of concern for other people—none of her talk about her friends or her children gave much sense of involvement with them. In general, however, the termination interviewer considered the treatment very successful and expected her to continue at the final high level.

Mr. Norris (#27)

Initial. At the start of treatment, when he was a third-year college student, Mr. Norris's main complaints were a fear of impotence and difficulty in speaking in front of groups. He had been guarded and suspicious with other people. He also felt he was floundering in finding his vocational direction, he had a sense of dissatisfaction with his performance, and he felt he was not working up to his level of ability.

Six months previous he had completed 8 months of psychotherapy aimed at similar symptoms, including the impotence and feelings of inadequacy. He benefited somewhat, but after termination he spent several months in drug taking, especially LSD, he limited his social contacts, and he consumed much time being "lost" in reading.

Termination. After 20 months of therapy he did not have the problem of impotence, but the improvement may have been situational. His general pattern was to be impotent when he started a new relationship with a woman. Later he would become potent, although his impotence would sometimes return. At termination he had been living with a woman for about 8 months and had experienced only the initial impotence with her. He felt that she was nonthreatening and that he was the stronger one in the relationship. He expected to be impotent again at the start of any new relationship.

The patient did seem to have become better able to tolerate anxiety. He said that in talking to people he was usually anxious at first but that when he exerted himself to carry on the anxiety usually subsided. He believed the speaking anxiety had become better but he was not sure. After his graduation from college (during therapy) he had not often been in front of groups, so it was difficult to test his adequacy. He sometimes still used marijuana and LSD, which may have been in part anxiety-related. The last LSD use was 3 months before termination, and he continued to use marijuana about once every 3 weeks.

His feeling of not accomplishing as much intellectually as he should remained something of a problem. He received a fellowship to study sociology and he hoped to do better in an academic environment. He was not sure whether he would pursue further education after his master's degree.

The termination interviewer felt that the patient had improved somewhat. Mr. Norris obviously felt that he had improved, and he gave the impression of a young man who had done some growing up over the two years of therapy. The interviewer thought there was something lacking in this patient's level of insight. The decision to terminate was a mutual one based on the fact that the patient had become more comfortable and had achieved some of his goals.

Mr. Howard (#44)

Initial. Mr. Howard, an 18-year-old white male who had completed part of his first year of college in New York State, came to psychotherapy with complaints of these problems: resentment of his parents, sporadic pain in the penis, difficulty in dealing with a new girlfriend, anxiety, and guilt. In growing up he never felt close to his father but was very close to his mother. He felt the need to comfort and take care of her.

On the one hand, he was expected to have a good prognosis with the help of psychotherapy. He seemed to relate well to doctors, he was warm and open. He appeared to be well motivated and able to learn. He had been reading some psychoanalysis and seemed to have gotten something from it. Also, his conflicts were seen as perhaps no more than an exacerbation of normal adolescent conflicts, chiefly intense guilt over sex.

On the other hand, his thoughts about wanting to be like an exalted spiritual leader were somewhat confused: "I'd like to have what he had, without the preliminary steps." By "what he had," perhaps he meant his spiritual power. This may simply be an expression of the patient's desire to be a great person, or it may reflect schizoid trends.

It was not clear whether there was prognostic significance in the fact that his guilt over sex took the form of a conversion symptom—pain in his penis—rather than just experience of guilt. The initial evaluation could predict only that failure to improve would indicate either that he had schizoid tendencies or that his underlying guilt was too strong, particularly his guilty attachment to his mother.

Termination. The initial contact with him revealed that he had difficulties in knowing how to be assertive, establish an identity, become separate from his family, be less passive, and relate better to his peers, especially women. Although there was no evidence of an active thought disorder, before therapy the patient described "panicky feelings" about not being able to keep himself "in control" and the sense that he was so weak that he would need to be a spiritual leader in order to obtain any of his desires. There was concern about the possibility of psychotic deterioration.

After his return from a holiday visit with his parents, the patient appeared to be remarkably more stable. He had not used the medication that had been offered because he felt that it was not necessary. During the spring he examined his fear of closeness in relationships; he also continued a relationship with a fellow freshman and experienced his first sexual intercourse with her. Through his relationship with his new girlfriend and with his therapist, he began to reexperience many of his oedipal conflicts.

As the summer vacation approached, the patient became increasingly anxious as he contemplated returning home to work. Instead he elected to stay and to continue therapy and to maintain contact with his girlfriend. During the summer he began more actively to examine his ambivalence in relationships. He experienced increased anxiety during which he described events that suggested referential ideation. However, when he visited his parents during the summer he found himself able to respond in a much more satisfactory and assertive fashion and felt encouraged by that.

In the fall the patient returned to school; he and his girlfriend made arrangements to live together. As the anticipated problems developed, the patient began to be able to evaluate the transference relationship in the triangle created between him, his girlfriend, and his therapist. He seemed to understand more clearly the mechanism of his "need to be better" and found himself able to maintain and form relationships.

He responded to the therapist's departure and the impending separation with a reawakening of his earlier feelings of needing to be all-powerful in order to survive and to gain his desires. But by the time of the final appointment the patient was able to understand much of his current difficulty not only in terms of transference but also in light of the way he had learned to respond to his situation at home during his earlier years. He agreed that in the future he would find himself better able to utilize many of the achievements of this period of therapy. He entertained (ambivalently) the idea of marriage to his current girlfriend and made plans involving education and training. He felt that the future held for him the probability of learning how to successfully accomplish those things that he wanted.

LESS IMPROVED PATIENTS

Ms. Kane (#6)

Initial. Ms. Kane was in her last year of college and thinking about graduate school. Her main initial relationship problem was, as she saw it, "I can't have a relationship with a guy." Her accounts of relationships showed that the problem of maintaining a relationship was a general one and included the one with her parents. Her relationships all seemed to her to be utterly frustrating failures. She explained that her relationship problem was based on having grown up with a mother who was incapable of mothering. She summed up her mother's level of functioning as "she couldn't boil water."

A highly emotional incident first brought her to the student health service. The women in her dormitory described her problem as a "nervous breakdown." The "breakdown" came on during and after a phone conversation in which her boyfriend informed her he was giving her up. She tried to find out why he had given her up but couldn't. She could not understand the problem in her relationships. Some nights she was unable to sleep as she tried to figure out what had gone on; at other times she slept an unusual amount. At times her thinking seemed loose, and she was extremely distractable. On some occasions she was suspicious, she avoided facing things, and she became full of suicidal thoughts.

Termination. She remained very much in need of treatment, and it was hard to see any gains. She explained her lack of progress in terms of the unsuitability of the therapist. She would have preferred that he give her overt direction. In contrast, she thought she had profited more from the six sessions she had at the student health service, as part of a time-limited treatment, because that therapy fulfilled her need for direction.

She was an intelligent person who could identify some of her relationship problems, but the awareness contributed very little to mastery of them. In each new relationship she seemed to choose people with whom she would reenact the lack of contact that characterized her relationship with her mother. When a person could provide direction, she sometimes experienced satisfaction in the relationship, but eventually the relationship would disintegrate. This pattern appeared to operate in her sexual behavior. She explained that she said yes too soon. Actually, saying yes appeared to be based on her yearning for immediate contact and direction. She claimed to understand that she was too open and got involved too soon, yet she had trouble modulating her involvement. Once she realized that she had become too involved, she felt disappointed in the response of the other person and wanted to withdraw.

With her intelligence and good school record, she could expect to get into graduate school; that training should serve as a source of structure in her life. She got some support from her dormitory, which she described as being "like a commune." The termination interviewer predicted that she might integrate briefly if she found a more suitable boyfriend. But it did not seem likely that without more successful treatment her severe relationship problems would alter very much.

Mr. Denny (# 77)

Initial. Mr. Denny started psychotherapy when he was a senior in college. He stated as his initial goals for the treatment to overcome nervousness and tension, difficulty with schoolwork—especially in concentration—and uneasiness in relationships. A few weeks before he came he had tried to kill himself by taking an overdose because a girlfriend had given up on him. He was briefly hospitalized and then went to live at home. In the initial interview he described his mother as meticulously neat and his father as calm, quiet, and kind of passive. The patient was excitable and very aggressive at the time.

Termination. His therapy lasted about 8 months. He reported slight improvement in one of the problems for which he sought therapy—nervousness and tension. But there was no change in his problem of uneasiness in relationships; his problem of poor school performance got worse. His global rating indicated that he was "very dissatisfied" with the result of his treatment because it seemed to him that the school problem was paramount. At termination it looked as if he would be asked to leave college. He still tended to attribute his problems to external events. He felt close to blowing up from his anxiety at falling further behind in his schoolwork; as a sophomore he had had to drop out one semester as a result of a similar predicament.

The same personality traits remained present at termination as were noted before therapy—passivity, inhibition, the feeling that others did not respect him, and a tendency to repress or suppress things: "I block things out of my mind." Blocking his schoolwork out of his mind left him unprepared for his courses.

His relationships with his peers remained meager and unsatisfying. He had not been dating during the preceding academic year. He had one fairly close, nonromantic relationship with a young woman engaged to someone else. It seemed to him that most of the people he knew were interested in him only when he could do them a favor. He felt pessimistic about his future. He described himself and his parents as part of a healthy family (although it was hard for the interviewer to imagine that he saw them clearly). He felt he was in treatment for his family, not for himself.

About his therapy, he says that he gained insight into his unconscious anger and the fact that his current interpersonal patterns were similar to those he had earlier in life. However, he did not believe that these insights had been helpful: "I don't know how to deal with them." Further, he was bothered by the new awareness of some of the personality traits to which he had been oblivious. Often he left the therapy sessions more depressed than when he had entered. His therapist was interested in hearing about the patient's early life, and he complied, but he did not think that speaking of that was helpful. Asked whether his therapist was warm, the patient replied that he was "professional" and seemed to accept that as satisfactory. Therapy did not make him feel less isolated. He would have liked advice from his therapist, but the therapist stated that it was not his job to provide that.

Ms. Innes (#5)

Initial. At the start of treatment the 22-year-old sales representative, Ms. Innes, appeared to have an adolescent adjustment reaction or a poorly defined personality disturbance. The symptoms of her acute episode (of overeating and stealing) went back to the previous winter. Her other symptoms included dependency on others—a trait that had been especially marked in prep school, where her whole life was guided by what others thought. She also had some possibly serious defensive detachment from others and some feelings of intellectual confusion at times. The patient experienced conscious guilt and perhaps unconscious guilt and need for punishment. Those feelings would be expected to influence the course of treatment. The patient's main reasons for treatment were trouble with making decisions, dependency problems on her parents, and problems with overeating and stealing.

Termination. Her therapy provided her with a good relationship, which she sorely needed. The therapist was somewhat older than she, but not so much older that she could not have fantasies about him. She did not speak of fantasies, but she did say that she felt dependent on her therapist and needed him. She also said that in her love life she was looking for a father figure.

The summer before termination, having broken up with the man she was living with, she started a relationship with an older man. "I convinced myself that I was in love with him so that I could sleep with him." However, he did not seem to reciprocate her feelings, and before long he went back to a previous girlfriend.

It seems that she then did not have any romantic interest for a while, then she had a date with a new man. She went to bed with him the first night and then felt very upset. She felt she had ruined the chance for a good relationship and that she had fallen back into her old pattern of too much sex too soon. (It is as though she could not tolerate the anxiety of letting the relationship develop first in a nonsexual way, probably out of fear that she would be rejected. The patient said that she did not bring any personality to the relationships.)

She went into a bad state for about 2 weeks. She was anxious, depressed, did not go to work, and must have had some dissociative periods: once she found herself lying on the bathroom floor in a building, and she did not know how she had got there: "I lost my perspective of space and time." She constructed a rationalization for what she was feeling during this period: "Since I felt like nothing I wanted to experience the center of my nothingness." She wanted her therapist to rescue her and to take responsibility for her. But she was able to accept his telling her in essence that what happened was up to her. She seemed rather sick, but the interviewer believed that she had probably experienced a hysterical dissociated state rather than a schizoid episode.

The therapy was a very strong source of support. Intellectual insights did not seem to have been very important for her, although she was quite bright and alert. The one insight she reported when asked for examples was, "I learned that I don't have parents." This interpretation, which had recently been offered by her therapist, seemed very important to her. Evidently, it represented a step toward independence and emotional divorce from her parents.

The interviewer predicted further improvement but was not certain whether the therapeutic relationship would prove to be the beginning of true growth, or would turn out to have been only temporary supportive help without underlying change.

COMMENTS

These selected examples taken from the larger group of 73 patients in the Penn Psychotherapy Project sample indicate that there were some patients who achieved their goals to a clinically meaningful degree and others who did not. The next section will give a more quantitative account of the amount of benefit achieved in the larger group of 73 patients.

Other impressions provided by this small sample of brief sketches will be examined in later chapters: (1) The improved patients clearly showed more of a positive helping alliance than the less improved patients (chapters 11–14). (2) The less improved patients gained very little usable insight; the more improved patients gained some but not an impressive amount (chapter 17).

Quantitative Measures of Benefits

The patients' benefits are estimated here by several measures: (1) general improvement, (2) specific improvement on target complaints, (3) amount of deterioration, and (4) comparisons of an effect size measure for the Penn Psychotherapy Project group relative to other similar psychotherapy and control groups. We did not include among these measures our two main outcome composites, residual gain and rated benefits, which are based on our own measures (transformed into standard scores with the mean defined as zero) and therefore do not permit comparison with other studies.

GENERAL IMPROVEMENT WAS SUBSTANTIAL

A standard numerical measure of the amount of benefits received from the treatment is the percentage of patients benefiting. These percentages tended to be large, whether they were estimated by the therapist or by the observer (table 3-1). For example, combining "moderate" and "much" improvement, the therapists rated 65% of patients as improved and the observers rated 56% as improved.

TABLE 3-1

Outcome Ratings from the Penn Psychotherapy Project (Percentages)

Variable and Source of Rating	Improvement				
	Got Worse	No Change	Slight	Moderate	Much
Global Improvement					
Therapist	1	7	27	43	22
Observer	3	14	27	51	5
Mean	2	10	27	47	14
Target Complaint 1					
Therapist	1	7	21	33	38
Patient	4	7	11	29	49
Mean	2	7	16	31	44

TABLE 3-2

Outcome Ratings of Five Samples Rated By Therapists
(Percentages)

Sample	Improvement				At Mode
	Worse	No Change	Small to Moderate	Large	
Menninger Foundation (N = 200)	2	9	64	24	34
Luborsky (N = 39)	2	0	69	28	46
Garfield et al. (1971) (N = 34)	3	6	56	35	44
Mintz et al. (1971) (N = 27)	7	26	52	15	44
Fiske et al. (1964) (N = 93)	3	15	59	22	59
All Samples (N = 393)	3	10	62	25	43

Source: Mintz, 1977, pp. 590–602.

The magnitude of the benefits in the Penn Psychotherapy Project tended to be similar to those in other studies. For example, the distributions of global benefits ratings in five studies (Mintz, 1977) with a total of 393 patients (table 3-2), showed 25 percent of patients with "large" change, 62 percent "small-to-moderate" change, 10 percent "no change," and 3 percent "worse." Bergin (1971) summarized many more studies and concluded that 65 percent of treated patients (excluding dropouts) showed "moderate improvement" or better. Therefore, in most studies about two-thirds of patients in psychotherapy were judged to show "moderate to much" improvement.

SPECIFIC IMPROVEMENT WAS LARGER THAN GENERAL IMPROVEMENT

Percentages of general improvement do not reveal the meaningfulness of the changes to the patient. In contrast, more specific information is offered by the Target Complaints measures (Battle et al., 1966). These "complaints" are statements in the patient's own terms of goals for the outcomes of psychotherapy. In fact, in our project, as is often true, the improvement on specific complaints for which the patients came to treatment was even greater than their general improvement (table 3-1)—38 percent of patients were rated by the therapists as "much improved" on their Target Complaints, but only 22 percent were in this category in terms of general improvement.

To amplify the meaning of the numerical measures we will give some examples of the kinds of Target Complaints that impelled these patients to come to treatment and of the degree to which the complaints were resolved by the time of termination. The examples chosen were Target Complaints 1 (primary complaint) and 2 (secondary complaint) for the six patients we described earlier (table 3-3). The rating scale for *severity* was "1" (most severe problem) to "11" (least severe problem); the rating scale for the *amount of change* was "1" (little change) to "5" (greatest change). The following are two of the six examples from table 3-3: Ms. Samuelson (#49), a more improved patient, listed as her Target Complaint 1 "unhappiness," by which she referred to her depression. She rated its severity pretreatment as "2," meaning "severe," and posttreatment as "9"; on the amount of change scale she gave it a "5," meaning it was "much better." Her Target Complaint 2 was "fear of heights," which improved similarly. Target Complaints 1 and 2 were also both judged by the therapist to be "much better." These examples illustrate some of the personal meanings of the benefits that accrue to patients who have improved.

A general conclusion emerges from the general and specific improvement figures. The benefits achieved by the more improved patients tend to be sufficient to make a meaningful difference in the patients' functioning, even though their earlier state tends to be still recognizable. For example, a patient who, like Ms. Samuelson, is prone to depression before treatment is not entirely free of proneness to depression at the termination

TABLE 3-3

Patient's Target Complaints (TC) and Ratings for Three More Improved Versus Three Less Improved Patients

Complaint	Pre[a]	Post[a]	Ratings of Change
Ms. Samuelson (#49)			
TC1: "Unhappiness"	2	9	5 "Much better"
TC2: "Fear of heights"	3	8	5 "Much better"
Mr. Norris (#27)			
TC1: "Sexual impotence"	3	11	5 "Much better"
TC2: "Can't talk in front of people"	5	6	3 "A little better"
Mr. Howard (#44)			
TC1: "Sexual problem"	3	10	5 "Much better"
TC2: "Feeling of lack of personal worth"	2	8	4 "Moderately better"
Ms. Kane (#6)			
TC1: "Relationships with men"	1	2	1 "Worse"
TC2: "Live up to the job"	2	not mentioned	3 "A little better"
Mr. Denny (#77)			
TC1: "Nervousness and tension"	7	6	1 "A very little better"
TC2: "Can't concentrate"	1	1	1 "Somewhat worse"
Ms. Innes (#5)			
TC1: "Trouble making decisions"	7	9	4 "Moderately better"
TC2: "Depending on parents"	5	7	5 "Much better"

[a]Rating Scale: 1 = couldn't be worse; 11 = doesn't bother me at all.

of therapy; instead she is less prone to it and has more mastery of it when it emerges. David Rapaport once recalled an old story about Moses to illustrate this conclusion (Gill, 1977, p. 724):

> Moses' portrait was brought to an oriental king whose astrologers and phrenologists concluded from it that Moses was a cruel, greedy, craven, self-seeking man. The king, who had heard that Moses was a leader, kindly, generous, and bold, was puzzled, and went to visit Moses. When meeting him, he saw the portrait was good and said: "My phrenologists and astrologers were wrong." But Moses disagreed: "Your phrenologists and astrologers were right, they saw what I was made of; what they couldn't tell you was that I struggled against all that and so became what I am."

Although later personality development can show major changes from the earlier personality, the earlier personality tends to remain evident. The wise men still recognized Moses's basic earlier personality despite changes in his appearance. This conclusion will appear again (in chapter 18) when we discuss the ways in which the patients overcome their core conflictual relationship theme problems.

DETERIORATION WAS INFREQUENT

Not all patients receive significant benefits from psychotherapy. In fact, a few deteriorate, according to some reviews (Strupp, Hadley & Gomes-Schwartz, 1977; Bergin & Lambert, 1978; Lambert, Bergin & Collins, 1977). For example, Lambert, Bergin, and Collins (1977) reviewed 47 studies and concluded that some patients deteriorated both in treatment groups and in control groups, but the percentages varied so widely that it was impossible to offer a typical figure. Nevertheless, based on their tables of results, we located 2–10 percent deterioration as the most usual and 0–1 percent as the next most usual figure. The combined categories apply to about 70 percent of the studies. Similarly, four other studies in our table 3-2 give data on therapist improvement ratings in which the percentages for deterioration were only 2–3 percent.

In the Penn Psychotherapy Project, according to our ratings of improvement, we found little that could be called clear-cut deterioration. In fact, table 3-1 shows that out of 73 patients only 1 percent were rated by the therapist and only 3 percent by the clinical observer as "worse." Not one of these few patients who were "worse" had seriously deteriorated; instead each was more accurately described as upset and disappointed with the outcome. Thus, what is really remarkable about our group of initially moderately to severely disturbed patients who were in treatment on the average 6 months to 1 year, is that so few of them got worse.

The Penn Psychotherapy Project offers additional data pertinent to this conclusion. If, instead of considering the improvement ratings alone, we examine pre–post changes on a sample of our assessment measures, the percentages of patients who got worse is slightly higher. The sample of assessment measures includes the Inventory of Social and Personality Functioning, the Symptom Checklist, the three MMPI measures, and the Health-Sickness Rating Scale. On these measures 7 percent of our patients showed a worsening on the (standardized) change scores of $-.1$ to $-.5$ standard deviation and another 6 percent had deteriorated more than $-.5$ standard deviation. Can these larger deterioration figures be reconciled with those from the improvement ratings? Such reconciliation is difficult because each assessment measure appears to have different meanings for clinical improvement; for example, to "get worse" on the Inventory of Social and Personality Functioning may not be exactly the same as to "get worse" on the global improvement scale, since the former measures a more limited aspect than the latter. Therefore, the estimate of the amount of deterioration depends on the measure.

EFFECT SIZES OF BENEFITS WERE SUBSTANTIAL

For a more precise way of estimating the benefits of psychotherapy, we relied on one of Cohen's (1969) effect size (ES) measures to describe the size of the changes in our outcome measures. Each effect size for each outcome measure was calculated as the pretreatment mean minus the posttreatment mean, divided by the pretreatment standard deviation. This is a within-group effect size measure and allows us to express the benefits in terms of standard deviations from the pretreatment status distribution. Comparisons of the same outcome measure in different studies and even comparisons of different outcome measures in these studies can be made directly since ESs are scores transformed into a standard unit. For example, measures with an ES of 1 indicate that a person who begins treatment in the middle of the patient sample (50th percentile) is expected to be one standard deviation improved (84th percentile) by the end of treatment (Glass, McGaw & Smith, 1981).

The advantages of the effect size measures seem obvious both because of their precision and because of the increased comparability across studies provided by their standard unit of change (Lambert, Christensen & DeJulio, 1983). Yet one objection has been raised: They do not necessarily convey the importance of the changes (as noted by Yeaton & Sechrest, 1981). At times such an objection may be justified, but it is not for the present research, since the main benefits represent achieving targets that are vital to the patient, as we noted earlier.

The remainder of this section will provide perspective on the benefits achieved by the patients in the Penn Psychotherapy Project. We will present the results of three sets of comparison data: (1) effect sizes of the Luborsky set of somewhat similar psychotherapy (SSSP) groups, (2) effect sizes of the Luborsky set of somewhat similar control (SSSC) groups, and (3) effect sizes of the Glass set of control groups.

Effect Sizes of the Luborsky SSSP Groups Were Substantial

The effect sizes are assembled in the major table 3-4 for the 10 studies of the SSSP treated groups—the Penn group and the 9 other groups. Five of these 9 psychotherapy groups had some form of control group. The table includes the effect sizes in both psychotherapy and control groups for all of the most usual outcome measures. We present these in detail

TABLE 3-4

Outcomes in Terms of Effect Sizes for the Set of Somewhat Similar Psychotherapy Control Groups

Study	Reference	Type of Therapy (N)	Outcome Measure	Treated Group Effect Size (N)	Waitlist Control Effect Size (N)	Untreated Group Effect Size (N)
U. of Pennsylvania	Luborsky, Mintz, et al. (1980)	Supportive-expressive Psy. (73)	HSRS	.63	—	—
			SCL	.80		
			MMPI			
			Hs	.52		
			Hy	.57		
			Es	.55		
			TC1	2.53		
			TC2	1.93		
			Average ES	1.05		
U. of Chicago	Fiske, Cartwright, and Kirtner (1964)[a]	Client-Centered Psy. (93)	MMPI			
			Hs	.49		
			Hy	.68		
			Es	.47		
			T-rated Adj.	.78		
			P-rated Adj.	.45		
			O-rated Adj.	.65		
			Average ES	.61		
Menninger Foundation	Kernberg et al. (1972)[b]	Psychoanalysis (21); Supportive-Expressive Psy. (21)	HSRS	.77		
Temple U.	Sloane et al. (1975)	Psychoanalytically Oriented Psy. (30)	TC1	2.72	.85	

TABLE 3-4 *(Continued)*

Study	Reference	Type of Therapy (N)	Outcome Measure	Treated Group Effect Size (N)	Waitlist Control Effect Size (N)	Untreated Group Effect Size (N)
Endicott	Endicott & Endicott (1964)[c]	*Dynamically Oriented Psy.* (17)	MMPI			
			Hs	.75		.16
			Hy	.53		.38
			Es	.34		.14
			Severity of Symptoms	1.20	.23	
			Average ES	.87	.78	
					.51	
Vanderbilt U.	Strupp & Hadley (1979)[d]	*Dynamically Oriented Psy.* (16 by Ts, 15 by Alternate Ts.)	HSRS	1.03	.28	
			MMPI	1.07	.85	.92 (19)
			D	.83		
			Psy 1	1.14		
			Soc Intro 1	1.23		
			Severity Rating	.95	−.09	
			PSS (3 scales)	.56	.20	
			Depression	1.13		
			TC1 (therapist)	1.69	2.20	
			TC2 (therapist)	1.12	.90	
			TC1 (alternate)	2.40		
			TC2 (alternate)	2.24		
			Average ES	1.10	.56	
Johns Hopkins U.	Liberman (1978)[e]	*Dynamically Oriented Psy.*	SCL	.60 (13)	.46 (13)	
			Soc/Ineffective	1.17 (13)	.15 (13)	
			Average ES	.89	.31	

TABLE 3-4 (Continued)

Study	Reference	Type of Therapy (N)	Outcome Measure	Treated Group Effect Size (N)	Waitlist Control Effect Size (N)	Untreated Group Effect Size (N)
Kaiser Foundation	Barron & Leary (1955)	*Psychoanalytic Psy* (42)	MMPI			
			Hy	.50	.25	
			Hs	.27	.19	
			Es	.76	.29	
University Hospital Leuven	Pierloot & Vinck (1978)[f]	*Dynamic* (9)	SCL	.30		
			PSS subjective distress	1.19		
			PSS denial of illness	.15		
			PSS summary role	.47		
			Average ES	.53		
U. of Queensland	Cross, Sheehan & Kahn (1982)	*Insight* (11)	TC1	3.60		
			Anxiety	3.00		
			Truax Adj. Rating	1.14		
			Average ES	2.58		

[a]Plus unpublished data supplied by Donald Fiske.
[b]Plus unpublished data supplied by Lolafaye Coyne.
[c]Plus unpublished data supplied by Noble Endicott.
[d]Plus unpublished data supplied by Hans Strupp.
[e]Plus partly unpublished data supplied by Bernard Liberman based on Frank et al. (1978).
[f]From a preprint of an article supplied by Jan Vinck.

because we expect that they will serve as a resource for researchers who wish to make their own comparisons.

Only four minimal requirements were used for admission into the Luborsky SSSP groups, a set assembled primarily for comparison with the Penn Psychotherapy Project group: The patients must be (1) referred by self or conventional sources (i.e., were not volunteers or recruits); (2) given psychotherapy, not analogue or group treatments, such as marathon therapy; (3) treated for general adjustment and neurotic problems (not primarily for specific and limited symptoms, such as enuresis or public speaking anxiety); and (4) evaluated by outcome measures that included some of the recommended general adjustment measures (e.g., by Waskow & Parloff, 1975) rather than outcome measures dealing only with changes in specific and limited symptoms. One further inevitable necessity for inclusion in the SSSP groups was that the data for the pre and post means and standard deviations of the outcome measures were available to us.[1]

Before telling more about the results from the SSSP groups, we need to explain why the set is so skimpy, especially in comparison with the hundreds of studies in Smith, Glass, and Miller (1980) and even after a wider search that tapped cooperative psychotherapy researchers' unpublished data. Mainly because of Smith, Glass, and Miller (1980) and the widening wave of meta-analyses, the impression has become widespread among clinicians as well as many researchers that wads of research data on psychotherapy-treated groups are tucked away somewhere. Unfortunately, that impression is mistaken. Our relatively few SSSP groups were all that could be found. It did seem to us extraordinary that the search within the 475 studies of Smith et al. had turned up only three studies for the SSSP groups: Endicott and Endicott (1963, 1964), Liberman (1978), and Barron and Leary (1955)!

Other researchers have tried to create their own sets for other special purposes. Andrews and Harvey (1981) searched for a subset of subjects within Smith, Glass, and Miller (1980) that would be especially relevant to the work of clinicians. They did succeed to some extent, for they identified 81 studies with patients who fit their admission profile: (1) patients diagnosed as having neuroses, true phobias, and emotional/so-

---

[1]The data for two potential SSSP studies were not available to us. Schlein et al. (1962) could not find their data (personal communication, 1980). Also, Sloane et al. (1975) could not provide their data. After several discussions with them they informed us (personal communication, 1980) that "all individual data were destroyed. We had to do this since at the outset we made this promise to patients in order to get their cooperation." Furthermore, their book does not report pre and post measures or standard deviations, so effect sizes can not be computed. We managed nevertheless to tease out a few target complaint effect sizes by visual estimation from one of the graphs in their book. Because Sloane et al. (1975) did not report pre and post measures, Smith, Glass, and Miller (1980) also did not include the Sloane et al. results.

matic complaints, and (2) patients who sought treatment on their own. Andrews and Harvey's subset showed similar beneficial results of treatment to those reported for the entire set by Smith, Glass, and Miller (1980). (Andrews and Harvey's subset of verbal psychotherapies has a fairly representative mean across-groups ES of .74.)

Landman and Dawes (1982) also reanalyzed the Smith and Glass meta-analysis (1977) to control for potentially serious methodological problems. They examined a subset of 42 studies, selected to ensure that each contained adequate controls, for either a randomly selected no-treatment or a placebo control group. In addition, they explored a second methodological problem: the effects of using each outcome measure as an independent unit of analysis, as Smith and Glass have done, versus using the whole study as a unit of analysis. Based on their reanalysis, Landman and Dawes (1982) concluded that the Smith and Glass (1977) findings were not flawed by these methodological problems, a conclusion that is consistent with Luborsky, Singer, and Luborsky's (1975) finding that the quality of the research design was not systematically related to the relative benefits found in the treatments compared.

The effect size measures and their comparison with the other groups in the Luborsky SSSP groups led to the following results.

First, the scores on the outcome measures in effect size terms for the Penn Psychotherapy Project were substantial (table 3-4), according to the descriptive labels for the ES, which were based on Cohen's (1969) suggestions. In the Penn Psychotherapy Project the general adjustment measures show the largest ESs (table 3-4): the self-rated Inventory of Social and Psychological Functioning .93, the self-rated Symptom Checklist .80, and the observer-rated Health-Sickness Rating Scale .63. The average effect size for the Penn study using the measures shown in table 3-4 was 1.05.

Second, the Penn Psychotherapy groups' effect sizes were generally like those of the other SSSP groups (table 3-4). These are a few examples of the effect sizes for general outcome measures: (1) For the Chicago study, the observer-rated adjustment composite ES was .65. That composite is probably similar to the observer-rated HSRS in the Penn study, where the ES was .63. (2) For the Menninger study the ES for the HSRS was .77 (from data supplied by Lolafaye Coyne). (3) For the Vanderbilt study the ES for the HSRS was 1.03 and the severity rating measure, which was probably like the HSRS, was .95. (4) for the Endicott study severity of symptoms had an ES of 1.20. The higher ESs in the Vanderbilt study, and possibly also in the Endicott study, may be a function of their smaller standard deviations. For the Vanderbilt study, the small standard deviation was probably based on their narrowly delimited criteria for selecting subjects into their study. Another basis for selection of subjects may also have played a part, according to the finding of Smith, Glass, and Miller (1980, p. 121): Clients responding to an advertisement for special therapy (as was true for the Vanderbilt study) had effect sizes of 1.00, but clients who had recognized a problem and independently sought assistance had effect sizes of .71.

The combination of subscales of the MMPI provides another measure of psychiatric severity (as noted in chapter 19). The treated groups in five studies (Penn, Chicago, Vanderbilt, Endicott, Kaiser) typically provided MMPI data on three scales: hypochondriasis (Hs), hysteria (Hy), and ego strength (Es). The ES means on the three scales for each study were, respectively, .55, .55, 1.07, .85, and .54. Again, the Vanderbilt and Endicott are higher, possibly for the reasons suggested earlier.

Turning now to comparisons of our treated groups on more specific outcome measures, we can see (table 3-4) that four studies used some version of the Target Complaints measure and achieved the following ESs: Penn 2.2 (mean Target Complaints 1 and 2), Temple 2.7 (Target Complaint 1), Vanderbilt 1.9 (mean of Target Complaints 1 and 2), and Queensland 3.6 (Target Complaint). The outcomes on Target Complaints are drastically higher than those for the general outcome measures, which again suggests that benefits measured by specific outcome measures may be larger than those measured by general outcome measures. We saw a similar result earlier in our comparison of benefits in terms of percentages of patients showing general improvement versus specific improvement on the Target Complaints. One reasonable implication is that patients improve most on the specific goals they set for their treatment. Finally, we calculated a mean ES for each study, averaging over each of the measures reported in table 3-4 under each study. The average of these composite ESs over the nine SSSP groups turned out to be 1.18, near the value of 1.05 for the Penn study.

So far we have shown that the magnitude of the benefits, in ES terms, achieved by the patients in the Penn Psychotherapy Project is (1) classed as "medium" to "large" by the Cohen (1969) usage, and (2) found to be within the range of the ESs reported for somewhat similar treated groups.

Effect Sizes of the Luborsky SSSC Groups Were Small

In the absence of a control group, it is hard to judge whether patients' improvement constitutes evidence of the effects of psychotherapy. The assumption is that the presence of a control group would reveal the extent of the non–treatment-related benefits. This is the usual view about the role of control groups of those who subscribe to the canons of evaluation research, and it is also our view, *in part.* Similarly, Berzins, Bedner, and

Severy (1975) pointed out in their presentation of data from a noncon-trolled treated group that for such treated groups changes might also be due to spontaneous remission, demand characteristics, selection effects, and other factors.

Accordingly, we devised a strategy to try to compensate for our lack of a control group: We have made comparisons with those SSSP groups that contained their own control groups, especially where sufficient informa-tion was provided to allow us to do matching of our psychotherapy pa-tients with their controls. The comparisons will be valuable for evaluating the changes of the Penn Psychotherapy Project patients, for, if our infer-ence is reasonably accurate that the Penn treated group and the other treated groups are somewhat comparable, then their control groups are also likely to have relevance to our psychotherapy group. We will compare our within-group ESs with the SSSC group's ESs.

The use of controls based on similar studies is not meant to supplant the usual indigenous controls used in many studies. However, even when the latter are present, similar studies' controls can be a useful supplement. In practice the usual indigenous controls tend to fall short of what they are intended to be: a properly matched sample of patients from the same population as the treated group, lacking only the benefits of the particular treatment and thus controlling for it. Therefore, the use of similar studies' controls offers certain attractive advantages. They make available addi-tional control comparisons at no additional cost. They supply a large array of comparisons, which is needed because there are many types of controls and the benefits of any one control may be a function of its type. The type of control may be an even more significant factor than the circumstance that the patients are selected from the same population. In fact, to utter an emperor-has-no-clothes opinion: We should not be misled by the halo around the words *control group*—the changes in the usual control group, like the changes in the usual treated group, are *also* a reflection of "spontaneous remission, demand characteristics and other factors," as Berzins, Bedner, and Severy (1975) note. Also the use of similar studies' controls provides a larger pool of patients with which to examine comparisons with treated groups. The usual indigenous controls are in actuality rarely matched with the experimental population on crucial variables such as psychological health-sickness, which is the best established pretreatment predictor of benefits (chapter 19). For some of these and other reasons the control design has been questioned (Parloff, 1986).

Therefore, we composed sets of control groups with known characteris-tics. One of them was achieved by returning to further consideration of the SSSP groups listed in table 3-4. Five of these 10 psychotherapy groups have control groups. Four of these 5 are wait-for-treatment groups: Temple, Vanderbilt, Endicott and Kaiser. The fifth, the Hopkins, is a minimal treatment control group. Note that all of these control groups deserve to be called minimally treated; the control patients could derive reassurance and support from knowing they were accepted for treatment and they also had moderate to considerable (as in the Temple study) contact during the wait.

The results of our analysis were generally positive: (1) The ESs of each treated group versus its own control group show the expected difference in favor of the treated group. (2) The ESs of the Penn Psychotherapy Project group versus the other SSSC groups show the expected differences in favor of the Penn group: for the Vanderbilt *control* group the HSRS is .28, which is considerably less than the Penn Psychotherapy group HSRS of .69. Likewise, the MMPI (three scales) of the Penn group is .55, while the Kaiser MMPI (three scales) *control* group is .24 and the MMPI of the Endicott *control* group is .23. However, the MMPI (mean of three scales) of the Vanderbilt wait-for-treatment *control* group MMPI is .85, which is probably raised by the Vanderbilt patients' selection to fit a particular MMPI pattern, because this restricts the variability. By averaging the ESs in each study together we derived a global ES for each of the control groups. The mean of these global ESs across the five SSSC groups was .49, about half the size of the global ES from the Penn study (1.05).

The Glass Set of Control Groups Did Not Serve as Somewhat Similar

We were fortunate in being able to try another set of control groups to be used for comparison with parallel data from treated groups. Gene Glass kindly supplied the data on 47 out of his 530 controls from the Smith, Glass, and Miller (1980) meta-analysis. These 47 were ones for which he had both pre and post information. For these 47 studies there were 124 ESs. We averaged the ESs within each study to reduce the data to 47 ESs. These 47 ESs ranged from −1.45 to 1.79 and had a mean of .14. Sixteen of the studies were waitlist controls. The mean ES for these studies was .00 (*SD* = .69). The remaining 31 studies had other types of control groups and the mean ES for these was .21 (*SD* = .34).

Unfortunately, this imposing assemblage of hard data melted away in the light of our reexamination of these 47, which revealed characteristics of the studies that reduced their value *for our purpose.* The studies were based mostly on very specific symptom outcome measures, for example, "reduction in snake phobia." Only 8 of the 124 ESs appeared to be based on general adjustment measures. Of these 8, 3 were based on wait-for-treatment groups and the other 5 on no-treatment or minimal treatment groups. These 8 were further examined and found not to fit our minimal admission requirements for being "somewhat similar" studies. Five of the 8 were based on a hospital maintenance program, another was a control group for psychoanalytic treatment with inadequate information provided about the treatment (Duhrssen & Jorsweik, 1965), and the other two were dissimilar in other ways. In summary, the net from this set of 47 control studies is 0 in terms of their similarity to the SSSP studies.

Summary

By the time of the termination of their psychotherapy most of the patients in the Penn Psychotherapy study had benefited. The magnitude of their benefits was illustrated by our clinical sketches of 6 patients and by a variety of numerical measures of the outcomes of the 73 treatments as well as by comparisons with other studies.

    1. In terms of ratings of general improvement, approximately two-thirds were "moderately" to "much" improved, a typical proportion of such patients. The patients' benefits were evident from all three of the usual viewpoints: the patient's, the therapist's, and the independent clinical observer's.

    2. In terms of ratings of specific improvement by the target complaints measure, more than two-thirds were "moderately" to "much" improved. The percentages of patients who were improved according to specific measures of improvement were slightly higher than those for the ratings of general improvement.

    3. In terms of measures of lack of benefit or deterioration, little evidence for deterioration was found among the 73 patients; only 1% of the patients were rated by the therapist and 3% by clinical observers as "worse." Pre–post change scores on some assessment measures were slightly larger, but it is more difficult to translate such assessment measures into their meaning for the question of deterioration. Our impression is that none of the patients was *seriously* worse. Therefore, a better description for most of these patients than is implied by the word *deterioration* would be that these patients were upset and disappointed with the outcomes of their treatment and slightly more symptomatic—as in the three less improved patients of the examples at the beginning of this chapter.

    4. In terms of effect size measures of the benefits, the Penn Psychotherapy Project group's outcomes were substantial according to the usual labels given to these effect sizes. The effect sizes in the Penn group were similar to those of groups from other somewhat similar psychotherapy studies. For

this comparison we were able to assemble an array of outcome measures from nine somewhat similar studies. The specific targets of the treatment, that is, the target complaints measure, provided much larger effect sizes than the global outcome measures. (As a resource for future studies, the array of outcome measures' effect sizes from the nine studies plus those from the Penn study can serve as a normative set of somewhat similar psychotherapy groups.)

5. The control groups of the somewhat comparable studies were pressed into service as stand-in control groups to compare with the Penn Psychotherapy Project group. As expected, the target complaints ESs showed superiority for the Penn group. Generally, these comparisons showed that the Penn Psychotherapy-treated group's effect sizes were larger than those from the set of somewhat similar studies' *control* groups.

In overall conclusion, the effect size measures analyzed in comparison with the stand-in control groups provide a good case for the benefits of the psychotherapy provided in the Penn Psychotherapy Project. This good case is consistent with the broadly based conclusion by Lambert, Shapiro, and Bergin (1986) from 14 meta-analytic reviews that bear on the question of the effects of psychotherapy: "The average effect associated with psychological treatment approaches is one standard deviation unit. By the standards developed by Cohen (1977) . . . the effects are large" (p. 159).

4

How Persistent Were the Benefits? A Seven-Year Posttreatment Follow-up

THE OBVIOUS PURPOSE of the follow-up was to learn how lasting the benefits of therapy were. Beyond that, our desire was to learn more about what factors produced the improvement and what factors sustained it, if it was sustained.

A follow-up of our entire group of patients was not possible for practical reasons, so we directed our efforts at trying to locate and reevaluate three subgroups: the 10 patients who improved the most, the 10 patients who improved the least, and a middle group of 10. We felt that this sampling was most likely to illuminate our questions. Furthermore, the most and least improved groups were the objects of intensive study for the investigation of the helping alliance (chapter 11).

The average time between the end of therapy and the follow-up examination was 7 years. The long interval provides perspective on the part played by the therapy experience in the patient's life. The disadvantages of such a long interval are that the patient's state at follow-up derives from many factors in addition to the previous therapy and that the patient's memory of the therapy experience may not be precise.

Procedure

Of the 20 patients in the most and least improved groups we were able to locate 14, and all but 1 agreed to cooperate in the follow-up. For the middle group, although 10 patients were originally chosen at random, not all of these were locatable and some were therefore replaced. There may thus be a bias in favor of locatability. This chapter reports the follow-up of 6 patients from the most improved group, 6 from the middle group, and 7 from the least improved group.

For the follow-up we mailed to each ex-patient a set of forms dealing with the issues in which we were interested. After they were returned, we invited the patient to our Center for Psychotherapy Research at the Hospital of the University of Pennsylvania for an interview. If it was not convenient for the patient to come, we conducted a tape recorded interview by telephone. We asked about issues that we knew were important from our previous contact with the patient as well as from the patient's answers on the forms. The same research staff who had seen the patients before did the follow-up; they knew the patient's background, and their previous contact made rapport with the patient easier to achieve.

Our goals in the follow-up study were to learn how the patient was currently functioning, whether life had generally been kind or unkind in the intervening years, and which elements in the therapy were especially influential in the total impact of the therapy. To reach these goals assessment instruments were chosen or devised. It should be noted that practical limitations made it impossible to attain each goal with the thoroughness we desired. The chosen instruments therefore represent a compromise with the reality of what could be obtained. The first two instruments, the target complaints and the general symptoms items, were meant to be an abbreviated sample of the general adjustment composites we used for measuring the outcomes at termination, since we knew these two were well correlated with the total composite. The list of instruments follows:

General symptom status was composed of items from two sources: (a) 14 representative items drawn from the Hopkins Symptom Checklist (HSCL) (chapter 6) and (b) the Inventory of Social and Psychological Functioning (ISPF) (chapter 6), a 101-item patient self-report questionnaire devised for the Penn Psychotherapy Project. The ISPF is somewhat similar to the HSCL but contains fewer somatic items and more items tapping social functioning. Analysis of the data obtained on these questionnaires (chapter 2) revealed that each checklist has a high degree of internal consistency (Cronbach's alphas are .96 for ISPF, .97 for HSCL), and that when a single score is computed for each, the two scores are highly correlated ($r = -.76$). We therefore decided to choose a small number (7) of the most representative items from each questionnaire to assess the patient's general level of symptom distress. The 14 items are shown in table 4-1. The internal consistency reliability (Cronbach's alpha) of the sum of the 14 items was found to be .92 with the sample of 19 patients included in the follow-up.

Target complaints (Battle et al., 1966) measures represent the problems for which the patient had originally sought therapy and their severity at follow-up.

Luck scale was a questionnaire on which we asked the patient to estimate and describe the kind of luck experienced in five life sectors since completing therapy. Our purpose was to assess roughly the quality of the events that have occurred in the patient's life for comparison with his or her present state. We recognize that such ratings are not only highly subjective but also may confound external events over which the patient had no control with those that the patient brought about. However, the patient was asked to try to differentiate these two conditions. The internal reliability (Cronbach's alpha) of the sum of the five luck items was .68.

Current level of performance was a single item on how the patient was getting along at the time of follow-up, compared with before psychotherapy.

Impact of therapy versus other experiences was a single item on the patient's

TABLE 4-1

General Symptom Status: Items from the Hopkins Symptom Checklist and the Inventory of Social and Personality Functioning

1. Feeling that you don't like yourself
2. Feeling lonely
3. Worrying or stewing about things
4. Your feelings are easily hurt
5. Worried about getting ahead in life
6. Feeling tense or keyed up
7. Feeling low in energy or slowed down
8. I get satisfaction and enjoyment out of life
9. I feel self-confident
10. I tend to feel helpless, as though I am not capable of working at and solving my problems
11. Certain situations or people make me anxious
12. When I feel anxious or depressed that discourages me and I then get more upset
13. When I have a problem I am able to think it through
14. I feel comfortable around people

estimation of the impact that the therapy had, relative to other influential life experiences.

Further therapy inquired whether the patient had further therapy after the completion of the original psychotherapy, and, if so, how much benefit was derived from the later therapy.

Influence scale was a 17-item checklist on which the patient reported which elements of the therapy were important. These items bear on various theories of the effective ingredients of psychotherapy. The questions put to the patient were in this form: "How important was_____in your therapy?" An examination of the intercorrelations of the 17 items revealed that 6 of the items that assessed the importance of feeling trust and warmth toward one's therapist were highly related to the therapist's displaying interest, genuineness, reassurance, and understanding. Thus, we chose to score this dimension of "positive relationship qualities" by summing the 6 items (Cronbach's alpha = .86). The remaining 11 items were used separately.

Results

GENERAL SYMPTOM STATUS: THE MIDDLE AND HIGH GROUPS IMPROVED MOST

Figure 4-1 shows the general symptom status (14 items from the HSCL and ISPF) at pretherapy, posttherapy, and follow-up. The figure is drawn so that a high score indicates freedom from symptoms and a low score indicates severe symptoms. Note that the three groups started therapy at almost the same point on symptom status. At the end of therapy the least improved group remained at about the same level, while the other two groups had improved significantly.

At follow-up the least improved group showed a slight improvement. The middle group improved still more, achieving almost the same freedom from symptoms as the most improved group, which had declined very slightly. The difference between the most improved and middle groups on the one hand and the least improved group on the other was statistically significant at $p < .05$ by t-test.

On Target Complaint status (figure 4-2) the pattern is similar: The least improved group again showed improvement in the period after therapy, although the other two groups showed a slight worsening of severity. The

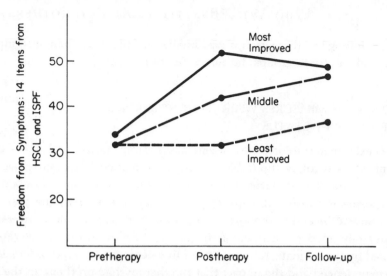

FIGURE 4-1. General Symptom Status at Pretherapy, Posttherapy, and Follow-up. Scoring has been reversed on the HSCL, so that a high score on the graph indicates *freedom* from symptoms. (HSCL-Hopkins Symptom Checklist; ISPF-Inventory of Social and Personality Functioning.)

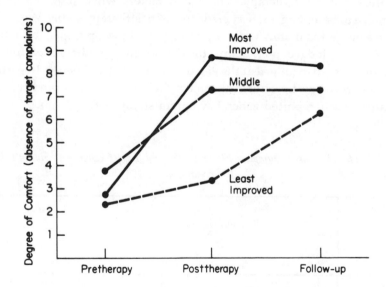

FIGURE 4-2. Target Complaint Status at Pretherapy, Posttherapy, and Follow-up.

spread among the three groups was smaller at follow-up than at termination, and the three groups did not differ significantly.

END STATUS MEASURES WERE THE BEST PREDICTORS OF FOLLOW-UP STATUS

We examined the correlates of general symptom status and Target Complaint status at follow-up (table 4-2) because their correlates might be the determinants of that status. It can be seen that the highest correlate for each test was the posttherapy status on that test; that is, the patient's condition at the end of therapy was the best predictor of follow-up status. Moderately good predictions of the patients' follow-up status were also yielded by the patients' ratings (sum of five items) of the kind of luck they had experienced and the impact that the therapy had on them. In the last four columns of the table are the correlations of follow-up status with two interviewer judgments: the Emotional Freedom and Level of Adjustment factors of the Prognostic Index. They are rated from interviews conducted before and after therapy. These two factors when judged pretherapy proved to be among our best predictors of posttherapy status. We therefore were interested in how well they predicted follow-up status. It can be seen that when judged pretherapy, they were poor predictors of follow-up status, but when judged at the end of therapy they did better. In particular, the posttherapy Level of Adjustment factor was a good predictor of the patient's self-reported general symptom status at follow-up.

TABLE 4-2

Correlates of General Symptom Status (GSS) and Target Complaint Status (TCS) at Follow-up ($N = 19$)

| | Patient Self-report | | | | | | Observer-rated | | | |
| | GSS | | TCS | | | | Emotional Freedom | | Level of Adjustment | |
	Pre	Post	Pre	Post	Impact	Luck	Pre	Post	Pre	Post
General Symptom Status Follow-up	.28	.63**	.00	.53**	.50*	.42	.06	.22	.22	.56**
Target Complaint Follow-up	.35	.47*	.35	.48*	.43	.40	.11	.21	.05	.26

*$p < .05$
**$p < .01$

MOST HAD FURTHER PSYCHOTHERAPY

Although the patients in the least improved group generally had unfavorable feelings about their therapies, they retained faith in psychotherapy. Every one of them had further therapy in the next few years, usually a significant amount, averaging about 1½ years. This fits with the conclusion in chapter 3—that the patients who had not benefited had not deteriorated but rather were disappointed in their therapy experience. Most of them benefited from the additional therapy, although they lost some of their gains after therapy. Half of the patients in the most improved group and one-third of the patients in the middle group also had further therapy. The implication here is that many patients, even in the most improved group, felt they wished to improve even more.

These findings about getting further treatment are similar to those reported by Fiske and Goodman (1965), who noted that patients who were lower in therapeutic improvement were more likely to have additional therapy. Sloane el al. (1975) also reported that some of their patients who had not improved got further treatment and then tended to achieve more benefits. This finding modified our original conception of the most versus least improved patients: They are most versus least improved in the one treatment occasion we studied. By engaging in another treatment with another therapist they sometimes achieve more of the benefits they seek. The new therapy may provide a therapist who the patient experiences as capable of providing more of what he or she needs. This explanation fits with our suggestion that the patient–therapist match is a significant factor in influencing outcomes (in chapter 19).

INCREASED HOPE AND SELF-UNDERSTANDING WERE HELPFUL

Through their responses on the Influence Scale patients reported their views of what was important in their therapy. Table 4-3 shows the average score given for each dimension by the patients in the most, middle, and least improvement groups. In general, patients estimated that the most important ingredients were (1) the elevation of their sense of hope and feeling that things could work out (mean rating on 4-point scale including all subjects = 3.8) and (2) the gain in understanding of the reasons behind their behavior and feelings (M = 3.6). The least important ingredients were (1) feeling irritated or angry with the therapist (M = 1.8) and (2) having feelings stirred up (M = 2.1). The mean ratings for the three groups were significantly different on 3 of the 11 influence scales. These were (1) the positive relationship factor [$F(2, 15)$ = 3.8, p < .05], (2) relief from getting things off their chest $[F(2, 15) = 3.7, p < .05]$, and (3) talking about their feelings toward or relationship with their therapist $[F(2, 15) = 7.8, p < .01]$. As can be seen in table 4-3, the most improved group, as expected, rated these aspects of therapy most positively. Surprisingly, however, the middle group rated these three ingredients the lowest, and their average rating for all of the ingredients was lowest. The possible explanation for this trend is that those patients who either improved greatly or not at all had the strongest feelings about therapy; these feelings, whether positive or negative, led to a greater sense of what factors were important in therapy. The middle group may have been less emotionally engaged in the therapy process and therefore may have viewed all of the ingredients as less important. On the other hand, with such small samples some of these findings may be chance fluctuations.

Clinical Impressions

To speak only of ratings and of central tendencies is to eliminate some of the nuances of what seems to have happened in the patients' therapies and in their lives. To compensate for this we will add some impressions that we gained from talking with them.

In interviews with us, patients elaborated on the views they conveyed via the Influence Scale. The opinions they expressed were familiar since they fit with the curative factors we describe in chapter 10: Patients said they were helped by being able to talk to someone who seemed interested in them (Curative Factor 1) and who understood them (Curative Factor 2). About half of them reported that they wanted their therapist to like them, but they became reconciled to the fact that the therapist's interest in them was primarily professional. The patients respected their therapist for that in the end. Most patients would have liked their therapist to be more active and to explain more to them. Patients who were helped said that they acquired a better self-concept.

When the patients were not helped, they felt it was because the therapist did not understand them (Curative Factor 2) or was remote or not sympathetic (Curative Factor 1). One of the most improved patients (Ms. M. H., #45) found qualities in her therapist that she did not like. He reminded her of her father, who was unresponsive and did not understand her. But she appreciated the opportunity to talk to someone and get things off of her chest. She also felt that a significant factor in her improvement was meeting and marrying a good man during the course of her therapy. She

TABLE 4-3

Mean Importance Ratings of Ingredients of Therapy for Most Improved, Middle, and Least Improved Groups at Follow-up

Ingredient of Therapy	Mean Importance Ratings		
	Most (N = 5)[a]	Middle (N = 6)	Least (N = 7)
Positive relationship	3.8	2.8	3.3
Talking about things that were not easy to talk about	3.8	2.8	3.0
Earning my therapist's approval	2.8	2.0	1.9
Gaining understanding of reasons behind my behavior and feelings	4.0	3.2	3.6
Having my feelings stirred up	2.4	1.5	2.3
Getting guidance	3.6	2.8	3.6
Getting a feeling of hope	3.8	3.3	4.0
Getting aware of and in touch with my feelings	3.8	2.5	3.1
Relief from getting things off my chest	3.6	2.3	3.1
Talking about my feelings toward or relationship with my therapist	3.2	1.2	2.4
My therapist making clear what he thought I should do in order to improve	2.2	1.5	2.9
Feeling irritated or angry with my therapist	2.2	1.2	2.0

NOTE: 1 = little or no importance; 4 = very important
[a]One patient in the most improved group had missing data on this measure.

did not directly attribute that happy event to the therapy although it probably had a facilitating role.

Ex-patients naturally looked at their previous therapy in the context of their life at the time. Most of the most improved group valued their therapy for having helped them get through a difficult time, which is congruent with the view of Frank (1971b) that this help is the chief benefit of psychotherapy.

The remainder of this section is organized around two basic but difficult questions: How much difference did therapy make to these people? How important was it in determining where they were at follow-up? Clearly, the therapy experience was only one of many influences on them. We must take what data we have and make reasonable inferences about the relative importance of the therapy experience and other influences.

Two findings from the follow-up can be taken as consistent with the argument that therapy *did* make a meaningful difference in their lives in the years since it was terminated. First, when asked to judge how they had been getting along since therapy as compared with before it, most patients said they had been doing much better since therapy, as shown in table 4-4. Second, the patients' follow-up status appears to have been determined

TABLE 4-4

Follow-up Responses:
How Have You Been Getting Along Compared with
Before Your Therapy? (N = 18)

	Much Worse	About the Same	Somewhat Better	Much Better
Most Improved		1		5
Middle[a]				5
Least Improved	1	1	1	4

[a]One patient felt she could not make this comparison.

more by their posttherapy status than by their pretherapy status. If it had turned out in the opposite way—that their pretherapy status had been the most important determinant of follow-up status—then we might have considered whether therapy produced only a temporary change, so that after it ended the patient's preexisting personality structures became dominant again. Given the findings as they are, it could be maintained that the change induced by therapy was not temporary, that it continued to operate and was the most important determinant of the patient's status at follow-up.

To look at it a little differently, we might view the therapy experience not so much as a determinant but as a preview of how things would be for the patient during the next 7 years. We have tried for each case in the sample of most versus least improved patients to decide whether the therapy outcome provided a reliable guide to how the patient would do in the next 7 years. (The patients in the middle group were not included in this analysis. The outcome of their therapy—"some" to "moderate" improvement—does not provide a sufficiently definite criterion against which to compare their subsequent life course.) This is, of course, another way of looking at the correlation between posttherapy status and follow-up, but here we do it case by case to permit the formulation of clinical impressions. These are subjective judgments based on interviews by Arthur Auerbach. For example, if a least improved patient at termination was found to be doing well in subsequent years, Auerbach counted the patient's follow-up status as not accurately foretold by the results of the therapy.

Based on the evaluation interviews of the most and least improved patients, the small numbers of table 4-5 suggest that there was about a 62% chance that the results of a period of therapy would give a general preview of how the patient would fare in subsequent years.

What about the other 38%? Why was their therapy outcome *not* an

TABLE 4-5

*The Observer's Assessment: Did
Therapy Outcome Accurately Foretell
How the Patient Would Do in the
Next Seven Years?*

Yes	Mostly Yes	Mostly No	No
7	1	2	3

accurate guide to how they would do subsequently? For these 5 cases we have constructed formulations based upon the patients' reports and our impressions.

With one most improved patient (Ms. R. W., #71) who subsequently had serious problems, there is first the question of how much she really had improved. At termination we suspected a defensive need to convince herself, her therapist, and the interviewer-clinician that she had done extremely well. Her strong positive transference to her therapist seemed to have contributed. In addition, her divorce, which she had decided on during therapy, led to more difficulties than she had anticipated. At the time of follow-up she was disillusioned with what therapy can accomplish, which was a marked contrast with her feelings at termination.

One patient (Mr. Denny, #77; see pp. 42-43), who had not improved with a therapist who did not deal with an unrecognized transference bind, had subsequent treatment with a more active and supportive therapist. The patient liked the give and take of the second therapy and improved. Furthermore, in the patient's view a change of colleges was very helpful. He felt that the atmosphere in his original college was cold and unfriendly. After failing in the original college he attended another one where he felt comfortable and was quite successful academically. (As with therapists, a good match with a college can have beneficial results!)

Another least improved patient (Mr. W. K., #101) felt that his therapist was aloof and not very interested in him. He later saw a therapist generally recognized as charismatic, whom the patient liked because the therapist understood him, was specific in his suggestions, and taught him by modeling what he needed to learn. Fortunate educational and vocational opportunities opened up at the same time, so that at follow-up the patient was definitely doing better, although many of his personality problems were still evident.

A young man who had been in psychoanalysis (Mr. T. H., #52) did not improve and, in fact, found the analysis itself to be an ordeal that he could no longer take. But he later ascribed his subsequent improvement to the analysis, stating that it was only about a year after its termination that he began to benefit from it. He believed the benefits resulted from the insights he gained into his personality. The inactivity and nonresponsiveness of the analyst had bothered him during his treatment, but in retrospect he thought this is what he had needed. Although he was no longer in treatment, he was continually working on his problems and trying to improve his situation. During the next 5 years he made a great deal of progress with the problems that had previously overwhelmed him, and at follow-up he was doing quite well.

One most improved patient (Ms. Samuelson, #49; see p. 38) was subjected to much stress after termination: the loss of her lover and later a disfiguring operation for cancer. Some of her symptoms recurred and she expressed some doubts about whether her therapy had been worthwhile. Nevertheless, she credited the therapy and the good relationship with the therapist with having strengthened her so that she could get through her crises.

These were the 5 cases in which the outcome of therapy did not accurately anticipate the patient's development in the next few years. We now will sum up our impressions of three factors that tend to be recurrent in the explanations in the retrospective clinical interviews: (1) the often positive impact of a change to a different therapist with a different therapeutic style and capability, (2) the negative impact of a loss of an important relationship, and (3) the impact of other major life situational changes, such as in education or vocation.

Summary

1. The most improved patients tended to maintain their gains from termination to follow-up 7 years later, although there was a tendency for a leveling off or a slight loss from termination to follow-up. This is evident in figure 4-1 and figure 4-2 for both the level of adjustment and the attainment of the patient's specific treatment goals (in the Target Complaints). The least improved patients made gains after therapy ended, bringing their status closer to that of the middle and high groups at follow-up. The middle group remained in the middle at follow-up, although it was close to the high group on one of our outcome measures.

The closer approximation of the three groups at follow-up than at posttherapy suggests the operation of a familiar pattern of extremes to move toward the middle—the regression toward the mean. We cannot rule out the possibility that such fluctuations unrelated to treatment account for part of our findings. Nevertheless, it should be noted that at follow-up the least improved group still differed significantly from the other two groups on general symptom status. Such a tendency for patients to hold on to their gains made in treatment, although with some attenuation, is well known; e.g., a review of studies that had both post-treatment and follow-up evaluations (Landman & Dawes, 1982) selected from Smith, Glass, and Miller (1980) found maintenance of gains. Their findings were consistent with Nicholson and Berman (1983). Andrews and Harvey (1981) found the same trend but reported that after termination improvement was stable for many months and then was followed by a slight decline at the rate of 0.2 effect size units per year. Liberman (1978) reported that despite some loss, some maintained gains were found at 5-year follow-ups over a 20-year period.

More research attention needs to be devoted to the best ways of ensuring the maintenance of the gains. One way is through providing environmental supports, such as through arranging for and supervising employment or arranging for participation in support groups (Atthowe, 1973; Karoly & Steffen, 1980). The more usual ways are based on the therapist's application of techniques for working through the meaning of termination (Luborsky, 1984).

2. Further treatment during the period from termination to follow-up was obtained by many patients: 50% of the most improved group, all of the least improved group, and 33% of the middle group. The patient's usual explanation for having obtained more treatment was a need to resolve problems further since they had not been worked out well enough in the previous treatment. This was true even for the most improved patients. Such high rates of obtaining further treatment are not uncommon, as we mentioned for the follow-up of patients in the Sloane et al. (1975) project, although their percentages of patients who had further treatment were not as large as ours, probably because their follow-up was conducted at the 1-year point. In the Menninger study (Wallerstein, 1986) the rate was almost 25%.

3. The outcomes of the subsequent treatments tended to provide further benefits. For example, in the Penn Psychotherapy Project, Ms. Kane (#6; see pp. 41-42), a less improved patient, made several tries at psychotherapy; one of these was experienced by her as moderately satisfactory. This experience of deriving benefits from psychotherapy should be no surprise since it is the typical experience of psychotherapy patients. The special circumstance in this case is that the benefits derive from subsequent treatments. (One novel implication about the benefits of successive attempts at further psychotherapy is that treatment evaluation studies should take

these into account rather than considering only the single therapy as the unit. It may be worth finding the degree of achievement of the patient's goals after as many courses of therapy as the patient has tried.)

4. The follow-up itself was generally a positive experience for these 19 patients. They tended to derive satisfaction from the opportunity for a retrospective review (Luborsky, 1987b). This conclusion is consistent with the suggestion of Schachter (1987) that follow-up after therapy be used as a routine clinical procedure.

5. The basis for the benefits achieved by the patients in the Penn Psychotherapy Project was investigated through the patients' attributions reported in their responses to the Influence Scale. The most important were (1) the renewal of a sense of hope and (2) the acquisition of understanding. Also important was the experience of a positive therapeutic relationship—referred to in later chapters as Curative Factor 1—where the therapist shows interest and understanding and the patient feels trust and warmth toward the therapist. The second attribution is similar to Curative Factor 2 (chapter 10). It may be that the presence of these curative factors engenders a sense of hope in the patient.

These attributions about the basis for improvement are not unusual. In Sloane et al. (1975), at least 70% of the successful patients in both psychotherapy and behavior therapy estimated as "extremely important" or "very important" the following causal conditions: (1) the personality of my therapist, (2) the therapist helping you understand your problems, and (3) the therapist encouraging you gradually to practice facing the things that bother you. The second condition appears again to be the emphasis on insight and understanding. The first and the third attributions appear to be the emphasis on the provision of therapeutic facilitative conditions, particularly the provision of the supportive relationship (Curative Factor 1) (Sloane et al., 1975, p. 206).

In general, patients' explanations of the bases for their improvement or nonimprovement have much in common with our list of the eight curative factors within psychodynamically oriented psychotherapy (chapter 10), particularly the two main ones, Factor 1 on the patient's experience of the helping relationship and Factor 2 on the achievement of understanding about the nature of the patient's problems.

5

A Sound Mind in a Sound Body:

Unanticipated Physical Health

Benefits of Psychotherapy

OUR CONCEPTION of the benefits of psychotherapy would be happily expanded if we found that "a sound mind in a sound body" implied that the healthier one becomes psychologically, the healthier one becomes physically, and the reverse. We were able to test this concomitance in the Penn Psychotherapy Project from patient reports of psychological and physical symptoms before and after psychotherapy.

Not only is the topic of intrinsic interest to patients and to some who are working on the frontier of psychotherapy research (such as Frank, 1975), but it also has a new economic timeliness. Recent surveys of the experience of insurance carriers show that there is a reduction in physician visits and hospitalizations for those who are engaged in psychotherapy (Durhssen & Jorswiek, 1965; Cummings & Follette, 1968, 1976; Mendelsohn, 1976; Mumford, Schlesinger & Glass, 1978; Cummings, 1975; Schlesinger, Mumford & Glass, 1980). For this economic benefit as well as for other reasons, a push has developed to include psychotherapy in proposals for national health insurance (Cummings, 1975, 1977).

The definitive surveys by Schlesinger, Mumford, and Glass (Mumford, Schlesinger & Glass, 1978; Schlesinger, Mumford & Glass, 1980) were the immediate impetus[1] to our study (Luborsky & McLellan, 1980). They

[1]The major stimulus for this research came from Lester Luborsky's participation in Herbert J. Schlesinger's ad hoc committee (along with Robert Wallerstein and Emily Mumford) of the American Psychoanalytic Association, *"Effects of Psychotherapy* and *Psychoanalysis on Emotional and Physical Health."* Our gratitude to Herbert Schlesinger and Gene Glass for their assistance.

showed that in virtually all studies reduction in physician visits and hospitalizations emerged for patients who started psychotherapy. The present study was aimed at determining why these reductions in the utilization of medical care services occurred for psychotherapy patients. Armchair speculation suggested several possibilities, but our data bear on only the first two:

1. The psychological improvement is associated with physical improvement because the patient actually gets healthier and therefore feels better and reports fewer physical symptoms.
2. The psychological improvement is associated with fewer reports of physical symptoms not because of real gains in physical health but because the patient experiences less stress and feels better.
3. The patient is less inclined to report physical symptoms because greater psychological competence may be associated with a reduced inclination to complain.
4. The patient realizes through the treatment that physical problems may be explained primarily on a psychological basis, so she or he pays less attention to them.
5. The psychological support sought from the physician who treats physical symptoms becomes less necessary for the patient who is in psychotherapy.
6. The decline in physical symptoms is simply an artifact, possibly a kind of regression to the mean based upon the concomitance of the patient's coming to therapy and a peak in utilization of medical services; if that is the case, medical utilization would be expected to decline after psychotherapy was begun.

Procedure

The 73 patients in the Penn Psychotherapy Project completed the Hopkins Symptom Checklist (Derogatis et al., 1970) at the outset of their psychotherapy and then again at the end of treatment. Each scale of the checklist had four choices from "1 = not at all" to "4 = extremely." The Symptom Checklist form had 85 items (the basic 58 plus the 27 we added); 16 of the 85 were physical items, such as headaches, faintness or dizziness, pains in the heart or chest, or constipation; 62 items were psychological, such as nervousness or shakiness inside, feeling fearful, or feeling critical of others; 7 could not be classed in either category.

Analysis of these data should allow us to test the relationship between psychological and physical improvement in terms of the correlations between the psychological and physical items from the checklist prior to treatment, and then the amount of change in the two measures over the course of treatment.

Results

INTERNAL CONSISTENCY OF PHYSICAL AND PSYCHOLOGICAL ITEMS WAS HIGH

The reliability (Cronbach's alpha) of the total of the 16 physical items (pretreatment) was .86. The comparable reliability for the total of the 62 psychological items (pretreatment) was .95. Therefore, both the physical and the psychological subscales showed high internal consistency. (These reliabilities, in fact, are much higher than the correlation of the two subscales with each other, $r = .63^{***}$.)[2]

Previous factor-analytic results also bear on the relative independence of these dimensions. Williams et al. (1968) did a factor analysis of the 58-item Symptom Checklist in a sample of 1,115 subjects. (The 58 items were included among the larger item pool of the Symptom Checklist form that we used.) Their factor analysis produced a large somatic factor, which included 11 of our 16 physical items (table 5-1). We had selected the items on clinical grounds, i.e., so that their content referred to clearly physical dysfunctions. Derogatis et al. (1970) showed similarly that items selected from the HSCL on clinical grounds tend to fall into the relevant factor. Furthermore, their reanalysis of the Symptom Checklist reported the somatic factor to be one of five underlying symptom dimensions that have been identified in repeated factor analyses. In summary, the sets of physical and psychological items, although related, were representative of separable dimensions.

BEFORE VERSUS AFTER PSYCHOTHERAPY WERE CORRELATED

Subjects' mean scores on the psychological items *before* psychotherapy correlated .52*** with their mean psychological score *after* psychotherapy (figure 5-1). Correlation of the physical items before versus after psycho-

[2]Level of significance is abbreviated throughout: * $= p < .05$; ** $= p < .01$; *** $= p < .001$.

therapy was .63***. We conclude that the physical and psychological items were reasonably consistent in level from before to after psychotherapy.

PHYSICAL VERSUS PSYCHOLOGICAL WERE CORRELATED

As indicated, the psychological and physical sets of items correlated with each other .63*** prior to treatment, while after treatment that correlation was .58*** (figure 5-1). This implies that before treatment as well as after it, a "sound mind" was moderately associated with a "sound body." This result appears to be similar to the reported association of physical and mental illness (Eastwood, 1975; Hankin & Oktay, 1979).

PHYSICAL AND PSYCHOLOGICAL SYMPTOMS WERE REDUCED BY PSYCHOTHERAPY

Intensive psychotherapy was associated with significant and pervasive reductions in virtually all psychological items on the checklist, resulting in a net reduction in mean severity of psychological complaints of .40 on the 4-point scale. This change was statistically significant at $p < .001$ by paired t-test. With regard to the 16 physical items, 8 (headaches, faintness or dizziness, pains or butterflies in the stomach, nausea or upset stomach, heart pounding, dry mouth, hot or cold spells, weakness in parts of the body) showed significant ($p < .05$) reductions (see table 5-1), 3 (pain in the chest, loose bowel movements, numbness or tingling in parts of body) showed marginally significant ($p < .10$) reductions, and 5 (itching, constipation, pain in lower part of back, soreness in muscles, trouble getting your breath) showed no significant change. These specific changes resulted in a net reduction in the mean severity of the physical subscale of .19 ($p < .001$ by paired t-test) on the 4-point scale. Results of a t-test comparing these change scores showed a significantly greater ($p < .001$) reduction in psychological symptoms than physical symptoms.

In order to examine the relationship between change in psychological symptoms and change in physical symptoms we first calculated residual gain scores for each of the subscales. This was accomplished through a regression analysis predicting posttreatment scores from the corresponding pretreatment measure with subsequent calculation of the residuals. Note that by removing the effects of initial level on change in physical symptoms and change in psychological symptoms we have removed from these measures the influence of a reporting bias (e.g., a personality tendency to complain); that is, the residual gain score rescales change relative to others with similar amounts of reporting bias. Through the method we found that the psychological symptoms residual gain measure correlated moderately

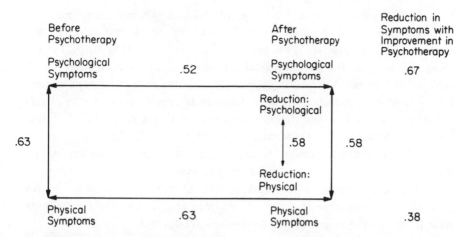

FIGURE 5-1. Correlations of Psychological Items and Physical Items on the Hopkins Symptom Checklist Before and After Psychotherapy. (All correlations are significantly different from zero.)

TABLE 5-1

*Pretreatment and Posttreatment Means on Physical Items
of the Symptom Checklist*

Physical Item	Mean Pre	Mean Post	Significance of t-test
Headaches	2.07	1.71	.001
Faintness or Dizziness	1.46	1.25	.01
Pains or Butterflies in Stomach	1.96	1.58	.001
Pains in Heart or Chest	1.50	1.33	.09
Itching	1.31	1.32	n.s.
Constipation	1.32	1.32	n.s.
Loose Bowel Movements	1.38	1.25	.07
Pains in Lower Back	1.50	1.49	n.s.
Nausea or Upset Stomach	1.72	1.33	.001
Heart Pounding or Racing	1.69	1.39	.006
Dry Mouth	1.50	1.18	.001
Soreness of Muscles	1.46	1.38	n.s.
Trouble Getting Your Breath	1.35	1.31	n.s.
Hot or Cold Spells	1.40	1.19	.02
Numbness or Tingling	1.38	1.24	.07
Weakness in Parts of Body	1.54	1.31	.007

SOURCE: Luborsky and McLellan (1980).

(r = .56***) with the physical symptom residual gain measure. This concomitance implies that patients who have benefited psychologically have also benefited physically. However, in the Penn Psychotherapy Project residual change in the psychological symptoms subscale correlated .67*** with a rated benefits measure (chapter 2) of improvement in psychotherapy. The corresponding correlation between the residual change in physical symptoms and psychotherapy improvement was only .38***. These two correlations were significantly different (Z = 3.25**).

The significant reduction in the psychological complaints on the Symptom Checklist is hardly a surprise; improvement was also shown by a variety of other measures for this sample of patients (chapter 2), and general improvement in psychological symptoms is expected for patients who have been engaged in psychotherapy (chapter 3).

The Meanings of Physical Improvement

Patients do not come to psychotherapy primarily for the relief of physical complaints; why then should there be a significant reduction in physical symptoms? Two main alternatives stated earlier may serve as explanations: (1) Psychological improvement is associated with physical improvement because the patient actually gets healthier and therefore feels better and reports fewer physical symptoms or (2) psychological improvement is associated with fewer reports of physical symptoms not because of real gains in physical health but because the patient experiences less stress and feels better.

The outstanding finding that physical symptoms, as reported on the Hopkins Symptom Checklist, improved during psychotherapy and that improvement in these symptoms was correlated with general measures of improvement in psychotherapy needs to be examined further to determine whether it reflects improvement in physical health or some other change. Several lines of evidence support the possibility of genuine physical improvement.

The patient is not just worrying needlessly—the reports of physical symptoms can be shown to be further demonstrated by a physical examination of the patient. The available data are based on 31 male drug-addicted veterans (mean age = 30) who not only filled out the symptom checklist but were also given an outpatient physical examination at the same time by a physician who checked symptom items in nine areas of physical health (from the study by Woody et al., 1983). The physician's judgment was based on the physical examination, which included the medical reports of previous treatments and the patient's physical examination chart (medical history), as well as patient's responses about his health (the physician did not have available the Symptom Checklist). Table 5-2 provides the results, which show significant correlations between the physical items on the Symptom Checklist (11 items rather than the 16—5 of the items were not available on the version of the checklist used in the study) and the symptoms found by the physician. (It is unfortunate that we do not have the physician's ratings at the end of treatment so that we could get a physician's improvement-in-health measure to compare with the patient's improvement-in-health measure.) It should be noted, however, that the source of much of the physician's knowledge of symptoms must have been the patient's responses about his health.

Another type of evidence supporting the direct effects of psychotherapy upon physical symptoms comes from studies comparing medical regimens alone with medical regimens plus psychotherapy (Luborsky, Singer & Luborsky, 1975); 9 of 10 such studies reported significant improvements in the physical illness through addition of the psychotherapy. On a larger sample of studies, Smith and Glass (1977) reported similar results.

A line of indirect supporting evidence derives from studies of the relationship between having physical symptoms and seeking medical attention, although, as Mechanick has shown (1966), the relationship tends to be only moderate. In the past few decades, as we have noted, several studies have shown reduction in physician visits and hospitalizations for patients in psychotherapy (e.g., Duhrssen & Jorsweik, 1965; Cummings & Follette, 1968, 1976; Mendelsohn, 1976; Mumford & Schlesinger, 1987). In

TABLE 5-2

Correlations of Physicians' Physical Examination
Items with Patients' Symptom Checklist of
Eleven Physical Items

General Health	.59
Ear, Nose, and Throat	.43
Musculoskeletal	.54
Respiratory	.55
Cardiovascular	.61
Gastrointestinal	.58
Genitourinary	.51
Neurological	.64
Psychiatric	.66
Total Number of Symptom Items Discovered	.57

NOTE: Based on 31 male VA patients.
SOURCE: Luborsky and McLellan (1980).

fact, our results can be thought of as providing a possible link explaining the association of psychotherapy with reduction in medical utilization. Our results imply that the patients are acting reasonably. Because they have fewer physical symptoms from before to after treatment, they seek medical attention less. A further comparison is noteworthy: The patients in our psychotherapy studies came to treatment primarily because of psychological, not physical, symptoms; patients in studies like Mumford and Schlesinger (1987) came because they were severely ill, and they subsequently got outpatient psychotherapy. Those patients also changed in physical health status, but the change was reflected in a significantly lower use of hospitalization.

Another line of indirect evidence comes from the rapidly mushrooming research on relationships of stress, mood, immunocompetence, and illness (Locke, 1982; Luborsky, et al., in preparation). Two outstanding symptoms, anxiety and depression, are prevalent within the initial psychological symptoms of the group of patients in the Penn Psychotherapy Project. These symptoms may be associated with immunosuppressive alterations in cellular immune function, which are likely to make the patient more susceptible to a variety of illnesses. An improvement in psychological functioning occurs during the treatment and may also improve immunocompetence and consequently lessen vulnerability to a variety of illnesses.

Taken together, therefore, these related results also imply that the reduction in patients' symptoms during psychotherapy has some physical basis and is not just a reflection of a reduction in complaining or other artifacts. But beyond that, these data cannot tell us how the changes came about. For that task we are thrown back on methods that may give us only slight illumination, such as interviews with patients on their reasons for reducing medical utilization, analysis of psychotherapy sessions for the conditions related to physical illnesses, and speculation on mind–body interaction mechanisms.

Summary

To explore the relationship of physical and psychological symptoms to each other and the amount of change in each through psychotherapy we examined the self-report Hopkins Symptom Checklist of physical and psychological symptoms for the 73 patients of the Penn Psychotherapy Project. Our main findings, as diagramed in figure 5-1, follow.

1. The physical symptoms subscale and the psychological symptoms subscale show high internal consistency. They were also moderately separable from each other, as identified by factor analysis in previous research.

2. The correlations between the subscales were, nevertheless, moderate—physical and psychological symptoms tended to be associated.

3. Both the physical and psychological symptoms show stability from before to after psychotherapy.

4. Evidence was available (from another sample) that the worries about physical health were not totally unfounded—a physical examination measure correlated moderately highly with the sum of the physical items on the Symptom Checklist.

Several findings about the interrelationships with reduction of symptoms during psychotherapy were reported.

1. Both psychological and physical symptoms were significantly reduced during psychotherapy. The reduction in psychological symptoms was significantly greater than in physical symptoms. Among the physical symptoms surveyed, those that were most frequent before treatment were the ones that most often were reduced during psychotherapy.

2. The reduction in physical symptoms was associated with reduction in psychological symptoms from before to after psychotherapy, after correcting for the influence of initial level on the change scores.

3. Reductions in both physical and psychological symptoms were correlated with improvement in psychotherapy, although the association was significantly less for the physical symptoms.

We have revealed that a physical improvement benefit from psychotherapy has some basis in reality, but our data are limited so that other possible explanations remain as agendas for future generations of researchers. Among these are that a change occurs in the patient's conception of which symptoms are physical versus which are psychological or that the patient has less need to complain because the patient's morale is better.

6

The Predictive Measures

Description of Predictors

TO INVESTIGATE which types of predictive measures from patients, therapists, and treatment conditions would have the best chance of predicting psychotherapy outcomes, we selected two broad classes of predictors: pretreatment measures, described in the Project A chapters, and during-treatment measures, described under Project B.

The initial list of predictors before data reduction is in table 6-1. The predictors were of three types. (1) Representative measures were selected from the qualities that had significantly predicted outcomes in several studies in our review (chapter 19). As one typical example, we chose measures of psychological health-sickness because the majority of studies using them achieved significant predictions. The predictive results in the Penn Psychotherapy Project therefore constitute a cross-validation of the measures in the previous studies. (2) Some largely exploratory measures were included on the basis of our special interests. The cognitive style measures were examples of these. They had never been tried as predictors of outcomes of psychotherapy, although they had been found to have significant relationships with initial therapy behavior (Witkin, Lewis & Weil, 1968). (3) We tested some completely "let's-see-what-happens" variables for which we had no hypothesis. Many of these were standard demographic variables.

The predictors themselves were of two types: direct predictive ratings of outcome by the patient, therapist, and clinical observer and scores derived from predictive measures. The 84 predictors were derived from seven domains: (1) patient measures, (2) therapist measures, (3) demographic information on the patients, (4) demographic information on the therapists, (5) clinical observers' measures (ratings), (6) patient–therapist

TABLE 6-1

Original Set of 84 Measures before Data Reduction

Patient Measures

1. Patient's Attractiveness for Psychotherapy (used as the therapist's prediction of outcome)
2. Hopkins Symptom Checklist (Uhlenhuth & Duncan, 1968)
3. Inventory of Social and Psychological Functioning (Auerbach & Johnson, 1978)
4–5. Target Complaints (rated by patient and by therapist). One measure each for ratings of first and second target complaints by the patient (Battle et al., 1966)
6–7. Five-Minute Speech Samples (for Anxiety and Human Relations scales) (Gottschalk & Gleser, 1969)
8. Social Assets Scale (Luborsky, Todd & Katcher, 1973)
9. Life Change Form (Holmes & Rahe, 1967)
10–12. MMPI: Hypochondriasis (Hs), Hysteria (Hy), Ego strength (Es) (Hathaway & Meehl, 1951; Barron, 1953a)
13. WAIS (four subtests weighted and summed: Comprehension, Vocabulary, Digit Symbol, and Similarities) (Wechsler, 1955)
14–15. Field Dependence-Independence: Rod-and-Frame (portable type) (Oltman, 1968); Embedded Figures Test (12-card set) (Witkin, 1950)
16. Rorschach Prognostic Rating Scale (Klopfer et al., 1954, pp. 688–699)
17. Prediction of Outcomes (during Prognostic Index interview): Patient's optimism about treatment

Therapist Measures

1–11. Therapist Orientation Questionnaire, 11 factors (Sundland & Barker, 1962)
    1. Training, planning and conceptualizing is important.
    2. Growth is inherent.
    3. Childhood experiences and psychoanalytic techniques are important.
    4. Verbal learning and cognitive gains are important.
    5. Affective gains are not important.
    6. Therapist feels secure.
    7. Social goals are important and directiveness should not be avoided.
    8. Involvement of the therapist is important.
    9. Informal behavior is all right.
    10. Interrupting the patient is okay.
    11. Unconscious motivation is important.
12. Sundberg Test of Implied Meaning: accuracy of recognizing the implied meanings of brief statements (Sundberg, 1964)
13–14. Raskin Tapes: Average difference-from-norm rating; discrepancy between self- and ideal concept of a therapist (Raskin, 1965, 1974).
15. Spence-Rubin Double Profile (Spence, 1966; Bachrach, Luborsky & Mechanich, 1974)
16–17. Field Dependence-Independence: Rod-and-Frame (portable type) (Oltman, 1968); Embedded Figures Test (12-card set) (Witkin, 1950)
18–20. Supervisors' Ratings of Therapist: competence as a therapist; competence as a psychiatrist; personal liking

Patient Demographic Measures

1. Age
2. Marital Status
3. Number of Children
4. Religion
5. Religious Activity

TABLE 6-1 *(Continued)*

6. Parents' Birthplace
7. Sex
8. Race
9. Education

Therapist Demographic Measures
1. Age
2. Marital Status
3. Number of Children
4. Religion
5. Religious Activity
6. Parents' Birthplace
7. Experience
8. Special Training
9. Style of Treatment
10. Academic Degree

Patient-Therapist Match Measures ("Similarities")
1. Age Match
2. Marital Status Match
3. Children Match
4. Religion Match
5. Religious Activity Match
6. Parents' Birthplace Match
7. Institutional Affiliation Match
8. Education Match
9. Occupation Match
10. Cognitive Style Match
11. Sum of 10 Matches

Clinical Judges' Ratings
1–10. Prognostic Index Interview Ratings (Auerbach & Luborsky, 1968a, 1968b, 1979; Auerbach, Luborsky & Johnson, 1972):
    1. Adjustment History
    2. Attractiveness as a Patient (composite of Insight, Motivation, Social Maturity, Attractiveness as a Patient, and Prediction)
    3. Duration (composite of Duration, Type of Onset, Precipitating Event, and Depression)
    4. Emotional Freedom (composite of Emotional Freedom, Initiative, Flexibility, and Patient Optimistic Expectations)
    5. Manifest Anxiety
    6. Anxiety Tolerance
    7. Interests
    8. Secondary Gain
    9. Extra Psychic Factors
    10. Control
11. Clinical Judge's Predictions of Outcome (Auerbach, Luborsky & Johnson, 1972)
12. Health-Sickness Rating Scale: mean of 8 ratings—7 specific criteria and the global rating (Luborsky, 1962a, 1975b)
13–16. Klein Adjustment Rating Scales: Sexual, Social, Self, Somatic (Klein, 1960)

Other Treatment Measures
1. Length of Treatment: number of weeks in therapy
2. Goals of Therapy: therapist's ratings of symptom relief versus personality change

TABLE 6-1 *(Continued)*

3.	Reason for Termination: natural versus unnatural termination (from the therapist's posttreatment questionnaire)
4–7.	Four Ingredients of Therapy: patient insight; therapist supportiveness; patient catharsis; therapist directiveness (from therapist's posttreatment questionnaire)
8.	Drug Use: prescribed medications

Recordings of Sessions and Variables Rated (Chapter 9)

1.	Ratings of two early whole sessions from each case made by two of six clinical observers
2.	Ratings of four 4-minute segments from the early and later parts of two sessions of psychotherapy made by four of six clinical observers.

match measures, and (7) early session measures. An eighth domain, other treatment measures, was included in the analyses although such measures (e.g., length of treatment, reason for termination) were not based upon pretreatment or early treatment information.

Most of the measures in table 6-1 are well known, and they need not be described here (there are references in the table). The less well known ones, such as the measures of therapist's sensitivity constructed for this project, are briefly described below.

PATIENT MEASURES

The 16 patient measures in table 6-1 are diverse standard measures that had been used in many other predictive studies (Waskow & Parloff, 1975). The Inventory of Social and Personality Functioning (Auerbach & Johnson, 1978) is a questionnaire developed for this study.

The Health-Sickness Rating Scale (HSRS) will be briefly described here because it has been used in the Penn Psychotherapy Project and in many other projects (Luborsky, 1962a, & 1975b; Luborsky & Bachrach, 1974). It is a clinician-rated measure of mental health based on an interview at the beginning and end of therapy. It was developed at the Menninger Foundation by a committee of clinical researchers. It consists of eight graphic 100-point scales: a global scale and seven specific criterion scales—capacity for autonomy, severity of symptoms, subjective distress, effect on the environment, utilization of abilities, quality of interpersonal relationships, and depth of interests. In order to rate the global scale, the judge considers the ratings on the seven specific criterion scales. The judge derives further assistance from placing the case under consideration in its position in relation to 30 HSRS-ranked sample case descriptions. Reliability and validity have been reported in many studies (Luborsky & Bachrach, 1974). In the Penn Psychotherapy Project, the sum of the eight scales was utilized;

this sum had an internal consistency (Cronbach's alpha) of .87 pretherapy and .92 posttherapy.

THERAPIST MEASURES

A wealth of anecdotal evidence attests to the power of the therapist as a determiner of the outcome of the patient's treatment. With that evidence in mind we were surprised to find so little in the quantitative predictive research about pretreatment characteristics of the therapist. Because predictive measures were even scantier for the therapist's sensitivity and treatment style, which seemed to have predictive potential, we concentrated on therapists in our test selection and development of new measures.

The Sundberg Test of Implied Meanings

The test consists of 40 simple declarative sentences on a tape recording (Sundberg, 1964). The task of the therapist who is being tested is to make a choice for each sentence from among four multiple-choice items consisting of possible intended messages implied by the sentence. What is measured by this test seems to be the ability of the therapist to recognize the intended message of a spoken sentence by the speaker's voice and expression.

The Raskin Tape as a Sensitivity Measure

The test was derived by us from a tape recording containing six 8-minute segments of psychotherapy, each carried out by a therapist who is a foremost expert in the exemplified form of psychotherapy. The tape had been constructed by Nathaniel Raskin to demonstrate the differences between forms of psychotherapy (Raskin, 1965, 1974). Raskin collected ratings of the six segments from a sample of 83 psychotherapists. The rating scales included 12 characteristics of the therapy, such as cognitive, experiential, empathic, therapist-directed, and so on.

Our measure of therapeutic sensitivity is based on the therapist's 12 ratings (plus 1 we added, "focuses on the transference") in comparison with the mean of the ratings by the normative group of 83 therapists. Each therapist's score is the degree of agreement with the normative group. A therapist's degree of agreement reflects the capacity to describe a sample of therapy in ways that it is typically described by others.

Another measure, also derived by us from these ratings, is a therapist's estimate of his or her competence relative to his or her ideal of a therapist's behavior. We had each therapist apply the rating scale to how he or she

typically behaved as a therapist (a self-description) as well as how a therapist should ideally behave (ideal description). The difference score represents the discrepancy between each therapist's own and ideal behavior as
a therapist.

The Rubin Double Profile as a Sensitivity Measure

We developed another procedure to use as a possible measure of sensitivity. The data to be judged by the therapist consisted of 30 pairs of
drawings (from a set loaned to us by Donald Spence). The therapist's task
is to judge which one of each pair of drawings was drawn by a subject who
had been flashed the Rubin double profile or a blank exposure, at .01
second. This test was intended to be a measure of the therapist's capacity
to detect very slight perceptual differences, a capacity we thought might
be relevant for psychotherapeutic skill.

The Therapist's Cognitive Style

We selected three of Witkin's measures of cognitive style (Witkin et al.,
1962): the Rod and Frame Test, Embedded Figures Test, and figure drawing
test. We were encouraged to use these tests by the results of Witkin, Lewis,
and Weil (1968), who had applied them to distinguish the behavior in
psychotherapy sessions of field-dependent versus field-independent therapists. Their study, although based on only 8 patients treated by 4 therapists, showed such impressive distinctions between field-dependent and
field-independent therapists that we decided to try the measures. According to Herman Witkin (personal communication, 1975), the more field-
dependent therapists seemed to do better with their patients than the
field-independent ones; *extreme* field-independence seemed to be associated
with nonresponsiveness and unconcern about the patient.

We used the measures also as similarity measures, since we supposed
that similarity of patients' and therapists' cognitive styles might improve
their relationship. In fact, for teachers and students, similarity in cognitive
style is associated with the teacher's positive estimate of the student's
ability (Witkin et al., 1977).

The Supervisor's Evaluation of the Therapist's Ability

The measure of therapists' ability was based on the annual evaluations
of the psychiatric residents by their supervisors during the 5 years of the
project. The form for the evaluation consisted of 5-point rating scales on
the therapist's abilities and style, partly derived from Holt and Luborsky

(1958a, 1958b). Three representative scales from these were used in our data analyses. For those therapists who were on the staff or in private practice, we obtained ratings from a few of their former supervisors and colleagues who had had an opportunity to know their work well. The ratings were made on the same type of form as was used for rating the psychiatric residents.

PATIENT DEMOGRAPHIC MEASURES AND THERAPIST DEMOGRAPHIC MEASURES

The 9 patient measures and the 10 therapist measures were derived from the Social Assets Scale (Luborsky, Todd & Katcher, 1973).

CLINICAL OBSERVERS' RATINGS

Most of the 12 clinical observers' measures were based on the Prognostic Index interview (chapter 7). The interview was conducted by a clinician from the research team. It contains questions covering the main areas that have been considered to determine the prognosis of psychotherapy.

PATIENT AND THERAPIST MATCH MEASURES

Ten matches or similarity measures were mostly derived from the Social Assets Scale (Luborsky, Todd & Katcher, 1973).

RECORDINGS OF SESSIONS

Recordings of whole sessions and segments of sessions were rated by clinical observers on 24 variables (see chapter 9).

OTHER TREATMENT MEASURES

Other measures provided broad descriptions of the treatment, such as its type, length, and goals.

The Structure of the Set of Predictors

Although we were tempted to try as many promising predictors as possible, we also made some effort to eliminate items that were highly redundant and to keep items that were representative of the range of dimensions established by a factor analysis of the predictors.

In reducing variables by the factor-analytic method, there is a danger that measures that are "specifics"—i.e., measures represented by only one item—might be thrown out. We were cautious about discarding such items since they might represent a legitimate point of view.

As a starting point, for multi-item tests we tried a simple sum of items and evaluated the result by the alpha reliability coefficient. We used an initial arbitrary criterion level of .85. When a test (i.e., set of items) did not reach this level, we constructed subscales, either by dropping poorer items or through the use of component analyses to suggest the cluster.

When all the appropriate pooling of items had been done, we computed principal components analyses within each set of predictors, looking again for composite scores that would carry most of the information more efficiently. Only composites with satisfactory reliability estimates were retained, though at times we settled for composites of borderline acceptability simply because the composite's individual items were themselves no more reliable than the composite and would have no convincing interpretation when retained as separate items. When we combined several tests, we first standardized them to weight them equally.

The results of our analyses are summarized in tables 6-2 through 6-4 for the patient test data and observer measures. These tables present the tests and single items retained in each area and the component analyses of patient and observer measures.

PATIENT PREDICTORS

Three components were retained for interpretation. The first was clearly a broad Adjustment dimension. The second appeared to tap the dimension of Field Independence—the correlation of two of its components, the Embedded Figures Test (EFT) and the Rod and Frame test (RFT), was .46. On the EFT, we noted an extremely high correlation between item means and standard deviations ($r = .86$); a log transformation removed this ($r = -.11$) and increased the estimated correlation of the EFT slightly.

The third component involved the two Gottschalk-Gleser (1969) measures—Anxiety and Human Relations. Since these two highly reliable scales correlated only $-.25$, we felt there was little to be gained by pooling them.

CLINICAL OBSERVER PREDICTORS

The factorial organization of the pretreatment Prognostic Index was explored in preliminary research (see chapter 7). Reanalysis of the instru-

TABLE 6-2

Reduction of Patient Measures

Test	No. of Items	Original r_{xx}	Decision	Final No. of Items
ISPF	101	.95	Sum items	1
Symptom Checklist (SCL)	85	.96	Sum items	1
WAIS	4 scales	.67	Sum items	1
MMPI	3 scales	.74	Use separate scales	
Hysteria (Hy)	26 + 7		Hy	1
Hypochondriasis (Hs)	49 + 11		Hs	1
Ego Strength (Es)	68		Es	1
Rod and Frame	8	.86	Sum items	1
Embedded Figure	12	.99	Sum items	1
Target Complaints	2	.32	Use separate items	
			TC1	1
			TC2	1
Life Change	1	—		1
Gottschalk Anxiety	1	—		1
Gottschalk Human Relations	1	—		1
Social Assets	1	—		1
Rorschach PRS	1	—		1

TABLE 6-3

Principal Components (PC) of Patient Measures

Test	Varimax Rotation		
	First PC	Second PC	Third PC
ISPF	.81[a]	.02	.07
SCL	−.88[a]	−.02	.05
WAIS	.45	−.56	−.29
Embedded Figure	−.12	.75[a]	−.12
Rod and Frame	.64	.69[a]	−.19
Hy	−.72	−.41	−.06
Hs	−.46	−.34	−.11
Es	.80[a]	−.01	−.10
TC1	.41	−.29	.35
TC2	.32	.20	.34
Life Change	−.25	−.45	.50
Social Assets	.68[a]	−.30	−.14
Human Relations	−.05	.15	.72
Anxiety	−.13	−.12	−.70
Rorschach	.06	−.22	−.06
Estimated r_{xx}	.86	.92[b]	—

[a]Item used in scoring the factor not scored due to low correlation ($r = .25$) between Human Relations and Anxiety; see text.
[b]Formula for reliability of sums used to estimate reliability; accordingly factor is *not* to be considered a randomly selected item composite.

TABLE 6-4

Observer Pretreatment Measures

Test	No. of items	r_{xx}	Decision	Final No. of Items	Loading on 1st PC
PI Adjustment	6	.78	Sum items	1	.80[a]
PI Attractiveness	5	.77	Sum items	1	.56
PI Acute Onset	4	.65	Sum items	1	.03
PI Emotional Flexibility	4	.64	Sum items	1	.55
PI Manifest Anxiety	1	—			−.30
PI Anxiety Tolerance	1	—			.54
PI Interests	1	—	These items did not fit into PI clusters; used as separate items		.50
PI Secondary Gain	1	—			.23
PI Extra Psychic	1	—			.19
PI Control	1	—			.34
PI Prediction	1	—			.11
Klein Ratings	4	.47	Use separately	4	
Social	1			1	.76[a]
Somatic	1			1	−.01
Self-esteem	1			1	.68[a]
Sexual Adjustment	1			1	.64[a]
Health-Sickness Rating Scale	8	.87	Sum items	1	.76[a]

[a]Used in scoring Adjustment component; estimated $r_{xx} = .82$.

ment with the current sample confirmed previous findings. The component involving educational achievement was omitted since more objective measures of these variables existed. The components retained from the Prognostic Index were interpreted as Adjustment, Attractiveness for Therapy, Emotional Flexibility, and Acute Onset. Several Prognostic Index items that were unrelated to these components were retained as single items. In an overall component analysis, including all observer measures, only the broad Adjustment dimension was scored, as no other composite of importance appeared.

DEMOGRAPHIC AND PATIENT–THERAPIST "MATCH" ITEMS

Several decisions were made regarding the scoring of demographic items. We treated religious affiliation as two dummy variables (i.e. coded "1" when the characteristic was present, "0" when it was absent) Jewish versus not Jewish and Christian versus not Christian. Data were available for scoring the match between therapist and patient on 10 items. The systems for deriving a match are outlined in table 6-5.

In general, overlap was slight among the demographic variables and match variables. In any event, it seemed inappropriate to generate derived composites of such variables (e.g., the "average" of marital status and number of children). Thus, all of the original items were retained.

THERAPIST TEST DATA

The therapist measures were all retained for separate examination because the sample size of therapists was too small for factor analysis.

RATINGS OF SESSIONS

The reduction of the 24 ratings of segments and sessions is fully described in chapter 9.

TABLE 6-5

Match between Patient and Therapist Variable

	Variable	Definition
1.	Age	Both P and T above respective median ($N = 10$) or both below median ($N = 33$)
2.	Marital Status	Both married ($N = 26$) or single ($N = 5$)
3.	Children	Both childless ($N = 16$) or both have at least one child ($N = 20$)
4.	Religion	Both "none" ($N = 3$) or Jewish ($N = 15$) or Christian ($N = 10$)
5.	Religious Activity	Both inactive ($N = 26$) or both active ($N = 17$)
6.	Parents' Birthplace	Both have both parents born in U.S. ($N = 31$) or both have at least one foreign ($N = 6$)
7.	Institutional Affiliation	Both affiliated in some way with University of Pennsylvania ($N = 29$)
8.	Education	Both have postgraduate education ($N = 23$)
9.	Occupation	Both are in the mental health field or allied fields ($N = 12$)
10.	Cognitive Style	Both have the same cognitive style, according to Rod and Frame and Embedded Figures scores ($N = 3$)
11.	Sum of 10 Matches	Sum of the above matches, allowing one point for each match

NOTE: N's are those who match.

Summary

This chapter has listed the 84 predictive measures from 8 domains that were selected for the study, as well as the methods for finding their structure based on many factor analyses and other methods of reduction of variables.

7

How Clinicians Predict Outcomes

TO GET MORE INSIGHT into how clinicians predict the outcomes of psychotherapy, we tried two methods: judgments of contrived cases and judgments of real cases. With the first method contrived patient data were systematically varied in order to examine clinicians' beliefs about prognostic signs. With the second method, clinicians used a semistructured Prognostic Index interview for judging patients' assets and liabilities for psychotherapy.

Judgment of Contrived Cases

Do clinicians share common beliefs about the prognostic significance of certain patient characteristics? To grapple with this problem, we will examine some data illustrating the types of beliefs held by clinicians about prognostic signs (drawn from the set of studies reported in Mintz, 1972). The novel method was to systematically vary prognostic indicators in a set of contrived patient data and then to obtain judges' prognostic reactions to these data.

The use of contrived clinical material is a methodological innovation in studies of this area and proves to be particularly useful for two reasons. First, it becomes possible to obtain a very large sample of "patients" for study without the huge labor involved in the typical study of therapy, since no real patients are necessary. Second, it is possible to systematically vary the aspects of the case that are hypothesized to be important.

Of course, this method is useful only for studying clinicians' judgments. No one would argue that invented materials can be experienced in the same way as a therapist experiences a real patient. Nevertheless, the method of contrived cases may begin to inform us as to how clinicians evaluate patients, yielding insights to test in actual practice.

METHOD

In our study four main dimensions of potential prognostic importance were examined, each represented by two levels: severity of difficulties (severe versus mild), chronicity (more than 2 years versus less than 6 months in duration), social assets (good versus moderate), and treatment setting (private practice versus clinic). Pairing all possible combinations on these four dimensions yielded 16 "patients."

A one-sentence description of each level was typed on a small piece of paper in capital letters. Each patient was described in a four-page booklet, each page containing the patient's level on one of the four dimensions. To balance order of presentation, each of the four dimensions appeared equally often in each position (i.e., page 1, 2, 3, or 4); also, there were as many "good" items as "bad" ones in each position.

The 16 booklets were presented to four judges—three Ph.D. clinical psychologists (relatively inexperienced) and one research assistant with substantial experience in rating psychotherapy. The judges were asked to read each booklet and rate each successively after reading each "fact" about the case in terms of how successful they would expect the patient's therapy to be. They were told that each patient started with a rating of "0," meaning "average in success," and that after reading each page of the booklet, they should rate (from −3 to +3) the probable success based on the total information to that point. Each "case" was rated four times by each judge; the final rating represented the overall prognostic judgment based on all four items.

An analysis of variance was computed for the predicted final success of therapy ratings and is summarized in table 7-1. Several trends emerged:

1. Agreement in assigning prognostic ratings was fairly high. The average correlation between judges was .76; the intraclass correlation was .69. Because of the small number of judges, all effects were tested against the pooled interactions with judges.

2. The main effects accounted for about 70% of the total variance and about 92% of the between-cases variance. By and large, then, the judges appeared to combine the bits of information in a simple linear manner.

3. Significant main effects indicated that three of the dimensions have clear prognostic significance to the judges. In decreasing order, recent onset, mild difficulties, and relatively good assets (education/income) were clearly seen as "good" prognostic signs. The significant interaction in-

TABLE 7-1

Analysis of Variance for Prognostic Study

Source	df	MS	F
Raters	3	.516	—
Setting (A)	1	1.891	3.51
Severity (B)	1	23.766	44.71**
Assets (C)	1	17.016	31.63**
Duration (D)	1	31.641	58.81**
A × B	1	.766	1.42
A × C	1	.391	< 1
A × D	1	.016	< 1
B × C	1	.016	< 1
B × D	1	2.641	4.91*
C × D	1	.391	< 1
A × B × C	1	.016	< 1
A × B × D	1	.141	< 1
A × C × D	1	1.266	2.35
B × C × D	1	.391	< 1
A × B × C × D	1	.391	< 1
Raters × Cases	45	.538	

*$p < .05$
**$p < .01$

dicated that the duration was a more salient variable when the problem was severe than when it was mild (table 7-2). This effect was small, however, relative to the main effects.

Prognosis affects perception of "success" in psychotherapy. The study just reported confirmed that contrived cases with good prognosis were seen as having better outcomes than cases with poor prognosis, although outcome data were identical. At least three aspects of a case description have powerful prognostic implications for these clinical judges. The next study was designed to explore this topic.

TABLE 7-2

*Mean Success Rating
(Four Judges) as a Joint
Function of Duration and
Severity of Problem*

	Severity of Problem	
Duration	Mild	Severe
Acute	1.375	.562
Chronic	.375	−1.250

Eight brief "personality sketches" of "patients" were written. Four of these patients were supplied with "good prognostic indicators": They had relatively mild problems of recent onset, and they were all professionals or white collar workers with college educations. Four of the "patients" had "poor prognostic indicators": They were seriously disturbed, had a high school education or less, were unemployed, and had problems of several years' duration. The cases were paired in terms of the *type* of problem: (a) aggressivity (a minister who lost his temper versus a construction worker with serious assaultive behavior); (b) addictive (a junior executive concerned about a mild dependence on sleeping pills versus a chronic alcoholic); (c) anxiety (a professional artist with mild "work blocks" versus an unemployed gardener with severe anxiety); and (d) somatization (a college professor concerned with occasional headaches during teaching versus a postal worker with chronic, severe migraine headaches).

Two measures of therapy outcome were devised. The first was a test of personality adjustment described as like the MMPI, with the same kind of scale values (i.e., 50 was average and 70 was abnormal). Judges were told that a change of "about 10 points is probably statistically significant." This "test" was called the General Personality Inventory (GPI).

The second measure was one of the patient's central problems (CPs), and was described in terms like those in the Target Complaints form. It was defined as a 9-point scale, anchored at 1 ("no problem at all at this time"), 3 ("a little"), 5 ("moderately"), 7 ("quite a bit"), and 9 ("couldn't be worse"). The measure represented how troubled the patient felt by the main problems.

All "patients" were given pretherapy "scores" on the GPI between 66 and 70 and scores on the CP of either 6 or 7. Two levels of change were defined for each measure. A large change on the GPI was a 9-point improvement and a small change was a 3-point gain. A large change on the CP was a 4-point improvement, and a small change was a 1-point improvement. Pairing these changes yielded four combinations—high change on both, low change on both, and high change on one only.

Exactly the same outcome data (pretherapy, posttherapy, and change score) were given to one high prognosis case and its matched low prognosis case. Any effects of prognosis were, therefore, independent of actual change. The "case description" and the "test data" were presented on separate pages so that the judges could respond to the case description before seeing the test data.

The eight cases were presented to seven judges—a psychiatrist, three Ph.D. clinical psychologists, and three psychotherapy research assistants. Inspection of the data showed no differences between the professionals and the nonprofessionals. Each judge was asked to read the case description and rate the patient's problem as mild or severe, the social assets as high or low, and the duration of the problems as acute or chronic. Then the judge was asked to look at the test data and rate the success of therapy on a 7-point scale, from −3 to +3, with 0 representing "average" in success.

Were the "conditions" of prognosis correctly perceived? By and large, they were. No judge misclassified a patient's social assets. There were 6 misclassifications (out of 56 possibilities) on duration. Since five different cases were involved, there is little reason to attribute this to the write-ups. On severity, there were 4 misclassifications, involving three different cases. There was only one case for which a judge misperceived two of the three conditions.

The analysis of variance of the success ratings is presented in table 7-3. Agreement among judges, indexed by an intraclass correlation of .50, was somewhat lower than we hoped, but it was adequate to warrant proceeding with the study.

The highly significant effects for GPI and CP are reassuring. Patients who made large changes were seen as having more successful treatments. In these data, the central problem measure was weighted somewhat more heavily than the measure of general personality change. Since the scales were not comparable, it was difficult to make much of this.

The striking finding is the significant effect for prognosis, since matched high and low prognosis cases had exactly the same set of test

TABLE 7-3

*Analysis of Variance for Contrived Cases
with Varying Prognosis and Change*

Source	df	MS	F
Raters (A)	6	3.66	—
Cases (B)	7	7.02	—
(a) Prognosis	1	4.57	5.24*
(b) GPI	1	18.28	20.98**
(c) CP	1	25.78	29.58**
(d) a × b	1	.29	< 1
(e) a × c	1	.07	< 1
(f) b × c	1	.07	< 1
(g) a × b × c	1	.07	< 1
A × B (Error)	42	.872	

$*p < .05$
$**p < .01$

scores. The result was, at first glance, paradoxical. The high prognosis patients, on the average, were judged to have had more successful treatment than the low prognosis cases. A difference in this direction was found for every judge.

One might expect that a large change in a patient who was not expected to improve would be seen as more successful therapy than the same size change in a patient with good prognostic signs. The reverse was true! Patients expected to have more successful therapies were seen to have had them, despite the presence of test data that failed to confirm this.

One explanation for this finding would be in terms of bias or "self-fulfilling prophecy." Research has also shown that mild problems, acute duration, and social assets are good prognostic signs (chapter 19). Here we see that judges will produce results confirming this even when test data contradict it.

When informed of the results, the judges contended that they were entirely reasonable in clinical terms. The gist of their views was that relatively healthy people with a history of "accomplishment" may well be expected to consolidate, maintain, and utilize their gains more successfully than those with fewer assets. Another view was that change at high levels of adjustment or organization is more difficult and should be weighted more. One judge suggested that as the goal of therapy is to produce "well-adjusted people," an important aspect of its success is the extent to which this is accomplished. Obviously, a patient who begins therapy as relatively well adjusted needs to change very little to end up well adjusted.

CONCLUSIONS

Three aspects of a prospective psychotherapy patient have been shown, with contrived systematically varied cases, to have clear prognostic significance in the minds of clinical judges: (1) recent onset of difficulties, (2) relative mildness of dysfunction, and (3) good social assets (education and income). In these beliefs, the judges echo the research findings in chapter 19.

Furthermore, we have shown that these prognostic findings about outcome can be reproduced with contrived case materials even when objective data provide *no* support for them. That is, contrived cases with good prognostic signs were seen as more successfully treated than those with poor prognoses, even though the objective test data as to pre- and posttreatment status given to judges were exactly the same for both groups.

Judgment of Real Cases

Because the Prognostic Index (PI) for psychotherapy was our best predictor, we will devote the rest of the chapter to describing its development and seeing how accurate clinicians were in using it to predict outcomes. When we began the Penn Project there was no convenient, compatible, and—in today's lexicon—"user-friendly" instrument for clinicians to use for systematic evaluation of patients for psychotherapy. We were encouraged to construct such an instrument by two observations: (1) Patient factors are more important than other factors in determining the patient's benefits (chapter 19); and (2) clinicians typically believe they can estimate the prognosis from a knowledge of the patient's personality gained through clinical interviews.

Our plan for developing the Prognostic Index interview was to assess patients on many variables that were reputed to have prognostic value and then, at the end of therapy, to see which of the variables actually predicted outcome. Like the researchers of the Menninger Psychotherapy Project, we assumed that clinically important patient qualities could be reliably assessed by trained clinicians (Sargent et al., 1968; Kernberg et al., 1972; Wallerstein, 1986). However, in some ways our project differed in approach from the Menninger Project, notably in the method of assessing patients. The standard Menninger Foundation procedures included extensive interviews with the patients and their relatives and a standard battery of diagnostic psychological tests. The Menninger Project interviews were only partly focused on the research variables, since the clinical interviewers did not even know which patients would be included in the research study. By contrast, our Prognostic Index interview was briefer and more structured, and it was not part of the normal clinical routine.

In the Penn Psychotherapy Project the interview was conducted by a research interviewer at the beginning of therapy. It provided the information needed to rate the patient on the 32 prognostic variables. (After the pilot study the number of variables was reduced to 29.) The manual for the Prognostic Index contains recommended questions for each variable for the interviewer's use in a semistructured interview format. Although the interviewer is not restricted to these questions the inquiry into each area should start with the suggested questions. Depending on the patient's reply, the interviewer may explore the area further in the usual clinical way. In our predictive study the interview was tape recorded so that ratings could be made not only by the interviewer but also by other independent judges who listened to the tape recording of the interview.

Each variable is rated on a 9-point scale, with 9 indicating the most favorable prognostic rating. In the later predictive study, the scale points were numbered 1–5, with half-step ratings, such as 3.5, permitted; this is another 9-point scale.

SOURCE OF VARIABLES

We were intentionally overinclusive in selecting variables. We included those that *might* prove to have prognostic significance, not only those that we thought *would*. The variables we selected were derived from the Menninger Psychotherapy Project; from the clinical lore about prognosis, especially as embodied in Wolberg (1967); and from our review of patient qualities that might predispose the patient to achieve a good outcome (chapter 19).

The variables of the Prognostic Index were classified in four categories: descriptive, psychodynamic, demographic, and global judgments (see table 7-4). The source of variables that were borrowed from other researchers is noted in the table.

Some of the variables need a few words of explanation about their predictive significance.

Anxiety and depression were tentatively considered to be good prognostic signs. Our reasoning was that these affects would serve as incentives for therapeutic work so that, in general, the presence of affect would be more desirable than the absence of affect. There was also research evidence supporting the favorable prognostic significance of these affects (chapter 19).

Early environmental trauma are poor prognostic signs.

Developmental history takes into account signs of stunted psychological development during childhood and adolescence, which are considered unfavorable prognostically, depending on their severity (as described by Freud, 1937).

Environmental and physical health limiting factors, if they include adverse environmental factors or poor health in the patient, may limit the improvement.

Patient's expectations from therapy have shown that a basic optimism is more favorable than its opposite.

Emotional freedom is defined as the ability to experience and express emotions. High emotional freedom is seen as a good prognostic sign.

Social maturity refers to the general impression of the patient's maturity, which should be a favorable prognostic factor.

Need for punishment is an inferential judgment made of whether the patient seems to have a need to suffer; one of the defining characteristics of this

TABLE 7-4

Prognostic Index Variables

Descriptive	Psychodynamic
Diagnosis[a]	Anxiety tolerance[b]
Duration	Adaptiveness of coping devices[e]
Acuteness of onset	Insight and psychological mindedness[b]
Recognizable precipitating event	Motivation for psychotherapy
Manifest anxiety[b]	Secondary gain[c]
Depression	Need for punishment
Quality of interpersonal relations	*Demographic*
Breadth and depth of interests	Intelligence[a]
Early environmental trauma	Education
Developmental history[c]	Occupation
Environmental and physical limiting	Marital status[a]
factors[b]	
Benefit from past therapy	*Global Judgments*
School or work adjustment[d]	Attractiveness for psychotherapy[f]
Flexibility	Interviewer's prediction of outcome
Initiative	
Patient's expectations of therapy	
Emotional freedom	
Self-control	
Social maturity	

[a]Dropped from the Prognostic Index since completion of the original predictive study.
[b]Wallerstein et al., 1956
[c]Wolberg, 1967
[d]Klein, 1960
[e]Menninger et al., 1963
[f]Nash et al., 1965

need is the habitual use of self-defeating patterns. A high need for punishment would be a poor prognostic sign.

Attractiveness as a patient for psychotherapy is the rater's impression in the form of a global judgment (Nash et al., 1965).

Rater's prediction of outcome is the rater's intuitive global judgment of how much the patient is likely to improve during psychotherapy. We included this variable to see how the rater's direct intuitive prediction compared with the more specific variables in predicting outcome.

RELIABILITY

Under the intensive, individual training condition, the median Pearson correlation for the items of the Prognostic Index was found, in separate samples, to be .71, .65, and .78, with a range from .25 to .99. Satisfactory agreement is apparently possible with proper training, during which the trainee listens to recordings of Prognostic Index interviews, makes ratings, and discusses points of difference with the trainer. The trainee is also taught how to conduct the PI interview so as to elicit the information needed for the ratings. It is important to note, however, that judges tend to have their own characteristic levels of rating these types of variables. The Pearson correlation used to assess interjudge reliability does not consider differences between judges in mean levels to be error variance. In the Penn Psychotherapy Project we employed a design where each of the 73 patients was rated by only a single judge (1 of 10 available judges). In this design differences in mean levels between judges adds error to the scores and lower reliability.

PROGNOSTIC INDEX STUDIES

In the first of two studies the Prognostic Index variables were rated on 20 patients. The database for the rating was as complete as usual; it was a two- to three-page summary of the history written by each patient's therapist at the beginning of therapy. The first published report on the Prognostic Index (Auerbach, Luborsky & Johnson, 1972) concerned these 20 patients (Group B) plus 27 patients from the predictive study (Group A). The reasons for combining the two samples were to produce a sufficiently large sample to justify a factor analysis and to compare predictive accuracy when the source of information about the patient varies.

Forty of the patients were given a DSM-II diagnosis of neurosis or personality disorder. Seven were considered psychotic or borderline psychotic; most of the latter were in Group B. Psychotherapy was the main treatment modality for all of the 47 patients, but a few also received tranquilizers or antidepressants. In almost all cases the treatment was outpatient therapy; a few patients were hospitalized. Forty-one of the patients were treated by psychiatric residents, most of whom were in their third or fourth year of training. Six of the patients had more experienced psychiatrists as therapists.

At the end of treatment all 47 patients had an evaluation interview similar to the initial one. This interview was designed to gather information about the patient's status and changes during the treatment. Most of the variables of the Prognostic Index were rerated at this time, providing an estimate of the patient's end-of-treatment status to compare with the initial status.

The group of diagnosticians who conducted the diagnostic and evaluative interviews at the beginning and end of therapy consisted of four psychiatrists and three clinical psychologists. For each patient, initial and termination ratings were made by two raters: one who conducted the interview and another who listened to the tape recording.

TABLE 7-5

Composition of the Factors in the Prognostic Index

Aptitude for Psychotherapy		Depression	.52
Motivation	.86	Precipitating event	.40
Insight	.67	*General Emotional Health*	
Secondary gain	.63	Interpersonal relations	.75
Anxiety tolerance	.55	Diagnosis	.72
Patient's expectations	.51	Coping devices	.72
Interviewer's prediction	.49	Absence of need for punishment	.71
Attractiveness	.41	Developmental history	.66
Emotional Freedom		Early environment	.65
Emotional freedom	.78	Social maturity	.57
Flexibility	.70	Self-control	.46
Initiative	.63	*Intellectual Achievement*	
Acute Depression		Intelligence	.76
Brief duration	.69	Education	.70
Onset	.59	Extrapsychic factors	.51

NOTE: Each variable is listed with the factor on which it loads highest. Variables with loadings less than .40 have been excluded.

In order to find the main dimensions that clinicians use in evaluating patients a factor analysis of the predictive variables was performed. Table 7-5 shows the principal variables that loaded each factor. Factor scores were calculated by summing the highest loading items on each factor.

OUTCOME CRITERIA

Seven criteria of outcome were used. Two are judgments made by the patient and five are judgments made by the interviewer. The criteria are as follows:

Target complaints, devised by the Johns Hopkins psychotherapy research group (Battle et al., 1966), refers to the patient's main complaints at the beginning of therapy. Those patients who had an initial diagnostic interview (Group A) were asked in the initial interview to name the three problems that they most wanted help with. The severity of each problem was indicated on a rating scale. In the final evaluation interview the patient, without seeing his or her initial rating, made a similar judgment on the severity of each of these problems at the time of the interview. These ratings gave a specific measure of the patient's improvement in terms of fulfilling his or her own goals. The Target Complaints procedure was also used for the patients in Group B, but since we did not have initial ratings for the severity of their problems, we relied on retrospective ratings by the patients in their posttherapy interviews.

Patient satisfaction indicates the patient's satisfaction with his or her treatment. The rating was made on a 9-point scale, from "extremely dissatisfied" to "extremely satisfied."

Interviewer's judgment of improvement was a global judgment of improvement based on the interview with the patient at the end of treatment.

Factor change scores, the last four criteria, reflect change on the factors that might be expected to change in therapy: General Emotional Health (now called Level of Adjustment), Aptitude for Psychotherapy, Acute Depression, and Emotional Freedom.

RESULTS

Three Factors Predicted: Acute Depression, Emotional Health, and Intellectual Achievement

The basic question in this study was how accurate were the clinicians in making predictions using the qualities in the Prognostic Index interview. Specifically, what are the correlations of the five factor scores—measured before therapy—with the outcome criteria? Table 7-6 shows the correlation of pretherapy factor scores and outcome criteria.

The outcome of psychotherapy was significantly predicted by the patient's initial scores on three of the factors: Acute Depression, General Emotional Health (Level of Adjustment), and Intellectual Achievement.

Acute depression in those patients who at the beginning of treatment were seen as having an acute depressive illness was likely to be judged significantly improved at the end of therapy (.27*). Depression has been found to be a favorable prognostic sign among schizophrenics (Stephens & Astrup, 1963; Vaillant, 1964). We found that it was also a good sign in our predominantly nonpsychotic population. The "acuteness" part of the Acute Depression factor supports the clinical and commonsense belief that it is better to have such a recent illness of brief duration than a chronic one.

Intellectual achievement predicted two outcome criteria: improvement in depression ($-.32^*$) and the patient's own rating of improvement on the Target Complaints (.29*). Thus, intelligent, well-educated patients were likely to recover from their depressions and to rate themselves improved on the main problems that brought them to treatment.

General emotional health (level of adjustment) was the most successful predictor of outcome. It correlated with three outcome criteria: improvement in depression ($-.37^*$), improvement in Emotional Freedom (i.e., greater Emotional Freedom) (.30*), and the rater's global judgment of improvement

TABLE 7-6

Correlation of Pretherapy Factor Scores with Outcome Criteria

	Patient's Judgment (Outcome)	
Predictor	Improvement in Target Complaints	Patient Satisfaction
Aptitude for Therapy	.01	.00
Emotional Freedom	.02	−.02
Acute Depression	.04	.19
General Emotional Health	.07	.00
Intellectual Achievement	.29*	.04

	Interviewer's Judgment (Outcome)				
		Change in Factor			
Predictor	Global Judgment of Improvement	Aptitude for Psychotherapy	Emotional Freedom	Acute Depression	Emotional Health
Aptitude for Therapy	.16	.05	.06	−.18	−.19
Emotional Freedom	−.09	−.21	.04	.02	−.04
Acute Depression	.27*	.22	.11	−.14	.08
General Emotional Health	.27*	−.15	.30*	−.37*	−.01
Intellectual Achievement	.16	.11	.08	−.32*	−.13

NOTE: Change scores used are regressed change scores. Each factor does not correlate exactly zero with regressed changes on that factor because of difference in methods of scoring the factors before and after therapy.

For changes in the Acute Depression factor, a negative correlation indicates *decrease* in depression.

*$p < .05$

(.27*). This finding lends support to the common belief that those patients who come to psychotherapy with greater personality assets are more likely to benefit from it.

Table 7-7 shows the correlation of the pretherapy global judgments—Patient Attractiveness and Interviewer's Prediction of Outcome—with the outcome criteria. These pretherapy global judgments predicted outcome about as well as General Emotional Health (Level of Adjustment) did, e.g., pretherapy global predictors correlated .32* with improvement.

If we look at the raters' global predictions and then at actual outcome, we naturally find that some outcomes were predicted less accurately than others. It is instructive to examine the incorrectly predicted cases in an effort to learn what misled the predictors. Most such cases fell into four categories.

1. In the initial interview it was possible for some patients to conceal from the interviewer (perhaps from themselves as well) the extent and severity of their problems. They presented themselves as relatively healthy, with only a few commonplace problems to work on, and the interviewer predicted a good outcome. In the course of treatment the full

TABLE 7-7

Correlation of Pretherapy Global Judgments with Outcome Criteria

	Patient's Judgment (Outcome)				
Predictor	Improvement in Target Complaints	Patient Satisfaction			
Patient Attractiveness	.34*	−.05			
Interviewer's Global Prediction	.18	.05			

	Interviewer's Judgment (Outcome)				
		Change in Factor			
	Global Judgment of improvement	Aptitude for Psychotherapy	Emotional Freedom	Acute Depression	Emotional Health
Patient Attractiveness	.28*	.11	.20	−.33*	.13
Interviewer's Global Prediction	.32*	.13	.01	−.28*	.00

*p < .05

extent of the patient's illness was revealed, and outcome was not nearly as good as expected.

2.   Conversely, some patients who were apparently very disturbed turned out to have important assets that were not apparent at the time of initial evaluation. In some of such cases there was a fortunate matching of patient and therapist so that a good relationship formed between them and allowed the patient's hidden assets to emerge.

3.   Many of the patients in this sample were university students, and there was a tendency for the interviewers to predict a good outcome for students. Students were usually seen as bright, sincere, and well motivated, and they often appeared attractive and appealing. But it was possible to overlook the resistances that would hinder therapy so that the actual outcome was not always so favorable.

4.   Predictions tended to be more accurate when based on a pretherapy evaluation interview (Group A patients) than when based on a protocol written by the therapist (Group B patients), although the difference in accuracy between the two groups did not quite reach statistical significance. This trend suggests that the information needed for a prediction can be obtained more efficiently from a systematic, semistructured interview than from the less structured write-up by a therapist.

CONCLUSIONS

Main Dimensions in the Prognostic Index

Factor analysis of ratings on the Prognostic Index revealed the main dimensions that clinicians use when they assess a patient for psychotherapy. These dimensions, with the variables that load each one .65 or above, are (1) aptitude for psychotherapy (motivation, insight), (2) Emotional Freedom (emotional freedom, flexibility), (3) Acute Depression (brief duration), (4) General Emotional Health (interpersonal relations, diagnosis, coping devices, absence of need for punishment, developmental history, early environment), and (5) Intellectual Achievement (intelligence, education).

Main Significant Predictions by the Prognostic Index

The outcome of psychotherapy was significantly predicted by scores on three factors: (1) General Emotional Health (Level of Adjustment), (2) Intellectual Achievement, and (3) Acute Depression.

General Emotional Health (Level of Adjustment) was the most success-ful predictor. It is similar to the variable, mildness of dysfunction, used by the clinicians in predicting outcomes of the contrived cases (in the first section of this chapter). (Another prediction from the contrived cases study is partially replicated here: "good social assets" corresponds in part with "intellectual achievement." The third, "recent onset," may correspond in part with "acute depression.") Emotional health is similar to the class of variables we refer to in chapter 19 as psychological health-sickness and in our Penn Psychotherapy Project predictive study (chapter 8) as pretreat-ment adjustment. In the Penn Psychotherapy Project and in more than 70 other psychotherapy studies the variable had a high percentage of signifi-cant predictions. The best predictor of outcomes of psychotherapy for depressed patients was the Prognostic Index interview rating of General Emotional Adjustment (Rounsaville, Weissman & Prusoff, 1981).

Level of Prediction by the Prognostic Index

The level of the correlations with outcomes, although statistically sig-nificant, reflects only moderately accurate predictions, since a correlation of .3 (the correlation of general emotional health with outcome) accounts for only 9% of the variance in the outcome measure. The interviewer's pretherapy global judgments—Patient Attractiveness and Global Predic-tion of Outcome—were about as successful as General Emotional Health in predicting outcome. It is our impression, and it is consistent with the findings in chapter 8, that the systematic assessment required by the Prognostic Index maximizes the accuracy of the global prediction by the interviewer.

Summary

Two methods were employed to understand how clinicians go about pre-dicting the outcomes of psychotherapy. In the first, clinicians made judg-ments of systematically varied contrived cases. Three aspects of a prospec-tive psychotherapy patient were shown to have clear prognostic significance in the minds of clinical judges: recent onset of difficulties, relative mildness of dysfunction, and good social assets (education and income).

With the second method, clinicians used the Prognostic Index interview with real patients. The interview covers 29 areas that clinicians believe are useful in predicting outcomes of psychotherapy. After the interview the clinician rates each area. A factor analysis of the ratings of 47 patients revealed five factors. The outcome of psychotherapy was significantly predicted by three factors—General Emotional Health, Intellectual Achievement, and Acute Depression—as well as by Global Prediction of Outcome.

8

Pretreatment Measures as Predictors of Psychotherapy Outcomes

THE PREVIOUS CHAPTERS have been prologue to a grand test of our pretreatment measures in predicting outcomes for the 73 patients treated in the Penn Psychotherapy Project.

Psychotherapists typically believe that the suitability of patients for psychotherapy can be estimated by a pretreatment evaluation or by some trial sessions. On this basis they try to predict not only which patients will benefit from psychotherapy, but even which types of psychotherapy will be most beneficial for each patient. This practice of pretreatment evaluation for suitability for treatment appears to them to be justified by their clinical experience and by the large clinical literature on how to go about these evaluations, for example, Dyrud (1975).

In contrast, another clinical tradition, generally associated with the "client-centered" Rogerian school, holds that psychotherapy is an adventure—its directions and outcomes are largely unpredictable and are to be discovered only as the treatment process unfolds.

The considerable quantitative research is also mixed in its verdict about the predictability of the outcomes of psychotherapy. Views in favor of predictability derive much support from our original review of 166 predictive studies (Luborsky et al., 1971), which revealed significant predictions based on certain qualities, including psychological health, intelligence, education, similarities of patient and therapist, patient experiencing, and therapist's experience and empathy. But not all studies showed significant levels of prediction, and it was not clear what distinguished those studies that succeeded from those that failed. In fact, one of the most well-designed studies (Fiske, Cartwright & Kirtner, 1964) found only a few barely significant predictors and concluded that psychotherapy is essentially unpredictable from the pretreatment information.

Research on the predictability of psychotherapy outcomes could have a practical value for assisting in the evaluation of patients for psychotherapy. It could also have more general value in directing our attention toward those aspects of the patient, the therapist, the treatment, and their interactions that are important determiners of its outcome; i.e., the research should contribute to our knowledge of the curative factors in psychotherapy.

The Penn Psychotherapy Project was designed to (1) try all the best predictors revealed by our review (Luborsky et al., 1971), (2) try these predictors against several representative outcome measures, and (3) try an adequate sample of measures of the therapist and treatment—not just patient measures or pretreatment information, as had been done previously. In this chapter we report on the pretreatment (or apart from treatment) predictive results of the project.

Procedure

First, we will review our methods briefly. Between 1968 and 1973, test and interview evaluations were made on the 73 patients at the time they began supportive-expressive psychoanalytically oriented psychotherapy and again when they completed treatment. The median length of treatment was 32 sessions during a median of 34 weeks.

The predictions were of two types: (1) direct predictive ratings by the patient, therapist, and clinical observer and (2) scores derived from predictive measures. These predictive measures were based mostly on standard procedures (chapter 6); one of the new ones was the Prognostic Index Interview for Psychotherapy (chapter 7).

What was to be predicted was the patient's benefits by the time of termination, as measured by residual gain and rated benefits (chapter 2). In our sample, raw gain and rated benefits correlated moderately highly ($r = .68$). The residual gain criterion correlated highly with rated benefits ($r = .76$). This suggests that the patient and therapist, as part of their usual way of judging benefits, made an estimated correction for initial level which was similar to the statistical one. What they did amounts to a subtraction of initial level from termination level and then a correction of that raw gain for the initial level! Not only did the outcomes show that the patients as a group had benefited but the outcomes varied considerably from patient to patient (chapter 3). The two positive attributes of the outcomes allowed us to move on more securely to the job of seeing how well we could predict outcomes.

Success of Direct Predictions by Patients, Therapists, and Clinical Observers

A direct prediction of a patient's outcome is made by a judge, not by a score on a predictive measure. A judge is free to use all of the available information and to apply it in any way he or she can to the predictive task. The patient and the clinical observer made their predictions in the course of the Prognostic Index interview, which was usually conducted after one or two psychotherapy sessions had been held. The therapist's prediction was to be made after one or two psychotherapy sessions but instead was often made retrospectively.[1] The predictions by the patient, therapist, and clinical observer showed low, although significant, agreement with each other (.27* to .32*).

Direct predictions were modestly successful. The accuracy of the predictions by the three types of judges was modest although statistically significant or nearly so (table 8-1): The patient's direct prediction correlated .23* with rated benefits; for the observer the correlation was .27*; for the therapist the correlation was .19 (just above the .05 level).

Therapists' clinical experience did not add to success. We expected that the more experienced therapists would be more successful at making predictions about the outcomes of the treatments they were about to conduct. This did

[1]The therapist data, although marred, probably remained representative. We could identify only 20 of the 73 patients for whom we are certain that the direct prediction by the therapist was made before treatment started. The other 53 therapists' predictions were made retrospectively in response to our instruction to predict as they would have done initially; many of the therapists used their original notes on the patient before completing the ratings. At the time this was done, most of the treatments were well under way or had been completed. The correlations with the outcome measures for the 20 therapists' predictions that were truly pretreatment predictions were, in fact, slightly (nonsignificantly) larger than they were for the total group. For example, for the 20, the correlation of the therapists' predictions for rated benefits was .31, for residual gain, .26—neither of these reached significance because of the small sample size. In predicting residual gain, none of the predictors was significant. In conclusion, the possible contamination for some of the therapist predictions did not increase predictive success as one might have expected.

TABLE 8-1

*Correlations of Direct Predictions by Patient, Therapist,
and Clinical Observer with Outcome Measures*

	Residual Gain	Rated Benefits	Posttreatment Adjustment Status
Multiple Correlations	.11	.32	.35*
Patient	.08	.23*	.27*
Therapist	.00	.19	.17
Observer	.08	.27*	.29*

NOTE: N = 69 due to missing data
*p < .05

not happen. Forty-one patients had therapists who were second- or third-year psychiatric residents, and 32 patients had therapists who were beyond their residency. The level of the correlations was not significantly different in the two groups.

Judges' experience in making predictions may have helped. Clinical observers who have had more experience in making predictions about patients' outcomes from psychotherapy should be able to make more accurate predictions. Table 8-2 shows that this may be true: The two judges who had the most experience in making predictions—they rated 27 and 33 patients, respectively—each had a significant prediction of one of the outcomes measured. However, this conclusion is limited by the small patient samples for the two judges with less experience.

Success of Scores from Predictive Measures

The correlations of predictive measures with the outcome measures, residual gain[2] and rated benefits, were generally low. This was true for all of the predictive domains: patient tests, patient adjustment measures, prognostic interview ratings, patient–therapist match measures, patient demographic variables, therapist demographic variables, therapist test measures, and therapy characteristics.

We offer a third outcome measure—posttreatment adjustment status (a composite of ratings and tests from the patient and observer)—as a matter

[2]Tests of significance of the correlations of predictors with the residual gain scores were based on *partial* correlation significance effects, i.e., the significance of the correlation between the predictor and posttreatment adjustment, controlling for pretreatment adjustment.

TABLE 8-2

Correlations of the Prognostic Index Interview
Predictions of Each Judge with Outcome Measures

Judge	n^a	Residual Gain	Rated Benefits	Posttreatment Adjustment Status
1	27	.33	.42*	.48**
2	11	−.13	.06	.25
3	10	−.16	.48	.24
4[b]	33	.34*	.32	.47***

[a]Number of Prognostic Index interviews.
For the first three judges ns totaled 48; the remaining 25 patients were distributed among judges who worked on too few cases to be included in these analyses.
[b]Based on listening to tapes of interviews of these and other judges.
  p < .05
 **p* < .01
***p* < .005

of general interest, not because the criterion is considered to be an adequate one. The predictive correlations with this measure reflect the consistency from pretreatment to posttreatment rather than the gains from treatment; correlations therefore tended to be higher than with residual gain and rated benefits. Nevertheless, because many previous studies have predicted posttreatment adjustment status, presenting it might facilitate comparisons with such studies. For example, Green et al. (1975) include posttreatment status although they properly qualify its inclusion as useful only if correlations between pretreatment status and posttreatment status are low. We would add that this condition is not often met in psychotherapy studies. Pretreatment status and posttreatment status tend to be highly correlated (.65 in our study).

MEASURES OF PATIENTS AND THERAPISTS

PI interviews were modestly successful. Predictions by clinical observers based on the Prognostic Index interview (table 8-3) tended to be slightly more successful than those based on patient test measures (tables 8-4 and 8-5), patient demographic information (table 8-6), or patient–therapist match measures (table 8-7). For example, the Prognostic Index predictive factors that correlated with rated benefits included "Duration" (an empirical composite of duration, type of onset, precipitating event, and depression), .23*; Emotional Freedom (a composite of emotional freedom, initiative, flexibility, and patient's optimistic expectations), .30**; overcontrol, −.24* (table 8-5). The highest correlations were with the Emotional Freedom composite (.30**), leading to the likely implication that patients who are considered flexible make more lasting gains. The Health-Sickness Rating Scale correlation was .25* with rated benefits and .30** with residual gain (table 8-5).

Similarities of patient and therapist were predictive. Successful prediction was expected in this area, since in our original review 10 out of 13 studies of similarities had achieved significant correlations (Luborsky et al., 1971). Of 10 matches examined in the Penn study, only marital status match (i.e., marital status of both was "married" or marital status of both was "single") was significantly predictive of outcome: .24* with rated benefits and .23* with residual gain (table 8-7). The occupational and age matches approached significance with one of the criteria. However, the sum of 10 similarities, based on a score of 1 for each similarity, was significantly predictive at about the same level as marital status.

Therapists' characteristics were not predictive. None of the demographic characteristics (table 8-8) or the tests and ratings (table 8-9) of the 42 therapists correlated significantly with the main outcome measures.[3] Not even the ratings of the therapist's competence by training supervisors were predictive of the patient's outcome, although in a few other studies these have been predictive (Luborsky et al., 1971).

Another type of analysis of the therapist's competence also did not show an expected effect on patient's benefits: a correlation between outcomes of patients of the same therapist. Such correlations were done for 20 therapists who had at least two patients in the study (for those therapists with more than two patients, two were chosen at random). The correlations were in the expected direction but did not reach significance: with rated benefits .37, and with residual gain .28. This indicates that each therapist's patients tend to have a diversity of outcomes. If each therapist had had a consistent performance level with all of their patients, the correlations would have been higher. These findings from the Penn study imply that therapists tend neither to be "supershrinks," with only successes, nor "subshrinks," with only failures. However, the Penn study was not designed with a sizable group of matched patients for each therapist, which would have permitted the success of their caseload to be compared. More recent studies with more comparable caseloads show significant differences in the level of therapist's success (chapter 19).

[3]Three of the nonsignificant correlations that are .28 or more are worth noting because they point in the same direction: Treatment outcomes are better, the more field dependent (Embedded Figures), the more sensitive in terms of recognizing implied meaning in the voice (Sundberg Implied Meanings), and the less Strong Test Type A (mechanical and engineering interests).

TABLE 8-3

Correlations of Prognostic Interview Measures with Measures of Outcome

	Residual Gain	Rated Benefits	Posttreatment Adjustment Status
Multiple Rs	.41	.54*	.49*
Attractiveness[a]	.03	.12	.23*
Duration[a]	.17	.23*	.07
Emotional Freedom[a]	.11	.30**	.37**
Manifest Anxiety	−.16	−.14	−.28*
Anxiety Tolerance	−.20	−.13	.14
Interests	−.16	−.19	.14
Secondary Gain	−.15	−.12	−.03
Extrapsychic Factors	.00	.11	.07
Overcontrol	−.17	−.24*	.07

[a]Composites of several items.
*$p < .05$
**$p < .01$

TABLE 8-4

Correlations of Patient Test Measures with Measures of Outcome

	Residual Gain	Rated Benefits	Posttreatment Adjustment Status
Multiple Rs	.36	.29	.47
WAIS	−.05	−.05	.20
EFT	.04	.00	−.01
Rod and Frame	.18	.03	.14
Hy	−.07	.00	−.22
TC1	.03	.04	.22
TC2	−.03	.01	.14
Life Change	−.02	.11	−.17
Gottschalk Human Relations	−.03	.03	−.08
Gottschalk Anxiety	−.17	−.19	−.20
Rorschach PRS	.16	.15	.11

TABLE 8-5

Correlations of Pretreatment Adjustment Measures with
Measures of Outcome

	Residual Gain	Rated Benefits	Posttreatment Adjustment Status
Patient			
Inventory of Social and Psychological Functioning (ISPF)	.01	.08	.53**
Symptom Checklist (SCL)	−.01	−.07	−.53**
Hypochondriasis (Hs)	−.06	−.04	−.41**
Ego Strength (Es)	−.08	−.11	.41**
Social Assets	−.09	−.10	.37**
Observer			
Prognostic Index Adjustment	−.16	−.16	.40**
Health-Sickness Rating Scale (HSRS)	.30**	.25**	.71**

NOTE: These were measures that were standardized and summed to create a pretreatment adjustment composite score; they are presented separately here. Multiple correlations were not done on this set of variables because of the high intercorrelations among them.
*$p < .05$
**$p < .01$

TABLE 8-6

Correlations of Patient Demographic Information with
Measures of Outcome

	Residual Gain	Rated Benefits	Posttreatment Adjustment Status
Multiple Rs	.26	.33	.39
Children	.06	−.02	.22
Religious Activity	.04	.12	.10
No Foreign-born Parent	.06	.14	.10
Sex (High = female)	.10	.20	.02
Race (High = non-white)	−.08	−.04	.01
Education	.05	.00	.17
Age	.09	−.05	.18
Marital Status (High = single)	−.18	−.12	−.18
Religion			
Christian	.07	.04	.02
Jewish	.05	−.03	.17

TABLE 8-7

*Correlations of Patient–Therapist Match Measures (Similarities) with
Measures of Outcome*

	Residual Gain	Rated Benefits	Posttreatment Adjustment Status
Multiple Rs	.38	.38	.50*
Age Match	.20	.12	.23*
Marital Status Match	.23*	.24*	.33**
Children Match	.10	.04	.24*
Religion Match	−.07	−.05	−.03
Religious Activity Match	−.04	.10	−.05
Foreign-born Parents Match	.03	.08	.09
Institutional Affiliation Match	.00	.03	.11
Education Match	.11	.08	.20
Occupation Match	.18	.20	.13
Cognitive Style Match	.03	−.06	−.03
Sum of 10 Matches	.23 (p = .056)	.24*	.36**

*p < .05
**p < .01

TABLE 8-8

Correlations of Therapist Demographic Measures with Measures of Outcome
(N = 42)

	Residual Gain	Rated Benefits	Posttreatment Adjustment Status
MD vs. Not MD	−.03	.07	.12
Special Training vs. No Special Training	.03	−.04	.00
Freudian vs. Non-Freudian	.07	.03	−.23
Experience	−.04	−.03	.15
Resident vs. Not Resident	−.14	−.08	−.01
Foreign-born Parent vs. No Foreign-born Parent	.03	−.07	−.01
Not Jewish vs. Jewish	−.09	−.12	.05
Not Christian vs. Christian	−.13	−.06	−.25
Degree of Religious Activity	−.05	−.06	−.25
Married vs. Single	−.09	.09	.20
Number of Children	−.05	−.06	−.02
Age	−.15	.06	.04

NOTE: For the dichotomous variables, the category on the left in the above description received the lower score.

TABLE 8-9

Correlations of Therapist Test Measures with Measures of Outcome (N = 38)

	Residual Gain	Rated Benefits	Posttreatment Adjustment Status
Double Profile (High = perceptually sensitive)	−.01	.00	−.08
Double Profile (High = confident in perceptual task)	.06	.22	.13
Rod and Frame (N=32) (High = field dependent)	−.02	.24	.03
Embedded Figures (N=35) (High = field dependent)	.08	.29	.15
Strong A–B (High = type A)	−.30	−.07	−.14
Sundberg Implied Meanings (Accuracy of recognizing the implied meanings of brief statements)	.28	.08	.17
Raskin Tapes			
Average difference from norm rating	−.23	.03	−.07
Difference between Ideal Concept of Therapist and Self-Concept	.01	.23	−.18
Supervisor's Rating of T.			
Competence as a T.	.02	−.02	.18
Competence as a Psychiatrist	.00	−.14	.05
Personal Liking	−.01	−.03	.13
Sundland Therapist Orientation Questionnaire			
Training, planning and conceptualizing are important	.25	.17	.28
Growth is inherent	−.09	.07	.27
Childhood experiences and psychoanalytic techniques are important	−.12	−.08	−.01
Verbal learning and cognitive gains are important	.04	.02	.16
Affective gains are not important	.26	.15	.33*
Therapist feels secure	−.19	−.02	.05
Social goals are important and directiveness should not be avoided	−.13	.04	−.35*
Involvement of therapist is important	.14	.13	.00
Informal behavior is all right	.10	.16	−.06
Interrupting patient is OK	−.12	.09	−.04
Unconscious motivation is important	−.12	.04	.08

*$p < .05$

THERAPY CHARACTERISTICS

A variety of treatment characteristics that were recorded on questionnaires administered at termination were correlated with outcome. Since this information was obtained posttreatment, these correlations were obviously not predictive, but it was still of interest to examine whether the outcomes of these therapies were influenced by such factors as length of treatment or use of medication. If treatment characteristics explained a large amount of outcome variance, it would be difficult for pretreatment factors also to be strong determinants of outcome, and we could then partially explain the lack of predictive success in the other domains.

Length of treatment was predictive. As would be expected, greater length of treatment, measured by number of sessions or length of time in weeks, was associated in most studies with greater benefits from psychotherapy (see chapter 19). This relationship appeared in 23 of 26 studies. In the present study, the level of the correlations was significant, but was not as high as in many other studies: .27* with rated benefits, and .20 (ns) with residual gain. The level of the correlations was probably reduced because a large number of patients in our own study had length of treatment determined by the length of the therapist's stay at the clinic; that is, the majority of the therapists were residents who changed services after 1 year. (The significance of these relationships is discussed further in chapter 19.)

Use of prescribed psychotropic drugs was not predictive. Since it is standard practice for some therapists to prescribe psychotropic medications to some patients under certain conditions, we explored its prevalence and association with outcomes (table 8-10). Of the 73 patients, 26 (36%) had some medications prescribed during the course of the treatment. The most frequently prescribed were small to moderate doses of ataractics, such as chlordiazepoxide hydrochloride (Elavil). The use versus nonuse of such medications had no relation to any of the outcome measures.

Reason for termination was significant but confounded. The significant correlation (table 8-10) between reason for termination and rated benefits is artifac-

TABLE 8-10

Correlations of Therapy Characteristics Measures with Measures of Outcome

	Residual Gain	Rated Benefits	Posttreatment Adjustment Status
Multiple *R*s	.47	.61**	.42
Length	.20	.27*	−.01
Goal (High = personality change; Low = symptom relief)	.05	−.02	−.11
Termination (High = unnatural termination)	−.35**	−.44**	−.21
Ingredients			
Patient Insight	.11	.24	−.02
Therapist Supportive	.04	.11	−.09
Patient Catharsis	.24	.30*	.23
Therapist Directive	−.11	−.06	−.15
Use of Medication (High = a drug was used)	.12	.07	−.16

*p < .05
**p < .01

tual: The reason for termination was one of the posttreatment measures included in the rated benefits composite. Unnatural termination (e.g., therapist left clinic) was, however, associated with poorer outcome on the residual gain criterion ($r = -.35^{**}$).

None of the other therapy characteristics was significantly related to outcome. In general, then, although there were some expectable associations between therapy characteristics and outcome, indicating some validity to our outcome measures, these correlations were high enough to rule out other possible influences on outcome.

Multiple correlations were modest predictors. As a preliminary step to examining multiple correlations, we looked into how much overlap there was among the significant predictors (table 8-11). Some of these intercorrelations are of interest, e.g., the one between the observer's prediction and HSRS is .38**—the observer could have been basing his or her prediction in part on HSRS, which would be sensible. The correlation between Emotional Freedom and patient's expectations is partly an artifact since patient's expectations form part of the Emotional Freedom composite. In general, these intercorrelations are low, which suggests that the significant predictors had low redundancy and therefore their multiple correlations could be high.

The multiple correlations were done within several predictive domains: patient test measures, Prognostic Index interview ratings, patient–therapist match measures, patient demographic information, and therapy characteristics (tables 8-3, 8-4, 8-6, 8-7, and 8-10, top row). These were generally disappointing. The best of these correlations was .54* for the Prognostic Index interview prediction with rated benefits. For a multiple correlation that combines nine predictive measures, its size is not impressive. The multiple correlation for therapy characteristics (table 8-10) was significant, but these are not true prognostications since they are based on what happened during or at the end of treatment. Within the other domains the multiple correlations were not significant. (Multiple correlations were not done across domains because of the large number of predictors and the limited success of individual predictors.)

Other outcome measures were predicted as well as our composite measures. So far, we have predicted our own two composite outcome measures. Now, in order to compare our results with those of others, we will revert to the use of the simple outcome measure that is most commonly relied on in other studies: the therapists' rating of improvement. Of the correlations of 84 pretreatment predictors with this outcome measure, only 4 were significant. The level of these correlations was only slightly less than that achieved by correlations with the residual gain composite outcome measure: 8 of these were significant. In summary, most of these correlations

TABLE 8-11

Intercorrelations Among the Significant Predictors of Outcomes of Psychotherapy
(Penn Psychotherapy Project)

	1	2	3	4	5	6	7	8	9	10
1. O[a] Prediction		.38*	.24*	.30*	.28*	.02	.25*	.05	−.05	.13
2. HSRS			−.02	.42*	.18	.20	.21	−.21	−.13	.28*
3. PI Duration				.01	.12	.14	−.11	−.08	−.12	.04
4. PI Emotional Freedom					−.18	.27*	.45*	−.03	−.02	.19
5. Overcontrol						.07	−.06	−.18	.03	.20
6. Match: Marital							.16	−.10	−.04	.38*
7. Patient's Expectations								−.05	.12	.18
8. Length									.18	−.15
9. Random Assignment										−.20
10. Sum of Ten Similarities										

NOTE: For the n = 73, a correlation of .23 is significant at p < .05. For random assignment, a correlation of .30 is significant at p < .05 (n = 45).
[a]Observer
*p < .05

with the therapists' ratings of improvement were not significant, just as we had found for our composite criteria.

The Target Complaint change (chapter 2) is another fairly commonly used outcome measure. For this measure we used both the patient and therapist version of the Target Complaint change, and both the first (TC1) and second (TC2) most severe Target Complaints. The correlations of our predictors with this outcome measure were at about the same level as those for predicting the composite criteria. For example, the Prognostic Index Emotional Freedom composite correlated .33 with TC1 change. (Target Complaint did form one component of rated benefits, but a very small part of it.)

Since dropping out of treatment probably often reflects a treatment failure, it constitutes an outcome measure and its predictability should be examined. For this reason, the 15 patients in our study who dropped out of treatment before eight sessions are of special interest. However, we found our predictions were not related to the outcome of these patients—the mean level of predictions for these 15 on the Prognostic Index was close to that of the 73 who continued in treatment.

The therapist's "preference assignment" was associated with better outcome. In the first year of the project some of the patients ($n = 17$) were randomly assigned to therapists, i.e., without any patient or therapist participation in the selection. Other patients ($n = 28$) were assigned after the therapist's review of each patient's intake psychiatric evaluation, i.e., the therapist's own preference. (For another 28, assignment procedure was not known.) We found that random assignment was associated with lower residual gain: for example, residual gain correlated significantly with method of assignment $-.37^*$ ($n = 45$).

Cross-validation for Emotional Freedom was successful. A study of the predictions of one judge illustrates an important direction for further research. This kind of analysis is advantageous—it avoids the problem of combining judges who may have different distributions, and even statistical corrections may not adequately take such differences into account. The Emotional Freedom composite by this judge (AA) correlated $.42^*$ ($N = 27$) with clinical observers' ratings of improvement. This level of prediction was sufficiently promising so as to warrant an attempt at cross-validation with a new group of 30 patients who had not been in our study. When this was done, the Emotional Freedom composite again correlated significantly with improvement at $.39^*$ Another successful cross-validation of the Emotional Freedom composite was done by Rounsaville, Weissman, and Prusoff (1981).

For the $N = 27$ validation group, the role of Emotional Freedom was clarified by a retrospective review of why prediction was wrong in those cases in which it was wrong. The therapy of those patients who did better than predicted (overachievers) was compared with that of those who did worse than predicted (underachievers). This retrospective analysis revealed that the underachievers dropped out of therapy sooner. Thus, prediction can be attenuated by the influence of such other factors as short duration of treatment. The underachievers also were rated higher on the Emotional Freedom composite at the beginning of therapy than were the overachievers. This indicated that a curvilinear relationship between Emotional Freedom was present to a degree: Those patients who were very high or very low on emotional freedom had worse outcomes.

Predicting after Limiting the Number of Correlations

In our analysis so far we have not done much to reduce the many predictors to more reasonable numbers because we viewed our study as a cross-validation of individual predictors. Also, many of the predictors were demographic ones and do not sensibly combine into factors. The only factor analyses were within our domains with the aim of forming composites to be used subsequently for outcome assessment.

Having been profligate with the number of predictors relative to the number of patients has meant that we have paid more than a piddling penalty. It has meant suffering with the possibility that even the few significant correlations we found might have been produced by chance (Nunnally, 1967). How can we take this into account? Because there were 84 pretreatment predictors (chapter 6) that we correlated with our two main outcome measures, we ran 168 correlations. Assuming independence of predictor variables, the conventional calculation for the number of significant correlations which might be expected by chance at $p < .05$ is 8.4. We found 10, which is better but not significantly better than chance, even considering that 2 of the 10 were at the $p < .01$ level (HSRS and Emotional Freedom).

However, the issue should not be tested and rested solely on the basis of that calculation. The result must also be considered in the light of certain qualifications derived from our study. These qualifications heighten the chances that some of the significant correlations reflect more than chance associations: (a) Some of the correlations are based on variables that are far from independent of each other. (b) Many of the correlations are based on predictors that were purely exploratory, and there was no reason to believe that they should be predictive, e.g., many of the demographic measures. (c) Some of the measures found to be significant in our study were subsequently successfully cross-validated in new studies; e.g., Emotional Freedom was found also by the Yale project (Rounsaville, Weissman & Prusoff, 1981), HSRS was found also by others (chapter 19), and match on marital status was found also by the Chicago study (Fiske, Cartwright & Kirtner, 1964). (d) The levels of the correlations for the predictors in the Penn (Luborsky et al., 1979) and the Chicago studies are parallel in the sense that their predictive correlations are significantly correlated with each other. (e) Our main predictive study was itself mostly a cross-validation of predictive measures that had been successful in previous studies (chapter 19). The last three of these qualifications deserve the most weight since they offer evidence that some of our predictors held up through cross-validation. The last one of these—that our main predictive study was itself a cross-validation of measures that had been successful in previous studies—is especially weighty.

Now we will explore the benefits of a sensible restriction on the number of predictors. We have listed in table 8-12 only those predictors for which a sufficient number of studies had been done—"sufficient" was arbitrarily

TABLE 8-12

The Most Promising Predictors to Be Cross-validated
by the Penn Psychotherapy Project

Predictor	No. of Studies Done	No. of Studies Significant	Percentage Significant	Cross-validation: No. of Significant rs[a]
P. Psychological Health-Sickness[b]	14	9	64	2
P. Intelligence	9	7	78	0
P. Education	7	5	71	0
P. Experiencing	6	6	100	0
T. Experience	12	8	69	0
P. Interest Patterns and Attitudes[c]	7	5	71	0
Similarities between P. and T.	13	10	77	2[d]

[a]The maximum is 2, i.e., when each variable is correlated with residual gain and rated benefits.
[b]The number of studies done includes the studies listed as "global psychological health-sickness measures" and "global MMPI measures." The additional category, "severity of diagnosis," was not included in the count although it could fit here.
[c]This category was included in order for the list of promising predictors to be complete. Actually we had only one possible predictor in the Penn study to serve as a test of the cross-validation, i.e., "breadth and depth of interests" in the Prognostic Index.
[d]The two significant predictors here were similarity in marital status. Two other significant predictors, with the sum of 10 similarities, could have been counted had we allowed ourselves more than two.

set to mean a lower limit of at least six studies, and at least two-thirds had to have reached significance. That limit was an objective basis as well as a serviceable floor level to try to ensure selection of measures with a record of predictive success. In this way 7 pretreatment predictors emerged as the most promising ones; they were then correlated with the two outcome measures, residual gain and rated benefits, for a total of 14 correlations. Although at the $p = .05$ level only .7 of a significant correlation could be expected by chance, we found 4 were significant predictors (see last column of table 8-12)—2 for psychological health-sickness and 2 for similarities. Assuming the predictors are independent, 4 significant predictors is significantly better ($p < .004$) than the chance expectation.

Predicting Within "Moderated Prediction" Subsamples

It is interesting to note that the similar University of Chicago Project's report (Fiske, Cartwright & Kirtner, 1964) ended with the suggestion that future studies should do what they did not do, that is, make predictions within more homogeneous subsamples. This condition for prediction is termed "moderated prediction." So far, as in the Chicago study, our data analyses have been based on a heterogeneous sample of patients.

Now we have examined predictions within several more homogeneous subgroups: (1) private practice patients ($n = 24$) versus clinic patients ($n = 42$) (7 patients were excluded because they did not fall into either category); (2) depressed patients ($n = 24$) (based on a Prognostic Index rating of "4" or "5" on a 5-point scale) versus nondepressed patients ($n = 49$); (3) male patients versus female patients (29 and 44, respectively); (4) student versus nonstudent patients (31 and 42); (5) neurotic versus other-diagnosis patients (30 and 43, based on the DSM-II diagnosis); and (6) high adjustment versus low adjustment patients (38 and 35).

To compare the success of the predictive measures for each of these dichotomies the correlations were Z-transformed and the significance of the difference between the two correlations was tested. Through these arduous analyses we found that strong relationships of interest emerged only in the private practice versus clinic groups and barely significant findings in the high adjustment versus low adjustment subgroups. Therefore, only these two will be discussed further.

There was greater predictability for private practice patients. The predictability of the outcomes of the private practice group was greater than that of the clinic group—there were 12 significant correlations in the private practice groups and 4 in the clinic groups (e.g., flexibility in the private practice group correlated .42 with residual gain and .57 with rated benefits; in contrast, in the clinic group the correlations were .07 for rated benefits and .12 for residual gain).

The lower predictability of the clinic patient group may be accounted for by two facts: (1) The clinic therapists, since they were psychiatric residents, had to leave the clinic at the end of the year and consequently often had to interrupt the treatment of some of their patients; (2) the clinic therapists were less experienced as therapists than the private practition-ers. Some of the other differences between the two groups may be worth mentioning, but their bearing is less clear: Private practice patients were older (29 versus 25 years mean age), more often female, and more often Jewish; they were superior on the experiencing measure, that is, they were more able than clinic patients both to deeply experience and to reflect on what they experienced; and they were more anxious, as judged from the Prognostic Index interview. The therapists of these patients were more often Freudian, older, and more experienced; they were judged to be more competent as psychiatrists and as therapists; they rated themselves as having less of a discrepancy between their performance as therapists and their ideal concept of performance as therapists; and they were markedly different on a number of therapist orientation questionnaire factors (Sund-land & Barker, 1962).

In terms of overall prediction results, (1) the outcomes of treatment for both clinic and private practice subgroups were only modestly predictable, but the private practice group was somewhat more predictable than the clinic group; (2) rated benefits seemed slightly more predictable than resid-ual gain when the subgroups were analyzed separately.

There were nonsignificant differences in predictability for high versus low adjustment subgroups. These two subgroups had many significant differences, but their number was not significantly more than chance. Yet the specific significant differences for both residual gain and rated benefits are worth noting. For example, one of these is for the Rod and Frame Test, which is considered to be a measure of field-dependence/independence (chapter 6). The corre-lations suggest that field-dependent patients with high adjustment make the best gains in psychotherapy: High adjustment patients have a signifi-cantly higher correlation of RFT with residual gain outcome (.39*) than low adjustment patients (−.07). The parallel correlations for high versus low adjustment with rated benefits outcome are .28 and −.25.

Summary and Discussion

1. *Treatment outcomes were significantly predictable from pretreatment information but the correlations were small.* By direct predictions by the patient, therapist, and clinical observers, as well as by scores on predictive measures, some significant levels of prediction were obtained. However, even the better correlations were in the .2–.3 range, which means that only 5–10% of the outcome variance was predicted.

These were the more specific results: (a) For the direct predictions by patient, therapist, and observer, the correlations hovered around the $p <$ .05 level for rated benefits; the highest was .27* for the observers' direct predictions of rated benefits (table 8-1). (b) For the 84 pretreatment predictive measures, the best predictor was the Prognostic Index (table 8-3), where the Emotional Freedom composite correlated .30** with rated benefits. For 27 of these cases predicted by one rater (table 8-2), the correlation of Emotional Freedom composite with rated benefits was .42*; in the impressive cross-validation attempt by the same rater for another 30 patients, Emotional Freedom composite correlated .39* with the therapist's rating of improvement. Almost as impressive in the context of these modest correlations was the Health-Sickness Rating Scale prediction (table 8-5): For observer ratings the correlation was .30** with residual gain and .25* with rated benefits. Multiple correlations within each domain were generally modest.

2. *Individual judges varied as predictors.* We found some variation in judges' success in making direct predictions (table 8-2). Judges 1 and 4, who predicted the largest number of cases, happened to perform the best, e.g., Judge 1's correlation with rated benefits was .42*. The same variation among judges was evident in another study (Luborsky & McLellan, 1978), involving 13 clinical observers' predictions of the outcome of treatment for drug-dependent patients. In both studies the variations among judges could have been chance variations. Coincidentally, however, the mean predictive correlations for these 13 clinical observers was .27, precisely the same as found in the present study.

3. *Therapist-selected patients did better than randomly assigned patients (−.37*).* Further research on the factors involved in patient–therapist matching should be done to follow up on this lead.

4. *The posttreatment level that the patient attained was easier to predict than gain scores.* The predictive correlations for posttreatment adjustment status are given in the last column in each table, although our regular outcome measures

measure only gains, not status at termination of therapy. The status measure tended to be predictable by pretreatment adjustment measures such as the Health-Sickness Rating Scale, which predicted posttreatment adjustment status .71** (table 8-5). Such correlations reflect only the patient's self-consistency: Patients with high pretreatment adjustment are those with high posttreatment adjustment, and vice versa. Such consistency is a usual finding, e.g., in the Menninger psychotherapy study the correlation of initial HSRS with termination HSRS for 24 patients was .74 (Luborsky, 1962b).

5. *Rated benefits tended to be easier to predict than residual gain as an outcome measure.* Although the predictability of the criterion is not strictly a reflection of its worth as a criterion, it is a useful rule of thumb. Of the eight pretreatment predictors, only two were significant in predicting residual gain while eight were significant in predicting rated benefits. Also for the direct predictions by patient, therapist, and observer, as we noted, rated benefits was more successfully predicted (table 8-1). Greater predictability for rated benefits was also observed in the subgroups for clinic and private practice. Again, for the Prognostic Index interview, more successful prediction was achieved for rated benefits (table 8-3). Similarly, the therapy characteristics more successfully predicted rated benefits.

The predictability of each outcome measure could not be drastically different since rated benefits and residual gain are moderately highly correlated (.76). Yet rated benefits is consistently a somewhat more predictable criterion than residual gain. It is difficult to understand this. The differences might derive from the way in which residual gain is computed—the correlation of pretreatment and posttreatment status is partialed out and the remainder represents the residual gain. Since the correlation between pretreatment and posttreatment status is high in this study, a large percentage of the remainder probably is error variance and therefore predictability is limited.

6. *The composite outcome measures, rated benefits and residual gain, appear to be better outcome measures than the single outcome measures.* We believe that our logic in assembling the composite outcome measures was sound. Composites have the virtue of a more respectable level of reliability than single measures.

7. *Clinic versus private practice patients differed in the predictability of their treatment outcomes.* Among the relatively homogeneous subgroups of the total group, only clinic versus private practice groups showed a number of significant differences favoring the private practice group, and rated benefits was slightly more predictable than residual gain. Possibly patients in the private practice group were more predictable because they were treated by more experienced, psychoanalytically trained therapists. Perhaps even more important, these therapists could continue with their patients as long

as needed; they did not have to break off treatment at the end of yearly rotations as the psychiatric residents often did.

We have shown that the final outcomes of psychotherapy are predicted significantly but only modestly from some types of initial information about the patient, while information about the therapist apart from the treatment adds relatively little to predictability. Why the level of prediction of the outcomes of psychotherapy is not higher is hard to understand in view of the reliability of the outcome measures to be predicted. Rated benefits showed considerable agreement between the patient and therapist, and residual gain is composed of measures showing substantial agreement between the clinical observer and the patient.

Several paths to a better perspective on these issues have been followed in other parts of the book.

1. Toward reconciling our conclusion about the low predictability of treatment outcomes with the clinical opinion that recommends routine prepsychotherapy evaluations: Should the field halt such evaluations? How could the opinions of so many good clinicians be wrong? (See chapter 19.)
2. Toward comparing these conclusions with those from other studies reviewed in chapter 19.
3. Toward considering which aspects of our research methods may have limited our ability to achieve more predictability (chapter 19).
4. Toward trying new paths in search of better prediction.

As long as the basis for prediction rests on pretreatment evaluation, not much improvement in prediction seems likely because the more crucial predictive factors may not be apparent until the patient and the therapist have had a chance to interact. Since most patients begin to show benefits in the course of psychotherapy, by examining sessions we should be able to discern when and how benefits develop. We report on some progress in this new direction: For the patients who benefited most, but not for those who benefited least, an early working alliance developed. Attempts to follow such new research paths should make the treatment venture safer, with clearer signposts to guide its progress, leading to predictably better outcomes.

PROJECT B

How the Benefits

Come About:

Predicting from Sessions

9

Conventional Process Ratings

as Predictors

HAVING COMPLETED the first part of this book, on prediction based on pretreatment data, we are ready to launch the second part of the book, on prediction based on the early sessions. We expected the early sessions to provide a fairly good basis for making predictions about the outcome of psychotherapy. After all, early sessions are a sample of the venture for which we aim to predict the outcome. In fact, our first review of quantitative studies based on judgments of early sessions supported this expectation (Luborsky et al., 1971). This review indicated, for example, that outcomes could be successfully predicted on the basis of early-session judgments of the patient's problem-solving attitudes, experiencing, and a variety of other patient measures. Likewise, significant prediction was achieved by early-session estimates of therapists' empathy, unconditional positive regard, genuineness, nonpossessive warmth, and a variety of other therapist measures.

Preliminary Studies with the Penn Pilot Sample

Before we could begin making predictions of treatment outcomes from psychotherapy sessions, we needed to do some basic preliminary studies (Auerbach & Luborsky, 1968a; Mintz & Luborsky, 1971; Mintz, Luborsky & Auerbach, 1971) to answer three questions: (1) How reliably could our major process variables be judged? (2) What are the major dimensions that underlie these variables? and (3) What are the relative advantages of brief segments versus whole sessions as units of measurement for judging the process of psychotherapy?

We decided to pose these questions on the Penn pilot sample of 15 therapists treating two patients each so that we would be in a more informed position to select measures for use in the Penn Psychotherapy Project.

To select the variables to be rated, we searched for ones that would be descriptive of therapists' behavior and patients' improvement through psychotherapy. A review of expert opinion on this issue revealed that certain assumptions are commonly held (Holt & Luborsky, 1958b, p. 354), e.g., response of patients is related to therapist's "warmth," "maturity," and "focus upon dynamic content." The list of variables we put together was designed to study these assumptions. It included several of our own variables, e.g., patient's level of anxiety (Luborsky, 1962b), and some borrowed from the research of others (e.g., Kiesler, Mathieu & Klein, 1964; Raskin, 1965; Strupp & Wallach, 1964; Wallerstein et al., 1956).

Our findings indicated that ratings of brief segments and of whole sessions of psychoanalytic psychotherapy could be made with acceptable levels of interjudge reliability (Mintz & Luborsky, 1971). Most of the pooled reliabilities (for three judges) ranged from .50 to .80. Even better, by combining variables into multi-item clusters, the levels of reliability were increased to above .80.

Four major dimensions underlying ratings of the process of treatment were interpreted from a factor analysis of ratings of whole sessions (Mintz, Luborsky & Auerbach, 1971). These included a broadly evaluative patient health versus distress dimension and three distinct therapeutic modes: (a) an optimal empathic relationship mode, describing a warm, accepting, natural, highly perceptive, and empathic therapist seen as skillful and as responding effectively, aiming at building self-acceptance by communicating understanding and acceptance of the patient in commonsense terms through reflection of feelings; (b) a directive mode, describing a firm, authoritative, and highly active therapist structuring, directing, advising, and attempting to elicit affect from an inactive patient, at times through open, creative self-expression—and even at times with some hostility; and (c) an interpretive mode with a receptive patient, describing a therapist attempting to foster insight in a receptive and highly involved patient through interpretation of unconscious motivation and of the patient–therapist relationship in terms of transference.

Our comparison of ratings of whole sessions with ratings of segments (Mintz & Luborsky, 1971) revealed that the brief segment appears to be a useful research unit for some problems in understanding the process of psychotherapy. Relationships between segment-based and whole session–based descriptions were high enough for most major dimensions of the process to justify taking advantage of the tremendous time savings achieved by using brief segments. However, several observed differences might be significant for particular research areas. Our interpretation of the findings suggests that session-based descriptions are more integrally tied to the interactional character of psychotherapy. Further, we concluded that some major qualities of the therapy relationship—those dealing with the therapist's relationship style—may be poorly judged from brief segments. Generalization from our findings *may* be limited by two main possibilities: (1) that some variables as we used them are not representative of those of other investigators (e.g., for experiencing), and (2) that the findings are limited to psychoanalytic psychotherapy.

Procedure in the Penn Study

TREATMENT PROCESS VARIABLES

Based upon our experiences with the Penn pilot sample data, as well as upon other research (e.g., Mintz & Luborsky, 1970) and the general psychotherapy process literature, we decided to apply ratings of eight primary dimensions of treatment process in the Penn Psychotherapy Project. Four of the dimensions captured aspects of the therapist's behavior, and four were descriptions of patient behavior. Dimensions included Therapist Empathic Understanding, Therapist Ideal Relationship Qualities, Therapist Active Directiveness, Therapist Interpretiveness, Patient Activity, Patient Involvement, Patient Distress, and Patient Hostility to Others. The dimensions of Therapist Directiveness, Therapist Interpretiveness, Patient Distress, and Patient Hostility conformed to Factors 2–5 of our factor analysis of whole-session ratings. The additional dimensions of Patient Activity and Patient Involvement were obtained from the factor analysis of segment ratings, which had included a broader range of patient variables than the whole-session analysis. Although our factor analysis of whole-session ratings had identified an optimal therapist relationship factor, which included both empathy and warmth ratings, we chose here to assess these two dimensions separately because of other factor-analytic evidence relating to their relative independence (Mintz & Luborsky, 1970).

For each of the eight dimensions, we selected three "marker" items to be rated. These items were for the most part the variables that had loaded most highly from the factor analysis. The dimension and the corresponding "markers" are given in table 9-1. Rather than applying the factor-analytic methods to the new set of items, our approach was to score these dimensions based on previous research. Internal consistency reliability coefficients would indicate the cohesiveness of a set of items within a given a priori cluster. This strategy allowed us to build on previous research while avoiding potential chance relationships.

We decided to apply the rating scales to both brief segments and whole sessions, based on the results from the segment versus session analysis in the Penn pilot sample, which indicated that whole sessions were the better unit for rating certain kinds of relationship variables, e.g., optimal empathic relationship (Mintz & Luborsky, 1971). We were also interested in comparing our predictions of outcome with those of other studies in the literature, which almost exclusively used brief segments.

TABLE 9-1

Predictors: Core Dimensions and Variables Judged from Early Sessions

Dimension	Marker Variables	
Therapist Empathic Understanding	T.	Empathy (Raskin)
	T.	Sensitive to undercurrents
	T.	Hits nail on the head
Therapist Ideal Relationship Qualities	T.	Unconditional positive regard
	T.	Warm and giving
	T.	Natural and spontaneous (congruence, genuineness)
Therapist Active Directiveness	T.	Directive and reinforcing
	T.	Active
	T.	Assertive
Therapist Interpretiveness	T.	Explores motivations
	T.	Emphasizes unconscious
	T.	Focus on transference
Patient Activity	P.	Activity
	P.	Amount of talking
	P.	Initiative
Patient Involvement	P.	Experiencing
	P.	Receptiveness
	P.	Focus on real concerns
Patient Distress	P.	Anxiety
	P.	Depression
	P.	Health-sickness
Patient Hostility to Others	P.	Hostility to others
	P.	Critical and disparaging
	P.	Superiority and condescension

SELECTION OF SESSIONS AND SEGMENTS

Two sessions from early in treatment were selected for each patient. These were usually Sessions 3 and 5. We chose not to use Sessions 1 and 2 because of the typical history-taking format of the first session and sometimes of the second as well.

Two 4-minute segments were extracted from each of the two sessions per patient. Based on our procedures in the Penn pilot sample, we sampled most of the segments starting from the 10th and 30th minutes of the 50-minute hour. Slight deviations in these guidelines were occasionally necessary to ensure that at least two of the therapist's and two of the patient's statements were included in the segments.

JUDGES

Six clinical judges were chosen to make process ratings. Their years of clinical experience (beyond Ph.D. or M.D.) were as follows: 25, 5, 3, 6, 5, and 7 years. One of the six was a psychiatrist; the other five were clinical psychologists.

Our initial assignment of segments and sessions to judges was guided by an attempt to conserve rater effort and an assumption that each judge would have adequate reliability so that they would be essentially interchangeable with the others. Each whole session was rated by only one judge.

In addition, a given judge would rate only one of the two sessions for a particular patient. Ratings of segments were done in the same fashion: only one judge per segment, and four different judges were assigned to the four different segments from each patient. Judges were not assigned segments from cases in which they had rated a whole session. Thus, each judge rated one session for one-third of the cases and one segment from each of the remaining (two-thirds) cases. Given these constraints, assignment of sessions and segments to judges was random. Note that our use of only one judge to rate a given session or segment assumed that the session-to-session or segment-to-segment variability within a patient would be relatively low compared to the across-patient variability. If not, low interjudge reliability would result.

Results

INTERNAL CONSISTENCY WAS ADEQUATE TO GOOD

Our first task was to examine whether the eight a priori clusters were internally consistent. This was assessed by applying Cronbach's alpha coefficient to the sum of the set of three items within each cluster. This was done separately for each judge's ratings. The results are presented in table 9-2 for the average of the six judges. Internal consistency reliabilities are given for the segment ratings and for the whole-session ratings. As can be seen, all of the clusters demonstrated adequate to good internal consistency reliability (.67 to .92 for segments; .72 to .92 for whole sessions), with the exception of patient distress (.51 for segments; .50 for sessions). Also of note is the finding that the average alpha coefficients were very similar for segments and sessions. Because of the low internal consistency of the Patient Distress cluster, the decision was made to use the three items comprising this dimension (Patient Anxiety, Patient Depression, and Patient Health-Sickness) separately in future analyses. This left us with 10 main variables, 7 clusters plus the 3 separate items.

INTERJUDGE RELIABILITY WAS LOW

Interjudge reliabilities were calculated for the segment and session ratings by performing analyses of variance, with subsequent calculations of intraclass coefficients from the mean squares. For the ratings of segments, two-factor ANOVA was performed with Segment (2 levels) as a random

TABLE 9-2

Average (of Six Judges) Internal Consistency
Reliabilities for Eight Process Variable Clusters

Dimension	Average Internal Consistency Reliability	
	Segments	Sessions
T. Empathic Understanding	.92	.92
T. Ideal Relationship Qualities	.77	.77
T. Active Directiveness	.83	.80
T. Interpretiveness	.67	.75
P. Activity	.87	.85
P. Involvement	.78	.75
P. Distress	.51	.50
P. Hostility to Others	.80	.72

factor nested within Session, and Session (2 levels) as a random factor nested within Patient. For the ratings of whole sessions, a single random factor (Session, 2 levels) nested within Patient was specified. The intraclass correlation coefficients calculated from these ANOVAs were generally extremely low (see Luborsky, Mintz, et al. [1980] for all of the values). For the ratings of segments, they ranged from .01 to .22, with a median of .06. For the ratings of whole sessions, they ranged from .00 to .38, with a median of .21.

To understand these results, we had three of the judges rate the same segments that the three other judges had originally rated. This allowed us to examine whether the low reliabilities were a function of different judges rating different segments for each patient. The per judge reliability coefficients for ratings of some segments were considerably higher (range = .18–.59, median = .38), but still unacceptably low. For whole sessions, no additional ratings were obtained.

The additional ratings on segments made it possible, however, to calculate a final set of reliabilities using all of the ratings obtained. We now had, on the average, 5.2 judges out of 6 who rated a segment for each case. We therefore changed the statistical model for the ANOVA from the nested design to a crossed design (Judges by Patients) with some missing data.

This design allowed us not only to calculate the standard intraclass correlations using all ratings but to calculate intraclass coefficients adjusted for anchor points (mean levels of each judges) (Winer, 1971).

Table 9-3 presents per judge and pooled judge versions of the standard

TABLE 9-3

Interjudge Reliability of Segment Ratings

	Standard Intraclass		Adjusted for Anchor Points
Dimension	Single Judge	Pooled Judges	Pooled Judges
P. Anxiety	.08	.29	.38
P. Depression	.23	.61	.65
P. Health-sickness	.17	.52	.54
P. Involvement	.09	.34	.39
P. Activity	.28	.66	.72
T. Ideal Relationship	.13	.44	.47
T. Empathy	.07	.26	.28
T. Interpretive	.09	.36	.42
T. Directive	.28	.66	.71
P. Hostility	.11	.39	.43

TABLE 9-4

Prediction of Outcome from Ratings of
Segments $(N = 72)$

Dimension	Rated Benefits	Residual Gain
P. Anxiety	.19	.19
P. Depression	.12	.24*
P. Health-sickness	.05	−.04
P. Involvement	.26*	.22
P. Activity	.03	.07
T. Ideal Relationship	.28*	.12
T. Empathy	.21	.19
T. Interpretive	.10	.00
T. Directive	.20	.08
P. Hostility	−.02	.15

*$p < .05$

intraclass coefficient for the 10 variables; the table also gives the pooled judge version of the "adjusted for anchor points" intraclass coefficients. Although still generally low, a few of the variables had pooled judges reliabilities within a marginally acceptable range. Using the adjustment for anchor points, three variables (P. Depression, P. Activity, T. Directive) yielded reliabilities of at least .65.

ONLY THREE CONVENTIONAL PROCESS VARIABLES PREDICTED OUTCOME

In our first published presentation of these data (Luborsky, Mintz, et al., 1980) we were led by the low reliabilities for segment ratings to examine prediction of outcome using each judge's data separately. As expected, the results were mixed. One judge with extensive experience and established reliability, however, showed several significant predictions.

With the increase in reliability coefficients found by combining all ratings, we made the decision to examine prediction of outcome averaging all judges' ratings for each case. The results are seen in table 9-4. Two variables, P. Involvement and T. Ideal Relationship Qualities, demonstrated statistically significant correlations with the rated benefits outcome measure. For the residual gain criterion, P. depression yielded significant prediction.

No prediction of outcome from ratings of whole sessions was attempted because the reliability of the ratings was too low.

Summary

In the Penn pilot study three basic "answers" were "obtained": (a) Ratings on conventional variables could be made with acceptable levels of reliability. (b) Four dimensions were interpreted from a factor analysis of the ratings of whole sessions. (c) Brief segments and whole sessions correlated highly except for those dealing with the therapist's style. In the cross-validation in the Penn study we made several conclusions.

1. The internal consistency of the variables within each cluster was adequate to good.

2. The reliability of our ratings of psychotherapy process for the pooled ratings of judges (after they were adjusted for anchor points) was generally low, although a few of the variables had pooled judge reliabilities within a marginally acceptable range. Three of the variables yielded reliabilities of at least .65: P. Depression, P. Activity, and T. Directive. Perhaps the marginal reliabilities in the Penn Study may be explained by the higher than anticipated segment-to-segment variability.

3. A few significant predictions of outcome were found, based on these process ratings and averaging all judges' ratings for each case. For predicting the patients' rated benefits outcome two variables reached statistical significance ($p < .05$), the therapists' ideal relationship ($r = .28$) and the patients' involvement ($r = .26$). (Consistent with this finding, three significantly positive studies of involvement are listed in the appendix.) For predicting residual gain outcome, patient depression demonstrated a significant relationship.

4. It is worthy of note that the best predictor was T. Ideal Relationship. In our extensive review (chapter 19) we found that positive relationship qualities were almost invariably successful in predicting outcomes—out of 17 studies all but 1 predicted significantly.

When we came to this point in the analysis of the Penn Psychotherapy Project process data, we were forced to take stock of our future research options. Our revised research directions, reports of which fill up the remainder of this book, involve three major steps: (1) a resurvey of the factors that are supposed to be curative in dynamic psychotherapies, (2) a transformation of these factors into operational measures, and (3) a test of these new measures against outcomes of psychotherapy.

10

Curative Factors and Operational Measures in Psychoanalytic Psychotherapy

THE WORK in this chapter was the beginning of our revised research strategy. It was aimed at identifying the most potent curative factors and the best-fitting operational measures of each of them within psychoanalytic psychotherapy as well as in the broader category of dynamic psychotherapies. We took stock of what had been written about curative factors based on clinical observation and on clinical-quantitative research. Eight factors emerged, which we then organized into a graded series according to their probable power for potentiating positive outcomes. We then proposed operational definitions of each of them to get a better research handle on them.

In the first phase of the work we expanded on the observations of a sample of clinical-theoretical sources of curative factors which had been assembled for a lecture (Luborsky, 1977a). The set of sources came to include Freud (1912b, 1913, 1914, 1937), Fenichel (1941), Luborsky and Schimek (1964), Stone (1961), Hollender (1965), Menninger and Holzman (1973), Mann (1973), Sifneos (1972), Malan (1963, 1976), and Luborsky (1976b, 1984). Most of the eight factors drawn or inferred from these sources were repeated in each of them. The factor most often discussed was the patient's self-understanding and how the therapist could facilitate it. Most of the authors of these works considered the therapeutic alliance to be basic, but they focused more on self-understanding.

The curative factors in psychoanalytic therapies are only partly special to them. Some of the factors are similar to those found in different treatment approaches, such as client-centered psychotherapy (Rogers & Dymond, 1954; Rogers, 1957) or the broad class of other psychodynamically oriented psychotherapies (Frank, 1971a, 1972b).

Compared with the clinical-theoretical sources, the quantitative research is more recent and based largely on studies still in progress. What we have learned from the quantitative sources is more limited in scope but more exactly confirmed. The relevant research includes that of Joseph Weiss, Harold Sampson, George Silbershatz and John Curtis at Mount Zion Hospital, San Francisco (e.g., Sampson, 1976; Horowitz et al., 1975; Weiss & Sampson, 1986); The Analytic Research Group of the Institute of Pennsylvania Hospital, Philadelphia (e.g., Luborsky et al., 1979); Hans Strupp and his group at Vanderbilt University (e.g., Strupp & Hadley, 1979); Hartvig Dahl and his group at Downstate Medical Center, New York (e.g., Dahl, 1972); Peter Knapp and his group at Boston University Medical Center (e.g., Knapp, 1972); Merton Gill and his group at the University of Illinois Medical Center (e.g., Gill & Hoffman, 1982a, 1982b) David Orlinsky and Kenneth Howard at the University of Chicago and Northwestern (e.g., Orlinsky & Howard, 1986); and Irving Janis and his group, until recently at Yale (e.g., Janis, 1982).

Each of the next eight sections is devoted to one of the curative factors, with the earlier ones considered to be relatively more potent than the later ones: (1) the patient's experience of a helping relationship, (2) the therapist's ability to understand and to respond, (3) the patient's gains in self-understanding, (4) the patient's decrease in pervasiveness of relationship conflicts (which permits decrease in symptoms), (5) the patient's capacity to internalize the treatment benefits, (6) the patient's learning of greater tolerance for his or her thoughts and feelings, (7) the patient's motivation to change, and (8) the therapist's ability to offer a technique that is clear, reasonable, and likely to be effective.

It was useful to prepare a diagram of the interrelated underpinnings of the clinical concepts (figure 10-1) to serve as a sketch of the process of dynamic psychotherapy within which the curative factors operate.

This diagram shows a succession of subsumed divisions in the process of psychotherapy. The largest natural division is in the *goals* to be achieved versus the *means* to achieve them. Bordin's (1975) overview of aspects of "goals, techniques, and bonds" gave backing to this main conceptual division. For example, at the beginning of therapy the patient may tell the therapist, "My goal is to be rid of my depressions." The psychodynamic psychotherapist usually suggests first a form of psychotherapy as the "means" (and to hold other forms of treatment, such as pharmacotherapy, in reserve).

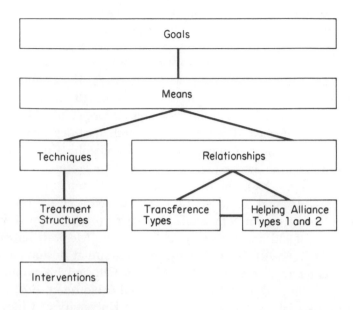

Figure 10-1. Components in the Process of Psychodynamic Psychotherapies.

The means, in turn, may be subdivided into another neat dichotomy: the *techniques* used and the *relationships* developed. This is a familiar dichotomy; for example, Strupp (1973a) proposed two main classes of effective ingredients in the process of psychotherapy—the relationship established by the therapist and the therapist's technical means.

The techniques themselves are of two main kinds: the *treatment structures* and the specific *interventions,* such as interpretations. The treatment structures include the time-limited versus open-ended dimension, the degree of focus on the search for understanding, and the degree of focus around working toward specific goals.

Curative Factors

1. THE PATIENT'S EXPERIENCE OF A HELPING RELATIONSHIP

Of the eight curative factors listed, relationship factors may be the most crucial for the outcome of psychoanalytic psychotherapy. We will examine especially the capacity of the patient to experience the relationship with the therapist as helpful.

The concept of a helping alliance is well established in clinical practice. It has been referred to variously as "the therapeutic alliance" (Zetzel, 1958), "the working alliance" (Greenson, 1965), or "the helping alliance" (Luborsky, 1976a). These terms all refer to the patient's experience of the relationship with the therapist as helpful, or potentially helpful, in achieving the patient's goals. The definition is traceable to part of Freud's (1912a) description of the transference as being composed of two kinds of attachment, one that interferes with cooperation and the other that induces cooperation. The cooperation-inducing part of the transference is the "conscious," "unobjectionable," positive feeling of the patient toward the analyst.

In figure 10-1 the relationship box is drawn larger than the techniques box because the development of a good working relationship is considered the more crucial vehicle for achieving benefits from treatment. Yet these two boxes do not operate in isolation. The technique of searching for understanding tends to provide much more than the value of the understanding itself; it may improve the helping alliance component of the relationship by offering both patient and therapist a common task on which they can collaborate.

The relationship box in figure 10-1 has two main branches: *transference types* and *helping alliance types.* Transference is usually defined by both clinical and metapsychological considerations, e.g., by Curtis (1973): "Transference is a revival in current object relationships, especially to the analyst, of thought, feeling, and behavior derived from repressed fantasies originating in significant conflictual childhood relationships." This definition suggests that the helping alliance concept is classed partly within the broader concept of transference because part of the revived or reactivated relationship pattern can include a transferred readiness to form an alliance with a helping person. The part of the helping alliance that is outside of the transference is a reality-based part rooted in the actual relationship. The alliance is usually further divisible into *negative* and *positive* (Freud, 1912a). The working through of the transference is generally hindered by the negative helping alliance and facilitated by the positive helping alliance.

The final bifurcation of the helping alliance is into two types (which partly follow Greenspan & Cullender, 1975): Type 1 is an alliance based on experiencing the therapist as supportive and helpful; Type 2 is an alliance based on a sense of working together in a joint struggle against what is impeding the patient. The emphasis here is on shared responsibility for working out the treatment goals. When Type 2 is present, the alliance qualities of the relationship are evident in a sense of "we-ness." The transition to a Type 2 helping alliance is often clearest as termination approaches. Then the patient frequently articulates fears about the difficulty of carrying on without the help that the therapist has provided during the sessions. A review of these fears often yields a recognition that the therapeutic operations the patient and therapist have so far performed in concert can be done by the patient alone. In a beneficial treatment, by the time of the termination goodbyes the patient realizes that in a real sense the jobs of patient and therapist have basic similarities; the knowledge further promotes a sense of being part of the same team.

What led to our viewing this curative factor as the most central one was the following line of reasoning: Patients usually achieve benefits from psychotherapy even though we cannot predict these benefits *with a high degree of accuracy* from the pretreatment information (chapter 8), from the designated type of the treatment (chapter 19), or from samples of the sessions (chapter 9). Numerous studies have found that 60–80% of patients improve in psychotherapy (as reviewed in Luborsky et al., 1975; Bergin, 1971; Meltzoff & Kornreich, 1970). This figure varies depending partly upon how it is computed; e.g., Bergin (1971) offers 65%, based on the exclusion of dropouts and inclusion of moderately improved or better. With the same exclusion and inclusion rules, in the Penn Psychotherapy Project, for example, we found the same percentage improved moderately or better (64.4%). Our reasoning from this point onward was the same as Rosenzweig's (1936) had been a half-century earlier and others' had been recently (Kazdin, 1986): Since a variety of differently designated psychotherapies showed similar percentages of benefits, common nonspecific factors in the treatments must be responsible for these benefits. One of these common elements must be the presence of a helping alliance.

Operational Measures

A review of miles of tapes of recorded sessions of the 73 subjects led to our recognition of the two types, Type 1 and Type 2, of the helping alliance. Our plan was to test our prediction that the capacity to form helping alliances would be related to the outcome of psychotherapy and then to see how early such an alliance might appear in the psychotherapy.

If the prediction was confirmed, then inquiries would be made about whether the patient's experiencing of a helping alliance was (a) primarily the product of the therapist's facilitating or inhibiting these helping relationships, or (b) primarily the product of the therapist's just happening to fit the patient's conception of a helping person who could be trusted. To investigate how the helping alliance is influenced by what the therapist does, we constructed the "Therapist Facilitating Behaviors" (TFB) manual (Luborsky, 1976a; chapter 13). The manual was applied to samples of transcripts of psychotherapy sessions, and judges rated every instance in which the therapist either facilitated or inhibited development of the helping relationship.

We did not plan to get systematic data on the second line of inquiry—whether the therapist fit the patient's conception of a helpful person—but we do have some supportive instances. In the first sessions one of the more improved patients, Ms. Samuelson (#49, described in chapter 3), had already begun to perceive the therapist as a person she liked and expected would be helpful to her. She noted a similarity between the therapist and the man she loved: Both had narrow feet. An example of negative perception of the psychotherapy and of the therapist was presented by a less improved patient, Ms. Kane (#6). In the third session, she said, "I know I have to open up and share my thoughts, but when I do it is upsetting." She meant that the structure the therapist imposed in the treatment, which required her to speak her thoughts, was one that she found unhelpful. The patient described her mother as exactly like herself in this respect—whenever her mother tried to open up and show her feelings, she could not.

The degree of fit between the patient's perception of the therapist and the patient's conception of a helpful person may be based on the patient's capacity to experience positive helpful relationships. If such object-relationship capacities are present, as shown in the object-relationship repertoire depicted or expressed in the treatment or in the past, very likely the person has a capacity to experience the present relationship with the therapist as helpful. Ryan (1973) made an early quantitative study on the capacity of the patient to enter a therapeutic relationship, as estimated from the initial psychotherapy interview. Indices of hope (based on independent interviews) and indices of object relations (based upon early memories) were found to be related to the strength of the "working alliance" as shown at the start of the treatment. A more recent study (Greenspan & Weider, 1984) on the capacity for helping relationships was set up to track the steps in the growth of this capacity in the course of psychotherapy by means of three scales: regularity, stability, and attachment. The sequence is considered to be generic in all therapy relationships.

Other factors may also contribute to establishing a helping alliance. Improving the patient's hope or faith in the treatment is likely to be beneficial (French & Wheeler, 1963). One way to improve the patient's positive anticipations, developed by Orne and Wender (1968), is called the anticipatory socialization interview. This interview, which is conducted with the patient before the start of treatment, offers the patient information about what to expect.

When a positive helping alliance is established and the therapist's interventions are reasonable, the relationship has considerable resilience so that even faults in technique tend to be glossed over. This may be what occurred in the experiences of an eager student of Zen who had come to his sessions many times and tried unsuccessfully to answer the favorite question of his Zen teacher, "What's the most important thing in the world?" On this occasion as soon as the student heard the question he thought, "I've got him now. I happened to have heard the answer from another student; I'm gonna say it and that will really get a favorable reaction from him." The student then answered, "The most important thing in the world is my sitting here talking to you." The teacher peered at him and said, "Wrong." Later the student described the incident to a friend who asked him if he wasn't disappointed in his teacher's answer because the teacher may have been at fault in not recognizing his student's right answer. "Well," he responded, "you've got to admit it. The guy was right. I wasn't fully convinced of the answer myself."

2. THE THERAPIST'S ABILITY TO UNDERSTAND AND TO RESPOND

Adequacy of the Therapist's Understanding

The therapist's capacity to understand the patient's communications is a highly desirable clinical skill which is supposed to be sharpened by the therapist's clinical training, although the foundation for this capacity is built up through a lifetime of experience.

Curative Factor 2 is displayed as part of an interactive feedback sequence. Initially, the therapist's capacity for understanding is applied in making a formulation of the transference. After the therapist's interpretation, the patient's response may alter the understanding of the transference and influence the therapist's next response.

When the aim is to search for understanding, the therapist must be devoted to the technique of being a good listener and must encourage the patient to do the same. For a large part of each session, the therapist's attention should be on listening to what the patient is communicating, evaluating it, and then deciding how to express the understanding. The process from the point of view of the therapist is an alternation of three phases within each session: listening, understanding, and responding (as described in the manual for psychoanalytic psychotherapy, Luborsky 1976b, 1984). In Phase 1, attention is on unreflective listening.

In Phase 2 a shift occurs to a more reflective, understanding attitude as hunches and hypotheses are generated. In psychoanalytically oriented psychotherapy the therapist conceives of the patient as being caught up in relationship patterns that have major out-of-awareness dimensions. At the same time the therapist listens for how the patient experiences the neurotic suffering at the moment. A tip-off to understanding the main theme of the neurotic suffering is redundancy: Themes that are central tend to appear again and again in the patient's communications, particularly those dealing with relationships. This observation about redundancy is incorporated in the procedure for the Core Conflictual Relationship Theme Method (Luborsky, 1977b). The therapist should be especially alert to occasions when the core relationship theme is experienced by the patient as involving the relationship with the therapist. Understanding the patient's relationship with the therapist, both its transference and its real components, is a valuable guide to the therapist, especially at times of special stress in the relationship.

Phase 3 is responding to the patient. The therapist's usual response should point to the essence of the main theme or some aspect of it.

The next phase is Phase 1 again, returning to listening, to an essentially unreflective or free-floating form of attention.

Adequacy of the Therapist's Responses

The second component of Curative Factor 2 is using the understanding to provide helpful interventions, which entails what Strupp (1973b) calls being a good manager of the relationship. Such good management requires (1) avoiding interfering with, and even when necessary, supporting the patient's experience of a helping relationship (Factor 1), and (2) responding adequately to the patient's communications and interpreting them correctly. Through the interpretations the patterns become more recognizable by the patient, both in and out of treatment, as familiar and often painfully pervasive.

Operational Measures

Our first venture into quantitative studies of Factor 2 was based on examining judgments of *the adequacy of the therapist's responses to the patient's main communications* (chapter 16). For making each judgment two initial evaluations are needed: (1) a formulation of the essence of the patient's communications in the session and (2) a formulation of the essence of the therapist's responses to these communications. The independent judge's rating of the factor represented the degree of convergence, i.e., the degree to which the therapist responded adequately to the patient's main communications.

CCRT as a help to making accurate therapist responses. Other aids are available to the therapist for making formulations of the essence of the patient's communications, specifically in terms of each patient's main wishes and the expected responses from others and from self. One of these aids is the Core Conflictual Relationship Theme method (Luborsky, 1977b), which was devised as a way to identify objectively the most pervasive relationship patterns of each patient (chapter 15). The method has two steps: (1) An independent judge selects relationship episodes within the transcripts of the early and late sessions. These episodes are typically spontaneously given narrative accounts by the patient of interactions with people. (2) Other independent judges review these episodes and extract the theme that is most pervasive across the most episodes. The theme contains three components: (a) the wish, need, or intention expressed in relation to the other person; (b) the responses of the other person to the patient; and (c) the responses of the self to the other person's response. The theme was found to be pervasive across relationship episodes and across different types of other persons (Luborsky, Mellon, et al., 1985; Luborsky, Crits-Christoph & Mellon, 1986). It was present both early and late in treatment, it tended to become more deeply experienced within the patient–therapist relationship later in treatment; for patients who improved, it became more easily mastered. In all these ways the core theme seems to behave similarly to the clinical concept of the transference pattern.

Therapist responses with "negative fit" to the patient's expectations. The therapist's interventions should be calculated to try to avoid fitting into the negative part expected by or even stimulated by the patient. Such "negative fit" responses by therapists do occur from time to time (Singer & Luborsky, 1977). For example when Ms. Kane was talking about her frantic need to borrow money to repay a loan, the therapist said, "Banks don't ordinarily give loans without collateral." The comment, although true enough, may have been stimulated by the patient and then perceived by the patient in terms of the expectations in her conflictual relationship theme: "I want to open up and share and be close, but instead I get a negative response from you and from other people." The patient seems to have experienced the therapist's telling her something she already knew as an expected put-down.

Whether or not the therapist actually negatively fits into the patient's expectations derived from the core conflictual relationship theme, patients will from time to time expect such actualization. It is an entirely commonplace observation that patients will reenact their core conflictual relationship theme patterns. Some theoreticians explain the repetition as in the service of a repetition compulsion, much like the rehearsing of a traumatic event (Freud, 1914, 1920); other theoreticians place more emphasis on the repetition as in the service of searching for eventual mastery (Mayman, 1959). At certain junctures in the treatment the patient may even consciously or unconsciously arrange tests to see whether the therapist will fit the anticipated negative expectations. Many of these tests occur when the patient first brings up a previously withheld idea, such as a negative attitude toward a parent or toward the therapist. The patient then watches for the therapist's response to see whether or how the therapist's behavior fits the expectation. This conception of tests of the ways in which the therapist responds was examined and shown to be applicable in studies at Mount Zion Hospital, San Francisco (e.g., Horowitz, Sampson & Siegelman, 1975; Weiss & Sampson, 1986).

3. THE PATIENT'S GAINS IN SELF-UNDERSTANDING

It is not the therapist alone who should search for understanding; the search for understanding should be a shared treatment agenda. Patients usually come to treatment with a set of explanations for their symptoms and suffering and they are interested in furthering their self-understanding. As the patient joins in with the therapist's attempt to provide understanding (Factor 2), he or she gradually becomes more deeply interested and involved in the therapist's method of acquiring understanding. One effect of this joint search is to develop further Helping Alliance Type 2.

In the psychoanalytic theory of therapeutic change, the major goal is to augment the patient's insight, and techniques for attaining it are the therapist's major tools. If our listing of curative factors had been done several decades ago, insight would have been given an even more central position (as it was in Luborsky & Schimek, 1964), but in recent years its limits have been recognized (e.g., Luborsky, 1984, chap. 2). However, the search for understanding remains one of the best agendas for the patient and therapist to work on, for several reasons:

1. It is readily acceptable as a goal by patient and therapist.
2. It has ethical virtues because it does not presume to teach the patient a system of values or a philosophy of life, as is the case in some schools of psychotherapy. Actually, even when there is no intent to teach the patient a system of values patients often work one out for themselves in the course of their treatment. Patients may identify with their impression of the values of the therapist, or they may become freer to attend to their own system of values during the treatment process.
3. It is consistent with promoting eventual autonomy. In the course of the treatment the therapist's and patient's search for understanding

can become a joint search. After treatment the patient can carry it on in the same manner.

In later phases of successful psychodynamic therapies, the result of the continued devotion to listening as a guide to understanding, especially for the core relationship theme, is that both therapist and patient become increasingly aware of evidences of transference (Graff & Luborsky, 1977). This increase undoubtedly represents more than just the actualizing of the transference potential in the patient–therapist relationship; it is also an increase in the therapist's and patient's *recognition* of the already existing transference.

The search for understanding can be subsumed under an even broader action-oriented heading: search for ways of improving the patient's skills in problem solving, as suggested by Katheryn DeWitt (personal communication, 1976) and as stressed by cognitive therapy (Beck, 1975). The hoped-for effect of increasing the patient's understanding is that it will also improve the patient's skill in getting what he or she wants or needs.

Operational Measures

The most usual measure used in quantitative studies has been unguided clinical ratings of amount of insight or self-understanding (chapter 19). With our principle of guided clinical judgment we decided to try a measure of accuracy of self-understanding using the CCRT as a criterion (chapter 17). It is also of interest to see the degree to which accuracy of the patient's self-understanding parallels accuracy of the therapist's interpretations.

4. THE PATIENT'S DECREASE IN PERVASIVENESS OF RELATIONSHIP CONFLICTS

In psychodynamic theories of psychotherapy, each patient at the beginning of treatment is thought to be suffering from relationship conflicts that are responsible for his or her symptoms. It follows that a lessening of the conflicts should lead to a lessening of the symptoms. Curative Factor 3 was a direct way to lessen the conflicts through increased self-understanding.

Operational Measures

For the purpose of making measures to evaluate Curative Factor 4, the CCRT should be evaluated both early and late in treatment for both kinds of conflicts reflected in the CCRT: (1) the conflicts between wishes and (2) the conflicts between wishes and the responses of others. We have constructed a pervasiveness measure for the CCRT components that reflects a reasonable operational translation of the concept of pervasiveness of conflict: the ratio of the frequency of each type of component within the relationship episodes divided by the number of relationship episodes. Results for early versus late sessions are described in chapter 18.

Each core conflictual relationship theme is composed of both the patient's recurrent wishes, needs, and intentions in relationships and expectations of the (usually negative) consequences of trying to achieve the wishes, needs, and intentions. During therapy the increased recognition of intentions and their consequences should help to get the proverbial monkey off the patient's proverbial back. The monkey is the fate of having to repeat unaltered the pervasive relationship problems in the core conflictual relationship theme. After treatment this monkey does not go away but remains in recognizable form but at a more comfortable distance that permits more effective surveillance and more mastery. The shift from before to after therapy is like the cartoon in figure 10-2: first, a patient is seen on her way to the therapist, riding on her motorcycle with a monkey on her back; second, after the visit the monkey is off the patient's back but still in view, riding in a sidecar.

FIGURE 10-2. The Shift from Before to After Dynamic Psychotherapy.

5. THE PATIENT'S CAPACITY TO INTERNALIZE THE TREATMENT
BENEFITS

Gains from psychotherapy that come about through internalization are
sometimes said to be based on structural changes in the patient's personality. *Structural* in this sense means that the gains are in aspects of personality
that have a slow rate of change and are therefore likely to be lasting. A
capacity to internalize gains is especially furthered by the Type 2 form of
helping alliance. Type 2 refers to a sense of joint endeavor in working on
the patient's goals and to the gradual development of ability to carry on
autonomously the same kind of work. Ms. Samuelson afforded an example
of this type of helping alliance in Session 89, in which she revealed in a
teasing way that she admired the therapist and felt that they shared an
awareness and method:

P: Well, I—my—you know, I want to tell you something, Doctor Freud
    (laughs). Don't know why I said that.
T: "Dr. Freud," you said?
P: I—that's what I thought when you went to L＿＿＿＿'s: "Hello, Dr.
    Freud." Well, they both begin with an *F.*
T: Both begin with *F-R-E,* as a matter of fact.
P: That's right. See, you're just as aware of it as I am. More so. Want me
    to analyze that?

At a 4-year follow-up, we learned that Ms. Samuelson had been able to
maintain her gains. Very likely, as Ms. Samuelson's follow-up illustrates,
a Type 2 helping alliance, which entails a sense of shared responsibility for
change, offers a better chance of gains being maintained after the treatment
than a Type 1 helping alliance.

Mr. Norris (#27) provided a contrast to Ms. Samuelson. Although he
was classed as an improver, within the year following the termination of
treatment he had lost most of the gains. When he resumed treatment with
another therapist 3 years later, he was described as having been in a
"prolonged withdrawal for about two years." During his first treatment,
prior to the one in our study, lasting about 8 months, with the initial
symptoms of "impotence" and feelings of inadequacy, he had managed to
overcome these problems; but after termination, he went into a period of
disorganization and drug taking. Thus, this patient provides a striking
example of a recurrent pattern for three periods of therapy during each of
which there was marked improvement, but after each of which the gains
were lost within 6 months to 1 year. In all three treatments the principal

curative factor lacking seemed to have been an ability to internalize and thereby to maintain the gains.

Capacities for internalization sometimes need to be bolstered by external support systems in order for treatment gains to be maintained. These may come from further contacts with the therapist, from friends, from family members, or from the patient's work. Support may be provided from the members of therapy groups, such as Alcoholics Anonymous. It may be offered by a hospital setting or by after-care systems; for example, for some hospital patients treated for incontinence, the hospital milieu and posthospital milieu are set up to reinforce continent behavior (Atthowe, 1973; Goldstein & Kanfer, 1979). Under such conditions of tangible external support, long-term maintenance of gains occurs; much more usual is a tendency toward attrition of gains.

Operational Measures

Research on internalization requires the development of methods of measurement. The concept implies a special capacity to maintain a sense of the aliveness and meaningful presence of relationships, especially when the object of the relationship is not physically present. This ability probably forms a part of the broader concept of psychological health-sickness and is consistent with "the lack of ego distortion" that Freud (1937) considered to be a positive predictor of the outcome of psychotherapy.

After immersion in conceptualization of internalization and after reading Geller (1986), we are better able to generate ideas for developing measurement methods. These might be applied to a sample of patients that includes some who have marked difficulties maintaining treatment gains and some who maintain them very well. These are some methods that need to be developed: (1) to construct rating scales for measuring internalization capacities in entire sessions; (2) to evaluate internalization capacities based specifically on a sample of the patient's relationship narratives; (3) to compare internalization ratings with ratings of psychological health-sickness (Luborsky, 1962a, 1975b) to see how much the two concepts overlap; and (4) to examine the patient's responses to interruptions in the treatment and to the termination, especially the capacity to maintain the gains and the nonrecurrence of the original symptoms.

6. THE PATIENT'S LEARNING OF GREATER TOLERANCE FOR THOUGHTS AND FEELINGS

Learning to tolerate one's thoughts and feelings is consistent with traditional observations about the growth that comes about in psychotherapy.

Freud (1914) remarked once that patients start treatment being afraid of their own reminiscences. This view was incorporated by Ekstein (1956) in his diagram of the process of psychoanalytic treatment. He identified as a basis for the success of the treatment process the patient's increased toler-ance for "regression," i.e., for experiencing and expressing unacceptable thoughts and feelings.

The concept of catharsis or abreaction partly overlaps with this factor since it means that when a traumatic idea is expressed it thereby becomes less traumatic. Another related curative factor is the achieving of increased self-acceptance by diminished self-criticism (Lewis, 1971). Also related is the concept that patients in psychotherapy develop an increased sense of mastery expressed in part as a greater tolerance for their thoughts and feelings.

Recognition of this curative factor is widespread even beyond mental health professionals. Consider the man who was sitting at a bar drinking a glass of beer. He drank half of it and then threw the rest in the bartender's face. The bartender became furious and said, "What the heck's the matter with you? You ought to go see a psychiatrist." A month later the man came back, sat down, drank half a glass of beer, and threw the rest at the bartender's face. The bartender got even more furious and shouted, "I thought I told you to go see a psychiatrist." The man replied, "I did. It did me a lot of good. Now it doesn't bother me to do this."

Operational Measures

Measures of the concept underlying Factor 6 need to be worked out and applied. The measures should estimate the capacity of the patient to expe-rience and to express threatening ideas. Judges could be asked, based on tape recordings, to make their estimates of the patient's capacity and to identify the ideas that are most threatening to express. The measures could be applied both early and late in therapy as a way to estimate changes in the capacity and to see whether the changes are correlated with the benefits of therapy. The ideas that are judged to be threatening may turn out to be the same ones that would be judged by the Horowitz, Sampson, and Siegelman (1975) method to be "warded off," that is, held out of awareness.

7. THE PATIENT'S MOTIVATION TO CHANGE

The patient's willingness and ability to go through the episodically painful and typically costly psychotherapy change system is a function of the motivation to change. Motivation to change is usually defined as the capacity of the patient to try to overcome the symptoms (the intentional aspect) and to persist in the attempt (the behavioral aspect) despite the difficulties of accomplishing the goals.

Operational Measures

There is a moderately large literature on measures of motivation, and these usually turn out to be successful predictors of the benefits patients have received (chapter 19). The most usual measure in these studies is a clinician's rating of motivation based on an initial interview. In the next paragraphs we suggest more specific measures that have not yet been tried. It should be valuable to do a study in which the patient, therapist, and an observer each make their own estimates of the patient's motivation to change. Then sample sessions would be rated for the ways in which several specific factors might contribute to the motivation. These factors include the following.

The prospect offered by the treatment for relief from the symptoms. This expectation serves as a carrot in motivating continuance of the treatment. Freud (1912b) recommended that the therapist's primary effort should be not on relieving the patient's immediate discomfort but on fulfilling the goals of the treatment. Furthermore, the setting up of goals to be achieved within the time available for the treatment makes more tangible the prospect of relief from the symptoms and can have a hothouse effect on the patient's growth.

The recognition of the need for self-change rather than just for environmental change. Although people generally seek help to relieve their suffering, they differ widely in the extent to which they believe they play some part in generating their own suffering. Some tend to blame others or to blame their circumstances and have little tolerance for or acceptance of the role they play. It was in these terms that a famous sage made a distinction in his reactions to two men who came complaining of their suffering. They asked for advice about whether their life would improve if they moved across the river. The first man said he was suffering but he thought his lot would be entirely different if he moved to the other side of the river.

SAGE: Why?
SUFFERER: I am told people are not bad there.
SAGE: Perhaps they are the same as here.
SUFFERER: You sound like all the others.
SAGE: Perhaps you *will* find a better lot there. Go in good health.

The second sufferer was asked by the sage why he thought things would be better on the other side of the river.

SUFFERER: I'm not sure why my lot here is what it is. Don't you think I will have a better response from people on the other side of the river?

SAGE: Perhaps the people are the same as here.

SUFFERER: I suppose they are, so I will stay.

SAGE: Tell me about your lot here so we will see how your staying or leaving is being decided.

The capacity to experience the therapist as providing support and as a helpful ally in the struggle against what is impeding the patient. This is an important basis for the patient's continuing the effort to change. The anticipated support and helping alliance usually increase the patient's hope and morale, which in turn augment the motivation to change.

Experiencing the transference relationship typically produces shifts in the relationship. As a result, sometimes the patient's motivation to change may decrease, even to the point of interrupting treatment; at other times, the patient may be encouraged to stay in treatment to satisfy the transference wishes. As an example, Ms. Samuelson, as part of her core conflictual relationship theme, wished to be given reassurance that she was a special person, and from time to time she felt that this wish was achieved in the relationship with the therapist. This intermittent reinforcement must have been a powerful motivation for her to continue. With other patients, similar wishes, such as the wish to be cared for and protected, may keep the patient coming to treatment even as the wish may, if not understood, interfere with the motivation to change.

All of these factors interact in producing the level of motivation. The level can be thought of as the resultant of a psychological cost estimate. The estimate's bottom line is obtained by balancing off (a) the *prospects of gains* from the therapy—i.e., the likelihood of benefits, such as relief of symptoms, (b) the anticipated psychological (and monetary) *costs* of the therapy, and (c) the *tolerability of the distress* from the symptoms.

8. THE THERAPIST'S ABILITY TO OFFER A TECHNIQUE THAT IS CLEAR, REASONABLE, AND LIKELY TO BE EFFECTIVE

The degree to which the therapist has a technique that is clear, reasonable, and likely to be effective is another curative factor. Such a technique serves as the basis for an agenda to bring the patient and therapist together in carrying out the job that they are to do. It is even better if the technique provided is believed by the therapist and patient to be effective. Different types of treatment have not usually been shown to have different effects on the outcome of treatment (Luborsky, Singer & Luborsky, 1975; Smith, Glass & Miller, 1980), and it seems likely that having a clear and reasonable technique in any therapy type serves as an understandable and hope-engendering agenda and, therefore, improves the therapist's relationship with the patient and the patient's motivation and capacity to improve.

Operational Measures

Measures of Factor 8 need to be tried in future studies. Estimates should be made by the patient and therapist of the degree to which the treatment is perceived as having a clear, reasonable, and likely to be effective technique. Both participants might also attempt to state what the technique is, and then have their statements judged for degree of concordance with each other and with the judged characteristics of the treatment.

Summary and Schema of the Psychotherapy Process

What was offered in this chapter was stimulated by the cold bath of our limited success in our first plunge into prediction based on conventional process variables (chapter 9). We regrouped and reimmersed ourselves in a review of clinical writings and of many transcripts of sessions of the more versus less improved patients to try to get a freshly focused view of the main curative factors. We emerged with the eight listed in the diagram in figure 10-3. The factors are presented there in a pyramid with the most powerful at the base. (The first four factors correspond to the three basic factors in Luborsky, 1984.) Most are patient factors (1, 3, 4, 5, 6, 7); two are therapist factors (2, 8). At the base of the triangle is Factor 1, the main relationship factor: the patient's experiencing the treatment relationship as a helping one. This factor depends on the patient's repertoire of past helping alliances and also on the therapist's ability to allow this experience to become established. Factor 2 is the therapist's ability to understand and manage the relationship, which includes interpreting the core conflictual relationship theme, a concept similar to the transference. Factor 3 is the patient's counterpart of Factor 2: It is the patient's involvement in the joint search for acquiring understanding. Factor 4 is the lessening of the pervasiveness of the relationship conflicts. Factor 5 is the patient's capacity to internalize and thus to hold on to the treatment gains; this capacity may

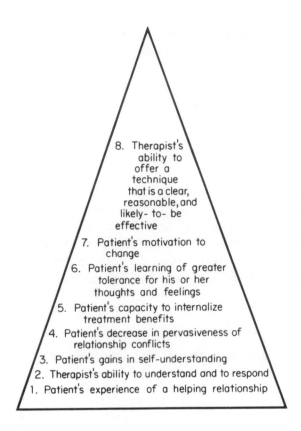

FIGURE 10-3. A Broadly Based Review of the Main Curative Factors within the Process of Psychotherapy.

depend on the patient's adequacy of personality functioning and, in part, on the availability of external supports. Factor 6 is the patient's ability to learn to tolerate his or her thoughts and feelings. Factor 7 is the patient's motivation to change. Last, Factor 8 is the clarity, reasonableness, and expected effectiveness of the therapist's technique.

From inspecting the factors as a whole, we can begin to see the outlines of a general theory of why these curative factors are curative. They can be grouped into a basic sequence that applies to many types of psychotherapies: (a) willingness to meet to talk about problems, (b) development of attachment, and (c) development of self-observing capacities that can be maintained in the face of separation from the therapist (Greenspan & Wieder, 1984).

More specifically, the successful operation of most of the eight factors, especially Factors 1, 2, 3 and 4, bolster the patient against falling into states of helplessness and hopelessness that would lead to heightened vulnerability to formation of symptoms (Engel & Schmale, 1967). These first four factors serve as an aid in dealing with what Freud (1926) calls expected and remembered situations and states of helplessness—which in turn are attendant on the activation of the patient's core conflictual relationship theme.

Most of the curative factors can be understood as providing support for the patient's wishes for self-efficacy, competence, and mastery. This dimension fits with a broad gamut of theories of therapeutic change and of symptom formation (e.g., Bandura's [1977] theory of self-efficacy as the key to therapeutic change; Frank's [1971a, 1971b, 1974] theory of the centrality of the patient's morale; Freud's [1926] theory of symptom formation, which gives a central position to the patient's expectation of helplessness; and Seligman's [1975] theory of the negative consequences of learned helplessness, especially the reliance on pessimistic explanatory style).

The remaining chapters of this book will report on our attempts to apply operational measures of these factors in our research studies and to discuss our findings in relation to research by other process research groups. More of this research genre is needed, but it must be remembered that the psychotherapy process research groups have come into being mainly in the last 20 years (as reviewed by Luborsky & Spence, 1978), which is recent for this difficult and time-consuming kind of research. Yet each of the research groups has already produced signs of helpful results, leading us to forecast improved knowledge of process predictors within the next few years.

11

The Helping Alliance:

A Global Rating Method

IN PREPARATION for Edward Bordin's 1975 panel at a Society for Psychotherapy Research conclave on the concept of the therapeutic alliance, Lester Luborsky reviewed the Penn study's transcripts of sessions to try to operationalize the concept in the light of the curative factors analysis (chapter 10). The result was the categories in the Helping Alliance Counting Signs Method (Luborsky, 1976a, chapter 12) and the version in this chapter called the Helping Alliance Global Rating Method.

Since that time research on therapeutic alliance measures has clearly moved beyond the era of reliance on the familiar concept-generating attitude of famous clinicians (e.g., Zetzel, 1958; Greenson, 1965) to the relentless "show me" attitude of research psychologists and research psychiatrists (as reviewed in chapter 19). We have attempted here to show two main points about the Penn Helping Alliance Global Rating Method.

Reliable and economical methods for estimating the helping alliance can be developed. We constructed the global rating method because it has some advantages over merely counting signs of the alliance. The global method allows a more clinical and more rapid assessment. Ratings can be based on whatever instigates the judge's inferences within the relevant segment of psychotherapy. In this way, the rating method may catch more of the helping alliance phenomena in briefer samples than the counting signs method.

Helping alliance measures will have power for predicting the outcomes of psychotherapy. Predictive power was estimated by correlations of the helping alliance measures with outcome measures. Since we were also interested in the relative predictive power of other measures from the clinical literature, we obtained ratings of therapist facilitative behaviors, patient resistance, and patient insight as well as pretreatment assessments of patient and therapist characteristics (Luborsky, Mintz, et al., 1980).

Procedure

The 10 most and the 10 least improved patients who were treated for at least 25 sessions were chosen from the 73 audiotaped cases in the Penn Psychotherapy Project on the basis of the two correlated composite outcome measures (chapter 2). Four 20-minute segments from the beginning sessions (each at least 10 pages of transcript), were drawn from each of the 20 cases: two segments from the initial treatment stage (Sessions 3 and 5), and two from the final stage (the session at which 90% of the treatment had been completed, and the prior session), making 80 segments. All ratings of each segment were made independently by two experienced psychoanalysts, not only on helping alliance but also on therapist facilitative behaviors, patient resistance, and patient insight. The segments were drawn from the beginning of the sessions, based on our view that the judge should know all that happened in the session from its beginning. The 20-minute unit was chosen as a compromise between the full session, which would have been too laborious to transcribe, and the usual 5-minute segment, which would have been too short. Five-minute segments seemed insufficient for a variable such as the helping alliance, which depends on judgment of the relationship between patient and therapist (Mintz, Luborsky & Auerbach, 1971). The 20 patients were treated in psychoanalytically oriented psychotherapy by 18 therapists (2 had two cases each and the rest one case each). Ten of the therapists were third- or fourth-year residents under supervision and 8 were more experienced. Demographic characteristics of the most versus least improved cases were similar. The patients had a mean age of 26. Thirteen of the 20 were female. All 20 were nonpsychotic outpatients, most at the psychiatric outpatient clinic of the Hospital of the University of Pennsylvania. The more improved patients' treatments lasted 61 weeks (median), and the less improved patients' treatments lasted 43 weeks (median).

THE SCALES

Both the Helping Alliance and the Therapist Facilitative Behaviors Scales represent the conversion of Luborsky's (1976a) counting signs manual into rating scales. The counting signs approach takes more time because the entire transcript has to be considered and some of it rated in terms of its applicability to each category in the manual. The rating approach is simpler and allows the judge more scope in evaluating the applicability of the concept.

The *Helping Alliance Rating Scale* is composed of 10 subscales; 6 are summed for Helping Alliance Type 1 (HA1) and 4 are summed for Helping Alliance Type 2 (HA2). Each item is rated on a 10-point Likert-type scale reflecting the degree to which each item was present. HA1 refers to the patient's experience of receiving help or a helpful attitude from the therapist; HA2 refers to the patient's experience of being involved in a joint or team effort with the therapist.

The *Therapist Facilitative Behaviors Scale* is also divided into two parts, which parallel the two types of alliances. As with the Helping Alliance Rating Scale, the two types of therapist behaviors are each rated on a 10-point Likert-type scale.

The *Patient Insight Scale* consists of seven categories of behaviors, each rated on a 10-point Likert-type scale and drawn from psychoanalytic and other research. The scale is influenced by the Reid and Finesinger (1951) definition of emotional insight.

The *Patient Resistance Scale* is based on patient behaviors that psychoanalytic theory and observations have designated as indices of resistance. Each of the seven categories is rated on a 10-point Likert-type scale according to the frequency and intensity of occurrence during the segment.

TRAINING RATERS AND INTERRATER RELIABILITY

The two independent raters were highly experienced psychoanalysts who had previously worked together clinically. A training session explained the rating procedures and used sample transcripts that were not part of the study proper. Following the training sessions the raters proceeded to rate the transcripts, and to ensure adequate agreement interrater reliability estimates were made after the first 10 segments were rated. Each of the segments was rated before the rater proceeded to the transcript of the next patient, and no ratings were changed after another transcript had been read.

OUTCOME MEASURES, SUBJECTS, AND DATA ANALYSES

The two outcome measures were rated benefits and residual gain (chapter 2). Since the two measures were highly correlated, cases chosen were extreme on either criterion. Seven of the most improved and eight of the least improved patients were chosen for study in terms of residual gain scores, and the additional 5 of the 20 were chosen in terms of rated benefits.

The main analyses involved a two-factor analysis of variance: one within-subjects factor (Treatment Stage, i.e., early versus late sessions), and one between-subjects factor (Outcome, i.e., more versus less improved patients). Given the findings of Luborsky (1976a), the main variables of interest were the helping alliance scores. The other variables—therapist facilitative behaviors, resistance, and insight—were of secondary interest in the sense that they were added later to help explore the meaning of any findings that might emerge with the helping alliance variables.

Because of the high interjudge agreement (see below), the two raters' scores were summed. We had no hypothesis about differences between the two early sessions or between the two later sessions, so we summed the ratings for the two early ones to yield an early treatment score and we summed the ratings for the two later ones to yield a late treatment score. Although the Helping Alliance Type 1 (HA1) and the Helping Alliance Type 2 (HA2) scores were highly correlated, they were analyzed separately because HA2 scores were expected to increase in the late sessions for the more improved patients.

Results

HELPING ALLIANCE RATINGS WERE RELIABLE

Interrater reliability for the two raters was more than adequate for Helping Alliance Type 1 (HA1), Helping Alliance Type 2 (HA2), Therapist Facilitative Behaviors Type 1 (TFB1), Therapist Facilitative Behaviors Type 2 (TFB2), resistance, and insight. For the 10 scales in the HA1 plus HA2, correlations ranged from .75 to .88, with most falling in the .80s. Reliability levels were similar for other variables.

Estimates of internal reliability (coefficient alpha) for HA, TFB, resistance, and insight scales were .96, .94, .86, and .92, respectively. It was concluded that all four scales had good internal reliability as well as good interrater reliability and were adequate in this respect to test our hypotheses.

HELPING ALLIANCE RATINGS WERE CONSISTENT OVER TIME

The extent to which helping alliance manifestations would vary over the course of the treatment was unknown. After such responses were expressed early in the treatment they might not occur as much later on, or they might become more frequent, especially in more successful treatments.

At the start of this research there were no precedents to guide us in the selection of sessions to measure the helping alliance. We chose an early and a late time in the course of therapy, using two sessions at each time period. For the early sessions we chose the fifth because Barrett-Lennard (1962) had used it for his relationship questionnaire; we added the third to enlarge the standard sample of sessions and to learn how early in treatment the helping alliance appeared. Subsequent studies of sessions by other researchers using the helping alliance measures followed suit by using the third, fourth, or fifth session (chapter 19).

We found that the helping alliance ratings of the early and late sessions were similar, as can readily be seen in figures 11-1 and 11-2. Essentially, there was no significant gain from early to late sessions in either HA1 or HA2; the HA2 scores for the more improved patients showed a nonsignificant increase—and an increase had been anticipated. Likewise, an analysis of variance using session scores showed no significant early versus late effects. The correlation of early versus late (table 11-1) was .57**. The correlation was high for the more improved patients (.69) but nonsignificant for the less improved patients.

PREDICTIONS OF OUTCOMES BY HELPING ALLIANCE RATINGS WERE MODERATELY HIGH

In terms of analyses of variance, for HA1 the test for treatment outcomes (more versus less improved) was significant, $F(1,18) = 5.9, p < .05$. The test for treatment stage (early versus late) and the test for treatment outcome by treatment stage interaction were not significant (both F-ratios were less than 1). The analyses of HA2 showed similar results.

The relationship of helping alliance ratings with outcome measures was examined. The rating of early sessions alone (HA1 + HA2) correlated .44* with the main outcome measure (more versus less improved). For HA1 and HA2 early plus HA1 and HA2 late sessions' ratings together, the correlation was .47*; for HA1 alone the correlation was .47* and for HA2, .46*. The within-group correlation of HA1 and HA2 was .91 for early plus late ratings. Therefore, the separate HA1 and HA2 results represent essentially the same finding. Some of the correlations with other outcome measures were even higher than those with the main dichotomous outcome measure of more versus less improved. For example, early HA1 + HA2 correlated

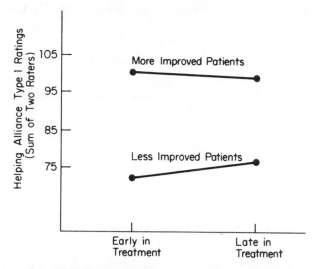

FIGURE 11-1. Sum of Helping Alliance Type 1 (HA1) Ratings for the More and the Less Improved Patients, Early versus Late in Treatment.

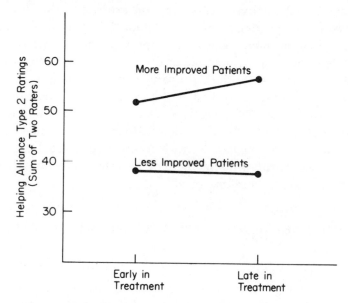

FIGURE 11-2. Sum of Helping Alliance Type 2 (HA2) Ratings for the More and the Less Improved Patients, Early versus Late in Treatment.

TABLE 11-1

Consistency of Helping Alliance Ratings:
Correlations of Early with Late Sessions

	Total ($N = 20$)	More Improved ($N = 10$)	Less Improved ($N = 10$)
Early HA1 vs. Late HA1	.57**	.69*	−.33
Early HA2 vs. Late HA2	.40 (.08)	.39	−.13
Early HA1 + HA2 vs. Late HA1 + HA2	.53*	.59 (.08)	−.32

Note: HA1 indicates Helping Alliance Type 1; HA2, Helping Alliance Type 2.
*$p < .05$
**$p < .01$

.58** with the three outcome measures summed: therapist's judgment of success, satisfaction, and improvement.

A direct and relatively easy way of expressing the differentiation achieved by the helping alliance as a predictive measure is in terms of a fourfold division: more versus less improved broken against more than versus less than the helping alliance scores' mean, median, or optimal cut-off. For example, for the eight patients whose ratings were more than the mean on early HA1 + HA2, 62% turned out to be more improved by the end of treatment. Taking early and late HA1 and HA2 ratings together, five of the six patients whose scores were higher than the mean were more improved. The early median ratings discriminated at about the same level, while all five patients who had helping alliance ratings above an optimal cut-off point were more improved.

PREDICTIONS BY RELATED VARIABLES WERE NOT USUALLY SIGNIFICANT

Even though the other variables—Therapist Facilitative Behavior, resistance, and insight—tended to be correlated with each other (table 11-2) and with the helping alliance ratings, none of them showed significant treatment outcome, treatment stage, or treatment-outcome-by-treatment-stage interactions.[1] In relation to outcome, the other variables tended to show differences between the more and the less improved which were in the same direction as the helping alliance scores but did not reach significance. By a correlational analysis, one was significant: TFB with rated benefits, $r = .45*$.

[1]We did not give up on insight, however, because it is central as a curative factor in the theory of change. In chapter 17 we report on the results of another attempt to analyze it and test its prediction powers.

TABLE 11-2

Intercorrelations of All Measures for Early and Late Segments ($N = 20$)

	HA1	HA2	TFB1	TFB2	Resistance	Insight
Helping Alliance Type 1 (HA1)						
Helping Alliance Type 2 (HA2)	.91					
Therapist Facilitating Behaviors Type 1 (TFB1)	.61	.50				
Therapist Facilitating Behaviors Type 2 (TFB2)	.85	.80	.74			
Resistance	−.60	−.69	.01[a]	−.52		
Insight	.67	.83	.43	.67	−.53	

NOTE: Correlations are within-group correlations, i.e., adjusted for differences in mean of the two groups.
[a]All rs but this one are significant at $p < .05$ or better.

PREDICTIONS BY PRETREATMENT WITH HELPING ALLIANCE MEASURES SHOWED THAT EACH CONTRIBUTED

Since combining factors from different domains might improve prediction further, we explored the predictive power of multiple correlations consisting of the best pretreatment variables, such as psychological severity, with the best in-treatment variable, the helping alliance measures. As a sample, the Health-Sickness Rating Scale (HSRS) ratings together with the helping alliance ratings provided impressive multiples, e.g., early HA ratings (HA1 + HA2) together with the HSRS ratings correlated with rated benefits .62* and with residual gain .58*. Both HA ratings and the HSRS ratings contributed significantly to the multiple correlation, which means that they were both uniquely contributing to the outcome.

Questions for Discussion

We have shown that the Helping Alliance Rating Method based on transcripts of sessions is reliable and has significant predictive power, accounting in our sample for about 25% of the variance of various outcome measures for the 20 patients. In evaluating these results several central questions were considered.

Is predictive power of the helping alliance measures greater than that of the pretreatment measures? As was reported, for these 20 patients the total early HA scores correlated .44 with the main dichotomous outcome measure, more versus less improved. For the same 20 patients, of the 57 pretreatment predictors in the Penn Psychotherapy Project, only a few variables achieved the same level of prediction as the rated benefits criterion (all at $p < .05$): the Rorschach Prognostic Ratings Scale (.48); the emotional freedom composite (.46) and interests variable (.49) of the Prognostic Index interview; HSRS (.47); age match (.46); and method of assignment ($-.46$, i.e., random assignment leads to poorer outcome than therapist's choice). Correlations were similar with the residual gain criterion. With treatment length, the correlations of rated benefits and residual gain were at about the same level, indicating that the longer the treatment, the better the outcome.

The implications were: (1) For the *same* 20 patients, the helping alliance predictive correlations were as good as the best that was achieved by the few significant pretreatment variables (e.g., for psychiatric severity as assessed by the Rorschach Prognostic Rating Scale and for the Health-Sickness Rating Scale). (2) Since these few significant pretreatment predictive correlations were somewhat higher for the sample of 20 than for the unselected sample of 73, it is likely that unselected samples will typically yield somewhat lower predictive correlations.

Does contamination explain the correlations of helping alliance ratings with outcome measures? An overlap in the content of the predictor and criterion might be present. Such an overlap could be considered as a contamination of prediction and criterion. An examination of the items in the manual manifestly suggests that HA1 item 3 might overlap with items in the outcome measures. However, when this item was omitted, the correlations remained substantially unchanged. The idea of overlap would be more relevant if the outcome measures, such as the helping alliance measures, were restricted to patient measures; instead, the outcome measures included observer and therapist measures (Luborsky, Mintz, et al., 1980). It should also be pointed out that the improvements represented by the helping alliance statements in the early sessions were only a feeble harbinger of final outcome. Early improvements tended to be minimal compared with the more substantial achievements by the end of successful treatment.

But even if there were some overlap, the present research nevertheless contributes to an important question: Do these very early indications of improvement anticipate the later outcome of the treatment? Our definitely positive answer delineates a discovery about the process of psychotherapy: Patients who are rated early in treatment as reporting evidences of being helped generally turn out to be those who are most helped in time, as indicated by our outcome measures. (A caveat about the interpretation of this association is required: The study does not demonstrate whether good outcomes are *caused* by good helping alliances or whether the significant association is caused by some other factor or factors that cause both good helping alliances and good outcomes.)

The possible presence of a contamination should also be considered in another sense, that is, the degree to which the raters were really "blind" as to the identity of the patient and the location of each segment in the course of treatment. In our view, these types of contamination were probably small since each judge rated, in random order and one at a time, 80 segments that were unidentified as to the patient and the time in treatment. Also, recognition of the session as early versus late was theoretically possible but probably slight since the late sessions represented the 90% point rather than the end of treatment. But even if both of these sources of contamination had occurred on a small scale, they would not be likely to have affected the main predictive findings much.

Can the beginning of the helping alliance be discerned? According to figures 11-1 and 11-2, the helping alliance was already present at Sessions 3 and 5 and showed a modest degree of consistency between the early and the late sessions. We do not know whether it was already evident in Sessions 1 and 2 as well or even whether it formed like an imprinting process at the patient's first sight of the therapist.

For a few patients we have evidence that the alliance seemed to begin as soon as patient and therapist met. We described one of these patients, Ms. Samuelson (#49), in chapter 3. At the end of the first session she said she expected things to go well with her therapist. She had noted some clues about his appearance that reminded her of someone to whom she was very positively attached.

Even before meeting with the therapist, the patient's expectations from helping relationships may be a measurable trait. Unfortunately, in the Penn Psychotherapy Project the only information that bears on this is the observer's rating in the Prognostic Index interview of "patient's optimistic expectations" about the outcome of the treatment, an interview that typically took place after the patient and therapist had had one or two sessions. Our correlation of that rating with early helping alliance ratings was not significant.

The helping alliance experience may result from the combination of a patient trait, such as prior needs and expectations in relationships, with the degree to which the therapist fits these needs and expectations for a helping alliance. For some patients, that estimate of fit probably begins even in the first session or two, as it did for Ms. Samuelson, but, as we mentioned, for the sample of 20 the patients' estimates of these expectations were not significantly associated with the helping alliance scores.

Are there simpler and better understood helping alliance measures? We need to

develop additional and simpler methods because the Helping Alliance
Rating Method is based on time-consuming observer judgments of sessions. The questionnaire method, for example, is much more economical
to use than the observer-judgment method. The success of the Barrett-
Lennard Relationship Inventory Questionnaire (1962) and the Orlinsky
and Howard (1975) therapy session questionnaire gave us reassuring indications that a helping alliance questionnaire would have some value in
predicting the outcome of psychotherapy. We therefore had reason to
expect the significant prediction we found from the Luborsky Helping
Alliance Questionnaire (used in the study by Woody et al. [1983] and
reviewed in chapter 13).

Do helping alliance measures measure what they are intended to measure? All of these
developing methods need to be better understood in terms of what they
measure. That will be accomplished in our research not only by predictive
studies but also by intercorrelations of measures and comparisons with
other personality measures (in chapter 12).

The high level of the intercorrelations noted in table 11-2 might imply
that the judges were largely making a global, undifferentiated assessment
of the patient's progress within each of the therapy segments they rated.
But the likelihood that they were doing more is bolstered by the fact that
the helping alliance scores had something else that resulted in significant
correlations with the outcome of treatment. Investigating that "something
else" was the target of the Helping Alliance Counting Signs Method,
which includes only specific examples of "signs" that define the helping
alliance concept. As an anticipatory peek at what is in chapter 15, predictions on the basis of those signs turned out to be at least as successful as
those based on the Helping Alliance Rating Method; two other independent judges' combined predictions correlated with outcome .51*!

Can helping alliance results be generalized to other patients and treatments? As a final
caveat, what we have learned may apply mainly to relatively short-to-
moderate length supportive-expressive dynamically oriented psychotherapy (as in our sample, with a median length of about 51 weeks) in comparison with traditional longer-term psychotherapy or psychoanalysis. In such
longer therapy, both because the interval between the early helping alliance measures and outcome measures is longer and because of factors
posited in clinical theories of psychotherapeutic change, the correlation of
the helping alliance measures and outcomes should be lower than what we
found.

Our speculation will have to halt here, however, because the bridges
between the clinical concepts of helping alliances and our limited operational measures of helping alliances may not be ready to carry the weight
of further theorizing about the results of future studies. In time we hope

to provide tested knowledge to permit generalization to longer psycho-therapy. Meanwhile, we are engaged in studies to extend our observations, including one on the predictive power of the helping alliance for patients who are given the choice of two therapists after having had two sessions with each therapist in succession (chapter 14).

Summary

This chapter is a report of the first of the studies of operational measures of curative factors.

1. Our main aim was to develop a reliable predictive method for rating psychotherapy transcripts in terms of the patient's experience of being in a helping alliance with the therapist. We succeeded through a method consisting of 10 observer-rated scales for judging the patient's experience of the helping alliance: (1) 6 scales for Helping Alliance Type 1 (i.e., statements in the form of "the therapist is helping me"), and (2) 4 scales for Helping Alliance Type 2 (i.e., statements in the form of "we have a helping alliance and are working together so that I can use the tools of therapy to help myself as well"). The 20-minute segments of psychother-apy (two from early and two from late sessions) of the 10 most and 10 least improved patients were rated by two clinically experienced independent judges. The interrater reliability and internal reliability of the ratings were high.

2. Helping Alliance Type 1 was highly correlated with helping Alliance Type 2 (.91). Helping Alliance Type 2 ratings increased from early sessions to late sessions in psychotherapy for the more improved patients, as ex-pected, but not significantly. The consistency of the early HA ratings (HA1) with the late HA ratings (HA2) was only moderate (.57) and mainly applied to the more improved patients (.69).

3. Both HA1 and HA2 predicted outcomes of psychotherapy signifi-cantly. For example, for the dichotomous outcome measure more versus less improved, the correlations for HA1 were .47, for HA2, .46 (for HA1 + HA2, .47); for the composite of ratings of success, satisfaction, and improvement, .58. Reliability was high for several related variables (thera-pist facilitative behaviors, resistance, and insight), but none predicted significantly.

4. The level of predictive success for helping alliance measures is as good as or better than for most of the pretreatment measures examined in the Penn Psychotherapy Project. In fact, only a few of the 57 pretreatment

predictors achieved correlations that were as high. Since psychological severity was relatively well represented among the few pretreatment predictive measures that were significant at about the same level, we tried a multiple correlation of the Health-Sickness Rating Scale with the helping alliance measures. What the multiple correlation (with rated benefits) of .62 implies is this: Favorable outcomes of treatment are contributed to independently (not interactively) by the patient's pretreatment psychological health as well as by the positive helping alliance formed during the course of psychotherapy.

12

The Helping Alliance:
A Counting Signs Method

IT WAS IMPORTANT to extend the applicability of clinicians' ratings of the helping alliance through identifying specific clues of its existence in transcripts from psychotherapy sessions. For that reason a quantitative "counting signs" manual was constructed (Luborsky, 1976a). The manual provides guidance for counting literal or almost literal signs of the patient's experience of a helping alliance.

This chapter specifically serves to (a) describe the helping alliance counting signs (HAcs) scoring manual; (b) provide more information about its reliability and predictive power; (c) compare the counting signs method with the Helping Alliance Rating Method (Morgan et al., 1982); and (d) examine a broad spectrum of the personality correlates of our helping alliance measures as a way of achieving further understanding of each measure.

Background

THE HELPING ALLIANCE COUNTING SIGNS MANUAL

The manual consists of two broad types of helping alliances together with examples.[1] The two broad types are Helping Alliance Type 1 (HA1), in which the patient experiences the therapist as providing or being capable of

[1]Manuals for the helping alliance methods may be obtained from the authors at the University of Pennsylvania, Philadelphia, PA.

providing the needed help, and, Helping Alliance Type 2 (HA2), in which the patient experiences treatment as a process of working together with the therapist toward the goals of the treatment. The manual contains four subtypes of HA1: (a) the patient believes the therapist or therapy is helping; (b) the patient feels changed since the beginning of treatment; (c) the patient feels a rapport with the therapist; and (d) the patient feels optimism and confidence that the therapist and treatment can help. Three HA2 subtypes are included: (a) the patient experiences working together with the therapist in a joint effort; (b) the patient shares with the therapist similar conceptions about the sources of his or her problems; and (c) the patient demonstrates qualities that are similar to those of the therapist, especially those connected with the tools for understanding. Each of these subtypes may appear in positive or negative form: The positive form is the one listed above and the negative form is its opposite. These types and subtypes were suggested by inspection of preliminary sessions, not part of the sample used in the present study, as well as by concepts of the helping alliance in clinical writings. Because the notion of HA2 came from these writings, it seems closer than HA1 to the clinical concept of the helping alliance. The present study will allow us to see how closely these two types are associated with each other, as was done for the global rating in chapter 11.

EVALUATING THE TRANSCRIPTS

The judge locates in the transcript all patient statements that are "signs" of each helping alliance subtype, classifies them as positive or negative, and then rates their intensity on a 5-point scale (from $1 =$ "very low" to $5 =$ "very high"). Each patient's score is the sum of the number of such signs in each session, weighted by the intensity ratings. Three scores were tried: (a) positive scores, (b) negative scores, and (c) difference scores, i.e., the difference between the positive and negative scores.

Two brief examples from patient Ms. Samuelson (#49), a more improved patient, will illustrate the scoring system. This patient had come to treatment with depression and suicidal thoughts and had also hoped through treatment to be able to break off an affair with a married man which she considered to have no future. One example is from Session 5 (p. 2, l. 25):

P: . . . Mmm. I feel much better. I don't know why I don't trust it, but it's fine while it lasts.

This example was scored by Judge 1 as "1b3" and by Judge 2 as "1b4." The "1" refers to HA1, the "b" refers to subtype b, and the "3" and "4" represent the intensity. Both judges were fairly close in identifying the statement as a positive Type 1 of moderate strength. The next example (familiar from chapter 10) is of HA2 and is taken from the same patient, Session 89 (p. 1, l. 23):

P: Well, I—my—you know, I want to tell you something, Doctor Freud (laughs). Don't know why I said that.

T: "Doctor Freud," you said?

P: How d' you like that. . . . Well, they both begin with an *F.*

T: Both begin with *F-R-E,* as a matter of fact.

P: That's right. See, you're just as aware of it as I am. More so. Want me to analyze that?

This example was scored by Judge 1 as "2c4" and Judge 2 as "2c3." These scores refer to HA2, subtype c, intensity 3 and 4.

Procedures

SESSIONS, PATIENTS, AND THERAPISTS

Both the Helping Alliance Counting Signs Method (HAcs) and the Helping Alliance Rating Method (HAr) were applied to sessions selected from the same 20 patients (described in the last chapter), the 10 most and the 10 least improved among the 73 in the Penn Psychotherapy Project. Improvement was based on the two moderately highly correlated (.76) composite outcome measures: rated benefits (RB) and residual gain (RG). As described in the last chapter, each transcript consisted of the first 20 minutes (or at least 10 typewritten pages) from four psychotherapy sessions: Sessions 3 and 5 and two late sessions.

JUDGES

The manuals for each of the two methods, the HAcs and the HAr, were applied to the 80 sessions by two different pairs of independent judges. All four judges were clinically experienced, which was requisite for their selection. They were given a practice session using the manuals with practice cases that were not from the Penn Psychotherapy Project. For the counting signs evaluations one judge was experienced in clinical psychology (MM) and one in social work (LA). They were affiliated with different teaching

institutions and did not know each other. They were trained separately by
one of the authors (LL). The rating method was applied as described in the
previous chapter.

Results

The focus of these results is on the counting signs method. Some results
of the rating method are presented here for comparison; full results are
available in the previous chapter.

THE MOST FREQUENT HAcs WAS "FEELS HELPED"

The scoring of the signs for the 80 sessions by the two judges provided
an opportunity to learn which among the seven signs appeared most frequently and, therefore, were most central to the manual. As table 12-1
shows, subtypes 1a and 1b were the most frequently scored. Subtype 1a
involves the belief by the patient that the therapist or therapy is helping.
Subtype 1b is a related variable in which the patient feels better, although
the change is not explicitly attributed to the therapist or the treatment.
Table 12-1 also reveals that both judges scored HA2 signs less frequently
than HA1 signs.

Positive signs were scored relatively more frequently than negative signs
for the 20 cases. This was due mainly to results from the more improved
group; in that group, as would be expected, positive signs were scored very
much more frequently than negative ones. For the less improved group
negative signs were scored only slightly more frequently than positive
ones.

HAcs WERE SCORABLE WITH MODERATE INTERJUDGE AGREEMENT

Determining agreements in scoring is harder for the HAcs method than
for the HAr method. With the HAcs method each judge must first locate
in the lengthy transcripts examples that might fit the subtypes in the
manual. Therefore, two types of unreliability in the HAcs approach must
be distinguished: (1) When one judge does not score a unit of the transcript
that another judge has located and specified as fitting a subtype of the
counting signs manual; this "locational unreliability" can sometimes be
ascribed to lack of attention by one judge to the particular statement and

TABLE 12-1

Frequency of Each Category of HAcs as Rated by Two Judges
(Early Plus Late Sessions)

	Judge 1 (MM)		Judge 2 (LA)	
	Positive	Negative	Positive	Negative
More Improved Patients				
Type 1 Signs				
a. Therapy is helping	13	14	16	8
b. Feels changed	39	11	41	8
c. Feels understood	1	1	13	11
d. Hopeful regarding change	1	5	6	9
Type 2 Signs				
a. A joint effort	2	0	14	1
b. Similar ideas of P. and T.	1	1	0	2
c. Devt. of self-understanding ability	3	0	1	0
Less Improved Patients				
Type 1 Signs				
a. Therapy is helping	1	6	0	5
b. Feels changed	3	7	4	4
c. Feels understood	0	3	2	19
d. Hopeful regarding change	2	3	2	3
Type 2 Signs				
a. A joint effort	0	0	3	0
b. Similar ideas of P. and T.	0	3	0	1
c. Devt. of self-understanding ability	0	0	0	0
Totals	66	54	102	71
		120		173

may not be as serious as the other type of unreliability. (2) When two judges assign different counting signs subtypes to the same portion of the transcript, which might be referred to as "agreement unreliability."

Turning now to the results of the HAcs scoring by the two judges: Many of their "errors" were of the first type and did not involve agreement unreliability. As expected, the judges did not score the same number of signs—Judge MM scored a total of 120 signs; Judge LA scored a total of 173 in the same 80 segments. The difference was due in part to overlooking some examples during the reading of the long transcripts and in part to differences in scorer style.

Nevertheless, whether or not the same signs were scored, there was moderate agreement in the number of signs scored by each judge across patients. Expressed correlationally, the positive items were agreed upon especially well (for early sessions, .69, for late sessions, .82; see table 12-2). The higher correlations for the positive items may be due in part to their slightly greater number.

TABLE 12-2

Agreement (Correlations) of Two Judges on Number of HAcs Scored (N = 20)

| | Judge 2 (LA) | | | | | |
| | Early Sessions | | Late Sessions | | Early + Late Sessions | |
Judge 1 (MM)	Positive	Negative	Positive	Negative	Positive	Negative
Positive	.69***		.82***		.81***	
Negative		.53*		.47*		.47*

$^*p < .05$
$^{***}p < .001$

However, only 74 signs among all those scored by both judges were exactly the same statements. Of these 74 signs only 33 (45%) were in exact agreement on all four scoring components: (1) the value, i.e., positive or negative; (2) the type, i.e., HA1 or HA2; (3) the subtype, i.e., a, b, c, or d; and (4) the intensity, i.e., the rating on the scale from 1 to 5. But agreement on all components simultaneously is well beyond the call of duty—very high agreement was obtained for each component alone: for value (100%), for type (97%), for subtype (82%), and for intensity (61%).

For the contrasting HAr method, interjudge agreement by the two highly experienced clinicians on these same 80 sessions was high: Correlations were in the .8–.9 range (chapter 11).

HAcs SHOWED AGREEMENT WITH HAr

Since both the HAcs and the HAr measures apply to the same concept, they should agree. They did. As it turned out, HAcs and HAr, each scored by two different pairs of independent judges, were significantly correlated for both early and late sessions' ratings (table 12-3). They agreed more highly for the late sessions (.83***) than for the early sessions (.57**), possibly because in the late sessions the probable outcome of treatment was sometimes evident in what the patient and therapist were discussing. The greater agreement for HAcs positive signs than for negative signs may result from the larger number of positive signs. The fact that the scores on the two methods by two different pairs of judges showed moderate agreement may imply some validity for both methods, especially since the counting signs method has a claim to some face validity because it is the sum of what was defined in the manual as literal examples of the helping alliance.

TABLE 12-3

*Agreement (Correlations) between
HAcs and HAr*[a]

HAcs	r
Early Sessions' Ratings	
Positive	.57**
Negative	−.21
Difference	.58**
Late Sessions' Ratings	
Positive	.83***
Negative	−.19
Difference	.80***
Early Plus Late Sessions' Ratings	
Positive	.86***
Negative	−.14
Difference	.81***

[a]The 3 HA scores are each correlated with
the single HAr score.
**p < .01
***p < .001

HELPING ALLIANCE SCORES FROM EARLY TO LATE IN TREATMENT WERE CONSISTENT

We had no basis to expect either much or little consistency from early to late in treatment, not even from the clinical writings about helping alliances. Our findings, therefore, represent new observations: (a) HA scores of the two early sessions are moderately consistent with scores of the two late sessions for both the HAcs method (positive items), $r = .58**$, and the HAr method, $r = .53*$. (b) For the more improved patients, the consistency of scores between early and late sessions was more evident than for the less improved patients. Within the more improved group the correlations were: by the HAr method, .59; by the HAcs method, positive, .54; negative, .47; difference between positive and negative, .47*.

PREDICTIVE POWER WAS FOUND FOR BOTH HAr AND HAcs

We wanted most for both of our methods to have the power to predict outcomes of psychotherapy. Our wish was granted for both the HAr and the HAcs methods.

Predictive success was examined in two ways: by a two-factor mixed model analysis of variance comparing the two extreme groups and by correlations using the continuous outcome measures. For the analysis of variance, the between-groups factor was based on dividing the subjects into two groups, more improved (MI) and less improved (LI), and the within-group factor was the early versus late sessions. Table 12-4 gives the means and standard deviations (judges summed) for the more improved and less improved groups. Table 12-5 gives the results of the analysis of variance, which showed significant F-ratios for the outcomes (for positive and difference scores), meaning that the MI had more HAcs signs than the LI. The stage-by-outcome interaction is significant only for the difference score measure. What is happening reflects a noteworthy difference in the scores of the MI versus LI patients (table 12-4): The MI scores are increasing from early to late (5.7 to 17.4), and the LI are decreasing (-1.1 to -10.9). With closer examination it can be seen that within the MI patients the positive scores go up over time and the negative scores do not change. In contrast, within the LI patients the negative scores go up and there is little change in the positive ones.

TABLE 12-4

Means and Standard Deviations of HAcs
(Two Judges Combined)

HAcs	Early Sessions		Late Sessions	
	Mean	S.D.	Mean	S.D.
More Improved Patients				
Positive	15.1	12.7	28.0	23.9
Negative	10.0	8.2	10.6	12.0
Difference	5.7	18.6	17.4	27.4
Less Improved Patients				
Positive	3.1	2.9	1.1	2.3
Negative	4.2	5.6	12.0	11.3
Difference	-1.1	4.4	-10.9	12.1

NOTE: Mean weighted frequencies, i.e., frequency weighted by intensity ratings, are used.

TABLE 12-5

Significance Tests on HAcs Scores (Two-factor Analysis of
Variance; Two Judges Combined)

	F-Ratios		
	Positive	Negative	Difference
Treatment Stage	2.0	2.4	0.1
Outcome	16.3***	0.4	7.1*
Stage × Outcome	3.8 ($p < .07$)	1.8	5.8*

*$p < .05$
***$p < .001$

Although the correlations for the late sessions were higher than for the early ones (table 12-6), we will present the early correlations since our primary interest is in early predictors. The highest correlations tended to appear for the early positive HAcs; it correlated .57** with rated benefits and .58** with residual gain. The early HAr correlations were significant but not quite as high: .46* with rated benefits and .44* with residual gain. The early HAcs difference scores (positive minus negative) were not significant.

The helping alliance measures were also useful in predicting simpler outcome criteria from the Penn Psychotherapy Project. For example, the combination of three simple outcome rating scales by the therapist—success, satisfaction, and improvement (SSI)—was significantly predicted by early positive HAcs (.59**) and HAr (.49*) (table 12-6). Similarly, with the criterion of the change in Target Complaints (Battle et al., 1966)—i.e., the specific symptoms for which the patient came to treatment—correlations tended to be significant: Early positive HAcs correlated .59* with change in the first Target Complaint, and HAr correlated .44* with change in the first Target Complaint. The fact that these correlations with SSI and Target Complaints were similar to the correlations with the composite outcome

TABLE 12-6

Correlations of Helping Alliance with Outcome Measures

	Rated Benefits	Residual Gain	SSI[a]
HAcs Positive			
Early Sessions	.57**	.58**	.59**
Late Sessions	.58**	.60**	.69***
Early + Late Sessions	.64**	.65**	.73***
HAcs Negative			
Early Sessions	.29	.23	.29
Late Sessions	−.08	−.10	−.21
Early + Late Sessions	.08	.04	−.02
HAcs Difference			
Early Sessions	.31	.34	.32
Late Sessions	.53*	.55*	.69***
Early + Late Sessions	.52*	.55*	.64**
HAr			
Early Sessions	.46*	.44*	.49*
Late Sessions	.33	.37	.44*
Early + Late Sessions	.45*	.46*	.53*

[a]SSI = Sum of success, satisfaction, and improvement outcome ratings by therapist
*p < .05
**p < .01
***p < .001

criteria is not surprising since SSI and Target Complaints were part of the rated benefits composite.

PERSONALITY AND TREATMENT CORRELATES WERE PLENTIFUL

What a measure assesses tends to be revealed by its correlates. Accordingly, this section is a first exploration of a large number of possible correlations derived from both during-treatment and pretreatment measures.

Correlates with During-Treatment Measures

During-treatment measures yielded eight scores: Therapist Facilitating Behaviors (TFB) scores as described in chapter 13 (TFB by the rating method and by the counting signs method, positive and negative and difference scores); Insight rating and Resistance rating (Morgan et al., 1982); Experiencing (Peak) and Experiencing (Sum) (chapter 8). The helping alliance measures were the usual four: HAr, HAcs positive, HAcs negative, and HA difference score. All early and late scores were summed. Therefore, the number of correlations between these HA measures and the other during-treatment measures was 32. By chance alone we might expect about 2 correlations to be significant; in this case 14 were (and 9 of these were even significant at the .01 level).

The TFB measures were constructed because of our interest in learning more about how the helping alliance was formed; as one likely basis we considered the therapist's facilitating or inhibiting behaviors. The Therapist Facilitating Behaviors Counting Signs Manual was fashioned to have parallel content to the Helping Alliance Counting Signs Manual; each subtype in the TFBcs manual has a corresponding subtype in the HAcs manual. Reliability estimates of the TFB measures were generally good. For example, agreement of two judges (MM and LA) with each other on TFBcs was high (early positive, .85***; late positive, .80***).

Some indications of the possible impact of TFB may be revealed by a sample of correlations of HA measures with TFB measures: Early HAr correlated .85*** with early TFBr, .76*** with late TFBr. Early HAcs positive was not significantly correlated with late TFBcs positive; late HAcs positive was correlated with late TFBcs positive .80***. These correlations of HAr and HAcs positive with TFBr and TFBcs positive suggest that the therapist's attempts to facilitate HA behavior were successful or eventually became successful.

The other process measures, those for insight and resistance, were correlated with the HA measure at about the same level. These correlations may imply that when there is a more positive helping alliance experienced by the patient, there is less resistance and more insight.

Correlates with Pretreatment Measures

The significant correlations of each helping alliance measure (early plus late) with pretreatment measures have to be interpreted with some skepticism since there were 84 pretreatment variables in the Penn Psychotherapy Project. The four helping alliance measures were each correlated with the 84 pretreatment measures, making a total of 336 correlations. By chance the number of significant ($p < .05$) correlations might be 17; we found 13. Thus, any of these significant correlations has to be considered with caution. To be safer in the selection of significant correlations for interpretation, we required the measures to have significant correlations with *both* HAr and HAcs; if the correlation was significant with only one of the methods, it had to be nearly significant with the other.

Similarities of patient and therapist. The similarity score was significantly correlated with both HAr and HAcs. The score was based on 10 mainly demographic similarities chosen a priori: age, marital status, children, religion, religious activity, foreign-born parents, institutional affiliation, cognitive style scores on Rod and Frame (Oltman, 1968) and Embedded Figures tests (Witkin, 1949) standardized and combined, education, and occupation. The sum of these 10 basic similarities (allowing 1 point for each item on which patient and therapist were similar) correlated .60** with positive HAcs and .62** with the difference between positive and negative signs, and .53* with HAr. Not all of the 10 similarities contributed equally: Age match and religious activity match contributed the most.

Somatic Problems. The Klein Somatic Scale (Klein, 1960) is a rating by a clinical observer of the patient's physical complaints. It correlated negatively with the helping alliance measures, particularly HAr, e.g., −.58* with total helping alliance as well as −.58* with total therapist facilitating behaviors.

Amount of Life Change. The measure was based on the Holmes and Rahe Life Change Scale (Holmes & Rahe, 1967). It correlated −.52* with HAr and −.48* with TFBr.

Random Assignment of Patients to Therapists. This tended to correlate negatively with both HAr and HAcs measures of helping alliances. The HAcs, for example, correlated −.60** and the HAr −.56** with random assignment.

Competence as a Psychiatrist. The measure was the mean of ratings by other members of the staff who had known the therapist's work over the years. The score was significantly correlated with HAcs difference score (.47*), and with HAcs negative signs ($-.61^{**}$); however, the correlation with the HAr was only .24.

Cognitive Style. Therapists' Embedded Figures Test (Witkin, 1949) correlated with early positive HAcs $.62^{***}$, and with HAcs difference score $.51^{*}$. The comparable correlation for the HAr method was .29.

Psychological Health-Sickness. Measures of psychological health-sickness were inconsistently correlated with the HA measures, e.g., the Health-Sickness Rating Scale (HSRS) (Luborsky, 1962a, 1975b) correlated with positive HAcs $.44^{*}$ but was not significant with HAr.

MULTIPLE CORRELATIONS OF PRETREATMENT WITH DURING-TREATMENT PREDICTORS WERE OF INTEREST

As a last step we tried multiple correlations of the most promising pretreatment with the most promising during-treatment predictors of outcomes of psychotherapy.

The HSRS qualifies as one of the best pretreatment predictors and the helping alliance as the best during-treatment predictor. Thus, standard multiple regression analyses were performed using these two predictor variables, HA and HSRS, with each of two outcome criteria. A sample of these multiple correlations includes: (1) HSRS and early positive HAcs as predictors of rated benefits produced a multiple R of $.61^{*}$. However, the two predictors did not both independently contribute significantly to the multiple; HAcs contributed the most with an F-value of 4.1, which is nearly significant at the .05 level. In separate multiple regressions in combination with the HSRS, the HA negative scores and the HA difference scores were not as strong predictors as the HA positive scores. (2) In multiple regressions with three types of measures—HSRS, HA, and TFB—the HA typically contributed most and TFB added very little.

Discussion

Our main aim was to further develop the Helping Alliance Counting Signs Method (HAcs) as another operational measure for evaluating helping alliances in psychotherapy sessions. As its name implies the method requires the counting of "signs" of the patient's experience of the treatment or the relationship with the therapist as helpful or potentially helpful. It has the merit of informing us about the frequency of different types of helping alliances signs—information that could not come from the HAr method. Two independent judges applied the HAcs manual to the transcripts of the same 20 cases as had been scored by the Helping Alliance Rating Manual (HAr) by two other judges. Twenty-minute segments (or at least 10 pages of transcript) from two early and two late sessions were scored for each patient.

RELIABILITY OF SCORING THE HAcs VERSUS THE HAr MANUALS

Two kinds of agreement were found. (a) The HAcs method showed moderate agreement with the HAr method. (b) The manuals were each applied with moderate interjudge agreement between their respective pairs of judges.

The agreement of the two judges on their sums of HAcs scores, even though they were not based on all of the same items, was moderately good. The sums of scores were not always based on the same two statements because the HAcs method suffers from locational unreliability, i.e., the difficulty of finding the same sentences in the transcripts to score. (Counting signs content analysis systems typically are vulnerable to this unless a separate judge is first assigned to locate the sets of scorable sentences so that the judges can be presented with the same units to score, e.g., as done by Johnston and Holzman, 1979.) However, in the present study, when the scores on the *same* statements are compared, the agreement between judges is satisfactory. Therefore, our conclusion that the inference process is simpler in the HAcs method than in the HAr method applies only to the scoring of the same sentences.

TYPES OF SIGNS SCORED MOST OFTEN BY HAcs

Of the seven subtypes in the manual, the two most frequently scored were those in which the patient reported feeling helped by the therapist or therapy and changed since the beginning of the treatment. From this evidence, these two subtypes form the core of the HAcs manual. They are part of the HA1, a type that we had anticipated would be more frequent than HA2 since it seems more difficult for a patient to develop a sense of working together with the therapist in a joint effort (Type 2) than for a patient to feel that the treatment or therapist was providing help (Type 1). HA2 was also expected to appear later than HA1 in the treatment of the improved patients. That was true for the HAr scoring, but the increase from early to late in treatment was nonsignificant. In fact, HA1 and HA2 were combined in our main scores since they were found to be highly correlated—for HAr the correlation was .93, and for HAcs it was .68.

PREDICTION SUCCESS OF THE HAr AND HAcs METHODS

The main news about prediction of the outcomes of psychotherapy from the HA is that although the two HA methods differ, they both attained moderately successful predictions, with correlations around .5, with the HAcs usually slightly higher than the HAr (table 12-6). In addition, of the four main helping alliance measures (HAr, HAcs positive, HAcs negative, and HAcs difference score) only the HAcs negative was not significantly predictive. The similar level of prediction for the HAr and HAcs also may suggest that the judges for both types were attending to similar signs of the helping alliance concept, which was just what we tried to achieve by giving the raters parallel manuals.

The fact that all HA predictions were based on early sessions, mainly the third and fifth, implies that many patients make an early appraisal of their treatment's benefits. At the same time, practitioners should keep in mind that HA assessments of these early appraisals yield levels of predictive correlations that explain only about 25–36% of the outcome variance, which leaves considerable room for change.

Another important implication for further studies of the predictive value of the helping alliance methods is that their future looks bright. Since the number of signs scored for the HAcs in the two early 20-minute segments of sessions was small, even a slight enlargement of the number of sessions or length of the segments might produce larger predictive correlations.

PRACTICAL VALUE OF EACH METHOD

The HAr method has the practical advantage over the HAcs method of being less time consuming. Eventually the HAr might become even more economical if research shows that it can be done from listening to tape recordings of therapy sessions, thus obviating the need to make transcriptions; by contrast, the HAcs method is likely to continue to require transcripts. Both methods could become displaced by simpler devices, such as the questionnaire method. Supporting this possibility is the work of Barrett-Lennard (1962) and Orlinsky and Howard (1967), which implies that it should be possible to construct patient questionnaires designed to measure something like our helping alliance measures based on the sessions.

Generalization from our results should be confined to samples of patients and treatments like those in the present study, that is, outpatients in moderate-length psychoanalytically oriented psychotherapy. The results reemphasize the importance of establishing a helping alliance as well as the positive impact of similarities of patients and therapists and, to some extent, of the therapist's facilitating behaviors.

EFFECTS OF USING EXTREME GROUPS

We have tried to evaluate the degree to which the predictive power of the two helping alliance measures was inflated by our reliance on the 10 more versus the 10 less improved patients from the larger sample of 73 in the Penn study. We had launched our studies by using these subgroups in order to avoid the huge expense of transcribing sessions from all 73 cases and as a way to get an initial estimate of the value of the methods. Later we tried to learn the effects of having used extreme groups by recalculating the predictive correlations with the 84 pretreatment variables in the Penn study for the 20 cases only. As discussed earlier, only a handful of these correlations were as high as the helping alliance correlations. We concluded that although using extreme groups may inflate some of the predictive correlations, the helping alliance remains the main treatment process predictor with a predictive power at least as good as that of any other pretreatment measure as well as of any early during-treatment measure.

POSSIBLE OVERLAP BETWEEN THE EARLY HELPING ALLIANCE
MEASURES AND THE OUTCOME MEASURES

There may be some overlap between the early helping alliance measures and some aspects of the outcome measures, since in both of these measures the patient is estimating the experience of being helped. To examine the degree of overlap, one approach we tried in the previous chapter was to see the effect of removing the HAr subtype that had the most obvious overlap. But removing that subtype did not affect the predictive correlations. Then, in another approach, we examined the early "improvements" described in the HAcs scores to see whether they were like the improvements in the outcome measures and found them to be pallid versions of the later improvements; for example, Ms. Samuelson reported in the early sessions that she was only slightly beginning to get control over the impulse to continue to see the man she wished to break up with, but in the later sessions she had given him up. Finally, the overlap of the early helping alliance and outcomes measures is only partial—the HA is a patient measure but the outcome measures also include a variety of therapist and clinical observer measures.

Does this partial overlap of predictors and outcome measures seriously limit the value of the research? It might be argued that the overlap should be considered as contamination, in test and measurement terms, which would invalidate the findings—in other words, that we have shown only that early outcome foreshadows later outcome. Yet to hold to this minimal view could miss the larger perspective of the contribution of these methods to psychotherapy research: The helping alliance research provides a novel quantitative examination of the impressive degree to which early helping alliance measures anticipate the outcomes of psychotherapy.

POSITIVE VERSUS NEGATIVE HELPING ALLIANCE SIGNS

Patients express fewer negative signs than positive ones. For the 20 patients, Judge MM scored 66 positive and 54 negative signs; Judge LA, 102 positive and 71 negative. The more improved patients had an overwhelming balance in favor of positive signs (for scores of both raters summed: 151 positive, 71 negative); the 10 less improved had more negative signs (54 negative and only 17 positive). Explanations for these proportions must recognize the fact that the more improved patients were beginning to get what they needed while the less improved patients generally did not get much of what they needed, although none of them could be described as clearly worse off than before treatment (see chapter 3) (Even the less improved patient Ms. Kane, #6, near the end of treatment was sadly disappointed but not markedly worse: T: "Why are you crying?" P: "You are getting worse and I am not getting better.").

Our interpretation of the positive signs as signs of progress is consistent with their predictive value—early positive HAcs signs are reliable harbingers of eventual positive outcomes; the negative HAcs signs are much less reliable as predictors. This correlational finding that early positive HAcs has some predictive value for treatment outcome should give pause to those who are inclined to believe the clinical lore that one should discount early positive relationships as merely a honeymoon phenomenon. Rather, as in love relationships, it may be that yes means yes and no means maybe. *No* here is equated with the negative helping alliance signs, which have relatively little predictive value; some of these patients became positive later and tended to improve, and some stayed negative and tended not to improve.

HELPING ALLIANCE MEASURES UNDERSTOOD THROUGH THEIR CORRELATES

Establishing the predictive success of the helping alliance measures was intended as another step toward a superordinate goal—that of understanding what the helping alliance measures measure. We will move closer to that goal by a discussion of some correlates of the HA measures.

We have seen that the HA measures most often measure the frequency of the patient's statements about beginning to be helped by the therapist or the treatment, or about being better off since starting treatment (although no explanation for the improvement may be given). Apparently the patient makes these kinds of statements because the therapist or the treatment is experienced as providing the kind of relationship that has begun to help the patient move toward the patient's goals. The HA statements obviously could, at times, have additional meanings, such as the patient's intent to commend or to complain to the therapist.

The correlates that we found for the helping alliance measures can be further understood as representing facilitating or impeding conditions that may influence the development of a helping alliance. Among these conditions are the following.

1. The presence of certain basic similarities between patient and therapist apparently facilitates the formation of the patient's experience of a helping alliance with the therapist. Even though the patient may not be told of all of these similarities, their existence may be sensed. This work on the helping alliance appears to fit with the research field sometimes referred to as human attraction. One of the findings in that research is that human attraction is partly mediated by perceived similarity (Byrne, 1971).

2. The presence of somatic problems is an impeding condition. The implication is that the more the patient is beset by somatic problems, the less he or she is likely to form a helping alliance (and the less the therapist is likely to use various ways of facilitating the helping alliance).

3. The amount of life change is an impeding condition. When the patient is engrossed in adapting to the demands posed by life changes, the patient may have less capacity for involvement in the treatment relationship, which would limit the formation of a positive helping alliance.

4. Random assignment of patients to therapists is an impeding condition. It tends to militate against the formation of a positive helping alliance, probably because the patient and therapist may experience the random assignment as a forced assignment. This conclusion is also consistent with the negative correlation of random assignment with outcome of treatment in chapter 8. Presumably, its counterpart, the patient's having a choice, would be facilitative (Luborsky & McLellan, 1981).

5. Competence as a psychiatrist is a facilitating condition for the development of the helping alliance.

6. Relatively field-dependent therapists may be more responsive to their patients and form a closer bond with them; this would be reflected in more positive helping alliance scores. *Relatively* is used to modify *field-dependent* because the therapists as a group had a mean (Embedded Figures Test) score on the field-independent side. Related trends have been reported with these measures, e.g., (a) relatively more field-dependent therapists and patients were found to have a shorter interval between each other's utterances (Witkin, Lewis & Weil, 1968), implying that field

dependence is related to greater social responsiveness; (b) dyads that included one or two field-dependent persons were found to reconcile their differences more often than dyads with two field-independent persons (Oltman et al., 1975). (c) Other leads about other correlates of the helping alliances can be found in the patients' statements within the session about the bases for their choice of the therapist. One patient, Ms. Samuelson, for example, had briefly tried and given up treatment with two other psychotherapists in succession just before the present study. She revealed at the end of the first session with the therapist in our study that she had discontinued with each of these other therapists because she felt they could not help her. But with the therapist in the present study, she announced toward the end of the first session that she expected she could be helped by him because he had narrow feet like the man she was having an affair with. From this and other patients' explanations for their choices of therapists we suggest that when the therapist is perceived as being like someone who was liked or loved, a rapid development of a helping alliance may occur. This perceived congruence might be a special but powerful instance of a version of the similarity principle—in this case between the therapist and a loved person—a kind of transference of positive feelings to the therapist (Freud, 1912a). Such congruence as a basis for the helping alliance, although hard to measure, may often be worth the research effort to determine.

Summary

This chapter reports on the development of a related measure of helping alliances in psychotherapy: the helping alliance counting signs measure. As its name implies, it requires the counting of certain types of patient statements: "signs" of the patient's experience of the treatment or relationship with the therapist as helpful or potentially helpful. The main findings with this method were: (1) the types of statements were found to be scorable with moderate interjudge agreement; (2) scores based on this manual showed moderate agreement with a similar helping alliance manual based on global ratings; (3) scores were fairly to moderately consistent from early to late in treatment; (4) scores predicted outcomes significantly; (5) basic background similarities between patient and therapist, such as in age and religious activity, attained highest correlations with the helping alliance measure.

13

The Therapist's Facilitative
Behaviors for the
Helping Alliance

AFTER CONSTRUCTING the patient measures for the helping alliance we turned our efforts to the next target in the master plan for making a set of operational measures—the therapist's role in facilitating or inhibiting the helping alliance.

As clinicians we expected to find that therapists could do much to foster the helping alliance. But as researchers we had to admit that there was no tested experience on how reliable a clinical judgment of the therapist's behavior could be and how much impact the therapist could have in developing the helping alliance. In fact, we realized that we might even find that the helping alliance was largely a function of behaviors and circumstances that could not easily be judged from a transcript—nonverbal influences such as the regularity of the sessions, the indirect side benefits that accurate interpretations can have for instilling a sense of helping alliance, and the partial recognition on the patient's part that the therapist is there to be helpful and tries to do the job effectively.

This chapter has as its specific aims (1) to describe two measures of therapists' behaviors for facilitating or inhibiting helping alliances, (2) to assess the reliability of the measures, (3) to test the predictive effectiveness of the measures, and (4) to examine correlates of the measures in terms of the conditions under which therapists convey facilitating behaviors or inhibiting behaviors.

Procedure

The subjects are the same sample of 20 patients, 10 more improved (MI) and 10 less improved (LI), and the same sessions as described in the earlier chapters on the helping alliance.

The Therapist Facilitative Behaviors Rating Scale (TFBr) consists of 10 items that parallel the items on the Helping Alliance Rating Scale (HAr). Like the HAr scale, the TFBr scale is divided into two types: Type 1 refers to the therapist's facilitating behaviors (e.g., the therapist conveys a sense of hopefulness that the treatment goals can be achieved), and Type 2 refers to the therapist's facilitating a joint effort (e.g., the therapist shows that he feels a "we" bond with the patient). Each item is rated on a 10-point Likert-type scale reflecting the degree to which each item was present in the session.

The Therapist Facilitating Behaviors Counting Signs (TFBcs) method consists of items similar to those in the TFBr, but the judge scores and counts all signs of each item in the transcript rather than providing only a global rating of their intensity.

Results

INTERJUDGE AGREEMENT FOR TFBcs AND TFBr WAS HIGH

The two judges who did the independent scoring of the helping alliance rating method and the two other judges who did the independent scoring of the helping alliance counting signs method did the scoring on the two present measures.

The TFBcs showed considerable agreement between the pair of judges (table 13-1). The agreement for the early sessions was considerably higher than the agreement for the late sessions. In the early sessions there may be more explicit evidences of what the therapist is trying to do in terms of facilitating behaviors. The agreement between the two judges for the TFBr ranged from .77 to .88 (median = .85) for the 10 items. Internal consistency (Cronbach's alpha) for the sum of the 10 items on the TFBr scale was .94. The sum score for the 10 items was used in all further analyses.

The two measures, TFBcs and TFBr, showed only modest agreement

TABLE 13-1

Agreement (Correlations) of Two Judges on Number of TFBcs Signs Scored
(N = 20)

	Judge 2 (LA)					
Judge 1 (MM)	Early Sessions		Late Sessions		Early + Late Sessions	
	Positive	Negative	Positive	Negative	Positive	Negative
Positive	.85***		.33		.54*	
Negative		.80***		.59**		.67***

*p < .05
***p < .001

TABLE 13-2

Agreement (Correlations) between
TFBcs and TFBr

TFBcs	r
Early Sessions' Ratings	
Positive	.25
Negative	−.06
Difference	.21
Late Sessions' Ratings	
Positive	.66**
Negative	−.21
Difference	.66**
Early Plus Late Sessions' Ratings	
Positive	.59**
Negative	−.24
Difference	.56**

NOTE: TFBcs scores are each correlated
with the single score for TFBr.
**p < .01

TABLE 13-3

Consistency of HA and TFB Scores from
Early Sessions to Late Sessions (N = 20)

	Positive	Negative	Difference
For HAcs	.58**	.18	.47*
For TFBcs	.16	.26	.32
For HAr	.53*		
For TFBr	.30		

*p < .05
**p < .01

with each other (table 13-2). The agreement was higher for the positive signs than for the negative signs. Very likely this results partly from the larger number of positive signs.

The consistency from early to late of the TFBcs scores was slight. To provide a contrast, we included in table 13-3 the consistency from early to late for HAcs, which can be seen to be much larger.

CORRELATIONS OF TFB WITH HA MEASURES WERE HIGH

One of the main reasons for constructing the TFB measures was our interest in learning more about how the helping alliance was formed. The helping alliance might be significantly facilitated by the TFB. At least, there is evidence of some considerable association between the two types of measures, e.g., early HAr correlated .85*** with early TFBr; late HAr correlated .76*** with late TFBr. Early HAcs positive was not significantly correlated with early TFBcs positive; late HAcs positive was correlated with late TFBcs positive, $r = .80***$. In addition, late positive TFBcs correlated .81*** with late HAr and late TFBr correlated .44* with late positive HAcs, which suggests that the associations between HA and TFB were not due solely to shared method variance. These significant correlations may imply that the therapists' attempts to facilitate HA behavior were successful. The correlations for late HAcs positive and late TFBcs positive perhaps suggest that the therapist's attempts eventually (i.e., at the late stage) became successful.

CORRELATIONS OF TFB WITH OUTCOME MEASURES WERE LOW

Therapist facilitating behaviors measures are not as predictive of outcome as are the helping alliance measures (table 13-4). For the two usual outcome measures, rated benefits and residual gain, TFBcs showed no significant correlation. For the TFBr, the early TFBr was significant at the .05 level ($r = .45$). We did not expect the TFB measures to relate as highly to outcome as the HA measures did. One possible explanation is that the TFB has its direct effects on the HA, and only indirectly affects outcome through its association with HA. In other words, the causal sequence would be: TFB → HA → Outcome.

CORRELATES OF TFB WERE LIKE THE CORRELATES OF HA

In order to understand the possible determinants of the TFB, we correlated with the TFBr and the TFBcs the wide range of predictive tests that were obtained in the Penn Psychotherapy Project. Data from early and late

TABLE 13-4

Correlations of TFB Measures with Outcome Measures
$(N = 20)$

	Rated Benefits	Residual Gain	SSI[a]
TFBcs Positive			
Early Sessions	.31	.18	.30
Late Sessions	.28	.31	.39
Early + Late Sessions	.39	.32	.46*
TFBcs Negative			
Early Sessions	−.19	−.29	−.09
Late Sessions	−.36	−.24	−.36
Early + Late Sessions	−.26	−.32	−.17
TFBcs Difference			
Early Sessions	.34	.32	.27
Late Sessions	.36	.35	.46*
Early + Late Sessions	.43	.41	.42
TFBr			
Early Sessions	.45*	.39	.45*
Late Sessions	.00	.21	.00
Early + Late Sessions	.27	.37	.19

[a]SSI = Sum of success, satisfaction, and improvement ratings by therapist.
*$p < .05$

sessions were summed for the TFB measures. Since the TFB measures were highly correlated with the HA measures, the TFB scales were significantly related to many of the same variables as the HA. For example, like HAr, TFBr was significantly correlated with the Life Change and Klein Somatic scales ($−.48*$ and $−.58**$, respectively). TFBr was also significantly correlated ($.50*$) with the supervisor's rating of competence as a psychiatrist, while the negative TFBcs was negatively correlated with the same rating ($−.44*$). Similar types of correlations with the HAcs difference score and HAcs negative had been found. The one major exception to the trend was that the similarity scale (sum of 10 different patient–therapist demographic match variables), which had correlated highly with the HA scales, was not significantly related to the TFB scales. Only one variable, the subscale "interrupting the patient is acceptable" from the Therapist Orientation questionnaire, demonstrated a significant correlation with a TFB measure ($.49*$ with TFBcs positive) but not with an HA scale.

Summary

Because the helping alliance measures were so highly related to outcome, we tried to understand them better by examining their correlates, especially how much the therapists' behaviors were associated with the alliance.

1. We constructed two moderately reliable measures of therapist facilitating behaviors for the helping alliance, a rated measure and a counting signs measure.

2. The evidence was strong that high levels of TFB were associated with high levels of the HA. One interpretation might be that the TFB is one of the factors influencing the formation of a positive HA.

3. But unlike the HA measures, the TFB measures were generally not significantly correlated with the outcome measures, with one exception: The TFB rated measure was significantly associated with the rated benefits outcome measures (.45*). Together with the evidence from the correlations of HA with outcome, this probably implies that therapists' efforts to improve the helping alliance end up at least slightly improving the outcomes of the treatments.

4. The correlates of TFB with other measures were generally similar to those of the HA.

14

The Helping Alliance
Questionnaire

THE MAIN AIM of this chapter is to examine the Helping Alliance Questionnaire (HAq) method and its performance in predicting outcomes of psychotherapy. It had already been clear when our study of the HAq started that the session-based Helping Alliance methods, HAr and HAcs, could predict the outcomes of psychotherapy. With the support of those results we (including A. Thomas McLellan and George Woody) were led to investigate whether the far simpler HAq method based on a self-report questionnaire could predict as well. Even more encouragement came from results of apparently related self-report questionnaires by Barrett-Lennard (1962) and Orlinsky and Howard (1975), which suggested that such an approach could be significantly predictive of outcomes of psychotherapy. The second aim of this chapter is to explore other correlates of the HAq as a way to gain further understanding of what might be measured by it.

To construct the HAq, the 11 categories of the Helping Alliance Rating Method and the Helping Alliance Counting Signs Method were recast in the form of a set of 11 questionnaire items. Each question was to be rated by the patient and therapist on a 5-point graphic scale from "1" (little or none) to "5" (very much) at the end of the third session; the ratings were summed to produce a total score.

Application of the HAq in the VA-Penn Study

The HAq was first tried in the VA-Penn study (Woody et al., 1983), which was getting underway when the HAq was on the drawing board. The aim of that study was to determine whether psychotherapy added significantly to the usual treatments for drug dependence provided in most clinics by methadone and drug counseling. The main results with the HAq are discussed in Luborsky, McLellan, Woody et al., 1985.

Drug-dependent patients were randomly assigned to one of three 6-month treatments: drug counseling (DC) alone, drug counseling plus supportive-expressive (SE) psychotherapy, and drug counseling plus cognitive-behavioral (CB) psychotherapy. A description of each treatment is provided in Woody et al., 1983.

Patients were encouraged to attend all of the once-a-week psychotherapy sessions. Their actual attendance ranged from the mandatory 3 to the maximum allotted of 24 sessions, with a mean of about 12 sessions for patients in psychotherapy and 16 counseling sessions for patients in drug counseling. The treatments were carried out by well-trained therapists who were guided by special treatment manuals for their respective therapies. The extent to which the therapists adhered to the techniques described in their manual was rated from tape recorded sessions by two independent, experienced judges. The benefits from the three types of treatments were judged by comparisons of admission and 7-month evaluations (Woody et al., 1983; Luborsky, Woody, et al., 1982).

THERAPISTS AND PATIENTS

Eighteen drug counselors and nine psychotherapists (five SE and four CB) participated. All but two psychotherapists had either M.D. or Ph.D. degrees; all had had at least 2 years of clinical experience since completing training, as well as some experience with addicts or alcoholics.

The patient samples included 39 in DC, 32 in DC plus SE, and 39 in DC plus CB. All were male veterans between 18 and 55 years of age, nonpsychotic, without a persistent or clinically significant organic brain syndrome, and at the beginning of a new drug abuse treatment episode. Only about 10% of new patients in our methadone maintenance clinic were eliminated by these criteria, which indicates that the subject pool was representative of the treated population. All patients received the Drug Use Disorder diagnosis based on the Lifetime Research Diagnostic Criteria (RDC). This group of patients had much in common with patients who are typically provided with psychotherapy: The most common diagnoses were affective disorder—especially major depressive disorder (43%)—and anxiety disorders (9%), although our patients had a higher percentage of antisocial personality (15%) than other psychotherapy-treated patient groups.

MEASURES OF TREATMENT OUTCOMES

Self-report psychological tests measuring affect, cognition, and other psychiatric symptoms were administered to each patient at the start of treatment and at the 7-month follow-up. These were the Beck Depression Inventory (Beck & Beck, 1972), the Maudsley Personality Inventory (Eysenck, 1959), the Hopkins Symptom Checklist-90 (SCL-90) (Derogatis et al., 1974), and the Shipley Institute of Living Scale.

The Addiction Severity Index, or ASI (McLellan et al., 1985), was also administered to all patients at the same times. The ASI is a clinical and research interview, designed to assess problem severity in seven areas of functioning commonly impaired in drug-dependent patients: medical, employment/support, drug abuse, alcohol abuse, legal, family/social, and psychiatric. In each of these areas, both objective and subjective questions are asked to measure the number, extent, and duration of problem symptoms in the patient's lifetime and in the past 30 days. Sets of objective and subjective items from each of the problem areas are standardized and summed to produce composite or factor scores that provide reliable and valid general estimates of problem severity at each evaluation point (McLellan et al., 1985). The use of the objective information base may have been an important contributor to the high reliability obtained.

Patients usually benefited from all three treatments, especially in terms of a reduction in drug use and criminal activity. However, in the two psychotherapies, significantly more than in the drug counseling alone, there was a reduction in psychiatric symptoms and overall use of medications, both prescribed and nonprescribed (Woody et al., 1983).

RESULTS

The HAq Predicted Treatment Outcome

The HAq was administered after the third therapy session to both therapists and patients. The total scores on the patients' HAq were correlated with the patients' 7-month outcomes to determine the degree of predictive capacity. The HAq was filled out by both the patient and the therapist independently. Because the results for each HAq were mostly similar, only the correlations between the patient's HAq scores and their 7-month out-comes are given in table 14-1. The correlations ranged from .51 with legal status to .72 with drug use, and all were statistically significant ($p < .01$). The predictive results tended to be higher than ones obtained through the HAr and HAcs, even though the HAr and the HAcs analyses had been done only on extreme groups. In addition, the level of the predictive correlations based on the HAq were as high or higher than those reported in other studies with therapeutic alliance measures (see chapter 19). In conclusion, our findings show that even this brief, uncomplicated Helping Alliance Questionnaire administered after only three sessions can perform quite well predictively in comparison with session-based measures, as well as in comparison with the results of other studies using either session-based or questionnaire-based measures.

The Therapists' Conformity to Their Therapy Manuals Predicted Treatment Outcome

Ratings of taped therapy session transcripts had been made by two independent raters using manual-based criteria. It was therefore possible to relate any differences in the performance of the therapy to the differences in treatment outcomes.

We proceeded in the following manner: The units of analysis were 15-minute samples of tape recorded therapy sessions randomly selected from each of the three treatments. Due to the time and cost of having these taped sessions transcribed and rated, we used a representative sample of each therapist's performance by including only those patients for whom

TABLE 14-1

Correlations between Patients' Helping Alliance and Seven-Month Outcomes

Outcomes	Helping Alliance Questionnaire Total Score[a]
Drug Use	.72**
Employment	.70**
Legal Status	.51**
Psychological Function	.58**

[a]Scores represent the total on eleven 5-point measures of patients' perception of the extent to which their counselor or therapist understood their problems and was able to help them. Scores are based on ratings by 77 patients of nine therapists.
**$p < .01$
Source: Luborsky et al., 1985.

we had at least three taped therapy sessions. Thus, for the purposes of analyzing therapy characteristics, the sample included 14 patients treated by three SE therapists, 15 patients treated by three CB therapists, and 12 patients treated by three DC therapists.

Measures of Therapists' Conformity to the Manuals. All taped therapy sessions were rated by two experienced judges using rating forms based on "core characteristics" of therapy derived from each of the three treatment manuals (Luborsky, Woody, et al., 1982). Examples of core SE characteristics included "degree to which therapy is focused on giving support," ". . . understanding feelings and relationships," and so on. Examples of core CB characteristics included "degree to which therapy is focused on cognitive distortions," ". . . on behavioral techniques," and so on. Examples of core DC characteristics included "degree to which treatment monitors current drug problems," ". . . initiates liaison functions," and so on.

The rating form included four characteristics for each therapy, and the presence of each characteristic was rated using a 5-point scale (0, "not at all" to 4, "very much"). Three global ratings were also made using the same 5-point scale: "the degree to which the session fit the specifications of SE," ". . . of CB, ". . . of DC therapy." Thus, every session was rated for the presence of all of the core characteristics of SE, CB, and DC. (Luborsky, Woody, et al., 1982, describes the manuals, the rating criteria, and the tape judging procedure.)

In table 14-2, we have given the mean global "conformity" ratings (SE, CB, and DC) for the tapes of each therapist, as well as what we will refer to as an index of "purity." This measure is simply the ratio of the intended therapy rating (SE for SE therapists, CB for CB therapists, etc.) to the total of all ratings (SE, CB, and DC). A "pure" session would have a high rating on the presence of intended therapy qualities and a low rating on the presence of the other therapy qualities.

Results of this examination indicate that there were clear differences among the therapists in the nature of their treatment techniques and in the purity of their sessions. A nonparametric analysis of proportions showed significant differences in purity among the SE therapists and among the DC therapists ($p < .05$) but not among the CB therapists, due to greater variability in session content among all CB therapists. In addition, the mean purity rating of the CB group was significantly ($p < .05$) lower than for either the SE or DC groups; these groups did not differ from each other.

Relation between therapy qualities and seven-month outcome. We examined the relationships among the therapy qualities and patient outcomes by performing Pearson product-moment correlations among the rated therapy qualities (SE, CB, DC, and purity) and their adjusted 7-month outcome measures for the 41 subjects. Positive correlations in table 14-3 indicate

TABLE 14-2

Ratings of Tapes for Specific Therapeutic Qualities

Therapist	N Patients	N Tapes	SE Qualities	CB Qualities	DC Qualities	Purity[a]
A	6	22	2.8	0.0	0.0	1.00
B	4	16	2.5	0.2	0.4	0.81
C	4	12	2.1	0.2	0.8	0.68
SE Average	14	50	2.5	0.1	0.4	0.83
D	5	28	1.0	3.2	1.0	0.61
E	6	16	1.7	2.6	0.6	0.53
F	4	12	1.7	2.4	0.8	0.49
CB Average	15	56	1.5	2.7	0.8	0.54
G	4	14	0.3	0.0	3.7	0.92
H	4	15	0.5	0.2	3.0	0.81
I	4	17	0.9	0.3	3.7	0.76
DC Average	12	46	0.8	0.1	3.4	0.83

NOTE: Scores reflect global ratings of the degree to which sessions contain qualities of the particular therapy (0, "not at all"; 4, "very much"). SE indicates supportive-expressive; CB, cognitive-behavioral; and DC, drug counseling.
[a]Purity is the ratio of the intended qualities (SE for SE therapists, CB for CB therapists, etc) to the total of all ratings (SE + CB + DC).
SOURCE: Luborsky et al., 1986.

that greater frequency of a particular therapy quality was associated with better outcome on a given criterion even after outcomes were adjusted for different pretreatment levels.

The coefficients in the first row of table 14-3 show that the presence of SE qualities in therapy sessions was highly related to patient improvement. The coefficients in the second row indicate a somewhat lesser degree of relationship between the frequency of CB qualities and patient outcome. The coefficients in the third row indicate that DC qualities in therapy sessions were not well related to patient improvement. In fact, DC qualities appeared to be negatively related to patient outcome in the measures of psychiatric status.

The correlations in table 14-3 are presented for the total patient sample. However, it is important and interesting to note that the same relationships seen between the therapy ratings and the patient outcome measures were also seen, although not always to the same degree, when the patients in the SE, CB, and DC groups were examined separately. Thus, even in patients in the CB and DC groups, there was a positive relationship between the frequency of SE qualities and better 7-month outcome. Similarly, even in patients in the DC group, the frequency of DC qualities was only modestly related to better patient outcome in the areas of drug use, employment, and legal status and negatively related to outcome in psychi-

TABLE 14-3

Correlations Between Ratings of Therapy Qualities ("Purity") and Seven-Month Outcomes in 41 Patients

Therapy Qualities	Outcome Measures						
	Drug Use	Legal Status	Employ- ment Status	Psycho- logical Status	SCL- 90	Maudsley N Scale	Beck Depres- sion Scale
SE[a] Rating	.44**	.39*	.41**	.46**	.40**	.30**	.37**
CB[b] Rating	.12	.24*	.26*	.29*	.34**	.21	.29*
DC[c] Rating	.18	.06	.11	−.10	−.26*	−.20	.04
Purity[d]	.47**	.50**	.49*	.42**	.40**	.36**	.38**

NOTE: Ratings were based on judgments by independent raters of the extent to which sessions contained "core characteristics" of each form of therapy (0 = "not at all," 4 = "very much").
[a]Supportive-expressive psychotherapy
[b]Cognitive-behavioral psychotherapy
[c]Drug counseling
[d]Ratio of intended qualities to total of ratings
*p < .05
**p < .01
SOURCE: Luborsky et al., 1986.

atric status; and, in fact, even in this counseling group therapy qualities (SE or CB) were related to better outcomes.

Significant relationships were also seen between the purity measure and the adjusted 7-month outcome measures (last row, table 14-3). These relationships were particularly significant (p < .001) for the two psychotherapy groups but were either nonsignificant or only marginally significant in the DC group. The result seen from these data was that at least in the two psychotherapy groups, a higher proportion of intended qualities in the therapy was related to better 7-month outcomes in all areas. The association can be causally interpreted in either direction—the more the therapists did what they were "supposed" to do, the better the patient outcome, or, the better the patient outcome, the more the therapists did what they were supposed to do.

Therapy qualities and seven-month outcome—an analysis within therapists. These results suggested two possible relationships. First, it was possible that the personality qualities, the relationship qualities, and the therapy qualities of the therapists were all somewhat independent and that each factor partially accounted for some separate portion of the differences seen in outcomes. Alternatively, it was possible that the most effective therapists were those who also happened to form better helping alliances with their patients and that their personality qualities and purity of treatment measures were all part of a single constellation of therapist personality qualities.

It is usually possible to partial out the unique contribution of several potentially related predictive factors through the use of multiple regression techniques. In this case, however, we were restricted by the fact that patients in each therapist's caseload would obviously have the same therapist characteristic scores, since they had the same therapist. This produced interdependent predictor measures and reduced the effective sample size to nine, which is the number of therapists.

As an alternative to this analysis, we noticed that even within the caseload of a given therapist, some patients had received relatively pure sessions while others had received sessions with more diverse therapy qualities. We reasoned that if we ranked a therapist's patients on the average purity of their sessions and also ranked them on their 7-month outcome status, it would be possible to compare the rankings to determine whether there was a relationship between receiving purer therapy and having a better outcome. Obviously, this type of analysis would control for some differences among therapists by giving a within-therapist measure of purity of therapy in determining a patient's outcome.

Three patients from each therapist were ranked on the average purity of the sessions they received and on their outcome criteria. The ranks for all therapists were summed and are presented in table 14-4. The data indicate that 6 patients who were ranked as having the purest therapy within their therapist's caseload also had the highest ranking within their therapist's caseload on the 7-month outcome criterion of drug use. Thus, 6 of the 27 patients (9 therapists times 3 patients) who scored highest in purity also scored highest in drug use outcome. Similarly, 6 patients who were ranked second in purity were also ranked second in drug use outcome within their therapist's caseload.

Results of the chi-square analyses of these rankings indicate a significant ($p < .001$) relation between receiving a high proportion of intended qualities (i.e., purer therapy) and having better posttreatment outcomes in drug use, employment, and psychological status. This relation is significant even within the caseload of a given therapist. These data suggest that the manner in which the therapist delivered therapy was also an important and independent predictor of outcome.

Therapists' Personality Qualities Were Only Slightly Related to Treatment Outcome

Qualities of the therapist tend to be less accessible to researchers than patient qualities, and probably for this reason they have not received

TABLE 14-4

*Analysis of Within-Therapist Purity Rankings and
Within-Therapist Outcome Rankings in Nine
Therapists (with Three Patients Each)*

	Purity Ranking	Outcome Ranking		
		1	2	3
Drug Use at 7 Months[a]	1	6	2	1
	2	2	6	1
	3	0	2	7
Employment at 7 Months[b]	1	5	2	2
	2	3	6	0
	3	0	2	7
Psychiatric status at 7 Months[c]	1	6	2	1
	2	1	6	2
	3	0	2	7

[a]$\chi^2 = 18.2$; $df = 4$; $p < .001$
[b]$\chi^2 = 16.6$; $df = 4$; $p < .001$
[c]$\chi^2 = 18.3$; $df = 4$; $p < .001$
SOURCE: Luborsky et al., 1986.

appropriate research attention, particularly as measured apart from the sessions. Two reviews attest to this deficiency (Parloff, Waskow & Wolfe, 1978; see also chapter 19). Furthermore, even within the studies reported, only a few promising qualities are found to be predictive of outcome: the therapist's adjustment, skill, and interest in helping patients. Based on this prior work and on the opinions of experts about well and poorly functioning therapists (Holt & Luborsky, 1958b) we developed eleven 5-point rating scales to measure these three qualities (Luborsky, 1982). A score of 1 represented the lowest level of development on that characteristic, and 5 represented the highest. Ratings were made by three judges who were not part of the psychotherapy study but who were clinically experienced and were familiar with the therapists' work. Reliability measures (Spearman-Brown rho) for the judges on their ratings of the nine therapists yielded correlations of .89 or higher on all items. These high correlations suggest a high level of familiarity with and agreement about the therapists.

To find how these 11 personality items were related, intercorrelations were carried out and factor analyzed. One large factor and one smaller one appeared. The large factor is best labeled "interest in helping patients" because of highest loadings on "tends to be very persistent in trying to help," "unusually interested in helping patients," "has a very supportive effect," and "is liked very much by patients." The smaller factor is best labeled "psychological health and skill," with the four highest loadings being on "unusually psychologically healthy," "unusually good adjustment," "very capable and skillful therapist," and "much above average in avoiding being directive and authoritarian."

We correlated the mean ratings on each of the two factors with the patients' mean adjusted 7-month outcome scores; as can be seen in table 14-5, there were moderately positive correlations between them. These data indicate that the effectiveness of a therapist is due in part to the therapist's interest in helping patients as well as his or her adjustment and skill, although in our data the association with outcome did not reach statistical significance because of small sample size.

The Three Correlates, HAq, Purity, and Personality, Were Interrelated

Since we found that each of the three correlates was separately related to outcome, we thought it would be helpful to see how they related to each other. The mean intercorrelation for the nine therapists was .63, which indicates much interrelatedness but some independence as well. This conclusion was also implied by our within-therapist analysis of the purity measure, which disclosed that regardless of the contribution from the therapist's personal qualities and from ability to form a helping alliance with the patient (themselves independently and jointly important to outcome), the extent to which the therapy was consistent with the manual was independently and significantly related to patient outcome.

To go further in understanding how these three types of correlates were interrelated and how they influenced treatment outcomes, we have to rely on a partly intuitive analysis of our findings:

First, the therapist's personal qualities were most highly correlated with

TABLE 14-5

Correlations among Therapists' Personality Qualities and Patients' Seven-Month Outcomes

	Therapist Characteristics[a]	
Outcomes	Interest in Helping Patients	Psychological Health and Skill
Drug Use	.41	.33
Employment	.34	.37
Legal Status	.31	.40
Psychological Function	.44	.41

[a]Characteristics were rated on a 5-point scale (see text). Ratings were made by three independent judges on nine therapists.
Source: Luborsky et al., 1986.

the helping alliance measure (.74), but not as highly related to treatment outcomes ($M = .32$) as were the helping alliance ($M = .65$) and the purity measures ($M = .44$). Therefore, we believe that the therapist's personal qualities may have exerted their main influence through the ability to form helping alliances.

Second, this interpretation of the helping alliance as a product of a therapist characteristic is supported by a previous study (Luborsky et al., 1983), which reported a moderately high correlation between therapist facilitative behaviors and the helping alliance. Furthermore, since the helping alliance measure was more highly correlated with outcome than were either of the other two qualities, we believe that the therapist's ability to form an alliance may be the most crucial determinant of effectiveness. On the other hand, there is some evidence that the helping alliance is also influenced by qualities that the patient brings to treatment. It is consistent with this view that moderately high correlations have been reported between similarities of patient and therapist and the helping alliance (Luborsky et al., 1983). On balance then, the helping alliance appears to be an interactive product of therapist and patient qualities.

Third, the high correlation between purity of technique and patient outcome suggests that once a helping alliance is formed, the therapists who do what they are supposed to do achieve their effectiveness in this way. However, an equally tenable, reverse-direction interpretation may apply, that it is the patient's experience of a helping alliance that enables the therapist to adhere to the therapist's intended technique.

Finally, we need to consider the extent to which our findings can be generalized to psychotherapy with nonaddicted patients. It is a natural issue to raise because of the range of professional opinion about the differences of addicted patients from other patients who more readily come to psychotherapy. Therefore, we have examined our findings with this question in mind. We noted that the diagnoses from the Schedule for Affective Disorders and Schizophrenia-Research Diagnostic Criteria have much in common with those of other patients receiving psychotherapy—except for addiction and antisocial personality, the main diagnoses are depression and anxiety (Woody et al., 1983). The psychotherapies had clear effects on these symptoms, much as they do for nonaddicted patients. Since many of the symptoms and the ameliorative effects of the psychotherapy are similar to those with other patients, it implies that many of the factors influencing outcome are similar to those with other patients. Furthermore, the main factors that predict outcome in this group are like those that generally predict outcomes. In conclusion, our view—which is shared by the therapists in our study—is that despite the differences mentioned for the addicted patients, the therapist qualities required for treating these

patients have much in common with those required for treating many
other types of patients.

The HAq was Related to Outcome Even within the Antisocial Personality Subgroup

It is well known that patients with antisocial personality (ASP) are
unlikely to benefit from the usual forms of psychological treatments, particularly psychotherapy (Woody et al., 1985). One of the main interpretations of these results is that these patients are not capable of forming a
meaningful relationship with a therapist and therefore are unable to benefit from psychotherapy. However, Woody et al. (1985) have shown that
not all ASP patients have a poor prognosis—an ASP diagnosis in combination with some other diagnosis, such as depression, was associated with a
somewhat better outcome of psychotherapy, although the poorest outcome was for those with a diagnosis of ASP alone.

The substudy to be described (Gerstley et al., 1988), from the Woody
et al. (1985) sample, examines the basis for treatability by measuring the
capacity of the patients to form a helping alliance and correlating this
capacity with the outcomes of psychotherapy. In this study 36 patients in
psychotherapy and 53 patients in counseling were diagnosed according to
DSM-III with antisocial personality. The findings showed significant correlations for the 36 ASP patients in psychotherapy between the HAq
(given at the end of the third session) and the 7-month treatment outcomes. However, for the 53 antisocial patients in drug counseling no significant correlation was attained.

The patients' HAq, for example, correlated .50** with the Addiction
Severity Index employment composite and .40* with the ASI drug composite. (The level of these correlations, predictably, is much like the level
for the entire group that was reported earlier.) Furthermore, a multiple
correlation of the patients' assessment of the helping alliance with all of
the outcome scores (for $n = 20$) was .76*. The multiple correlation coefficient indicates the correlation between the complete set of adjusted outcome measures (that is, the ASI composites of drug and alcohol, employment, legal, and medical and the SCL-90 total) and the helping alliance
measure.

The implication is that even among methadone-maintained opiate addicts with a DSM-III diagnosis of antisocial personality disorder, there is
considerable variability in the ability to form a therapeutic alliance; although this patient group has an especially poor prognosis for psychotherapy, the ability to develop a helping alliance is significantly associated with

the outcome from professional psychotherapy. It is not clear why the drug counseling patients did not also show such an association, although the HAq scores for the drug counseling group within these antisocial patients were significantly lower than those of the psychotherapy groups. It is likely that the counselors were less able to develop a beneficial relationship with many of the patients.

Application of the HAq within the Re-pairing Opportunity Program

We designed the re-pairing study to provide more knowledge about the best bases for optimal patient–therapist matching. We call it that because each patient was given the opportunity to pair with two different therapists for two sessions each and then choose one of the two to re-pair with for further treatment.

PAST RESEARCH

The present study builds on the Penn Psychotherapy study finding that random assignment of patients to therapists was not as beneficial as therapist-selected assignment of patients (chapter 8). The patients of therapists who had had some choice in selecting their patients improved more than patients whose therapists had no part in the patient selection process.

In spite of the widespread view that clients have privileges and rights as consumers, only a few studies were found where the client rather than the therapist had some choice in the selection process. Three of these will be noted here; all found that having a choice is beneficial to the subjects or patients. In one analogue study (Devine & Fernald, 1973) choice was based on the subjects' having viewed videotapes of four therapists who had described and illustrated their techniques for treating fear of snakes. In another analogue study (Gordon, 1976) choice was based on a brief verbal description of two different relaxation treatments. In both studies, the subjects who were involved in a treatment selection procedure had higher ratings of actual or possible improvement than did control subjects.

Another study of client choice (Ersner-Hershfield, Abramowitz & Barren, 1979) used a community mental health center to study the effects on the frequency of attending the first session for patients who had a choice of two therapists with different therapy styles versus patients who were assigned on the usual rotating basis. In a phone interview one group of subjects was given two descriptions, one of a therapist with a relatively active therapeutic style and another of a therapist with a relatively reflective style. Patients stated their choice over the phone and were scheduled with the next available therapist who had the selected style. As predicted, a significantly greater proportion of choice- than nonchoice-condition patients appeared for the initial interview. A significant proportion of these patients also favored the active over the reflective therapy style. But there were no significant differences on client and therapist evaluations of the initial interview. Also there were no data on the effects over the course of the therapy.

AIMS

The aims of our study were (1) to examine the degree to which the helping alliance was involved in making the choice and (2) to examine the degree to which a positive helping alliance as measured by the helping alliance questionnaire predicted the outcome of psychotherapy.

Our main hypotheses were: (1) Patients choose a therapist with whom they feel they can establish a helping alliance, and (2) a positive helping alliance will be associated with greater benefits from psychotherapy.

PROCEDURE

This study was set up somewhat like the VA-Penn study, so as to examine the predictive power of the HAq for the outcomes of psychotherapy. In terms of its design, this study is unique in providing patients an opportunity to choose a therapist, based on an actual therapy experience. We felt that having actual experience with the prospective therapist would better guide the patient's choice than just hearing about styles of therapy or watching a videotape of the therapist in action.

The basic plan was that each patient who elected to be part of the Re-pairing Opportunity Program would be randomly assigned to one therapist with whom he or she would have two psychotherapy sessions and then switch to a second therapist for another two sessions. At the end of the second session and at the end of the fourth session, the patient would be interviewed about the basis for a choice. At the end of the fourth session the patient would choose the therapist with whom to continue treatment. The main measure used was the HAq.

The therapists were third- and fourth-year psychiatric residents and

Ph.D. postdoctoral psychologists at the outpatient psychiatric department of the Hospital of the University of Pennsylvania.

All patients were selected from those applying for treatment at the outpatient psychiatric department. Patients were not eligible for the study if they were (1) emergency cases in need of immediate treatment, (2) organically impaired, (3) clearly schizophrenic, or (4) significantly cognitively impaired. Eligible patients were told of a special program at the clinic that allowed some patients to work with two different therapists and then choose one to continue in treatment with.

The major psychotherapeutic orientation in the outpatient department was psychodynamic, and the therapists primarily were engaged in psychodynamic psychotherapy, mostly following principles in the *Manual for Supportive-Expressive Treatment* (Luborsky, 1984).

RESULTS

The response of most of the patients who were offered the Re-pairing Opportunity Program was favorable. The patients liked the idea of having some choice of therapist. When presented with the description of the program, patients often said, "It sounds interesting," or "It should be helpful to me because I relate better to some people than to others." (At the time of this writing, further results on the prediction of outcomes by the HAq are not available.)

Summary

Two experiences with the Helping Alliance Questionnaire (HAq) were examined for the predictive capacity of the method. The first, in the VA-Penn Psychotherapy Study, yielded these findings:

1. The HAq significantly predicted treatment outcome. The level of prediction was as least as good as that for the session-based helping alliance methods.

2. The therapists' conformity to their treatment manuals ("purity") significantly predicted treatment outcome, both across and within therapists.

3. The therapists' personality qualities were slightly, but not significantly, related to treatment outcomes.

4. The three measures, HAq, purity, and personality, were moderately related to each other (mean $r = .63$).

5. Even within the antisocial personality subgroup, the HAq was significantly related to outcome. The second experience with the HAq was with the Penn Re-pairing Opportunity Program. With this sample the HAq has not yet been related to outcome.

Another study of the HAq is needed in which in the same sample the intercorrelation of the HAq with the two session-based helping alliance methods can be examined.

15

The Central Relationship Pattern:
The Core Conflictual
Relationship Theme Method

AFTER each success in prediction based on measures of Curative Factor 1, the helping alliance, we were further convinced that this factor had the most curative power and that the other factors, such as accuracy of interpretation and self-understanding, were not likely to be as predictive.

A heavy emphasis on Factor 1 is not consistent with psychoanalytic psychotherapy's most written about theory of psychotherapeutic change, which is copiously cognitive. It concentrates on the need for the therapist to acquire and communicate understanding of the patient's conscious and unconscious cognitions about relationships with others and with the self. Much of a psychodynamic psychotherapist's attention during a therapy session is on forming an accurate concept of the patient's central relationship pattern. As the concept becomes further articulated, the therapist becomes more able to distinguish the most maladaptive problems within the pattern, as well as the way it may instigate the main symptoms. The concept of the relationship pattern provides the therapist with a treatment focus to draw upon for responding with the most helpful interpretations. This interpretive process is more fully described in Luborsky (1984) and Luborsky (in preparation).

Because of the integral technical utility of these cognitive concepts it is obviously worth fashioning operational measures of them. Yet quantitative research on the relationship pattern was scant when we began the Penn studies. The few quantitative studies tended to rest on unguided clinical judgments of therapist's skill or of patient's insight (chapter 19).

In contrast, our new measures (to be described in this chapter and those that follow) have been based on guided clinical judgments. In this chapter we describe our earliest method of extracting the core theme of patients' communications and a later method of identifying the Core Conflictual Relationship Theme (CCRT).

The First Core Theme Measure: Effective Response to the Patient's Main Communications

We will begin with an operational definition of Curative Factor 2: the adequacy of the therapist's response to the patient's main communications. First, the therapist formulates the main themes of the patient's communications; second, the therapist tries to respond adequately to them.

We proceeded to try independent ratings of this two-phase measure on a sample of sessions in which the therapist was judged to have responded adequately versus inadequately to the patient's communications (Auerbach & Luborsky, 1968a). Our aims were to see how reliably this measure could be judged and also what other qualities were associated with it. Of 60 sessions rated by the two professional judges on the Penn pilot sample (chapter 9), we selected approximately the best 18% and the worst 18% according to the rating on "therapist responds effectively." We chose sessions where the two professional judges agreed: for better hours, a rating of 4 or higher on the 5-point scale; for poorer hours, a rating of 2 or lower (or 2.5 by one rater, 2 by the other). The final sample consisted of 10 better hours and 11 poorer hours. As expected for the criterion variable Therapist Responds Effectively, there were highly significant differences in ratings between those two groups of hours.

"THERAPIST RESPONDS EFFECTIVELY" WAS JUDGED RELIABLY

Judges achieved fair agreement with each other in rating "therapist responds effectively": Judges 3 and 2 correlated .65; Judges 2 and 1 correlated .62; Judges 3 and 1 correlated .47. (More on reliability was given in chapter 9.) But what actually were they considering in rating "therapist responds effectively"? One way to expose the judgment process is to see what cluster of variables went along with an effective therapist response.

"THERAPIST RESPONDS EFFECTIVELY" CORRELATED WITH SKILL, EMPATHY, AND POSITIVE REGARD

The other variables with ratings significantly different for the two groups of sessions according to both judges were (in order, with the most different first): (a) "therapist skill," (b) "therapist empathy," (c) "therapist unconditional positive regard," (d) "therapist security and maturity," (e) "therapist warmth," (f) "therapist creativity," and (g) "therapist emphasis on unconscious." These are all therapist variables; the patient variables, in general, were not associated with the criterion variables. The central core of the differentiating therapist qualities seemed to be the triad empathy-warmth-acceptance, with the relatively more intellectual qualities, such as "creativity" and "emphasis on the unconscious," on the outer rim.

Some of the differentiating therapist variables call for further explanation. The variable "therapist security and maturity" is one of these. Our effort in rating it was to capture one dimension of the therapist's self-presentation. Our interest in this variable was stimulated by Strupp's (1964) use of it. We have added to its definition Butler, Rice, and Wagstaff's ideas (1962) on therapist voice qualities (which could be rated because the judges listened to the tape recording). In a general way, the variable is intended to estimate (a) the therapist's apparent self-confidence and (b) devotion to the task of helping the patient. Our assumption is that the therapist's security facilitates the capacity to serve as a helper.

In rating "therapist creativity" we ask whether the therapist is repetitious or follows Butler's dictum (Butler, Rice & Wagstaff, 1962) that for therapy to be a growth experience there should be "a continuing search for new elements (of experience), and the forming of creative re-combinations of new and old elements. . . . the therapist's style should be original and stimulating . . . (p. 188)."

The variable "emphasizes unconscious" is derived from Raskin (1965). It inquires into the therapist's concern with what underlies the patient's manifest communications. The variable could equally well have been called "emphasizes psychodynamics," since none of our therapists was inclined to interpret deeply unconscious material.

EVALUATION OF THE MEASURE

Some deficiencies remain in the identification of good therapy hours by ratings of "therapist responds effectively." The first is the issue of inter-rater reliability, which needs to be further improved. The chief reason for divergence is the complexity of the variable. Therefore, judges have different opinions about which content should be stressed by therapists and which interpretations are most appropriate. Furthermore, the adequacy of the patient's performance during the hour tends to be a contaminating factor, even though the patient's behavior does not enter into the definition of "therapist responds effectively." It is too easy to assume that when a patient is making gains, the progress comes from the effectiveness of the therapist's response—or, conversely, that when the patient is showing resistance, the therapist is at fault.

Other studies and ours seem to be roughly convergent in their delineation of the good hour. At least the different studies do not point to any obvious contradictions in the views of a good hour by patients (Lennard, 1962; Orlinsky & Howard, 1967), therapists (Duncan, Rice & Butler, 1968; Orlinsky & Howard, 1967; Strupp, Chassan & Ewing, 1966), and judges (Fiedler, 1950a; Hoyt, 1980). It seems that the kind of therapy session that feels good *to* a patient is also the one that therapists and judges say is good *for* the patient.

An Improved Core Theme Measure: The Core Conflictual Relationship Theme Method

Our work on the good hour was our first experience in the then-new field of quantitative studies of the therapist's interpretative process and our first attempt at a system for identifying the main theme of a session. Only now, through the perspective afforded by retrospection, are we able to see that the view of the good hour as the therapist's effective response to the patient's main communication had brought us to the growing edge of our studies based on the more objective Core Conflictual Relationship Theme (CCRT) Method (Luborsky, 1976a). This method is based on clinical judges' inferences about the core thematic components of the narratives patients tell about their relationships.

Luborsky had been searching for a way to measure the transference relationship concept for many years before his 1976 publication. His search gained momentum when he joined the Psychoanalytic Research Group of the Institute of the Pennsylvania Hospital, which met weekly for 4 years trying to accomplish the task. Although several collaborative studies were completed (e.g., Lower et al., 1973; Luborsky et al., 1975; Luborsky et al., 1973), our shared wish remained unfilled. The measures in that era used only ratings of the *amount* of transference in sessions but not of the *content* of the transference theme.

Several years later, while he was working on the construction of the helping alliance measures based on therapy sessions (Luborsky et al., 1983; Morgan et al., 1982), the idea for the CCRT measure happily appeared (Luborsky, 1976a). After the helping alliance method was fashioned, the logical next question was how the helping alliance fit into the general relationship pattern. A measure of the general relationship pattern was needed. The germinal ideas for the CCRT emerged during the examination of transcripts of sessions to discover how the general relationship pattern could be inferred. Luborsky noticed that *narratives* about relationships helped most to generate a formulation of the general relationship pattern. Within these narratives, the three components that seemed most meaningful were wishes, responses from others, and responses from self. Later, the division into wishes and responses was recognized as approximately corresponding with the psychoanalytic concept of an impulse-defense dichotomy.

APPLYING THE CCRT METHOD

The CCRT method (Luborsky, 1976a, 1977b, 1984) is a system to guide clinical judgment of the content of the central relationship patterns in psychotherapy sessions. The primary data to be scored are the patient's narrative episodes about relationships, which are common in psychotherapy sessions. Typical narratives are about father, mother, brothers, sisters, friends, bosses, and the therapist. These relationship episodes (REs) are identified by a separate set of independent judges before the transcripts are given to the CCRT judges. A minimum of 10 relationship episodes are usually used as a basis for scoring the CCRT. The reliance on narratives as well as the choice of some of the scoring categories bear a resemblance to the Thematic Apperception Test (TAT) (Murray, 1938). A major difference is that for the CCRT the narratives are told as accounts of real events, not—as in the TAT—as fantasies or stories.

The CCRT judge next reads the relationship episodes in the transcript and identifies content about these three components within each episode: (a) the patient's main wishes, needs, or intentions toward the other person in the narrative; (b) the responses of the other person; and (c) the responses of the self. Both positive and negative types of each are identified. Positive responses refer to gratification of the wish, and negative responses refer to lack of gratification of the wish. Within each component the types with the highest frequency across all relationship episodes are identified; their combination constitutes the CCRT.

The steps in the CCRT method represent a formalization of the usual inference process of clinicians in formulating transference patterns. The clinician-judge first identifies the wishes and the responses to the wishes in each of the REs and from these makes a preliminary CCRT formulation (Steps 1 and 2); then the same judge reidentifies and reformulates (Steps 1' and 2'). The specific steps are as follows.

Step 1. Identify the types of wishes, responses from other, and responses of self in each relationship episode.

Step 2. Formulate a preliminary CCRT based on the frequency of each of the types of each component.

Step 1'. Reidentify, where needed, the types of wishes, responses from other, and responses of self based on the Step 2 preliminary CCRT.

Step 2'. Reformulate, where needed, based on the recount of all wishes, responses from others, and responses of self in Step 1'.

The CCRT judges work independently of each other. Judges are trained by first reading the CCRT guide (Luborsky, 1986a) and trying several standard practice cases, receiving feedback from the research team about their performance after each one.

Although we have preferred to use experienced clinicians with a psychoanalytic orientation as judges, some graduate students have also performed well as judges because the task does not require that the judge be committed to a particular school of therapy. In fact, the CCRT may belong in a family of related conceptualizations of relationship patterns, which includes Tomkins's (1979) concept of a nuclear script and Meichenbaum and Gilmore's (1984) concept of core organizing principles.

RELIABILITY AND VALIDITY

The method has come along far enough for us to cite evidence for its good psychometric properties. Reliability has been shown (Crits-Christoph et al., in press) for the selection of the narratives and for the scoring of the CCRT components.

Four different kinds of evidence for validity have been assembled. The first three will be only briefly presented because they are described in the next three chapters, but the last will be described in some detail.

Validity 1

A measure of the degree of the congruence of the CCRT pattern and the content of interpretations has been shown to correlate significantly with the outcomes of psychotherapy (chapter 16).

Validity 2

Changes during psychotherapy in pervasiveness of relationship conflicts as measured by the CCRT were significantly correlated with changes in standard measures of outcome of psychotherapy (chapter 18).

Validity 3

Studies of the correspondence of the CCRT with other relationship pattern measures are just beginning. Three unpublished ones indicate a correspondence (Perry et al., in preparation).

Validity 4

To discover correspondences of the CCRT with Freud's (1912a) 10 observations that led to his "transference template" we examined each of the observations, some more fully than others. The findings of the CCRT tend to converge with Freud's observations. We will illustrate here how Freud's observations are paralleled by observations derived from the CCRT. The illustrations will be drawn from the patients who were part of the Penn Psychotherapy Project (see chapter 4).

The simplest way to learn more about how the CCRT system works in practice is to inspect the first six relationship episodes in Session #3 for Mr. Howard (#44) (figure 15-1). They are purposely drastically shortened in order to make the job of reviewing them easier, although in actual practice the entire episode is considered.

The reader can judge these very condensed relationship episodes in figure 15-1 in terms of each of the three components: the types of wishes, responses from others, and responses from self. What emerges from scoring the actual narratives is the following most frequent relationship pattern: the wish is "I wish to maintain close relationships and not have them cut off"; but the response from other is "The other excludes me and rejects closeness with me"; the response from self is "I feel angry, self-blaming, anxious, guilty, and passive."

Freud's 10 observations, beginning with each of the next 10 paragraphs, provide a framework for presenting more of the CCRT results from Mr. Howard and for presenting some samples of the kinds of research completed or planned on the CCRT.

1. There is one main pattern. Mr. Howard shows the one high frequency theme we have presented. In this patient and in others there are two commonly found characteristics of the main pattern: (1) The main pattern

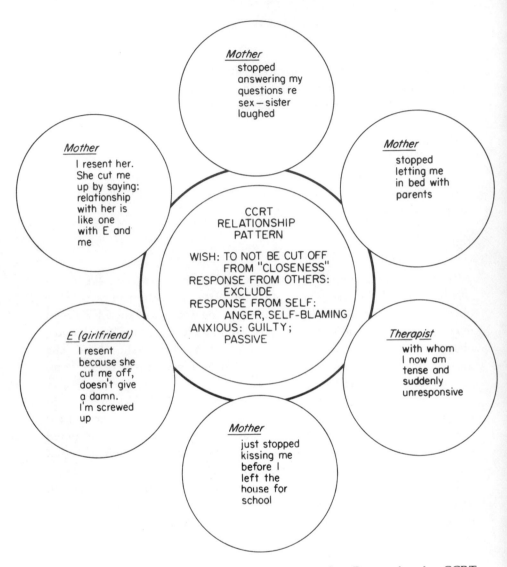

FIGURE 15-1. Relationship Episodes and Relationship Pattern by the CCRT Method (for Mr. Howard [#4], Session 3).

is present across relationships with many other kinds of people. We are just beginning research to determine the degree to which the generality across different kinds of relationships is evident. (2) The main pattern appears not just in the narratives used as the basis for the CCRT but also in dreams (Popp et al., in preparation).

   2. The pattern is distinctive and specific for each person. The CCRT for Mr. Howard is distinguishable from the CCRT patterns of other people (Luborsky, Crits-Christoph & Mellon, 1986). We have many examples for this observation, but a large study is needed.

3. *The pattern is especially evident in erotic relationships.* This appears to be true for Mr. Howard. For example, in five of the six REs drawn from his life the content is manifestly erotic. Only the RE with the therapist shows no manifest sign of erotic content.

4. *Part of the pattern is out of awareness.* We have examined clinical judgments based on the CCRT to find the principles that clinicians use in making inferences about the parts of the pattern that are out of awareness. For example, one principle is that a frequent and conscious wish is often paired with a less frequent and less conscious wish. For Mr. Howard the conscious wish is to be close and to receive affection from women, the less conscious wish is to be passive in relation to father figures (perhaps out of guilt over competition with them). The set of unconscious conflict inference principles is being tried by independent judges to determine the degree of reliability of judgments based on their use.

5. *The pattern tends to be consistent over time.* The CCRT pattern for Mr. Howard is quite similar early (Sessions 3 and 5) and late (Sessions 82 and 82). However, in Session 82, RE 1 shows that there has been a deepening involvement with the therapist—the patient feels more resentful toward him than he had earlier. There is an increased awareness of having to pay too big a price for being close, that is, to have to give up being aggressive and sexual. At the time of a follow-up session about 9 years after termination, Mr. Howard provided 10 REs as part of a special interview (the Relationship Anectodes Paradigms [RAP] interview). In these REs the CCRT remains consistent enough to be recognizable, but there is a considerable increase in positive responses. This consistency over time has been investigated systematically (chapter 18) in terms of the concept of the pervasiveness of conflictual relationship patterns.

6. *The pattern changes slightly over time.* This is reported also in chapter 18. We found that the wishes remained relatively stable from the beginning to the end of the therapy but the response from others and the response from self undergo more change.

7. *The pattern becomes evident in relation to the therapist.* In figure 15-1 Mr. Howard's RE 3 dealt with a suddenly experienced state of tenseness and unresponsiveness, which gives him a headache. The unresponsiveness is his own but it proves to him that "no perfect rapport exists," meaning that people do not respond to people. This pattern with the therapist dovetails with the general pattern in the CCRT. A significant degree of correspondence of the pattern with the therapist and with other people has been shown by Fried et al. (1987).

8. The early-in-life pattern of relationships with the parents is like the current pattern. The correspondence appears to be evident for the REs of Mr. Howard in Session 3 and other sessions. This has not yet been systematically studied.

9. The pattern inside the treatment is like the pattern outside the treatment. The RAP-based interview with Mr. Howard done years after the treatment showed a considerable correspondence. This appears to be generally the case, although our study of this observation is not yet completed.

10. The components of the pattern can be judged to be positive or negative. This appears to be a readily judged aspect of the CCRT components, although it has not yet been systematically studied.

Summary

Our first core theme method was part of the judgment of "therapist responds effectively." We learned from it that:

1. Two professional judges agreed fairly well in distinguishing better from poorer hours when these were defined in terms of the therapist's responding effectively to the patient's main communications.

2. When this definition was applied, the *therapist* variables that were most differentiating were "skill," "empathy," "unconditional positive regard," "security and maturity," and "warmth." But no *patient* variables were differentiating for both judges' ratings.

3. An impressionistic inspection of the poorer and better hours confirmed and extended these findings: In poorer hours the therapist tended to be either inactive and nonresponsive or impatient and hostile. The therapists in the better hours showed some differences among themselves, notably in the dimension of spontaneity and expressiveness versus reserve; but all of them seemed interested and energetic in engaging the patient in an examination of important topics.

The second method, the CCRT, was the payoff of a long preoccupation with operational measures of relationship patterns for evaluating psychotherapy sessions. The CCRT measure showed desirable psychometric properties in terms of good reliability and four kinds of validity.

In the next three chapters we will report on more systematic study of three of the observations about the main relationship pattern. A forthcoming book on the CCRT (Luborsky & Crits-Christoph, in preparation) will provide much more extensive coverage of the principles of scoring the CCRT from narratives and dreams based on psychotherapy sessions as well as special RAP interviews.

16

The Central Relationship Pattern: The Accuracy of the Therapist's Interpretations

THE IDEA for the earlier method of measuring the accuracy of interpretation described in chapter 15 prefigured the idea for the method described in this chapter. With hindsight it is easy to see that the earlier measure—convergence of the therapist's interpretations with the patient's main communication—has a parallel with the later measure—convergence of therapist's interpretation with the patient's CCRT (Crits-Christoph, Cooper & Luborsky, in press). But a major problem with the earlier measure is its impressionistic assessment of the patient's main communications. In this chapter we report on the gains to be garnered by the safer reliance on the CCRT as a criterion for judgments of accuracy. The basis for the improved assessment was the hypothesis that a cogent measure of accuracy is the extent to which the therapist's interpretations in a session deal with the main theme in the CCRT of the session.

A caveat is in order here. Our use of the word *accuracy* is only shorthand for convergence of the interpretation content with the CCRT content. A measure of accuracy is not an external criterion of validity, and it does not deal with the larger concept of the adequacy of the interpretation, i.e., accuracy plus timing and tact.

Our initial aims in the current work were (1) to develop the improved measure of accuracy of interpretation and (2) to examine the predictive capacity of the measure for the outcomes of psychotherapy. Our subsequent aims were (1) to learn whether accuracy of interpretation would predict outcome only in the context of a positive therapeutic alliance and (2) to learn the relative predictive capacity of a broader measure of the therapist's responses, the Therapist's Errors in Technique scale (Sachs, 1983).

Design and Procedures

The design of the study to carry out these aims was as follows: Of the 73 patients in the Penn Psychotherapy Project, 43 were selected for this study. A preliminary step was to apply our CCRT measure of patients' central relationship themes to transcripts of two sessions drawn from early in treatment. Sets of independent judges could then rate the interpretations for their accuracy.

With the exception of one judge who coded interpretations and one judge who marked off relationship episodes (both trained research assistants), judges were experienced clinicians (clinical psychologists and psychiatrists) trained in each task. All judges were blind to treatment outcome and worked independently. Separate sets of judges scored each measure.

Two previously developed measures, the Helping Alliance Counting Signs method (Luborsky et al., 1983) and the Errors in Technique Subscale (Sachs, 1983) of the Vanderbilt Negative Indicators Scale (O'Malley et al., 1983) were also applied to the sessions. The Errors in Technique scale was utilized to examine its overlap with our measure of accuracy of interpretations. The helping alliance scale was applied to examine whether alliance and accuracy measures contribute independently to the predictions of outcome and to test the hypothesis that interpretations have more impact in the context of a positive therapeutic relationship.

PATIENTS

The patient sample consisted of 30 females and 13 males, ranging in age from 18 to 48 years, with a mean age of 25.2 years. About two-thirds of the patients were between the ages of 18 and 24. Descriptive characteristics of the patients are presented in table 16-1. The majority of patients were

TABLE 16-1

Descriptive Characteristics of Patients
$(N = 43)$

Characteristic	Number
Age	
15–19	3
20–24	25
25–29	6
30–34	4
35–39	4
40–44	0
45–49	1
Sex	
Female	30
Male	13
Race	
Black	3
White	40
Marital Status	
Single	29
Married	8
Divorced-Separated-Widowed	6
Education	
High School Degree	5
Some College	21
College Degree	6
Some Graduate or Professional School	7
Graduate or Professional Degree	4

diagnosed as dysthymic disorder, generalized anxiety disorder, or a variety of personality disorders (table 16-2).

THERAPISTS AND TREATMENT CHARACTERISTICS

Twenty-eight therapists participated in the research project. Each therapist usually treated one or two patients. The therapists ranged in age from 27 to 55 years, with a mean age of 35.6 years. The therapists had between 1 and 22 years of prior clinical experience, with an average of 5.4 years. Twelve of the therapists were psychiatrists in private practice; the remaining 16 were psychiatric residents. The residents attended weekly 1-hour therapy supervision sessions with supervisors who were experienced clinicians.

All patients were seen in individual psychodynamic psychotherapy. Approximately two-thirds of the patients were treated at the outpatient clinic of the Hospital of the University of Pennsylvania; the rest were seen

TABLE 16-2

Patient Diagnoses (N = 43)

DSM-III Axis I	Number	With Axis II
Atypical Eating Disorder	1	—
Dysthymic Disorder	16	8
Ego Dystonic Homosexuality	2	1
Generalized Anxiety Disorder	11	4
Inhibited Sexual Excitement	2	—
Obsessive Compulsive Disorder	2	—
No Axis I Diagnosis	13	13

DSM-III Axis II	Number
Atypical Personality Disorder	1
Compulsive Personality Disorder	4
Histrionic Personality Disorder	4
Narcissistic Personality Disorder	1
Passive Aggressive Personality Disorder	4
Schizoid Personality Disorder	8
Schizotypal Personality Disorder	3
Mixed Personality Disorder	1

NOTE: Numbers total more than 43 because several patients had more than one diagnosis.

in private practice settings. Treatment length ranged from 21 to 149 weeks, with an average of 53.5 weeks.

MEASURES

Identifying Interpretations

Two judges (an experienced clinician and a research assistant very familiar with the task) coded therapist statements into interpretations versus all other types of responses. A response was considered an interpretation if it met at least one of the following criteria: (a) the therapist explained possible reasons for a patient's thoughts, feelings, or behavior (e.g., "Yes, but one of the benefits of using drugs is that it keeps you in the role of the child"); and (b) the therapist alluded to similarities between the patient's present circumstances and other life experiences (e.g., "And what's happening is that you keep getting yourself into these kinds of situations like what happened on Saturday where you put yourself in for a hell of a big rejection experience").

The judges were kept blind to treatment outcome and independently read the typed transcripts of two therapy sessions. Responses that were scored as interpretations by *both* judges were included in the study. If a case yielded no interpretations in the two sessions (as occurred for two patients), judges read additional sessions until agreement was reached on at least one interpretation. The number of interpretations obtained per patient ranged from 1 to 16, with a mean of 6.1.

Interrater reliability, based on the judges' ratings for all 43 cases, was assessed for distinguishing interpretations versus other statements. The interjudge agreement was 95%; Cohen's (1960) kappa statistic, a measure of chance-corrected agreement for nominal scales, was .56 ($p < .0001$).

Combining Judges' CCRT Formulations

Two, or occasionally three, experienced clinician judges scored each of the 43 patients for the CCRT (chapter 15). For each case the final CCRT selected for inclusion in the study was a composite of the judges' independent CCRT formulations. It included three components: wish, negative response from other, and negative response of self (positive responses from other and positive responses of self were of low frequency in this sample). Since judges occasionally used different wordings in describing their CCRT formulations, their specific wordings were coded into a standardized language to permit direct comparisons (Luborsky, 1986b). This task was accomplished by having three judges independently code the CCRT judges' formulations into the wordings provided by standard lists of wishes, responses from other, and responses of self. The coding was highly reliable, i.e., greater than 95% agreement between judges.

A composite CCRT was derived by selecting the most frequent wishes and responses among the CCRT judges. The final CCRT formulation for each patient consisted of up to two wishes, three negative responses from other, and three negative responses of self.

Accuracy of Interpretations

Accuracy of interpretation as scored here represents the degree of congruence between the contents of a patient's CCRT and the contents of the therapist's interpretations. Since the CCRT is composed of three main subtypes, accuracy is conceptualized as a multidimensional concept. Consequently, the assessment of accuracy involves multiple ratings on each interpretation. A 4-point rating scale was used to assess the degree to which a clinical judge believed that the therapist addressed a particular CCRT wish, response from other, or response of self in his or her interpretation.

The following CCRT and therapist interpretation, drawn from one of the cases used in this study, is presented to illustrate the nature of the accuracy ratings. The patient's CCRT consisted of one wish ("to make contact with others, be close"), one negative response from other ("rejects, distant"), and three responses of self ("lonely," "depressed," "anxious"). One of the therapist's interpretations was this:

> Well, I'm beginning to get a picture of a—a lot of involvement that you have with this guy still, even though he's cut things off; you haven't. And you're not able to begin replacing him yet and, uh, the emotional investment, emotional tie you've got still to him, and pretty strongly. And that's inhibiting you. Now, what's behind that, y'know, obviously he was very important to you, more important than any other guy has been. And that makes it harder to give him up. And the fact that he really is the one who decided—made the choice to break, not you, makes it harder to give him up too. I—I see some reaction: What's going on?

This interpretation was rated as accurate in regard to the wish and response from other, but not for the responses of self. For the wish, the average of the accuracy judges' ratings for the congruence of content was 3.67; for the response from other, 4.0; and for the three responses of self, 1.33, 1.33, and 1.0, respectively.

For each case, three experienced clinician judges who were kept blind to treatment outcome were presented with composite CCRT formulations and interpretations which were extracted from transcripts for each case. The judges, working independently, were directed to familiarize themselves with the patient's CCRT formulation and make ratings of accuracy on each wish, response from other, and response of self contained in that patient's CCRT formulation.

Ratings for the wishes were averaged to form a composite wish dimension for each patient. Similarly, ratings for the responses from other and responses of self were averaged to yield composites on each. For each patient, these accuracy scores were then averaged across all interpretations. Interrater reliability of the accuracy scales was computed using the intraclass correlation coefficient. Based on the sample of 43 cases, the pooled interjudge reliabilities were as follows: (a) .84 for accuracy with respect to the patient's wishes; (b) .76 for accuracy with respect to the patient's responses from other; and (c) .83 for accuracy with respect to the patient's responses of self.

Intercorrelations between the accuracy scales were computed to examine the overlap between these dimensions. The correlation between the wish and response from other scales was .68. Virtually no correlation was found between the response of self and wish ($r = .07$) or between the response of self and response from other ($r = .04$). Given the sizable correlation between the wish and response from other, these two dimensions were combined into a composite dimension to avoid problems of multicolinearity of predictors (Cohen & Cohen, 1975) in subsequent multiple regression analyses.

Errors in Technique Scale

The Errors in Technique Subscale of the Vanderbilt Negative Indicators Scale (O'Malley et al., 1981) is a set of 10 items, all of which are hypothesized to be inversely related to beneficial treatment outcome (Sachs, 1983). The 10 items are (a) failure to structure or focus the session, (b) failure to address maladaptive behaviors or distorted apperceptions, (c) insufficient examination of potentially harmful behavior or attitudes, (d) failure to address signs of resistance, (e) failure to examine the patient–therapist interaction, (f) superficial interventions, (g) poorly timed interpretations, (h) destructive interventions, (i) inappropriate use of silence, and (j) inflexible use of therapeutic techniques. Possible ratings for each item range from 0 (errors not present or "within normal limits") to 5 (strong evidence for errors).

In Sachs's (1983) study of negative factors in short-term therapy, interrater reliability was calculated for the Errors in Technique scale. Of the original 10 items, 7 had adequate levels of interrater reliability (i.e., $> .60$). The average interrater reliability of the 7-item scale (Sachs, 1983, p. 559) was .73. The level of internal consistency (coefficient alpha) was .46 (Sachs, 1983, p. 559). In addition, the scale was significantly correlated with treatment outcome ($r = -.56^{**}$) in a sample of 18 male college students in brief therapy.

For each case in the present study, two experienced clinician judges (including the author of the scale) independently listened to the audio tape recordings while reading the typed transcripts of the first 30 minutes of each of two early therapy sessions. To reduce the complexity of the task, each 30-minute segment was divided into two 15-minute segments, which were separately rated on the 10 items of the Errors in Technique scale. The ratings of each item were averaged across the two segments, and then the scores of the two sessions were combined. Of the original 10 items on the scale, only 6 had nonzero variance. These 6 items were summed to form a final scale score. The 6-item version of the Errors in Technique scale used in the current study had a mean of 5.5 (out of a possible 30 points) and a standard deviation of 3.4.

Based on the sample of 43 cases, the pooled interjudge reliability (intraclass correlation) of the 6-item scale was .61. Additionally, the level of internal consistency of the scale, as assessed by Cronbach's alpha, was .60.

Helping Alliance Counting Signs Scale

The Helping Alliance Counting Signs (HAcs) method (chapter 12) was applied by two experienced clinician judges to the first 30 minutes of each of the two early sessions for each patient. The score for positive helping alliance signs was selected for use in this analysis because this measure had proven to be the most successful predictor of outcome in the comparison of the 10 most improved and 10 least improved cases from the Penn Psychotherapy Project. The pooled judge reliability of this measure (intra-class correlation = .57) was lower than expected and appeared to be a function of one judge's scoring many more indicators of a helping alliance than the other judge. Nevertheless, we combined the two judges' scores for a final helping alliance measure.

Treatment Outcome

Test and interview evaluations were conducted on the 43 patients when they began therapy and again when they terminated treatment. From these data two outcome measures had been devised, residual gain and rated benefits (chapter 2). Residual gain and rated benefits scores were highly correlated ($r = .76$).

Results

The average level of accuracy was low. Table 16-3 gives the means and standard deviations of the accuracy dimensions. As can be seen, the average level of accuracy was low, yet enough variability was present to allow for relationships with other variables to emerge.

The predictors were unrelated to each other. The relationships among the predictors were examined as a preliminary to the prediction of outcome. An intercorrelation matrix for the four predictors is given in table 16-4. None of the correlations attained statistical significance.

Accuracy on the wish and RO scale was the best predictor of outcome. Multiple regression analyses were performed using the two accuracy measures (wish plus response from other; response of self), the Errors in Technique scale, and the helping alliance scale as predictors, and rated benefits and residual

TABLE 16-3

Means and Standard Deviations for Accuracy
Dimensions ($N = 43$)

Accuracy Dimension	Mean	Standard Deviation
Response of Self	1.69	.41
Wish	1.81	.56
Response from Other	1.49	.38
Wish plus Response from Other	1.65	.43

NOTE: The accuracy dimensions were rated on a 1 to 4 scale, with "1" indicating no congruence between the content of the interpretation and the patient's CCRT and "4" indicating high congruence.

TABLE 16-4

Intercorrelations of Predictors

Measure	1	2	3	4
1. Accuracy Wish Plus Response from Other		.06	.12	−.11
2. Accuracy Response of Self			.17	−.21
3. Helping Alliance				−.08
4. Errors in Technique				

gain as outcome criteria. Simple correlations between each predictor and the two outcome measures are given in table 16-5, as well as partial correlations (each variable controlling for the others) and a multiple correlation combining the predictors.

Most striking is the fact that the accuracy on the wish plus response

TABLE 16-5

Prediction of Outcome from Accuracy, Helping Alliance, and Errors in Technique

Measure	Simple Correlations		Partial Correlations	
	Rated Benefits	Residual Gain	Rated Benefits	Residual Gain
Accuracy Wish Plus Response from Other	.38*	.44**	.36*	.43**
Accuracy Response of Self	.16	.07	.07	−.02
Helping Alliance	.31*	.36*	.26	.35*
Errors in Technique	−.21	−.10	−.16	−.04
Multiple Correlation			.49*	.54**

*$p < .05$
**$p < .01$

from other scale is the best predictor of outcome, yielding statistically significant results in all cases (both outcome measures, simple and partial correlations). The Errors in Technique scale and the accuracy on the response of self scale were not significantly related to outcome. The helping alliance measure showed significant simple correlations with both outcome measures, as had been expected from the studies reported in chapter 12, which included a sample of 20 patients that overlapped with the sample of 43 used here. In addition, the helping alliance scale demonstrated a significant partial correlation with residual gain and a near-significant result with rated benefits. Thus, the predictive effects of the accuracy and helping alliance scales appear to be independent.

Accuracy of interpretation does not interact with the alliance. In order to test the hypothesis that accuracy interacts with helping alliance (i.e., accurate interpretations have an impact only when the therapeutic alliance is positive), cross-product terms between accuracy on the wish plus response from other and the helping alliance were entered after main effects in the multiple regressions. These interactions were nonsignificant.

Because one item ("failure to address maladaptive behaviors or distorted apperceptions") of the Errors in Technique scale overlapped conceptually with the concept of accuracy of interpretation, it was of interest to examine the correlations of this one item with the accuracy scales. For both accuracy scales the correlations were nonsignificant ($r = -.11$ for wish plus response from other; $r = -.19$ for response of self).

Discussion

The results of our study suggest that the accuracy of interpretation has an impact on psychotherapy outcome; it will be important to investigate further its role in treatment.

RELIABILITY OF THE ACCURACY MEASURE

It is important to note that the interrater reliability of the accuracy of interpretation scales was reasonably high compared with the level of reliability usually found in psychotherapy process research (see, for example, Luborsky, Mintz, et al., 1980). The very specific nature of the rating task (the scales were tailored to each patient's CCRT) and the use of experienced clinical research judges probably contributed to the reliability level. By combining the ratings made on all interpretations identified in each of two complete therapy sessions, as well as averaging the ratings over three judges, a robust measure was constructed.

ACCURACY AS A PREDICTOR OF OUTCOME

The major hypothesis of this research received strong support: A statistically significant and moderately strong relationship was found between accuracy of interpretations (i.e., the wish plus response from other dimension) and treatment outcome. These results extend the findings of Silberschatz, Fretter, and Curtis (1986), who studied the immediate impact of accuracy (i.e., convergence of the interpretations with the patient's "plan diagnosis") in the psychotherapies of three patients. Although a relationship between accuracy and therapy outcome was observed in that study, the significance of the finding was limited by the size of the sample. In the current research, larger and more diverse groups of patients and therapists were examined, allowing for the first systematic investigation of the relationship between accuracy of interpretations and treatment outcome.

The results suggest that the therapist's technical performance in dynamic psychotherapy has an impact on outcome. The overall pattern of results also suggests that a specific technique factor, not a more general one, accounts for the finding. The predictive strength of accuracy on the wish plus response from other was not accounted for by other variables such as errors in technique or quality of the therapeutic alliance.

The approach used in the current study has possible implications for research concerning the effects of other treatment techniques on psychotherapy outcome (Frank, 1979; Orlinsky & Howard, 1978). Assessing the "quality" or "skillfulness" of the treatment techniques under investigation, as we did, may be necessary before real relationships between treatment techniques and outcome are observed. This type of research strategy has recently been advocated by a few psychotherapy researchers (e.g., Schaeffer, 1982, 1983; Silberschatz, Fretter & Curtis, 1986).

It is of interest that accuracy with respect to the wish plus response from other, rather than accuracy with respect to the response of self, predicted treatment outcome. It appears that correctly addressing the patient's stereotypical patterns of needs and wishes, followed by the responses of others, is an effective strategy. In contrast, limiting the focus of interpretations to the patient's usual responses (typically feeling states) in interpersonal situations may offer more limited benefits.

DOES ACCURACY INTERACT WITH THE HELPING ALLIANCE?

The helping alliance predicts outcome significantly, as we know from chapters 11, 12, and 14, but it is independent of and noninteractive with accuracy. The lack of a significant interaction between accuracy of interpretations and the quality of the therapeutic alliance was surprising, given the clinical lore that a strong alliance is necessary for patients to tolerate and make use of interpretations. Perhaps this relationship would emerge with more severely disturbed patients than the sample used here, particularly if there was a higher frequency of poor alliances present. In our study, only three therapist–patient dyads showed no signs at all of a positive alliance.

THE ERRORS IN TECHNIQUE SCALE AS A PREDICTOR

The results for the Errors in Technique scale are discrepant from the findings in Sachs's (1983) study, which showed a significant inverse relationship between errors in technique and outcome. There are a few possible reasons for the nonsignificant finding for errors in technique in the current research. For one, the relatively limited reliability of the Errors in Technique Subscale may have partly explained the results. The limited reliability may have been a function of the generally low level of errors in this sample (four items did not occur and several others occurred infrequently). In addition, items on this scale may be more appropriate for time-limited psychotherapy. Treatment in Sachs's (1983) study was specified as brief therapy (maximum of 6 months) as compared to the open-ended therapy in the current research (mean length of close to a year).

LIMITATIONS OF CORRELATIONS

Interpretation of the main findings in the study is subject to the inherent limitations of all correlational research. First, the direction of the relationship between interpretations of the wish plus response from other dimension and treatment outcome is not clear. For example, it is possible that patients who are making good progress in treatment may be more likely to elicit accurate interpretations from their therapists, particularly if they are becoming aware of their own relationship patterns and can articulate these issues during the sessions. However, the fact that the finding was observed very early in treatment (usually by the fifth session) provides some support for the opposite position—that accuracy leads to favorable outcome.

It is also possible that an alternative hypothesis or "third variable" accounts for the relationship between accuracy and treatment outcome. For example, the complexity of a patient's CCRT may influence both accuracy and outcome. Perhaps therapists are more likely to make accurate interpretations with patients who have less complicated, and therefore easier to discern, relationship patterns. And these patients may improve in treatment, not as a result of the impact of accuracy, but simply because patients with less complicated relationship patterns may make better treatment gains. An informal inspection of the CCRTs in the sample, however, did not reveal any major differences in the complexity of the relationship patterns.

It should be mentioned that focusing interpretations on issues not captured by the patient's CCRT may also be important. For example, it would be interesting to learn whether focusing on defenses is related to patient improvement. (The CCRT does not make clear distinctions between defenses.) Inspection of the interpretations in the sample did not reveal any consistent differences between therapists in focusing on defense mechanisms. In fact, with only a few exceptions, the content of the interpretations appeared to fit the structure of a typical CCRT formulation (i.e., wishes, responses from others, and response of self). Formal research in this area is obviously needed.

WHAT'S NEXT? ONWARD TO NEW VISTAS

New ideas, after reflection about their origins, often can be seen as having been anticipated. The hope of the generator of the ideas, of course, is that they have some worthwhile novelty. We believe that the present operational definition of accuracy has advantages over our initial measure and that both of them have advantages for research and clinical practice over the clinical definition from which they sprang. That is, in clinical terms an interpretation tends to be a therapist response that presents to the patient a part of the patient's relationship pattern with others or with self; in addition, the selection of the part of the patient's relationship pattern that is presented in interpretations is intended to be not too far removed from the patient's awareness (Freud, 1912b; Bibring, 1954).

Several other operational recastings of the clinical concept of interpretation have also been suggested, as we mentioned earlier. One of the best known is that proposed by Weiss and Sampson (1986) in which accuracy of interpretation is to be evaluated by the congruence of the interpretation with the patient's "unconscious plan" as measured by the "plan diagnosis" method (Rosenberg et al., 1986). We expect many more operational measures to be generated in the next few years for the concept of accurate interpretation, and clinicians and researchers will be able to choose from these the best for their purpose.

If our accuracy finding is replicated, it could have several implications for the teaching and practice of psychodynamic psychotherapy. For example, therapists could be trained in formulating their patients' CCRTs and in correctly addressing these issues in their interpretations. Assuming that the therapists in this study are representative of the general population of psychodynamic clinicians, the relatively low mean scores for accuracy in this study's sample of therapists suggest that they have much room for improvement in the quality of their interpretations; our findings further imply that when the improvement occurs it will be associated with an additional increment of improved patient outcomes.

Our study has also provided new information about the validity of the CCRT measure: We based the assessment of accuracy of interpretations on the CCRT method and found a significant relationship between accuracy, in terms of the wish plus response from other, and treatment outcome.

Summary

1. We developed a reliable measure of the accuracy of therapists' interpretations based upon their congruence with the Core Conflictual Relationship Theme (chapter 15) and examined its relationship to the outcome of dynamic psychotherapy. Accuracy was assessed on therapists' interpretations from two early-in-treatment sessions of 43 patients receiving moderate-length therapy.

2. The results indicated that accuracy with respect to the main wishes and responses from others that were contained in the relationship themes was significantly related to outcome, even controlling for the effects of general errors in therapist technique and the quality of the helping alliance.

3. A test of a hypothesis that accurate interpretations would have their greatest impact in the context of a positive helping alliance was not confirmed.

17

The Central Relationship
Pattern: Self-Understanding
of Core Relationship Themes

ONE OF the central concepts in clinical theory is the importance of self-understanding or insight as a curative factor in psychoanalytically oriented psychotherapy (Luborsky, 1984). Yet it is astonishing to see how few quantitative studies exist on the measurement of self-understanding and its relationship to the outcome of treatment.

Our review of studies of self-understanding and similar concepts is a part of the survey of the prediction of outcomes of psychotherapy (chapter 19). The Appendix lists studies of insight before and during treatment. Two of the three pretreatment studies showed significant prediction of outcomes. But of the four studies of insight measured during treatment, only one was significant. It is a fair verdict that so far insight has been an inconsistent predictor and that it is especially likely to be nonsignificant when the measure is taken during treatment. Furthermore, several investigators employed single-item ratings of insight and did not present reliability data. Only two of the studies employed psychodynamic psychotherapy.

Our main point, however, is that all of the existing measures of self-understanding are unguided clinical ratings, i.e., each judge defined insight as he or she saw fit. In contrast, the measure that we have begun to develop is a guided clinical rating. The judge assesses the extent to which the patient has self-understanding relative to a specific, independent criterion: the Core Conflictual Relationship Theme (CCRT). Guided clinical ratings have frequently been found to have better predictive validity than un-guided ratings (Holt, 1978). Thus, our use of a guided clinical rating represents a potential methodological advance.

The purpose of the present study was to attempt to develop a set of ratings that would allow us to assess the extent to which patients in the Penn Psychotherapy Project were acquiring self-understanding of their central relationship patterns. If we could develop such an operational measure, we could then explore one of the main principles of psychoanalytic psychotherapy—that improvement from treatment is related to gains in self-understanding.

Procedure

SAMPLE

The sample used for this study was the same 43 patients used in the project on accuracy of interpretation (chapter 16). These 43 were a subset of the total sample of 73 patients in the Penn Psychotherapy Project.

SESSIONS

Two sessions drawn from the early part of treatment were used to score our measures of self-understanding and also the CCRT, on which they are based. We scored the CCRT method generally on Sessions 3 and 5 but occasionally used a third session to obtain the minimum number (10) of relationship episodes (REs) for the method.

For the ratings of self-understanding, only the two sessions that contained the most REs were used. Thus, the occasional third session employed to find more REs was not used for self-understanding ratings.

Trained judges working independently were used for each task. The judges were clinical psychologists, psychiatrists, and research assistants highly familiar with the methods.

MEASURES

The Core Conflictual Relationship Theme Method

A description of the CCRT method is given in chapter 15. Final CCRTs represented a composite of individual judges' CCRTs; they were composed of up to two wishes, three responses from other, and three responses of self.

Self-Understanding of the CCRT

The items that comprised the self-understanding (SU) rating scale were derived mostly from the principles provided in Luborsky's (1984) manual for supportive-expressive psychoanalytic psychotherapy. The items (each rated on a 5-point scale from "none" to "very much") tap the patient's self-understanding in different areas. Ratings were made of self-understanding of (1) the CCRT in general, (2) the CCRT in relationship to the therapist, (3) the CCRT in relationship to parents, and (4) the CCRT in relationship to each of two main other people discussed by the patient within each session (these people were the most frequent topics of relationship episodes).

For each of these areas, separate ratings were made for each wish, response from other, and response of self present in each patient's CCRT. The ratings of all wishes, responses from others, and responses of self were averaged for each patient to create four final scores corresponding to the four areas listed above.

The judges who rated self-understanding were given the following information on each patient: (1) transcripts of two early sessions and two late sessions, (2) a list of the two main "others" for each session, and (3) the CCRT formulation. Judges read each session and then rated the session as a whole on the SU scale items.

Health-Sickness Rating Scale

The HSRS was included in the current study so that we could examine gains in self-understanding controlling for the patient's general level of psychological health-sickness. The scale is described in chapter 6.

Outcome Measures

Two outcome measures, rated benefits and residual gain, were employed (see chapter 2 for a description).

Results

Interjudge reliability was good. Interjudge reliability was assessed for the four scores from the SU scale, (i.e., global, therapist, parents, other people), and a total combining the four subscales, using the intraclass correlation coefficient. The results are given in table 17-1. As can be seen, interjudge reliability was quite good. Scores for the two judges were combined for subsequent analyses.

Level of self-understanding was low. The mean level of self-understanding in Session 3 was compared to that in Session 5 to assess whether there was any noticeable increase in self-understanding over these early sessions. Means, standard deviations, and the results of paired t-tests on each of the four subscales are shown in table 17-2. In general, the level of self-understanding of the CCRT toward the therapist was low in these early sessions. It remained at about the same level for Sessions 3 and 5, except that a small but significant decrease in self-understanding toward the therapist was observed. No other significant changes were observed.

Level of SU predicted outcome; change in SU did not. Prediction of outcome of treatment was performed in three ways. First, level of self-understanding (averaging Sessions 3 and 5) was correlated with the two outcome measures. Because it might be expected that the healthier patients would display more insight, these correlations were done controlling for patient's pretreatment level of health-sickness using the HSRS. Second, change in self-understanding from Session 3 to Session 5, correcting for initial (Session 3) level via regression analysis, was correlated with outcome, again partialing for pretreatment HSRS. Although this is a short length of time to assess gain in insight, and, as described in the previous section, there were no significant increases in insight over this period, previously reported results (chapter 16) had indicated that the therapist's interpreta-

TABLE 17-1

Interjudge Reliability of the Self-Understanding Scale

Self-Understanding Scale	Pooled Judges Intraclass Correlation
Global	.77
Therapist	.87
Parents	.89
Other People	.87
Total (Sum of Subscales)	.85

TABLE 17-2

*Mean Self-Understanding for Session 3 and
Session 5 (Five-point Scales)* $(N = 43)$

Self-Understanding Scale	Session 3	Session 5	Paired t-test
Global	2.21 (.7)	2.31 (.9)	.7
Therapist	1.66 (.9)	1.33 (.5)	2.4*
Parents	2.31 (1.1)	2.13 (1.1)	.9
Other People	2.50 (.7)	2.74 (.8)	1.6
Total Score	2.16 (.5)	2.12 (.5)	.4

*p < .05

tions in these sessions did have an impact on outcome. It might be possible, therefore, to detect trends toward increasing self-understanding in those patients who improve the most in treatment.

The results of the predictive analyses are given in table 17-3. *Change* in self-understanding from Session 3 to Session 5 yielded no significant partial correlations with the two outcome measures. *Level* of self-understanding of CCRT, however, produced two significant relationships with out-

TABLE 17-3

*Prediction of Outcome from Level of
Self-understanding and Change in
Self-understanding* $(N = 43)$

	Outcome Measure	
	Rated Benefits	Residual Gain
Level (Session 3 + Session 5)		
Global	.03	.16
Therapist	.31*	.29
Parents	−.28	−.30
Other People	.22	.34*
Total	.04	.12
Change from Session 3 to 5		
Global	.06	.11
Therapist	.23	.25
Parents	−.23	−.22
Other People	−.07	.11
Total	−.07	.04

NOTE: Coefficients are partial correlations, controlling for HSRS, and, in the case of change in self-understanding, also controlling for Session 3 level.
*p < .05

come. These were: (1) self-understanding of the CCRT with the therapist correlated with rated benefits (.31*) and (2) self-understanding of the CCRT with other people demonstrated a significant partial correlation with residual gain (.34*).

Summary and Discussion

Overall, the results provide evidence that our measure of self-understanding of specific relationship themes can be rated reliably and that there are associations between the level of self-understanding and outcome. Even these associations are small, however, and we are not able to decide at this time whether the results mainly reflect that self-understanding is hard to operationalize or that any measure of it will achieve low associations with outcome.

Several methodological issues lead us to be cautious in interpreting these data. The specific hypothesis that *gain* in self-understanding is related to more favorable outcome was not confirmed, although it is likely that this hypothesis was not given an adequate test. It may be necessary to evaluate change in self-understanding over a longer period of treatment rather than simply from Sessions 3 to 5. In order to evaluate change over a longer period of time on a specific criterion (i.e., the CCRT), it would be necessary for that criterion to be relevant to both points in therapy. In the case of the treatments studied here, the relatively larger number of sessions on the average (mean number of sessions was 53.5 for the 43 patients) compared to the usual brief, focal dynamic treatments meant that it was likely that some change in the content of the clinical material would occur over therapy. In a brief, focal dynamic therapy, it might be possible to track level of self-understanding of the same content over the course of the whole treatment.

Although the significant results for *level* of self-understanding are suggestive, the correlational nature of the study limits inferences about the causal role of self-understanding. Statistical control of one major variable, psychological health-sickness, allows us to rule out one potential third-variable explanation of the results, yet other third variables may exist.

To the extent that we can speculate from these data, it is of interest that ratings of self-understanding of the CCRT with the therapist and with other people were predictive but self-understanding of the CCRT in a global sense or with parents were not. The major importance of the relationship pattern with the therapist is of course evident in many clinical theories of psychodynamic psychotherapy (Luborsky, 1984; Strupp & Binder, 1984). The data may be more consistent with a focus on the "here and now" relationships of the patient and less on the past, parental relationships, although we did not specifically code each relationship for past versus present.

The data presented here have taken us one more step toward testing aspects of the clinical concepts of dynamic psychotherapy. This study provides the groundwork for investigating the role of self-understanding in therapy and offers suggestions about where to look in future studies for the therapeutic "action" in the patient's level and change in self-understanding during treatment.

18

The Central Relationship Pattern: The Reduction in Pervasiveness of Conflicts

---

IN CASE DESCRIPTIONS by psychodynamic psychotherapists, relationship conflicts typically are identified as fomenters of symptom outbreaks. These same relationship conflicts are reported to be reduced when the symptoms recede. This sequence of reduction in relationship conflicts and their consequent symptoms is clearly evident in the examples we described of improved patients before versus after psychotherapy (chapter 3). In one of these, for example, Mr. Howard (#44), the following conflictual relationship pattern emerged from a review of the patient's narratives of interactions with other people: I wish not to be cut off from closeness and affection; the other person cuts me off; then I respond by becoming highly anxious (i.e., by developing a symptom). The patient's relationship problems were considerably better controlled by the end of treatment, although when they reappeared from time to time the patient's anxiety symptom reemerged, as in the episode reported many years later (described in this chapter) when the patient's supervisor appeared to be cutting him off. At that time the patient's relationship conflicts were reactivated and anxiety symptoms started to develop, but he showed that he had acquired a greater capacity to recognize the reappearance of a familiar relationship conflict and even to see the humor in its recurrence.

Not only do the changes in the conflictual relationship patterns operate as a curative factor through fostering reduction of the symptoms, but the amount of change in itself constitutes a theoretically relevant measure of the outcome of dynamic psychotherapy. One of the most significant needs of research on psychotherapy, particularly dynamic psychotherapy, is for the development of measures of outcome of therapy that are relevant to the theory of psychodynamic change. Behaviorism and DSM-III have pulled the field of psychotherapy research toward the use of bare measures of overt behavior and symptoms as outcome criteria. For psychodynamic psychotherapies, the lack of a reliable and valid measure of psychodynamic change has forced studies to rely on other types of assessment, such as general symptom inventories or global ratings of improvement. Such measures have the virtue of simplicity and applicability to many different kinds of treatment. However, measures derived from each theory of therapy are lacking. For psychoanalytic psychotherapy, relevant measures would include change in the main conflictual relationship pattern and changes in the patient's awareness of this pattern.

An exception to the trend toward non–theory-related outcome measures is the work by Malan and his associates (Malan, 1963; Malan et al., 1968). Malan has argued against the reliance on behavioral manifestations alone and has developed an individualized method of assessment that is guided by psychodynamic hypotheses. In brief, his method involves: (1) an initial detailed account of the patient's presenting problems, (2) a consensus formulation of a dynamic hypothesis by a group of clinicians, and (3) specification of emotional and behavioral changes that would indicate favorable outcome for each case. Posttreatment assessment is based on a clinical interview. An account of the interview is given to the group of clinicians in order for them to rate improvement on a global 9-point rating scale. The problems with Malan's method have been detailed by Mintz (1981) and include the lack of reliability and validity information about the psychodynamic hypothesis and the reliance upon one interviewer's account after treatment rather than independent assessment of outcome by different clinicians. Using Malan's published case reports, Mintz (1981) has also demonstrated that a large component of the Malan outcome rating is simple symptomatic improvement that can be readily assessed by non-clinician judges.

Other individualized methods of outcome assessment have been developed, such as the Target Complaints method (Battle et al., 1966) and Goal Attainment Scaling (Kiresuk, 1973), but these measures are not psychodynamically based and have been criticized on psychometric grounds (Mintz & Kiesler, 1982). Still other measures go beyond assessment of symptoms (e.g., Weiss et al., 1985), yet these methods do not assess the types of individual themes and conflicts that are important in psychoanalytic psychotherapy.

It is clear that the major stumbling block to the development of an outcome measure suited to the evaluation of outcomes of psychoanalytic psychotherapy has been the lack of a reliable and valid measure of the *nature* of the patient's particular dynamic conflicts and themes. Without a measure of the *relevant* conflicts for each patient, researchers cannot determine whether improvement that is consistent with the theory and techniques of the therapy has occurred.

Several studies (Seitz, 1966; Dewitt et al., 1983) comparing independent clinicians' formulations of patients' dynamic themes have reported a lack of consensus among clinicians in open-ended judgments of such themes. More recently, however, guided clinical formulation methods that are applied to psychotherapy session material have arrived on the scene and appear to be more promising. These include the Plan Diagnosis Method (Rosenberg et al., 1986), the Cyclical Maladaptive Pattern (Schacht, Binder & Strupp, 1984), the Frame Method (Teller & Dahl, 1981) and Configurational Analysis (Horowitz, 1979). The Core Conflictual Relationship Theme (CCRT) Method (Luborsky, 1976a, 1977b) is the oldest of this genre of methods applied to sessions and has developed evidence for a promising level of reliability and validity, as reviewed in chapter 15. In brief, the CCRT method is a system to guide clinicial judgment of the content of the central relationship patterns in psychotherapy sessions. It is based upon clinical judges' scorings of certain types of thematic components in the narratives patients tell about experiences in relationships.

Aims

To the degree that the focus of dynamic psychotherapy is on maladaptive, repetitive relationship patterns, i.e., particular sets of wishes, expectations, reactions, etc., that are inappropriately applied to relationships, we propose that one index of change in dynamic therapy is the extent to which the maladaptive theme becomes less prevalent in the relationships of a patient by the end of treatment. For the CCRT method, this concept translates into a decrease in the percentage of relationship episodes in which the maladaptive theme is present at the end of treatment compared to the beginning of therapy (Crits-Christoph, Cooper & Luborsky, in press).

The purpose of the study presented here is to report data on the reliability of such a measure of change based upon the CCRT and to give descriptive outcome results from applying the measure to sessions early and late in treatment for a sample of patients in psychoanalytic psychotherapy. In addition, we will examine the relationships between the psychodynamic measure and the more conventional measures of change in self-reported symptoms and change on clinician-rated health-sickness.

Design and Procedures

MEASURES

The Core Conflictual Relationship Theme (CCRT) Method is described in chapter 15, and the Health-Sickness Rating Scale (HSRS) is described in chapter 6.

Combining Judges' CCRT Formulations

For each case the final CCRT selected for inclusion in the study was a *composite* of the judges' independent CCRT formulations. It included five components: wish, negative response from other, negative response of self, positive response from other, and positive response of self. Judges' specific wordings were coded into a standardized language to permit direct comparisons between their formulations (Luborsky, 1986b). Three judges independently coded the CCRT judges' formulations into the wordings of the lists of wishes, responses from other, and responses of self. This coding task was done with greater than 95% agreement between judges. The standard list of CCRT components included in the original CCRT formulations were those components that were selected by all three judges. On only a few occasions one of the judges disagreed with the other two judges about the selection of a CCRT component. In these cases the CCRT component included in the original CCRT formulation was the one selected by two out of three judges.

For each case, each judge's CCRT formulations were examined. A composite CCRT was derived by selecting wishes and responses that were in common among the different judges' listings of the most frequent CCRT components. Frequency scores were derived for each type of component by taking the average of the different judges' frequency scores.

Finally, these average frequency scores were divided by the number of relationship episodes used for each case to derive a percent score. This percent score we have termed the "CCRT pervasiveness score" or the "pervasiveness of conflicts across the relationship episodes." Because it is a central measure in the current study we set it off as a fraction below:

$$\text{CCRT Pervasiveness} = \frac{\text{Number of REs with the CCRT component}^{1}}{\text{Number of REs in the session(s)}}$$

This measure reflects a theory-derived expectation of changes to be gained from successful psychoanalytic psychotherapy: The main conflictual relationship patterns should become less pervasive across the relationship episodes because the patterns should become less stereotyped as more different relationship options are opened up to thought and expression.

Although multiple wishes and responses are generally evident for each patient, the highest frequency of each of the five types of CCRT components was chosen for study. Because we were examining *change* on these components it was necessary to use the percent score for the same thematic category both early and late in treatment, although the same category was not necessarily the one with the highest frequency at both times (e.g., if "anxious" was the most common negative response of self early in treatment it was not always the most common response of self late in treatment). For the wish, negative response from other, and negative response of self the highest frequency early-in-treatment category was selected as the focus to examine change. For the positive response from other and positive response of self, the highest frequency late-in-treatment category was chosen first, and then we noted the frequency of this same component at the early-in-treatment point.

Hopkins Symptom Checklist

A modified version of the Hopkins Symptom Checklist (Derogatis et al., 1970) containing 85 items was used as a general measure of level of self-reported symptoms. The internal consistency (Cronbach's alpha coefficient) of this measure was .96. The measure was obtained from patients before the start of therapy and at termination.

PATIENTS, THERAPISTS, AND JUDGES

A sample of 33 patients drawn from the larger sample of 73 patients in the Penn Psychotherapy Project was used for this study. The sample consisted of 8 males and 25 females, with a median age of 24 years. The DSM-III diagnoses included dysthymic disorder (13), generalized anxiety disorder (7), schizoid personality disorder (7), and histrionic personality disorder (4); the rest of the diagnoses are represented by only 1 to 3 patients each. All patients were nonpsychotic.

[1]For example, wish A: "I wish not to be cut off from closeness and affection."

A total of 25 therapists (all psychiatrists) treated the 33 patients, with each therapist generally working with one or two patients. The therapists ranged in age from 26 to 55 years, with a median age of 34. Thirteen of the therapists were fourth-year psychiatric residents who were supervised by experienced clinicians. Eight therapists had less than 10 years of post-residency experience, and four therapists had more than 10 years of post-residency experience.

Trained judges working independently were used for each task. The judges were clinical psychologists, psychiatrists, and research assistants highly familiar with the methods.

TREATMENT AND SESSIONS

All patients were in psychodynamic psychotherapy, typically once or twice per week, although two patients attended four sessions per week. Treatment length varied from 21 to 149 weeks, with a median length of 43 weeks.

Sessions drawn from the early and later parts of treatment were used to score the CCRT. The number of early and late sessions was a function of the number of sessions needed to obtain the minimum of 10 relationship episodes. This was generally two sessions, but for a few patients it was as many as three or four.

The early-in-treatment sessions were typically Sessions 3 and 5. For the late sessions, we chose to avoid sessions close to termination so that issues related to termination (e.g., resurgence of symptoms) would not affect our data. On the average, the late sessions represented the point of treatment at which 80% of sessions had been completed.

Results

CCRT pervasiveness scores were highly reliable. The agreement between judges in the pervasiveness of the main CCRT components was examined by calculating intraclass correlation coefficients for early session data in which the same two judges had scored the cases.

The results indicated relatively high agreement, with pooled judges' intraclass correlation coefficients as follows: wish, .82; negative response from other, .90; negative response of self, .80; positive response from other, .84; positive response of self, .85. Judges' pervasiveness scores were therefore averaged for all subsequent analyses.

Measures of CCRT change were moderately intercorrelated. Pearson correlations among residual gain scores on each of the CCRT pervasiveness measures are presented in table 18-1.

Of the 10 intercorrelations, 3 were statistically significant: (1) Residual change (Manning & DuBois, 1962) on the wish measure significantly correlated (.45**) with residual change on the negative response of self scores; (2) change on pervasiveness on the positive response from other dimension was related to change on the negative response from other ($-.52**$); and (3) change in positive response from other correlated (.41*) with change in positive response of self.

CCRT pervasiveness decreased from early to late in treatment. The early treatment CCRT pervasiveness and late treatment CCRT pervasiveness on each of the five CCRT measures was subjected to a two-factor repeated measure analysis of variance. One factor, Measure, had five levels corresponding to the five types of pervasiveness measure (i.e., wish, negative response from other, negative response of self, positive response from other, and positive response of self), and a second factor, Time, consisted of the early–late dimension. The interaction term, Measure by Time, addressed the question of differential change across the five CCRT measures, and was of primary interest.

The ANOVA produced statistically significant main effects for Measure [$F(4,128) = 93, p < .001$], Time [$F(1,32) = 7.4, p < .01$]; in addition, the Measure $\times$ Time interaction was highly significant [$F(4,128) = 12.6, p < .001$], indicating that the early–late changes were not uniform across the five measures.

Table 18-2 presents mean early and late pervasiveness scores on each of the five CCRT measures. For each measure, the statistical significance of the early to late changes was tested via paired t-test.

TABLE 18-1

Intercorrelations of CCRT Pervasiveness Change Measures
(Residual Gain Scores)

	Negative RO	Negative RS	Positive RO	Positive RS
Wish	.25	.45**	−.24	−.24
Negative Response from Other (RO)		.28	−.52**	−.28
Negative Response of Self (RS)			−.22	−.16
Positive Response from Other (RO)				.41*

*$p < .05$
**$p < .01$

TABLE 18-2

Mean Percent Early in Treatment and Late in Treatment CCRT Pervasiveness Scores $(N = 33)$

	Early	Late
Wish	66.3 (15)	61.9 (25)
Negative Response from Other	40.7 (14)	28.5 (18)
Negative Response of Self	41.7 (14)	22.8 (18)
Positive Response from Other	8.6 (10)	18.7 (12)
Positive Response of Self	13.4 (12)	19.1 (16)

NOTE: Standard deviations in parentheses.

As can be seen in table 18-2, the pervasiveness of the CCRT main wish decreased from 66.3% to 61.9% over the course of treatment, but this difference was not statistically significant. Changes on the negative response from other (12.2% decrease), negative response of self (18.9% decrease), and positive response from other (10.1% increase) were all highly significant ($p < .001$, two-tailed). Change on the positive response of self (5.7% increase) was also significant ($p = .055$, two-tailed). Thus, small but reliable changes occurred on four of the five CCRT measures.

Initial CCRT pervasiveness was unrelated to initial symptoms and to initial health-sickness. Pearson correlation coefficients were calculated to assess the relationship between the five CCRT pervasiveness measures and (1) initial symptoms as measured by the total score on the Hopkins Symptom Checklist, and (2) initial scores on the composite clinician-rated Health-Sickness Rating Scale. With the SCL, four of the five measures yielded correlations near zero. The positive response of self pervasiveness measure, however, correlated significantly ($r = -.48$, $p < .005$) with the SCL, indicating that higher symptom levels were associated with fewer positive responses of self in relationship episodes. A significant correlation ($r = .41^*$) was also found between the HSRS and the positive response of self pervasiveness measure. Additionally, the HSRS correlated significantly ($r = -.34^*$) with the negative response from other measure.

Change in CCRT pervasiveness correlated with change in symptoms and change in health-sickness. The relationship between change in CCRT pervasiveness and both change in symptom levels and change in the HSRS was assessed through partial correlation analyses. The purpose of this method was to allow for an assessment of change corrected for initial level on each type of measure. Posttreatment SCL scores were correlated with late-in-treatment pervasiveness, partialing out the effects of pretreatment symptom scores and early treatment pervasiveness. The same analysis was done using the HSRS.

TABLE 18-3

*Partial Correlations of Change in CCRT
Pervasiveness Measures with Change in Symptoms and
Change in Health-Sickness*

	Hopkins Symptom Checklist	Health-Sickness Rating Scale
Wish	.41*	−.14
Negative Response from Other	.34[a]	−.27
Negative Response of Self	.40*	−.53**
Positive Response from Other	−.32[b]	.11
Positive Response of Self	−.40*	.14

Note: Initial level of CCRT pervasiveness and initial HSCL or HSRS were partialed out in each analysis.

[a] $p = .06$
[b] $p = .08$
* $p < .05$
** $p < .01$

Table 18-3 presents the partial correlations between change on each of the five CCRT measures and change on the SCL and HSRS. Of the five CCRT measures, three showed statistically significant partial correlations with change in the SCL, and the other two evidenced near-significant partial correlations, all in the expected direction. For change in the HSRS, only change in the negative response from self was significantly correlated ($r = −.53**$).

Discussion

This study presented one approach, based upon the Core Conflictual Relationship Theme method, to fashioning a theory-relevant measure of psychodynamic change. Good interjudge reliability was obtained with the measure of pervasiveness of the CCRT across relationship episodes. Relatively small but consistent changes from early to late in treatment were obtained on the measure. Changes in pervasiveness were significantly correlated with changes in other outcome measures, namely changes in symptoms and changes in clinician-rated health-sickness. Each of these findings will be discussed in turn.

The relatively good reliability of the pervasiveness score can be attributed to several factors. First, the system is really a two-step task: It involves assessing the content of the main relationship theme and then recording its pervasiveness. Attempting to judge dynamic change in one step without breaking the complex judging tasks down into substeps is likely to result in lower reliability. Second, the CCRT method on which the pervasiveness measure is based is a guided clinical scoring system with demonstrated interjudge reliability. A dynamic formulation method of questionable or unknown reliability would, obviously, be problematic as a basis for assessing change in dynamic conflicts. The use of a straightforward concept such as "percentage of interactions with other people that contain the main relationship theme" allows for easy quantification, and has theoretical appeal for psychoanalytic clinicians as well.

In terms of the pattern of changes from early to late in treatment on the pervasiveness scores, it was found that the responses changed more than the wishes. Apparently, tendencies toward certain wishes, needs, and intentions in relationships are relatively intractable, yet the expectations about others' gratifying or blocking one's wishes and the consequential emotional responses to these actions or expectations have more flexibility or malleability. Patients of a successful therapy learn to recognize and cope with their inclinations in a way that leads to fewer negative and more positive responses. In essence, the reduction in pervasiveness of the conflictual relationships can be seen as a theoretically crucial curative factor.

The magnitude of the changes seen on the pervasiveness scores also raises important questions. Despite the fact that on standard outcome measures the patients in the Penn Psychotherapy Project improved as a group by the usual amount (65%) for psychotherapy outcome studies (chapter 3), the dynamic changes were small on the average, and even patients who improved considerably retained some of their basic relationship components. These results have implications for theories of psychoanalytic psychotherapy. Clinical discussions of the theory of change have two somewhat different views of what happens in the course of psychoanalysis or psychodynamic psychotherapy. One view holds that the transference pattern and the conflicts within them are resolved (see, for example, Davanloo, 1980). Another view (e.g., Pfeffer, 1963) holds that transference patterns and the conflicts within them remain evident even in the most successful psychotherapy, while some components of the pattern are altered. Our results clearly favor the second clinical view of change.

The example of Mr. Howard will help to illustrate the types of consistency and changes that occurred for relationship themes. As we described in chapter 3, he improved considerably in psychotherapy. His most frequent wish in therapy was "to maintain close relationships and not have them cut off." The response from other was "the other cuts me off—the other excludes me and rejects closeness with me." The responses of self were: "I feel rejected, angry, passive, anxious, and guilty." This patient was evaluated through a follow-up interview 8 years after therapy ended. By that time he was well along in his training to become a lawyer. One of the relationship episodes he told at the 8-year point was about an evaluation session with one of his supervisors. He had been hoping of course to get a good report from him, but was astonished and disappointed in what he heard. At the conclusion of the evaluation the supervisor had said, "You are a loaf." After his surprise and initial disappointment he asked for an explanation. He repeated, "You are a loaf." The patient suddenly realized what the supervisor was trying to say, but it was distorted by his Hungarian accent: "You are aloof." At this point in the interview the patient smiled because he could see some humor in the reappearance of his old inclination to disappointment through his expectation of being deprived of approval, followed by the recognition that nothing really bad had been said about his performance.

Although small, the changes in pervasiveness found in our data apparently were meaningful, as evidenced by the significant correlations between CCRT pervasiveness change and symptom reduction. Whether the dynamic change is driving the symptom reduction or is merely a correlate cannot be rigorously answered with the current data. Assessing both dynamic and symptomatic change at multiple time points would allow for testing hypotheses about whether dynamic change precedes and predicts symptom change.

The correlations between CCRT change and symptom change were not so high, however, as to suggest that change in the CCRT is redundant with change on symptom inventories. Our data indicate that change in the CCRT provides reliable extra information that is not captured by symptom inventories or clinician ratings.

Despite the promising results obtained, there are several limitations of the methods used here. The CCRT pervasiveness measure is based on all of the (relatively complete) relationship episodes that we found in the two or three sessions used at each time point. Variations in the size of this data base may affect the final measure of dynamic change. For example, it is conceivable that a larger number of episodes than the 10 early and 10 late ones used here might be necessary to obtain a more representative index of the frequency of the main relationship theme in the person's life. Also there was no control for the main other person of the relationship episodes. For some patients, the same central type of other person may be present in several of the episodes early in treatment but not included in the episodes sampled late in treatment, thereby potentially biasing the data. Of course, simply the fact that the patient chooses which episode to tell means that the group of episodes can not be considered a truly representative or random sampling of the interpersonal interactions in the patient's life. On the other hand, similar relationship patterns tend to emerge with different other persons, and it is our impression that the main relationships in most patients' lives are covered by the sampling used here. In addition, the reliance upon material as it unfolds to the clinician allows our measure to have a closer tie to the clinical theories and methods. But more research is necessary to examine the role of the choice of significant other in affecting the early versus late changes in the frequencies within the CCRT.

Finally, our index of pervasiveness of the CCRT is only one criterion that might be used as an outcome measure for psychoanalytic psychotherapy or psychoanalysis. Other aspects of the psychoanalytic process, such as changes in defenses and changes in awareness of relationship patterns, have yet to be studied and might serve as criteria for improvement in psychoanalysis or psychoanalytic psychotherapy.

Summary

The purpose of the study was to examine a theory-relevant measure of change in moderate-length psychoanalytic psychotherapy. The measure chosen was change in pervasiveness of the CCRT from early to late in therapy and its relation to more usual measures of change, the self-reported change in symptoms and the clinician-rated health-sickness rating. The database was 33 patients' psychotherapy transcripts from the Penn Psychotherapy Project. The main results were as follows.

1. CCRT pervasiveness scores showed high agreement among judges.

2. There were small but meaningful changes from early to late in treatment, although the changes were not uniform across the five pervasiveness measures. For example, wishes did not decrease significantly, but responses did change significantly. The largest changes were a decrease in negative responses of self, a decrease in negative responses from other, and an increase in positive responses from other.

3. Initial CCRT pervasiveness of the positive response of self was significantly correlated with initial level of symptoms and clinician-rated health-sickness. Health-sickness ratings were also significantly correlated with pervasiveness of negative response from other.

4. Change in CCRT pervasiveness was significantly correlated with

change in symptoms for three of the five CCRT measures, and change in health-sickness correlated significantly with change in the negative response of self measure.

As a whole, these results demonstrate some validity to this new method of measuring dynamic change. In addition, the data have implications for psychoanalytic theories of change, and in particular lend support to clinical theories that hold that aspects of the core conflictual relationship pattern are still apparent even after successful treatment.

CONCLUSIONS

How the Penn

Psychotherapy Project

Measures Up

19

The Penn Studies in
Perspective of Past Studies

<hr />

THE PERSISTENT WISH of the Penn Psychotherapy Project over the past 20 years has been to find the factors in the patient, therapist, and treatment that influence the outcomes of psychotherapy. By now the knowledge that has been gained can offer to clinicians and researchers more reliable guides than have been available before for (1) pretreatment evaluation of patients for psychotherapy and (2) understanding and dealing with the factors that influence the progress of the treatment.

The main findings take off from the best bases of the Penn Psychotherapy Project and other predictive studies of the past four decades. Most of this chapter is a summary of past studies as a context for the Penn study, because no single study in this field, no matter how well executed, can be expected to achieve representative results. In this chapter we remind the reader of our basic findings on the benefits of psychotherapy, compare our Penn studies with past studies, and point the way for future researchers.

The Benefits Achieved by Psychotherapy

Our work was done in a sequence of two predictive projects: Pretreatment Project A examined factors in the patient and therapist apart from the treatment; Treatment Process Project B examined the within-treatment factors that had most influenced outcomes. The first part of Project B tested conventional types of ratings of psychotherapy sessions (chapter 9). The second part developed new measures of key concepts of the curative factors in psychotherapy sessions (chapter 10), including the methods based on the helping alliance (chapters 11–14) and on the Core Conflictual Relationship Theme (CCRT) (chapters 15–18).

It would not have been worth doing the predictive analyses if the overall benefits of psychotherapy were small or narrow in variation among patients. We will give on the following pages the conclusions from this review of the benefits both for the Penn Study and for related projects.

Conclusion 1: Most patients who remain in psychotherapy at least for a few sessions will benefit. Especially in the last decade, researchers have reached the consensus opinion that the evidence strongly supports the positive conclusion that most patients *will* benefit from psychotherapy. This issue had been controversial and conjectural in the past, at least since Eysenck's (1952) review raised the issue by asserting a challenging negative conclusion.

The positive conclusion on benefits agrees with clinical opinions as well as with the quantitative results. In the Penn study a high percentage of the patients showed significant treatment benefits. The therapists' ratings of patients' benefits were: 22% large improvement, 43% moderate improvement, 27% some improvement, 7% no change, and 1% got worse. The corresponding observers' ratings were: 5%, 51%, 27%, 14%, and 3%; the patients' ratings were similar. These percentages are close to those reported by Mintz (1977, p. 591), who summarized the therapists' ratings of improvement of 393 patients in five studies, including our own. He found 25% large improvement, 62% small-to-moderate improvement, 10% no change, and 3% got worse. Bergin and Lambert (1978) also arrived at the usual 65% improvement rate in their review by including moderately improved or better and excluding dropouts. When we combined our top two categories, moderate and large improvement, our percentage likewise was the magically recurrent 65%.

The Penn study offers other outcome measures besides percentages of patients who improve, and these support the same conclusion. The size of the improvement is expressible more precisely by an effect size measure (Cohen, 1969), defined as the posttreatment mean minus the pretreatment mean divided by the pretreatment standard deviation. A sample of such effect sizes for the Penn study (chapter 3) are the following: The change in the observer-rated Health-Sickness Rating Scale (HSRS) is represented by an effect size of .69; the patient-rated Symptom Checklist's (SCL) effect size is .80. The size of the effects for both of these measures, reflecting improvement in general adjustment, would be classed as "large" by Cohen's (1969) categories.

We compared the Penn study effect sizes with those in other studies (chapter 3) and found them to be similar. After an intensive search, data were assembled from 10 somewhat similar psychotherapy-treated groups: Penn, Chicago, Menninger, Temple, Endicott, Vanderbilt, Hopkins, Kaiser, Leuvan, and Queensland. Despite all of the comparative treatment research until 1987, only these 9 other studies met our relatively undemanding criteria for being comparable to our own in design, treatment, and patients. Here is a simple comparison of effect sizes: For the Chicago study the observer-rated adjustment composite effect size was .65; in the Penn study the observer-rated HSRS, which is probably similar to the Chicago measure, was .63; in the Menninger study the observer-rated HSRS effect size was .77; in the Vanderbilt study it was 1.03.

Since the Penn study did not include a control group, the five control groups within the set of 10 somewhat similar psychotherapy studies provide some pertinent comparisons (i.e., Temple, Vanderbilt, Endicott, Kaiser, and Hopkins studies). As would be expected from nontreatment or minimal treatment control groups, their effect sizes were markedly smaller than those of the Penn treated group (chapter 4).

Conclusion 2: Although changes occur in the basic relationship pattern, the pattern is still recognizable at the end of therapy. The Penn study provided a new observation about the nature of the changes offered by psychodynamic psychotherapy. The observation was made possible through the CCRT method of measuring the pervasiveness of relationship conflicts (chapter 18). Pervasiveness of conflict is defined as the percentage of the relationship episodes in psychotherapy sessions that repeat the same conflicts, that is, that contain the same wishes and responses from self and others. We found that this percentage decreased during psychotherapy, slightly for the wish component and more in terms of responses from others and responses of self. From those observations about the pervasiveness of the basic relationship pattern we have concluded that at the end of treatment the later pattern is still recognizable as similar to the earlier pattern.

Conclusion 3: Only a few patients ended psychotherapy in a worse psychological state than they were in before treatment. According to the global improvement measures, very few patients changed for the worse from the beginning to the end of their psychotherapy (chapter 3). The percentages of such patients are small, just as in the Lambert, Bergin, and Collins (1977) review in which the majority of the studies showed a range of 0–10% worsened. The percentages are somewhat higher for pre–post difference scores than with the global improvement measures, but they remain within the 0–10% range.

With either measure the decline in scores does not appear to represent serious deterioration. In fact, it is impressive that among the 73 patients in the Penn study who started psychotherapy, many with serious problems, few got worse—even though it can be presumed that some of them would have gotten worse without treatment (see the control group comparisons with similar studies in chapter 3). The most likely explanation must be the one in Conclusion 1, that patients are generally helped by the psychotherapy; in those few instances in which they are not, they are not harmed seriously.

After his speech on the therapeutic action of psychoanalysis, Robert Waelder (about 1965) got a familiar question from the audience: "Is it advisable for people with unusual talents, such as gifted writers, to undergo psychoanalysis?" Waelder replied that he was not worried about harming the person's talent because he was not impressed with the power of psychotherapy, for good or ill. Our research-based conclusion agrees with the premise that psychotherapy usually does not have harmful effects, but our study and others show that psychotherapy usually does provide patients with meaningful benefits.

Conclusion 4: Improvement in physical health also tends to occur during psychotherapy. A further benefit of psychotherapy appears to be improvement in physical health—even though physical improvement is not usually a main treatment goal. Schlesinger, Mumford, and Glass (1980) and Mumford et al. (1984) showed that, in more than a dozen studies, after the advent of psychotherapy medical utilization decreased. These results stimulated our investigation of health benefits in the Penn sample. We obtained evidence for improved physical health from patients' reports on the Hopkins Symptom Checklist about the lessening of a variety of physical symptoms (chapter 5). As would be expected, the improvement in psychological symptoms was significantly greater than for physical symptoms, although both were significantly reduced during psychotherapy. The amount of the reduction of both psychological and physical symptoms during psychotherapy was correlated with the amount of overall improvement in the treatment outcome measures.

Conclusion 5: Patients tend to maintain their gains after psychotherapy, although with some loss. The small sample of the Penn Psychotherapy study patients who were included in a long-term follow-up ($n = 19$) showed a tendency for gains to be maintained, although with some loss from termination levels (chapter 4). Such results are usual in follow-up studies of psychotherapy (e.g., Frank et al., 1978).

Within the follow-up sample we were able to identify two types of changes that occur during the period after psychotherapy. The first is shown by a patient, Mr. Norris (#27), who improved during therapy but was unable to retain his gains after its termination. Patients in this category tend to suffer from an intrapsychic problem that involves difficulty in internalizing the gains from relationships and the sense of availability of helping relationships. A second type also includes only a few patients. It is illustrated by Mr. Denny (#77), who did not improve during his Penn study psychotherapy. Yet subsequently, with a new therapist and a better relationship, he was able to make a highly significant and lasting change in his life and personality. If a patient has not improved in one psychotherapy, a different one may provide a better match and better results.

Factors Predicting Outcomes in the Penn Psychotherapy Project

THE PENN PRETREATMENT PREDICTORS

One aim of the research was to learn which pretreatment qualities of the patients are associated with their gains. The best pretreatment predictors were: (1) psychological health (from the Health-Sickness Rating Scale), (2) Emotional Freedom (from the Prognostic Index interview), and (3) Overcontrol (from the Prognostic Index interview). The measures that were most predictive apart from the treatment were (4) the similarities of patient and therapist and (5) the matching of patients and therapists according to therapist's preference.

These pretreatment predictors represent only a few of the many potential predictors that were tried in the Penn Psychotherapy Project, and they explained only about 5–10% of the outcome variance.

Yet even that modest level of success has to be evaluated in relation to the large number of correlations run. We had correlated 84 pretreatment predictors with the two outcome measures, rated benefits and residual gain, for a total of 168 correlations. The number that would be expected to be significant by chance is 8.4 at the 5% level—we found 10 significant correlations, with 8 at the 5% level and 2, Health-Sickness Rating Scale and Emotional Freedom, at the 1% level. We concluded that for the large number of correlations computed the number of significant ones we found was slightly, but not significantly, above chance level. But beyond these results, there are cogent reasons for inferring that more than chance factors determined some of the significant correlations we found.

First, our results must partly reflect our having violated Cohen's principle (1969) that with such prediction studies, more predictors are not better. Some of the correlations might be discounted as the expected yield of an incautious overinclusion of possible predictors. In fact, most of the demographic measures were listed as predictors even though they were never considered by us to be so—they were counted as predictors only because we had measured them pretreatment. When we appropriately reduced the predictors to those whose record (table 1 in the Luborsky et al. [1971] review of studies) had earned them a right to further cross-validation, we achieved more significant correlations than would have been expected by chance (chapter 8). Furthermore, in a set of somewhat similar predictive studies (chapter 3) in which the number of predictors had already been prudently pared down—as in our reanalysis of the data on the Chicago Psychotherapy Project (described below)—the number of significant correlations exceeded chance expectations.

Second, we correlated the set of predictive correlations in the Penn study with the corresponding ones in the Chicago study for 13 similar predictors; we found considerable correspondence for prediction of rated benefits (.62, $p < .025$) and moderate correspondence for predictions of residual gain (.48, $p < .10$). This comparison is especially cogent because the two projects have much in common as predictive studies, notably, the same type of criterion measures because of our reanalysis of the Chicago study data. In addition, when the Penn study's significant predictors were compared with those of other somewhat similar predictive studies, we found some consistency of results.

Third, some of the significant predictors in the Penn study were subjected to further successful cross-validation studies, for example, Emotional Freedom in the Penn study and in the Yale study (Rounsaville, Weissman & Prusoff, 1981). Both provide strong evidence for above chance results. Furthermore, some of the significant predictors in the Penn study were consistent with the main trend of the predictive results in other studies and in that sense can be considered to be a cross-validation.

Finally, when we compared the predictions of outcomes for the clinic versus private patients (chapter 8), we found higher levels of prediction success in the private practice patients. One of the explanatory factors may have been that the clinic therapists needed to break off treatment at the end of their rotation, but the private therapists did not, of course.

We did further comparisons after our study to see whether in other studies the outcomes of other kinds of patients and other kinds of treatments could be predicted more readily than ours had been. Generally, they could not be—we found the same modest levels of prediction in other studies. For example, for predicting outcomes of treatment for alcoholic patients (Luborsky & McLellan, 1978), the mean of the predictive correlations for each of 13 clinical judges' direct predictions of outcome of treatment was .27 (for 50 alcoholic patients). This is exactly the same level found for the direct predictions in the Penn study.

Since the levels of prediction in our study and other studies turned out to be lower than we had expected in 1966, when we planned our Penn study, we naturally pondered about why we had ever expected higher levels than those we found. One likely basis must have been that in the decade leading up to the Penn Psychotherapy study we were imbued with optimism, which was especially heady at the Menninger Foundation, about the capabilities of psychiatry and clinical psychology for predicting human behavior. At the Menninger Foundation in those years, that spirit was instilled by the innovations in diagnostic testing by David Rapaport (1946) as further disseminated by Roy Schafer (1948, 1958), Robert Holt (1960), and Martin Mayman (1960). Most pertinent, we were not confronted then by the recurrently modest levels of prediction to be encountered in rigorous research on the prediction of later personal developments through psychotherapy. The moderate results of the Chicago Psychotherapy study (Cartwright, Kirtner & Fiske, 1963; Fiske, Cartwright & Kirtner, 1964) were known to us, but they had little dampening effect on our hopes and plans. We were inclined to believe then—though we are wiser now—that the Chicago project's results were likely to be limited to that study.

TI IE PENN DURING TREATMENT PREDICTORS

After the poor predictive showing of the conventional psychotherapy process measures (chapter 9), we set about on a new course: to create operational measures of the theoretically relevant curative factors in psychodynamic psychotherapy (listed in chapter 10 and in Luborsky, 1984). An operational measure is one that translates a theoretical concept into specified, measurable components of the clinical data; operationalizing a concept requires simplifying it to some extent. Yet despite its limitations, the process of operationalizing can offer significant compensations in terms of reliability and validity, as it has done for us.

The Penn process measures that show the greatest promise include: (1) three forms of helping alliance measures (chapters 11, 12, 14), (2) a measure of the degree to which the therapist engaged in behaviors that facilitate the helping alliance (chapter 13), (3) the accuracy of the interpretations (chapter 16), (4) the patient's self-understanding (chapter 17), and (5) the pervasiveness of conflictual relationship patterns (chapter 18). Finally, as a basic building block for each of these measures, we relied upon (6) our measure of the general relationship pattern, the CCRT (chapter 15). Together these form our armamentarium of measures.

The helping alliance measures were the first to show themselves to be significant predictors of outcome. Correlations for the Penn predictive measures during psychotherapy (table 19-1) show that all three types of helping alliance measures were significant predictors. The experience with these measures reveals that an early positive helping alliance is to be taken

TABLE 19-1

The Main Significant Predictions in the Penn Studies $(N = 73)$

	Outcome Measures	
Pretreatment Predictors ($N = 73$, approx.)	Residual Gain	Rated Benefits
Health-Sickness (HSRS)	.30**	.25**
Emotional Freedom (PI)	.11	.30**
Overcontrol (PI)	−.17	−.24*
Similarities		
Marital Status	.23*	.24*
Sum of 10 Matches	.23*	.24*
Treatment Length	.20	.27*
Random Assignment to Therapist ($N = 45$)	−.37*	−.24
During-Treatment Predictors		
Helping Alliance		
HAr (early) ($N = 20$)	.44*	.46*
HAcs (early positive) ($N = 20$)	.48**	.57**
HAq (early) ($N = 77$)	.51** to .72**	
Therapist's Facilitative Behavior		
($N = 20$) (early)	.39	.45*
Accuracy of Interpretation		
($N = 43$) (Wish and Response from Other)	.43**	.36*
Self-understanding (SU)	.34*	.31*
($N = 43$)		
Pervasiveness of Conflict (CCRT)		
($N = 33$)		
Wish	−.20	−.03
RO	−.18	.02
RS	−.38*	−.26

$^*p < .05$
$^{**}p < .01$

seriously as a harbinger of a positive treatment outcome. In the light of this evidence, an early positive alliance should not be minimized as a honeymoon phenomenon.

The biggest surprise among the operationalized measures was the accuracy of interpretation measure. The findings with this measure, examined for the first time on a moderate-size sample, confirmed the clinical lore about the benefits of the therapist's accuracy of interpretation. We demonstrated significant predictions based on accuracy defined as convergence of the content of the interpretation with the content of the main relationship pattern, as measured by the CCRT.

In its broader significance, the research with these measures is providing the field of psychodynamic psychotherapy with remediation for its previous deficiency in research support. Our exercise in operationalization shows which measures of clinical concepts can be judged by clinicians reliably and validly. The larger implication of these measures is that clinicians can now agree with each other when using some concepts but only when their attention is focused on the well-designated operational definition. This conclusion dovetails with the obverse observation that if concepts are not operationalized interclinician agreement will often be ambiguous (e.g., Seitz, 1966).

Next we turn to how our Penn study predictors, both pretreatment and during treatment, fit with the large body of predictive results from the review of relevant past studies.

A Review of Past Studies and the Penn Studies of Factors that Influence the Outcomes of Psychotherapy

We began our review of the literature by rereading the clinical works because they have been the most sustaining source of guidance for practice. Among these, three classic clinical overviews stand out: Freud (1937), Rogers (1957), and Rosenzweig (1936). We also reconsulted two compendiums of clinical opinions, one about the necessary qualities of the therapist, by Holt and Luborsky (1958a & 1958b), and another on the necessary qualities of the patient, by Wallerstein et al. (1956). These five articles made the biggest impression on the shape of our research plans; they also served as the basis for our comparison of clinical wisdom with quantitative results.

The quantitative studies required a review because they were more like the research we were planning: It is fitting that this final chapter is dedicated to them. This section is an update of the widely cited original survey by Luborsky et al. (1971). Many of the quantitative studies have also been reviewed—with a different orientation—in the massive periodic review books of Bergin and Garfield (1971), Garfield and Bergin (1978), and Garfield and Bergin (1986). Although much of our review covers many of the same studies, only ours provides the mean predictive correlations.

Compared with the impact of the clinical lore, that of the quantitative research on the practice of psychotherapy has been slight. Clinical and quantitative researchers have been inclined to keep their distance, and those who know one type of research tend not to know the other. The distance has come about more from the clinicians' side; clinical researchers are likely to be guided almost entirely by the writings of other clinicians. In fact, when a clinician ventures to present data gathered by clinical quantitative methods, he or she is at risk to forfeit clinician status. This happened on an occasion in 1987 when a clinician-researcher was to present a paper to a clinical organization and asked another clinician-researcher to join him as a discussant. When this plan was reviewed with the arranger of the program, he said, "Good, but we will need to add to you two on the panel a person who is a clinician." Unfair it is, but it must be admitted that the clinicians have had some good reasons for their doubts, as a clinical-quantitative researcher once wrote in an article titled, "Research can not influence clinical practice" (Luborsky, 1969). The quantitative studies sometimes lack clinical sophistication, and clinicians have become generally skeptical of quantitative research. Whether or not such an attitude is still justified by the quantitative research can only be judged from our review. Be it noted that because of the new knowledge in this review, the same clinical-quantitative researcher has now changed his tune: "Research can *now* influence clinical practice" (Luborsky, 1987a).

Our review is intended to serve several purposes: (1) We offer guidelines for clinical practice in the form of a set of qualities of the patient, the therapist, and the patient–therapist interaction that have been shown to relate to various criteria of outcome. Many of these qualities can be assessed by clinicians or researchers by an easily applied Prognostic Index interview (Auerbach, Luborsky & Johnson, 1972; chapter 7). Some of these guidelines suggest modifications in the practice of psychotherapy that should improve therapeutic results. (2) We systematically compare the clinical and quantitative lists of factors. We highlight areas that should be investigated by quantitative research. (3) We provide a critique of the existing research to serve as a guide to improved future investigations.

CRITERIA FOR INCLUSION IN THE REVIEW

Method

Quantitative studies of the factors that influence outcomes of *individual psychotherapy* for *adult* patients were examined. Studies were included if there was an attempt to provide reasonably controlled conditions, and if the conclusions were passably supported. This meant the exclusion of poorly conceived studies, usually on these bases: (1) inadequate correction of outcomes for each patient's initial level, (2) reliance on retrospective data, (3) post- but not pretreatment assessment of predictors, (4) poor descriptions of outcome measures, which made their utility difficult to assess, (5) outcome measures consisting of only the length of the treatment or whether the patient remained in or dropped out of therapy. (Actually, the predictive characteristics of drop-outs [Baekeland & Lundwall, 1975] have much in common with those in the present review.)

Diagnoses

The review includes studies of mostly nonpsychotic patients with a variety of diagnoses—mostly depression, anxiety, and mixed—of the kind seen in outpatient psychotherapy practice. The virtue in this naturalistic variety is that the results are of special interest to practitioners of outpatient psychotherapy. In contrast, the style of more recent research is to delimit the sample to specific diagnostic groups; but such research is as yet only a small proportion of studies.

Types of Therapy

For the definition of psychotherapy, we followed the lead of Zax and Klein (1960) in their review of the types of changes that occur via psychotherapy. They put limits on the scope of their research by following Snyder's (1947) definition of psychotherapy, which rules out research based primarily on educational and guidance activities emphasizing the giving of information. Also not included were occupational therapy, shock therapy, chemotherapy, behavior therapy, and laboratory analogues of psychotherapy unless these were part of a comparison with psychotherapy. We have excluded behavior therapy since its outcome predictors may differ from those of nonbehavioral psychotherapy (e.g., Sloane et al., 1975). The advent of manuals to define adherence to the type of treatment is an important advance; however, at this time only a small proportion of the treatments are manual-guided.

Availability

We omitted many studies that were available only in the form of unpublished theses or in difficult-to-obtain foreign language journals. In addition, it is noteworthy that many investigations whose results never made it to publication were necessarily excluded. This obvious limitation to any review is likely to result in a biased sample of studies and has been termed the "file drawer problem" (Rosenthal, 1979).

Number of Studies

Governed by these limitations, 166 studies were included in our original review (see Appendix, dates of 1970 or earlier). They cover a period of 24 years—from 1946 through 1970. Most of them are from Strupp and Bergin's (1969) bibliography of individual psychotherapy research through 1967. The studies before 1970 were our basis for planning the Penn Psychotherapy Project.

In this chapter we have added studies from the 15-year period 1971 through early 1986, bringing up the total of findings reported from 378 to 486.

DISCERNING THE FINDINGS

The body of this section contains the factors influencing outcomes of psychotherapy and the research support for them. A model for classifying the factors (by Sanford, 1962, p. 155) suggested the divisions under which we classified results of each study: (1) patient factors (before treatment and judged from the session), (2) therapist factors (before treatment and judged from the sessions), (3) the match (similarity) between patient and therapist (patient and therapist assessed apart from treatment), and (4) treatment factors. A reader can see at a glance the direction and consistency of the findings in each division by the convenient list in the Appendix.

We should note that there is a distinct asymmetry in the weights that should be attached to significant and nonsignificant findings—the latter receiving much less weight. Obviously, a nonsignificant result does not warrant the positive conclusion of no relationship, merely the absence of evidence sufficient to conclude that a relationship exists. Given the likely poor statistical power of much of this research (small samples, relationships attenuated by measurement error), this point takes on particular force (Cohen, 1962; 1965, pp. 95–101).

The predictive associations reported in the vast majority of studies were simple correlations, t-tests, or ANOVAs, without partialing or covarying out the influence of other potential outcome predictors. Thus, information about the independence of predictor variables is not readily available in the literature. Because there is potential statistical overlap between predictors, or between a reported variable and a third unmeasured variable, we are limited in our ability to draw causal inferences from the associations of predictors with psychotherapy outcome, and we must question the size of reported effects. Nevertheless, this review can serve as a summary of the main trends found for simple correlations with outcomes and help future researchers determine which variables to take into account in outcome prediction studies.

Our method of estimating the strength of a trend is a "box score" of significant versus nonsignificant studies, supplemented where possible by the mean correlation of all studies. For the box score results we have paid special attention to trends based on 4 or more studies, where all of them were significant in the same positive direction or where the number of studies that were significant was double the number of nonsignificant studies. The lower limit is 2 or more significant correlations in the same direction.

It is supportive of the two aspects of our methods of showing trends, the box score and the mean correlation, that they tend to agree. There is a positive relationship, which is most apparent at the extremes, between the mean correlation and the percentage of significant findings ($r = .75**$). For example, the highest mean correlation based on at least 4 studies is .57 for the patient involvement studies, and all 4 of the 4 studies are significant. The lowest of the mean correlations is $-.08$ for fee payment, and only 1 out of 4 is significant in the same direction.

Even though the box score system is a rough summary, it will catch the fact that some qualities remain significantly predictive across several studies, despite different patients, different forms of treatment, and different outcome criteria. By accomplishing this feat they become more worthy of our attention. These qualities are listed in table 19-2 and are reviewed in more detail below. To simplify this chapter only the numbers of studies will be given; citations for each category are given only in the Appendix, with a few exceptions needed to explain the text. Not all categories listed in table 19-2 will be discussed; only the main ones or the ones that require explanation.

For certain categories all the studies for which a correlation coefficient (r) was available or obtainable through conversions (following Glass, McGaw & Smith, 1981) were combined to reach an average correlation coefficient. This r was calculated by (1) averaging the correlations within studies, that is, obtaining a single r for a given study, which may derive from the mean r of the predictor with several similar global measures of outcome; and (2) averaging the correlation coefficients across the studies within each category. All correlations were first transformed by the use of Fisher's Z before averaging; then the average Z was transformed back to a correlation.

PRETREATMENT FACTORS: PATIENT FACTORS BEFORE TREATMENT

Psychological Health-Sickness

A medley of words in various psychological languages have meanings subsumed under the broad continuum psychological health-sickness (PHS): mental health versus sickness, mental pathology, integration, ego

TABLE 19-2

*Number of Significant versus Nonsignificant Predictive Findings
and Mean Correlations*

	Outcomes			
	Sig.		Non-sig.	Mean
Predictor	+	−	0	r (N)
Patient Factors as Assessed before Treatment				
1. Psychological Health-Sickness Measures				
Global Adjustment Measures	10		4	.27 (11)
Severity of Diagnosis	10	2	0	
MMPI Severity Measures	4	1	0	
Barron Ego Strength Scale	4	1	4	.24 (6)
TAT: Adequacy of Functioning	2		0	
Rorschach Prognostic Rating Scale	6		3	.49 (5)
Symptom Checklist Severity	2		0	.54 (2)
Chronicity	4		3	
2. Affect				
Anxiety	6		4	.26 (6)
Depression	3		0	
Other Affects	3		2	
3. Motivation and Expectations				
Motivation	5		3	.31 (4)
Expectations	6		4	.36 (7)
Other Motivation Measures	0		4	
4. Positive Attitudes toward Self, Therapist, and Treatment	4		1	
5. Interest in Human Relations	8		0	
6. Intellectual Functioning				
IQ	6		3	.31 (6)
Intellectual Skills	3		0	
Ability in Perceptual Tests	0		1	
7. Authoritarian	0		1	
8. Ethnocentrism	2		1	
9. Somatic Concern	2		1	
10. Self-understanding and Insight	2		1	
11. Attractiveness, Suitability, or Prognosis in Psychotherapy	2		0	
12. Healthy Traits and Coping Styles	8	1	3	
13. Mastery vs. Helplessness and Passivity	2		0	
14. Miscellaneous Test Findings and Traits				
MMPI Scales	5		0	
Figure-Drawing Test	1		0	
Rorschach: General Scores	11		7	
Locus of Control Scale	1		1	
Other Psychological Tests and Ratings	9		4	
Patient Demographic and Life Situation Factors				
1. Age	3	2	6	
2. Sex	3		8	
3. Race	1		1	

TABLE 19-2 *(Continued)*

Predictor	Outcomes			
	Sig.		Non-sig.	Mean
	+	−	0	r (N)
4. Religion	0	1	1	
5. Social Achievements				
Socioeconomic Status (SES)	5	1	2	
Occupational Adjustment	3		3	
Educational Level	5		2	
Marital or Sexual Adjustment	2		5	
Social Competence	1	1	0	
6. Student Status	3		1	
7. Early Home Situation	1		1	
8. Previous Psychotherapy	0		3	
9. Health Insurance	1		0	
10. Other Demographic	0		1	
Patient Physiological Factors	2		0	
Therapist Factors Assessed Apart from Sessions				
1. Skill as Judged by Others	3		1	
2. Experience and Training	7		9	.36 (3)
3. Interest Patterns	6	1	5	
4. Therapist's Personal Therapy	0	1	4	
5. Healthy Qualities of Therapist	4		3	
6. Favorable Attitude toward Treatment	2		1	
7. Expectation of Patient Improvement	2	1	2	.17 (3)
8. Therapist Demographic Variables	3		3	
9. Authoritarian	1		0	
Patient Factors as Judged from Sessions				
1. Psychological Health-Sickness	1		0	
2. Affect	3	2	1	
3. Likability	2		0	
4. Problem-Solving Attitudes	5		0	
5. Process Continuum of Psychotherapy	4		0	
6. Experiencing	4	2	5	.38 (3)
7. Motivation	1		0	
8. The Therapeutic Alliance				
Therapeutic and Helping Alliance	8		0	.50 (8)
Other Positive Relationship Qualities	9		1	
9. Self-understanding and Insight	1		3	
10. Involvement	4		0	.59 (4)
11. Amount of Patient Talking	2		1	
12. Other Patient Factors	6		2	
Therapist Factors as Judged from Sessions				
1. Skill	4		0	
2. Empathy				
Empathy as Judged from Sessions	8		5	.26 (9)
Empathy as Judged by Other Measures	6		2	.20 (5)
3. Accuracy of Interpretation	1		0	
4. Focus on Transference	2		1	.50 (2)
5. Positive Regard and Warmth	9		4	.32 (11)

TABLE 19-2 *(Continued)*

	Predictor	Sig. +	Sig. −	Non-sig. 0	Mean r (N)
6.	Genuineness (or "Congruence")	3		2	.21 (3)
7.	Empathy, Warmth, and Genuineness	1		1	
8.	Liking the Patient	3		3	.19 (3)
9.	Hostility and Negative Attitude	0		1	
10.	Encouraging Independence	2		0	.21 (2)
11.	Directive and Advice-giving	2		1	.06 (2)
12.	Supportive	2		0	.61 (2)
13.	Amount of Therapist's Talking	2		4	
14.	Therapist's Prognostic Expectations	3		1	.31 (2)
15.	Other Therapeutic Performance Factors	13		1	
	Match (Similarity) between Patient and Therapist				
1.	MMPI Similarity	0	1	3	
2.	Rorschach Similarity	2		0	
3.	Interest and Values Test Similarity	4		0	.31 (2)
4.	Social Class Similarity	2		0	
5.	Racial Match	0		2	
6.	Other Similarities	12		5	
	Treatment Factors				
1.	Number of Sessions and/or Duration	23		3	.46 (20)
2.	Frequency of Sessions per Week	3		3	
3.	Fee Payment	1	1	2	−.08 (2)
4.	Waiting Interval between Applying and Starting Psychotherapy	3		0	
5.	Role Preparation Provided to Patient	4		2	
6.	Comparisons of Different Forms of Psychotherapy				

strength, psychological or psychiatric severity, adjustment, adequacy of personality functioning, and mental dysfunction. Research on this topic began with Freud's (1937) review of the factors influencing outcomes of psychoanalytic treatment. He listed three factors: "the influence of traumas, constitutional strength of the instincts and alterations of the ego" (p. 224). The last of these most closely refers to degree of psychological health-sickness. A total of 59 PHS studies[1] use these and similar terms for their predictive measures (Appendix). We grouped the findings under eight headings, each corresponding to a method of measurement: global PHS measures (13), severity of diagnosis (12), MMPI severity (5), Barron Ego Strength Scale (9), TAT Adequacy (2), Rorschach Prognostic Rating Scale (9), Symptom Checklist (2), and chronicity (7). We cannot be entirely

[1]Four studies in the previous review were omitted from the present one because they suffer from a method deficiency: a correlation of an initial measure with a nonresidualized difference score. These studies include Cartwright & Roth, 1957, Klein, 1960, Luborsky, 1962b (omitted in part), and Stone et al., 1961.

sure of the common kinship of each of these measures with psychological health-sickness. In judging each measure we had to rely on what is known about it from the available validity data. Of the eight headings, chronicity is least clearly a PHS measure, but it is included here because in the studies cited it is considered a facet of PHS.

Of the 59 findings, 41 (or 69%) showed this main trend: Greater psychological health at the start of treatment is associated with greater benefits, and vice versa. The trend in the studies after the 1971 review was the same as that found earlier. Of the remaining studies, 14 were nonsignificant; only 4 reported a significantly negative correlation.[2] A reexamination of the 4 negative studies did not reveal a basis for their negativity. Similarly, reexamination of the 14 nonsignificant studies, as compared with the significant studies, did not suggest a basis for their nonsignificance.

Since the measures are grouped according to the eight methods of assessment, we examined the results with each method.

Global measure of PHS (mean r = .27 for 11 findings).[3] The largest group, 13 PHS findings, consists of the global measures; 10 were positively significant and 4 were nonsignificant. Since the variety within this group is large, we will mention only a few of its most recurrent and useful measures.

The Health-Sickness Rating Scale (HSRS) (Luborsky, 1975b; chapter 6) was positively significant in 3 studies: Luborsky (1962b), Luborsky, Mintz, et al. (1980), and Free et al. (1985).

The Addiction Severity Index—Psychiatric Severity Subscale (as described in chapter 14) is represented by 2 significant studies (McLellan et al., 1983; Woody et al., 1984).

The Global Assessment Scale (GAS) (Endicott et al., 1976) has become a widely used simplification of the HSRS. One of its developers, Robert Spitzer, was granted permission by Lester Luborsky to simplify the HSRS; the new version was renamed the GAS. The main changes were to eliminate the HSRS sample cases and to dispense with the seven criteria. Further research comparing the two formats is needed.

Severity of diagnosis. This is a most impressive category because it has 12 studies, and all but 2 follow the main trend. The trend is that the more serious diagnoses, involving such terms as schizophrenia, psychotic trends, or psychosis, were associated with less improvement in psychotherapy. Within the schizophrenic groups, the more severe forms, represented by

[2]The negative correlation in Woody et al. (1983) refers only to a small subgroup of 13 cases all diagnosed DSM-III antisocial personality. The 13 cases are part of the 110 patients, who as a group showed the usual significant trend for high psychiatric severity to be associated with low improvement. Although this subgroup of antisocial personality patients did not show a high level of psychiatric severity, they did show an abysmally poor response to the psychotherapy.

[3]The number of findings refers only to those on which the mean r was based, since not all findings offer an available or calculatable r.

the diagnosis of process schizophrenia, had worse outcomes than the less severe, nonprocess, diagnosis (Stephens & Astrup, 1963).

The only exceptional diagnosis is that of psychopath (or antisocial personality) among methadone-treated substance abusers. These patients are not severe in terms of health-sickness rating and yet they do not show improvement in the course of psychotherapy; in fact, these patients are the only ones in the diagnostic lexicon who show minimal improvement in psychotherapy. In contrast, the group diagnosed psychopath *plus* depression shows moderate improvement, and the group diagnosed depression alone shows even more improvement.

We do not have precise data from the studies of severity of diagnoses to examine the *amount* of improvement in relation to diagnostic category. However, it is amply clear from the analyses we have presented that most of the differences in outcome of the different diagnostic groups are functions of differences in severity of psychological health-sickness.

The MMPI Severity Measures. These results show the same trend. Four of the 5 studies showed that less maladjustment on the MMPI is associated with more improvement, but 1 study showed the opposite.

TAT Adequacy of Functioning. Both studies using ratings based on TAT protocols showed that patients with greater judged adequacy of functioning did better in psychotherapy.

Barron Ego Strength Scale (Mean r = .23 for 6 Studies). This single MMPI scale showed the trend in 4 of the 9 studies, but in 1 study the opposite trend was found.

Rorschach Prognostic Rating Scale (RPRS). Among the prognostic tests this time-consuming measure by Klopfer et al. (1951) turned out to be a big surprise. In 9 studies in which the RPRS had been applied before therapy, 6 showed a significant positive relationship; a high RPRS score was associated with improvement in psychotherapy (mean $r = .43$ for 5 studies). These Rorschach scores are weighted combinations of six variables thought to be related to adequacy of personality functioning.

Chronicity. This concept and measures of it have considerable overlap with PHS. It has a fairly good predictive record: 4 of 7 studies were significant.

In conclusion, a definite trend emerges within the whole set of PHS studies. The initial severity of the patient's illness is a fairly consistent predictor of the outcomes of psychotherapy: Initially sicker patients as judged on many types of PHS measures do not improve as much with psychotherapy as the initially healthier do. The mean correlations for some of the PHS categories are low to moderate.

These findings suggest an interpretation about the nature of PHS which helps to explain its predictive capacity. People who have the greatest assets in terms of psychological health and adequacy of personality functioning and the fewest liabilities in terms of psychiatric disabilities can profit more from psychotherapy because these assets help them make use of such interpersonally mediated growth-potentiating experiences as psychotherapy. This interpretation, made after having assimilated the accumulated wisdom about PHS, has remained remarkably similar to the earliest one (Luborsky, 1962b): Like wealthy people, those with psychological endowments are able to recognize good "investments" (e.g., the treatment venture) and are able to invest in them and profit when they come along. There is also a bit of evidence that the trend is less likely in untreated groups— Sloane et al. (1975) found nonsignificant predictions with a PHS measure in their control group.

Affect

For *anxiety,* 6 of 10 studies yielded a significant relationship between high initial anxiety and a criterion of change (mean $r = .26$ for 6 studies). High initial anxiety probably indicates a readiness, or at least an openness, for change.

For *depression,* 3 of 3 studies showed that a higher initial level of depression is significantly predictive of better outcomes.

Other affects also tended to be a good sign in 3 studies, while flattening of affect signified a poor prognosis. Guilt, however, did not predict outcome.

The overall conclusion about affects is that almost any affect is better prognostically than no affect, and that anxiety and depression are probably the two "best" initial affects. These findings about the prognostic potential of affects are not unique to psychotherapy; they are also prognostic for a variety of other treatments, such as treatment by drugs (Beecher, 1959). The presence of these strong affects may indicate that the patient is in pain and is asking for help. The absence of affect very likely goes along with a state in which the patient is not reaching out for help or has given up.

Motivation or Expectations

The common clinical opinion of the value of good motivation for treatment was upheld by 5 out of 8 studies (mean $r = .31$ for 4 studies).

Although *amount* of motivation tended to be positively related to outcome, *type* of motivation was not predictive (Gliedman et al., 1957). Unexpectedly, patients with congruent motives for treatment did not fare better than those with noncongruent motives (such as, treatment should change their life situation rather than change them). Similarly, type of transference expectation was not predictive (Apfelbaum, 1958).

Patient's expectation of change was similarly predictive in 6 out of 10 studies (mean $r = .36$ for 7 studies). In one study the patient's general tendency to be hopeful, as measured from speech samples, predicted good outcome (Gottschalk, Fox & Bates, 1973).

Positive Attitudes Toward Self, Therapist and Treatment

Four of 5 studies reported significant predictive results based on positive attitudes to self, to therapist, and to treatment. This pretreatment category seems to reflect the same trend that is shown more strongly during the treatment, as reviewed under "The Therapeutic Alliance."

Interest in and Capacity for Human Relations

All of the 8 studies showed this to be a valuable characteristic of patients who enter psychotherapy. The measures in these studies eventually may be shown also to be related to the positive relationship and helping alliance qualities as measured during treatment.

Intellectual Functioning

An impressive array of studies, 6 out of 9, using various ways of estimating intelligence showed that patients with higher initial intelligence improved more in psychotherapy (mean $r = .31$ for 6 studies). All but 2 of the 9 studies were based on the Wechsler Adult Intelligence Scale, either the full scale or four subscales.

As further confirmation, 3 out of the 3 more diverse estimates of intellectual skills produced results in the same direction. One obvious principle that may explain these findings about intellectual functioning is that profiting from psychotherapy requires learning, and those who learn most readily do better.

Self-understanding and Insight

Two out of 3 studies showed that these qualities, as assessed by a variety of pretreatment measures, were positively related to outcome.

Healthy Personality Traits and Coping Styles

The presence of healthy personality traits and coping styles is the most common characteristic of 12 heterogeneous studies; such traits and styles are often associated with better outcomes in 8 of the studies. Among these studies, defensiveness was one obvious subtype shown to be negatively related to improvement.

Mastery versus Helplessness and Passivity

Two studies out of 2 reported that more mastery and less helplessness were predictive of good outcomes for psychotherapy.

PRETREATMENT FACTORS: PATIENT DEMOGRAPHIC AND LIFE SITUATION FACTORS

Age

There is no strong trend in the relation between age and outcome, although older patients tend to have a slightly poorer prognosis. Of 11 studies, only 3 showed that younger patients profited more from psychotherapy. Nonsignificant results were obtained by 6 studies. The 2 negative studies that found older patients did better were based on a limited age range (Conrad, 1952; Knapp et al., 1960).

Sex

Of 11 studies of men versus women, 8 found nonsignificant differences in benefits from psychotherapy; in 3 studies, the women did better.

Social Achievements

Patients with higher social achievements tended to be better suited for psychotherapy. This would be expected, because people who can achieve in spheres requiring social skills should also do so in psychotherapy; the benefits of psychotherapy are mediated by the relationship between patient and therapist. Various social achievements have been examined: socioeconomic (5 of 8 significant but one significantly negative), occupational (3 of 6 significant), educational (5 of 7 significant), and marital status and sexual adjustment (2 of 7 significant). Of these, socioeconomic status and educational achievement had the most supporting studies. In addition to these separate categories of social achievements, combinations of measures of social competence have been successful predictors of improvement with psychotherapy (Stone et al., 1961) as well as with hospitalization (Zigler & Phillips, 1961).

Student Status

Three studies reported that student status was associated with improvement, and 1 found that it made no difference. The main trend appears to be a function of the facilitating effects of educational achievement and probably partly a function of the similarity felt between the patient and the therapist. The same reasoning may explain some of the finding that professional people, including patients who are analytic candidates or psychiatrists, are more likely to complete treatment than the general population of patients (Hamburg et al., 1967).

Previous Psychotherapy

Findings in all 3 studies were in agreement that just having had previous psychotherapy made no significant difference in predicting the outcome of a patient's current psychotherapy. Each new treatment venture, therefore, can be thought of as a fresh start. For further research, however, it would help if the studies had information on the degree of benefit from each of the previous treatments.

PRETREATMENT FACTORS: THERAPIST FACTORS AS ASSESSED APART FROM THE SESSIONS

We present results on only a small sample of the most often investigated characteristics of the therapist, such as skill, experience, psychological health, and interest patterns.

Skill and Success with Patients

The only estimates of therapist's skill reported in the studies are ratings of skill by others. This is significant in 3 of 4 studies.

A more tangible estimate of therapist's skill has recently begun to be explored: therapists' success with their caseloads. What is needed to develop this measure is first more information on differences in therapists' success and then an examination of whether the present level of success predicts outcomes with later caseloads, i.e., whether success really reflects a therapist's skill or a patient's difficulty. But very few studies give information on the level of each therapist's success with his or her caseload. The best known of these few studies is Ricks (1974); it reported a phenomenally large difference between one therapist, a "supershrink," and another, a "subshrink." A Johns Hopkins study (Nash et al., 1965) found differences among four therapists' levels of success. Our first study in this area (Luborsky, McLellan, et al., 1985) examined (1) the differences in the average level of each therapist's success with patients, and (2) the bases for each therapist's level of success. We found differences in performance for nine therapists, ranging from an improvement of the patients in one therapist's caseload of 82% to a worsening in another therapist's caseload of -1%. Because of the potential importance of these results we also reanalyzed data from three other studies (Luborsky et al., 1986) and found comparable differences in therapists' level of success. Then, to help in understanding the bases for each therapist's level of success, the VA-Penn study (Luborsky, McLellan, et al., 1985) examined these correlates of each therapist's success: (1) peer judgments of the therapists' "interest in helping patients" and "adjustment and skill" (mean $r = .32$), (2) patients' and therapists' judgments of the helping alliance (mean $r = .65^{**}$), and (3) rater's independent judgments of the therapist's use of the techniques of the intended treatment recommended in the treatment manual ($r = .44^{**}$). The mean intercorrelations of these three predictors was .63. These results suggest that therapists who help their patients most establish a helping alliance and do what they are supposed to do according to their treatment manual.

Experience

Seven of 16 studies indicated that patients of experienced therapists improved significantly more than those of inexperienced therapists. Although experienced therapists do not consistently achieve better results, there is a small trend in that direction.

Other reviews have been less positive in their conclusions. Parloff, Waskow, and Wolfe (1978) were less impressed with the evidence for the relationship because "the body of data available is not sound enough to permit us to draw any firm conclusion," and a similar conclusion emerged from the review by Auerbach and Johnson (1977) about the capacity of the therapist's level of experience to predict outcome.

However, even though the results are inconsistent across studies, there are enough significant studies to constitute a slightly positive trend. The results of each study probably depend on interactions with other variables, such as the association of experience and skill. Consistent with this view, Auerbach and Johnson (1977) noted a "heartening consistency" in a related finding: In about a dozen studies a better quality of the therapeutic relationship was found for the more experienced therapists. This is shown in a variety of ways, including better communication; higher positive regard, empathy, and congruence; less of a tendency to distance themselves defensively from the patient; and greater likelihood of being direct, focused, involved, and expressive.

Interest Patterns

The division of therapists into Types A and B based on their pattern of scores on the Strong Vocational Interest Blank seemed important at the time of the earlier review in 1971, because Betz (1963) had found that Type A therapists were much more likely to be successful with schizophrenic patients. But time has not been kind to the A-B variable. Razin (1977) reviewed the literature and drew the following conclusions about the A-B variable. (1) It has a certain validity in that it reflects some personality differences. (2) It is not a good predictor of any important psychotherapy process or outcome variable. (3) It may have some usefulness in matching patients and therapists in brief encounters, such as crisis intervention. We mostly agree with these conclusions, and we note that the previous flood of studies on the A-B variable has dried up completely. However, our review shows that the studies were not entirely nonsignificant. Six of 12 studies had a significant advantage for Type A therapists, and 1 study showed an advantage for Type B therapists.

Therapist's Personal Therapy

The amount of the therapist's personal therapy or satisfaction with that therapy clearly is not related to the improvement of the patients the therapist treats—in 4 studies the relationship is nonsignificant and in 1 it is negatively significant (Garfield & Bergin, 1971). A significant positive relationship might have been expected because psychotherapy helps patients (chapter 3) and it must also help the therapists when they are patients themselves. However, there is no control in these studies for the amount of therapy each therapist gets; probably the ones who need it more get more. The effects of such natural selection would be to reduce the chances of a significantly positive relationship between amount of the therapist's personal therapy and the benefits the therapists provide to their patients.

Therapist's Psychological Health

Of the 7 studies of the therapist's healthy personality qualities, 4 are significantly predictive of the outcomes of their patients' treatments, for example, therapists with healthier MMPI profiles (Garfield & Bergin, 1971), and therapist's absence of "pathogenesis" (Vandenbos & Karon, 1971).

DURING-TREATMENT FACTORS: PATIENT FACTORS AS JUDGED FROM THE SESSIONS

Because predictions from these factors are based on the treatment itself, such predictions should be more closely related to treatment outcomes than those based on pretreatment data. This expectation was borne out.

Within the area of process predictors of outcome a larger review than ours is now available (Orlinsky & Howard, 1986).[4] Its findings overlap considerably with our own, but its framework of categories at times differs conceptually.

Psychological Health-Sickness (PHS)

Only 1 study of PHS was done and it was significantly predictive. Because PHS was so often predictive on the basis of pretreatment measures, we would have expected more PHS studies based on sessions to have been done.

Affect

This showed no consistent trend: In 3 studies expression of affect was positively related to outcome, in 2 studies it was negatively related, and in 1 it was unrelated.

Likability

In 2 of 2 studies the patient's quality of being likable was positively associated with outcome. (This is closely related to the therapist's liking, reviewed with therapist's qualities.)

[4]The much larger number of findings in their review is mostly a function of three differences: (1) They include studies of group therapy and studies with children; we use only individual therapy. (2) They include every correlation of a predictor with an outcome measure as a different finding; we average the correlations with the outcome measures within each study. (3) We excluded many more studies because of major design flaws.

Problem-Solving Attitude

A problem-solving attitude is a useful attitude in psychotherapy—it was significantly predictive in all 5 of the 5 studies. This attitude, therefore, appears to express the patient's actual ability to deal with problems.

Process Continuum of Psychotherapy

Because a problem-solving attitude involves reflecting on one's experience, it is a component of the experiencing concept, which is part of Rogers's (1959) process scale. His scale is composed of seven strands, which he called relationship to feeling, degree of incongruence, manner of experiencing, communication of self, construing of experiencing, relationship to problems, and manner of relating to others. All 4 studies were related to outcomes.

Experiencing

One of the most predictively successful strands is manner of experiencing (first suggested and later reported by Gendlin et al., 1968). It implies that the patient is capable both of experiencing deeply and immediately *and* of being reflectively aware about this feeling. The scales are usually applied to very brief segments, such as 4 minutes, of the treatment session. A low score indicates that the patient is remote from experiencing and unable to understand its implicit meanings. Scales have been developed by Gendlin et al. (1968), Klein et al. (1969), and others, and they show fairly good interjudge reliability.

Experiencing has only a fair record of predictive performance within the client-centered psychotherapy and not as good a record in other psychotherapies. For 3 studies the mean r is .38. Of the 11 studies involving the Experiencing scale, 4 are significantly positively related to the patient's improvement. Two are negatively related, although both may involve extenuating circumstances: (1) Ryan (1966) is negatively related based on the second interview and positively related based on the middle interview; (2) Richert (1976) is negatively related but in a very restricted sample of high experiencers.

The Therapeutic Alliance

The patient's experience of alliance with the therapist. Measures of the therapeutic or helping alliance—we use the terms interchangeably—have performed with impressive consistency: Eight studies using somewhat similar systems have appeared and all significantly predicted outcomes; the mean r for 8 studies is moderately high (.50). The first manual-based system for scoring transcripts of psychotherapy sessions involved counting signs in the transcript (Luborsky, 1976a; Luborsky et al., 1983). Our helping alliance rating system (Morgan et al., 1982) and the helping alliance questionnaire (Luborsky, McLellan, et al., 1985) also achieved successful prediction. Another system also involved rated transcripts of sessions (Marziali, Marmar & Krupnick, 1981). One of the Vanderbilt systems for rating therapeutic alliances in transcripts achieved significant prediction only for the session that was at the 25% point in the treatment (Hartley & Strupp, 1982).

All of these measures are intended to be operational definitions of an old and established clinical concept (Freud, 1913). The therapeutic alliance is believed to develop through therapist empathy and supportiveness, or through fortuitous matching of patient's expectations and therapist's attributes which facilitates the patient's experience of a helping relationship.

In the Penn studies, the helping alliance is defined as the patient's experience of a helpful relationship with the therapist. It is further defined by its two main types and seven subtypes or "signs." The judge rates or counts signs of positive or negative expressions of categories of helping alliances within transcripts of psychotherapy sessions.

Significant predictions of outcome were achieved by scores on the seven subtypes of helping alliance categories by all three helping alliance measures (Alexander & Luborsky, 1986). This success must have been furthered by the use of sizable segments of the sessions, e.g., 20 minutes from the beginning of each of Sessions 3 and 5. In support of this supposition, we also found in an earlier study (chapter 9) that although many types of variables could be judged reliably just as well from brief segments as from whole sessions, there was one big exception: "Optimal empathic relationship" could not be judged reliably from brief segments. The helping alliance appears to be a similar exception since it also depends on assessing the patient–therapy interaction and therefore requires large segments.

The pattern of correlations between helping alliance measures and other measures offers bases for understanding the nature of helping alliance measures. One of the highest correlations, both by the rating and counting signs methods, was with basic demographic similarities between the patient and therapist. The sum of 10 similarities correlated between .50 and .60 with the helping alliance measures, e.g., .60 with positive Helping Alliance Counting Signs (HAcs) and .53 with Helping Alliance Global Ratings (HAr). The highest of the correlations for the 10 individual similarities were with similarity in age and similarity in level of religious activity. These significant correlations are even more impressive because similarities were assessed apart from the psychotherapy and the judge reading the transcript "blind" had no direct way of knowing the existence of these similarities.

The presence of such basic similarities between patient and therapist as age or religious activity appears to have a facilitating effect on the establishment of a helping alliance, although it is not obvious how these similarities exert their impact. Very likely the patient and the therapist somehow acquire awareness of these similarities and that awareness augments the patient's experience of the helping alliance.

The correlations of helping alliance measures with the method of patient assignment may point to another condition that facilitates or inhibits the formation of the helping alliance. These correlations suggest that random assignment tended to inhibit the helping alliance: HAcs $-.60^{**}$ and HAr $-.56^{**}$. Further, the therapist's facilitating behavior (TFB) may encourage the helping alliance. Several correlations were consistent with this view, e.g., early HAr correlated $.85^{**}$ with early TFBr.

In summary, these three types of correlates suggest that the chances of forming a positive helping alliance will be increased by the existence of some basic demographic similarities, by the opportunity of the therapist to express preference in patient assignments, and by the therapist's efforts toward facilitating the helping alliance.

Other positive relationship qualities. Research on a variety of other positive attitudes to the therapy and the therapist supports the conclusion that variables based on the early sessions tend to be more consistently predictive than those assessed pretherapy. A total of 10 findings have been reported, and 9 of the 10 were significantly predictive. This category of positive relationship qualities has become an actively investigated area with almost consistently positive findings. For example, a study of early increases in positive attitudes to self and others (Rosenman, 1955) showed these to be predictive of the outcomes of psychotherapy. Likewise, the Relationship Inventory by Barrett-Lennard (1962), which grew out of Rogers's ideas of the conditions for effective psychotherapy, found that such positive attitudes predicted the outcomes of psychotherapy.

Self-Understanding and Insight

Four studies of psychotherapy sessions showed only 1 significant and 3 nonsignificant correlations. In view of the theoretical centrality of insight as a curative factor, it is astonishing that there are not more significant results and that there is not more research on insight as measured within psychotherapy sessions. It must be admitted, however, from the Penn study experience (chapter 17) that finding operational measures of this category is no easy task.

Involvement

All 4 studies measuring the patient's involvement in the treatment (lack of inhibition, active participation) were significantly predictive of positive therapeutic outcome at an impressive level of correlation (mean $r = .59$).

DURING-TREATMENT FACTORS: THERAPIST FACTORS AS JUDGED FROM SESSIONS

Skill

Whenever sessions have been judged for aspects of therapist's skill, they show significant prediction of outcomes—in 4 of 4 studies (much like the pretreatment judgments of skill). Research in this area should go on to examine the types of therapist behavior that are the basis for the judgments of skill.

Empathy

Judges' ratings of empathy based on samples of sessions generally predicted the outcomes of psychotherapy—in 8 of 13 studies correlations were significant (mean $r = .26$ for 9 studies). An even better record was achieved for empathy as judged by other measures, such as by the Barrett-Lennard Relationship Inventory. Six of 8 studies were significant (mean $r = .20$ for 5 studies). Empathy is obviously an important variable in relation to the success of psychotherapy; it deserves a place in the theory of psychotherapeutic change as well as further research to understand the basis for its contribution.

Accuracy of Interpretation

Only the Penn study confirms the core clinical concept that therapists' accuracy of interpretation predicts the outcomes of psychotherapy (chapter 16). After this study had been completed and the results were to be entered in the Appendix, its location in the outline was decided by the realization that Empathy and Accuracy of Interpretation, although they originate in different schools of psychotherapy (the client-centered and the psychodynamic), may well be within the same family of measures.

The Penn study is based on a methodological advance in the criterion for evaluation of accuracy of interpretation (Crits-Christoph, Cooper & Luborsky, in press): the degree to which the interpretation is congruent with the relationship problems presented by the patient in the session, as these are independently evaluated by the Core Conflictual Relationship Theme (CCRT) method (Luborsky, 1977b; Luborsky, Mellon, et al., 1985; Luborsky, Crits-Christoph & Mellon, 1986).

Focus on Transference

This therapist's behavior is prized in dynamic psychotherapy's theory of therapy. Two of 3 studies support its potential benefits. The verdict may become even more positive in time because the limited operational measures tested so far may not give enough attention to the appropriate conditions for making transference interpretations, as shown by Silberschatz et al. (1986).

Positive Regard and Warmth

As this is judged from sessions, 9 out of 13 studies were significant (mean $r = .32$ for 11 studies).

Genuineness (or "Congruence")

In 3 out of 5 studies this quality was significantly predictive (mean $r = .21$).

Liking the Patient

The findings tend to agree with clinical opinion that it is desirable to like one's patients. Three of the 6 studies showed significant correlations with outcomes. The mean r, however, is only .19 for 3 studies.

Encouraging Independence

This category would elicit considerable concurrence from clinicians, and the 2 studies are both significantly in its favor (with a mean r of .21).

Directive and Advice-Giving

Dynamic therapy especially tends to abhor this therapist behavior, and the studies are somewhat in agreement: Of 3 studies 2 are with the trend (but the mean r is only .06 for 2 studies).

Supportive

The two studies both support this quality at a correlation level that is impressive (mean $r = .61$ for 2 studies).

Amount of Therapist's Talking

There are 6 studies of this exactly measurable aspect of therapy, but only 2 are significant. What is said by the therapist must matter more than how much is said.

Therapist's Prognostic Expectations

Of 4 studies 3 are significant. The finding can be interpreted in two ways at least: (1) the therapists can predict the patient's outcomes and (2) the therapists are partly involved in a self-fulfilling prophecy.

THE SIMILARITY BETWEEN PATIENT AND THERAPIST, ASSESSED PRETREATMENT

A frequently studied basis for matching patient and therapist is on their similarities to each other: 29 studies dealt with some form of similarity between therapist and patient assessed apart from the therapy sessions. Twenty showed a positive relationship: Greater similarity was associated with better outcome. One report contained a significant negative relationship between similarity of patient's and therapist's "subtlety of defensive patterns" (Wogan, 1970). The forms of positive similarity include social class, interests, values, and compatibility of orientation to interpersonal relations. Of these, similarity of interests had the most supporting evidence (4 studies of 4). A variety of other similarities were generally predictive. In one, from the Penn study, the measure was the number of similarities that apply from among a set of 10 similarities.

Similarities were also relatively outstanding predictors in the Smith and Glass (1977) meta-analysis based on 120 effect size (outcome) measures derived from 50 studies. Their table 4 (p. 758) offers correlations with effect size of many predictors: group versus individual, duration of therapy (in hours), years of experience of therapists, therapists' diagnosis of clients (severity as measured by the assigning of "1" to psychotic and "2" to neurotic), IQ of clients, age of clients, similarity of therapists and clients, internal validity of the study, date of publication, reactivity (i.e., subjectivity) of the outcome measure, and number of months posttherapy for the follow-up. Among all of these, the largest correlations were the similarity of therapists and clients, $r = .19^{**}$ (similarities included ethnic group, age, and social level), and IQ of clients, $r = .15^{**}$, was a close second.

Since the predictive capacity of similarities is broadly supported, we should search for the sources of its strength. The most likely source is that the similarities facilitate close relationships: basic demographic qualities, interests, values, and orientation toward interpersonal relations. The presence of similarities furthers the formation of a helping relationship because the patient and therapist can see each other as having a shared background, as being alike, and thus as able to understand each other. In turn, the better relationship that forms helps the patient achieve the goals through the treatment. It is at least consistent with these views that a high correlation was found between the number of these similarities and the helping alliance (HAcs) scores (chapter 12).

Further useful hypotheses about the basis for good matches of patient and therapist emerged from a review of the reactions of different patients in the Penn Project to the same therapist. The following is an example of one of these reactions: An alcoholic patient (Ms. Q. M., #17) who was in the most improved group said of her therapist in the follow-up interview, "He was the best damn brick wall I ever found," meaning that he did not allow her to become too dependent and for this reason she valued him. In contrast, another of the therapist's patients, who was in the least improved group (Ms. Kane, #6), while crying, said to him in one late session before she discontinued treatment, "I haven't changed and you've gotten worse." These two patients were reacting differently to the same therapist quality, but the different reactions were in line with their special needs from helping relationships. We therefore formed this hypothesis: The basis for a good match may lie in the fit between (a) the patient's core conflictual relationship theme, which succinctly specifies what is wished for and what is expected in relationships, and (b) the patient's perception of the therapist's characteristics and responses in terms of how they fit with what is wished for and expected in relationships. Ms. Q. M. needed someone who could lightly and humorously brush off her tremendous inclination to become overdependent, and this kind of brush-off came naturally to the therapist. Yet Ms. Kane needed someone who was not a "brick wall" but could understand her need to open up and her fantastic fear that she would be brushed off when she did. Ms. Q. M. improved partly because she experienced this crucial aspect of a good match; Ms. Kane did not improve partly because she did not have this crucial aspect of what she needed, nor did the therapist try to help her to understand what it was in relationships that she most wished for and felt she was denied.

CHARACTERISTICS OF THE TREATMENT

Through reliance on his clinical observations Freud (1913) arrived at the conclusion, expressed in his well-known analogy between chess and psychotherapy, that we have a grasp of only some of the opening and closing moves; for the rest, we have only intuitively applied guidelines. Therefore, "this gap in instruction can only be filled by a diligent study of games fought out by masters" (p. 123). But technical advances have changed things for chess: Endgames by masters have been improved on by certain computer analyses. A parallel kind of change is beginning to apply to psychotherapy. While tutorial exercises and apprenticeship, coupled with self-scrutiny, will remain as primary means of ferreting out factors affecting the benefits of psychotherapy, the findings of quantitative psychotherapy research can now supplement and assist clinical judgments (Luborsky, 1987a).

The research to be described is a long way from the finesse of a master clinician's sensitive techniques, but it can offer some broad guidelines within certain areas.

Effects of Number of Sessions and Duration of Treatment

In 23 out of 26 studies the length of treatment was positively related to outcome: The longer the duration of treatment or the more sessions, the better the outcome (mean $r = .46$ for 20 studies).

It is tempting to conclude—and it may be accurate to do so—that because psychotherapy is beneficial, then the more the better. But, to tell the whole truth, other interpretations may also fit: (a) Patients who are getting what they need stay in treatment longer; those who are not, drop out sooner. (b) Therapists may overestimate positive change in patients who have been in treatment longer. A complementary trend may also operate— therapists often assume that some minimum number of sessions are needed before real change can occur, so that early drop-outs tend to get poor outcome ratings.

The Penn study was one of these studies, with duration of treatment correlated .27* with rated benefits and .20 with residual gain. Data from a much larger sample of studies examining treatment outcome in relation to number of sessions is provided by Smith, Glass, and Miller (1980). They report a curvilinear correlation of .29 between the effect size achieved in a study and the number of sessions, with almost none of the relationships being linear. However, their sample of studies is quite different from our own. It is short-term treatment in which the average duration was about 15 sessions, with over two-thirds involving 12 or fewer sessions. Their results would be more comparable if their sample of studies involved dynamically oriented open-ended psychotherapy, as ours did.

Furthermore, the Smith, Glass, and Miller (1980) review was based on between-studies comparisons. The results of Howard et al. (1986) show that there is not necessarily a relationship between analyses based on between-study results and analyses based on within-study results. Howard et al.'s (1986) study was based on panels of data from their own and other studies covering 2,400 patients. A probit analysis resulted in a generally good fit, indicating for specified "doses" of psychotherapy what would be the expected benefits of the therapy. They report, for example, that it would be expected from their data that by 8 sessions about 50% of the patients would have improved; with once weekly psychotherapy (26 sessions) about 75% of patients would have improved after 6 months, and about 85% of patients would have improved by the end of a year. In addition, they suggest that the "dosage" for establishing a treatment group should generally be 6 to 8 sessions and that patients who have had fewer than that should probably be considered for purposes of research "as subjects who have not been effectively exposed to treatment." (Note the coincidence that in the Penn Psychotherapy Project we limited our sample to patients who had 8 sessions or more.)

Frequency of Sessions

There is some inconsistent evidence that a greater number of sessions per week is associated with greater benefits: Three studies are significant and 3 are not. This kind of study needs especially careful control of psychological severity because greater frequency of sessions is often provided to patients who are *lower* in psychiatric severity.

Fee Payment

The results for the impact of the fee on psychotherapy outcome are mixed: One significantly positive, 1 significantly negative, and 2 not significant. These results do not fit well with the clinical lore that the payment of a fee is an ingredient to a successful treatment, but more research should be done in this area.

Effects of Waiting for Treatment

In 3 out of 3 studies, a long and mandatory wait between the time of applying for psychotherapy and the time of beginning it is negatively related to outcome. Two main implications may be drawn from this result.

First, the practice of using the patient as the patient's own control by having the patient wait for psychotherapy and then be retested during the waiting period has in itself a negative impact on potential benefits from psychotherapy. The experience appears to be a negative one; therefore a wait-list design cannot be accepted as fitting the researchers' intention to provide a neutral, no-therapy period. Second, clinics with long waiting lists should be aware of these studies and should try to provide service close to the time the patient applies for it or refer the patients to a facility where they can obtain more immediate care.

Role Preparation Provided to the Patient

Six studies used a preparation interview (role-induction) that provided patients with expectations for the psychotherapy process. In 4 of these the preparation was associated with significant benefits. In the preparation interview the interviewer introduces patients to what will be expected of them and how the therapist and therapy will proceed. For example, the therapist is described as a person who will try to understand the patient so that the patient will become more aware of issues that have been preventing development. Through this preparatory interview patients probably become more ready to feel suitably matched to the intended form of psychotherapy. An example of one preparatory socialization interview (Orne & Wender, 1968) has been reproduced, with instructions for its use, in the treatment manual for psychoanalytic psychotherapy (Luborsky, 1984).

Relative Benefits of Different Psychotherapies

A factor that many clinicians believe in and often fill books about is the special benefits of one type of psychotherapy over another. In fact, different types of treatment may well have different effects, but it is difficult to know, even from systematic research, what type of treatment has what effect. Yet in the last four decades the number of studies comparing different types of treatments with each other has increased dramatically (as reviewed by Luborsky, Singer & Luborsky, 1975; Smith, Glass & Miller, 1980). We will note only their main result: Most comparisons of different types of psychotherapy show nonsignificant differences in their outcomes. In our review (Luborsky, Singer & Luborsky, 1975) the types of psychotherapy compared were group versus individual, time-limited versus unlimited, client-centered versus other psychotherapies, psychotherapy versus pharmacotherapies, psychotherapy versus or plus medical regimens for psychosomatic illnesses, and psychotherapy versus control groups of no psychotherapy or minimal psychotherapy. Just as Rosenzweig (1936) had anticipated 40 years before, our principal finding was that for comparisons of different psychotherapies, there were no consistent winners; thus the subtitle given to the paper was taken from *Alice in Wonderland*'s Dodo bird's verdict after judging the race: "All have won so everyone shall have prizes." A much larger version of this kind of review (Smith & Glass, 1977; Smith, Glass & Miller, 1980), with almost 475 studies, came to similar conclusions. Not only does this conclusion apply when psychotherapies or behavioral treatments are compared with each other for psychiatric patients, it also applies in other treatment comparisons, such as the intercomparison of different behavioral treatments for hypertensive patients (Luborsky, Crits-Christoph, et al., 1980; Luborsky, Crits-Christoph, et al., 1982; Wadden et al., 1984).

A still unpublished update of the Luborsky, Singer & Luborsky (1975) review shows that the effect is as strong as ever. This updated review includes a comparison that is highly relevant for this book: psychodynamic psychotherapy versus other psychotherapies. We located 13 studies with a total of 20 comparisons. These showed the typical box score result: 16 of the 20 comparisons showed nonsignificant difference effects between psychodynamic psychotherapy and others; in 1 study psychodynamic psychotherapy was better and in 3 it was worse. These studies dealt with patients with a variety of diagnoses. In only 1 of all of these comparisons was manual-guided psychotherapy used (Woody et al., 1983). Also of interest is that most of these studies were done by researchers from nonpsychodynamic fields; as Smith, Glass, and Miller (1980) have shown, the orientation of researchers tends to have some recondite effect in the direction of support for their orientation!

But the recurrent perplexing conclusion that nonsignificant differences are the main effect in comparative studies still needs to be accepted cautiously. Some limitations in the research methods in these treatment comparisons may have unfairly fostered the finding.

1. The major limitation is that the outcomes of the studies were almost always based only on a global measure, such as the percentage of patients improved, which offers no information about the composition of the improvement. More specific outcome measures would offer more opportunity to reveal some possible differences among treatments in the quality of the outcomes.

2. Another limitation is the overreliance in almost all of the studies on the treatment label for information about the nature of the treatment. The label does not give an independently verified estimate of what the treatment actually comprised. The small revolution in research and practice based on the new technology of treatment manuals (Luborsky & DeRu-

beis, 1984; Luborsky, 1984; Luborsky, in press) has begun to correct this. Manuals and their associated performance scales permit independent observers to judge how much of the intended treatment was actually employed by each therapist and how much each of the "different" therapies compared actually differed (Luborsky, Woody, et al., 1982).

3. The studies do not adequately match the groups being compared on psychological health-sickness measures. It is true that the studies do use random assignment of cases to the groups, but this step alone may not achieve the needed matching on this variable.

4. The studies do not adequately match the groups to be compared in terms of an important index of the therapist's skill: the therapist's past record of success with patients (as discussed earlier in this chapter).

Nevertheless, despite the limitations of the comparative treatment studies, we have paid serious attention to this finding of nonsignificant differences. Our belief in it played a role in our research planning. Because most patients benefited, it was natural to suppose that some common elements in these different treatments must serve as the curative factors. We searched for these common elements and were led most directly to the patient's ability to experience a helping alliance with the therapist.

Matches of type of patient with type of psychotherapy. Although different types of psychotherapy have not so far been shown to have different effects, it still may be possible that some types of patients will do better with some types of psychotherapies. Cogent clinical opinions (such as Horowitz et al., 1984) affirm that because psychotherapy is helpful to most people who need it and because people may require different forms of treatment, research may eventually show that people with certain needs will do better in treatments with the qualities that meet these needs. Our review (Luborsky, Singer & Luborsky, 1975) confirmed the sparsity of proven special matches, but noted three—one a probable match and two very tentative matches:

1. For those illnesses that are usually called psychosomatic, the addition of psychotherapy to a medical regimen makes a helpful match.

2. For the treatment of circumscribed phobias, behavioral therapy may be especially well suited. However, only 1 study so far supports this possible match (Gelder, Marks & Wolff, 1967).

3. For schizophrenic patients, group psychotherapy as part of after-hospitalization care may be especially valuable. O'Brien, et al. (1972) found a significant advantage for group psychotherapy over individual psychotherapy in the after-hospitalization care of schizophrenic patients. This finding was subsequently replicated in another study, by Claghorn et al. (1974). However, in a slightly different marshaling of studies by Parloff and Dies (1977), this special optimal match was not clearly supported.

The search in psychotherapy research for patient–treatment matches may also derive some leads from studies of matches between type of student and type of instructional mode in comparative instructional research in education. Cronbach (1957) devoted his presidential address to the American Psychological Association to the need for finding such matches. However, the search for these student–instructional mode interactions, like the ones for psychotherapy, has turned up only a few that have held up on cross-validation (Cronbach & Snow, 1977). The counterpart of the following three matches also should be tried in psychotherapy research studies, especially the last.

1. The student's level of intelligence interacts with different types of instruction. This means that the relationship between ability, learning time, and efficiency is altered by different kinds of instruction.

2. The student's previous experience interacts with instructional technique. Experience with a particular instructional technique generalizes so that the person learns how to profit from that kind of instructional technique.

3. Two instructional techniques may be selectively effective for different types of students. Students who score high in independent achievement motivation are better able to profit from instruction that is less directive than students who are more anxious and introverted; the latter do better with more directive instruction.

General Conclusions about the Main Factors Influencing Outcomes

Although many of the single studies are weak reeds because of their small sample size, unreliability of measures, and brevity of treatment, some of the predictors that have emerged will probably stand up to further testing. It adds fiber to a finding when it is resilient enough to appear in different samples and by different assessment methods. In this field of research it is a source of some safety to seek trends based on a series of studies; it is necessary to give up the hope that a single really well designed study will clear the way once and for all to a conclusive conclusion. When there have been divergent results on the same factors, it has sometimes been possible— though less often than anticipated—to review the studies and locate the probable responsible agent in the nature of the patient groups or criterion measures. Much more of this type of reviewing remains to be done.

The summary list in table 19-2 contains the essence of the quantitative research on the best predictors of benefiting from psychotherapy in terms of numbers of significant versus nonsignificant studies. The size of the list shows considerable progress since the 1971 review. It should have value as a guide in the selection of patients and therapists, as well as in the delineation of crucial facets of the process of psychotherapy. Because table 19-2 is so long, two subsidiary tables are offered.

As we see in table 19-3, by far the most studied area is the patient measured apart from treatment—a total of 250 findings. To date much less research has been carried out to examine therapist factors assessed apart from the treatment—only 56 findings. There are only 63 treatment process findings of the patient and 87 of the therapist, although they have had a long history, beginning with Rogers (1957). Many new studies in this area are being done, especially with the therapeutic relationship qualities.

The area with the greatest relative concentration of significant findings (table 19-3) is for the patient during treatment, where the ratio of significant to nonsignificant findings is about 4. There are only twice as many findings significant in the area of the therapist during treatment. It is easy to see, and well worth seeing, that predictive studies of patient qualities show many more significant findings than predictive studies of therapist qualities *both apart from treatment and in treatment.*

Now we come to the topic with the greatest payoff in implications for practice—the qualities that are most predictive and the level of their mean predictive correlations (table 19-4).

TABLE 19-3

Numbers of Findings, Proportion Significant, and Qualities Most Often Significantly Predictive (All Studies)

		Sig.	Nonsig.	Ratio Sig. to Nonsig.	Qualities Most Often Significant
P.	Apart from Treatment	161	89	2×	PHS, Motivation and expectation, Positive attitude, Human relations orientation, IQ
T.	Apart from Treatment	28	28	1	—
P.–T.	Match Apart from Treatment	20	10	2×	Similarities in interests and other similarities
P.	in Treatment	50	13	4×	Problems-solving attitude, Experiencing, Helping alliance, Other positive relationship qualities
T.	in Treatment	61	26	2×	Empathy
Total		320	166		

TABLE 19-4

Rankings of Categories of Predictors from Highest to Lowest Mean Correlations

Category of Predictor	Mean r	No. of Studies
Therapist Supportive	.61	2
Patient Involvement	.59	4
Symptom Checklist Severity	.54	2
Therapeutic Alliance	.50	8
Focus on Transference	.50	2
Rorschach Prognostic Rating Scale	.49	5
Number of Sessions or Duration	.46	20
Process Continuum	.38	3
Patient Experiencing	.38	3
Therapist's Amount of Experience	.36	3
Patient Expectations	.36	7
Therapist Positive Regard and Warmth	.32	11
Patient Motivation	.31	3
Interests and Values Similarity	.31	2
IQ	.31	6
Therapist's Prognostic Expectations (Early Therapy)	.31	2
Global Adjustment Measures	.27	11
Therapist Empathy as Judged from Sessions	.26	9
Patient Anxiety	.26	6
Barron Ego Strength Scale	.24	6
Encouraging Independence	.21	2
Genuineness	.21	3
Therapist Empathy as Judged by Other Measures	.20	5
Liking the Patient	.19	3
Therapist's Expectation of Patient Improvement (pretherapy)	.17	3
Directive	.06	2
Fee Payment	−.08	2

In the area of the patient apart from the treatment, the significant findings that are most impressive are: psychological health-sickness (Barron Ego Strength mean $r = .23$; Global Adjustment mean $r = .26$; Rorschach Prognostic Rating Scale mean $r = .43$), motivation (mean $r = .33$), expectation (mean $r = .35$), positive attitudes, human relations orientation, intelligence (mean $r = .30$), and anxiety (mean $r = .25$).

The therapist apart from the treatment is an area where there are no frequently significant qualities.

For the patient during the treatment process the significant findings are: problem-solving attitude, experiencing (mean $r = .23$), the helping alliance (mean $r = .57$), and other positive relationship qualities and involvement (mean $r = .57$). For the therapist during treatment, empathy (mean $r = .26$) and related qualities, such as warmth (mean $r = .26$), are important.

For the patient–therapist match apart from treatment two very significant areas are similarities in interests and other similarities. The predictive value of such similarities was already evident in the 1971 review, and the more recent results remain equally predictive.

A related type of research on finding the best match between type of patient and type of treatment is still neglected, even though reviews routinely present it as a topic that researchers should investigate.

Although studies in the area of the impact of specific techniques of psychotherapy started more than 40 years ago, such studies are still less common than they should be. Studies of specific techniques are being revitalized by the advent of psychotherapy manuals, which define the therapist's use of different techniques.

TO WHAT TYPES OF PSYCHOTHERAPY DO THESE PREDICTORS APPLY?

The predictors probably apply to most of the more usual forms of psychotherapy represented in this review, including psychodynamic, client-centered, and cognitive psychotherapies. The form of psychotherapy is occasionally specified in the citation in the Appendix. It would especially interest those who share the concerns of members of the Society for the Exploration of Psychotherapy Integration to see whether there are any predictors that are specific to particular forms of psychotherapy. The strong impression from this review is that within the realm of the different psychotherapies included there are few, if any, specific predictors for each type.

SOME PROMISING PREDICTIVE INTERACTIONS

It must be a safe overall conclusion that factors in the patient, in the therapist, and in the patient–therapist combination interact to eventuate in the gains of psychotherapy. Such interactions have been shown very neatly for pharmacotherapy studies in which factors such as the manner of giving the drug, the expectations of the patient, and the patient's qualities are as important as the nature of the drug itself in determining the effects of the drug (Rickels, 1968). But, so far, within psychotherapy research only a few promising interactions have been investigated.

High psychological health with high affect. The section on patient factors apart from treatment points to an interactive conclusion suggested by Luborsky (1962b): High affect (anxiety, depression, and other forms of distress) together with high integration (or ego strength, or other descriptors for psychological health) form a good combination of prognostic conditions for change through psychotherapy.

High psychological health, high affect, and high capacity to form relationships. A combination of low severity of illness, high level of anxiety, and capacity for relationships with people may make for good outcomes of short-term psychotherapy. Some of these are suggested by Gottschalk, Mayerson, and Gottlieb (1967).

High motivation with high therapist empathy. A combination of high patient motivation with high therapist empathy was found to be especially advantageous by Cartwright and Lerner (1963).

Appropriate match of type of patient and type of psychoactive medication. It seems unlikely, based on the results of our review, that the conclusion by Astrup and Noreik (1966) for psychotic patients applies equally to nonpsychotic ones. They found that it is almost entirely the patient's initial state that determines the future course, either with or without psychotherapy! Their implication for psychotic patients is still controversial (Karon J. Vanden-Bos, 1981). Their broader implication is that for these patients only diagnosis matters and there are no interactions with form of treatment. That conclusion now appears to be outdated not only for psychotic patients but also for other types of patients, in large part because of greater sophistication about combinations of types of patients with types of psychoactive medications (Klerman, 1986). Consensus has increased for the types of medications considered appropriate for schizophrenic and affective disorders. Consensus is lower for anxiety disorders and for opiate dependence.

COMPARISON OF THE QUANTITATIVE FINDINGS WITH CLINICAL WISDOM

Clinical knowledge lays claim to much more wisdom than the quantitative has managed to garner. Even though the clinical lore has a higher degree of undetermined validity, it has the advantage of addressing the array of issues that the clinician must confront. What follows is a listing of the outstanding specific discrepancies in the two types of literature and of what research needs are implied.

1. Quantitative studies, with their stress on the qualities of the patient, the therapist, and their relationship, give far less attention to the techniques of treatment than do clinical writings. Above all, accuracy of interpretation has had relatively little quantitative work done on it, except for the work on empathy, which is an unclearly related concept. Our work (chapter 16) has begun to remedy this deficiency.

2. Despite the tremendous emphasis in the clinical literature on the importance of providing insight to the patient, little quantitative investiga-

tion of insight in relation to outcome variables exists. There is somewhat more now than in the 1971 review, but more is needed of the kind that is begun here in chapter 17.

3. Very little exists in the quantitative literature on which qualities of the patient make him or her amenable to one form of treatment versus another. In contrast, the clinical literature is full of such discussions, as summarized by Wallerstein et al. (1956) and Horowitz et al. (1984). For example, one reason for conducting a diagnostic evaluation is to decide on the patient's suitability for psychoanalysis versus other forms of treatment. There are dozens of clinical articles on how to make this judgment, but no quantitative ones (Bachrach & Leaff, 1978). At the present time the best conclusion from the quantitative literature is that those patients who are most suitable for expressive psychotherapy are also the ones most suitable for psychoanalysis.

4. A large part of the clinical literature is based on long-term psychotherapy; most of the quantitative research is on short-term psychotherapy. We hope researchers will gather patients and patience to tackle this issue of the relative benefits of the two treatment modes.

Guidance for Theory and Practice of Psychotherapy

THE VALUE OF PRETREATMENT EVALUATIONS

The practice of performing pretreatment evaluations to determine suitability for psychotherapy should be continued, even though it might be held to be questionable because of the modest level of predictive success of the pretreatment predictors. Four arguments are on the side of continuing such evaluations: (a) The fact that the correlations were modest does not mean they were zero; some better than chance prediction was achieved. (b) The follow-up of predictions is based on patients who went on into psychotherapy instead of also following up those who did not. A basic comparison of the two groups has never been tried and may show a much greater measure of success in the treated group. (c) Our experience in the Penn Psychotherapy Project with random assignment of patients who have applied for treatment suggests that random assignment is less beneficial than assignment after the therapist has examined some pretreatment information. (d) The pretreatment information appears to provide some helpful guidelines to the therapist about the types of issues that need to be resolved in the psychotherapy.

The evaluation should be based on the pretreatment predictors that were found in our review of predictive studies. These methods can be helpful. However, it is noteworthy that some clinicians who do pretreatment evaluations have a mistaken impression of the high level of accuracy that can be achieved by unguided interview methods. Without a careful record of the predictions and their outcomes based on a sizable sample of patients, it is easy to be fooled. The most common mistake is to retrospectively overestimate the accuracy of pretreatment and even early-in-treatment predictions of outcomes. How do such mistaken impressions occur? If a therapist is generally optimistic in initial evaluations about patients' prognosis, then the therapist soon comes to believe that he or she is generally right since, as we have documented, about two-thirds of patients in psychotherapy do improve (chapter 3). By the time the termination of treatment occurs, it may be hard for the evaluator to recall which of the few patients who made only slight gains or did not improve were the ones the evaluator had expected to improve the least.

Clinicians' impressions of their accuracy are also likely to be bolstered in another way. They probably are able to predict the types of issues that will be prominent during the psychotherapy, yet they probably are not very good at predicting the degree of eventual resolution of these issues. As an example, they may be able to discern the patient's core conflictual relationship theme, but they may not be able to forecast whether improved ways of dealing with it will be developed. More research is needed to determine whether these suppositions are correct. Only a bit of evidence now exists to suggest that some individual predictions for each patient can be made about what will happen in the course of each treatment (Sargent et al., 1968).

APPLICATION TO MATCHING OF PATIENT AND THERAPIST BY PREFERENCE FOR EACH OTHER

The assignment of patients and therapists for psychotherapy by the therapist's preference was a significant predictor in the Penn study (chapter 8). That observation has led to a radically different approach to matching than the conventional assessment-based assignment model, in which patients are assessed and then assigned according to matching principles. This usual approach has not achieved much by way of tested, confirmed, and generalizable principles. In contrast, in the newer approach, the participant preference assignment model (Luborsky & McLellan, 1981; Dahl, 1983), the patient and therapist are given information about each other so that they can express their own preferences and make their own choices.

The assignment-by-preference principle is similar to the one discovered by the long-term Army research project whose purpose was to find which people would be best able to withstand cold weather. After years of developing objective measures the project found that the best predictor was based on simply asking how well the person could stand the cold. Presumably, people who have had opportunities to experience cold weather can judge whether they and the cold make a good match. Analogously, it seems likely that arranging for patients and therapists to make informed choices of each other will usually be advantageous for them. In fact, we have found a positive result for the procedure of allowing the therapists to have their preference in the choice of patients as compared with random assignment of patients.

Two variations on participant preference assignment procedures appear to be useful aids for patients in making informed choices of therapists: (1) the patient is given an opportunity for a "re-pairing" program and is allowed to have two sessions each with two different therapists before making a decision about which therapist to continue therapy with; (2) a procedure, which is like that used by dating bureaus, in which the patient does not actually have sessions with the therapist but instead is given information about the therapist (background data and pictures of the therapist) and then is allowed to make a choice. These two procedures could be applied in ways that allow for patient or therapist preference or both.

The first procedure has already been tried in the University of Pennsylvania Department of Psychiatry Outpatient Clinic. There it is called the Patient–Therapist Re-pairing Opportunity Program. At the end of the two sessions with each therapist, the patient and therapist are interviewed about how their preference was formed. They are also evaluated on choice-related dimensions, such as demographic and attitudinal similarities, which might have played a part in their choice. Two findings are already evident (Alexander et al., 1982): Patients like having a choice, and they often have a clear preference for one or the other therapist.

Even before having completely analyzed the data derived from these two procedures, it already appears justified to recommend to patients that they shop around and have interviews with different therapists before making a choice. Such a systematic search for the most suitable therapist occurs much less often than it should. Patients tend to settle in with the first therapist they see rather than go through the cost and discomfort of prolonging the choice process. It also appears justified to suggest to researchers that more studies be done of preference in relation to outcome.

APPLICATION OF FINDINGS TO THE REFERRAL OF PATIENTS
FOR PSYCHOTHERAPY

Our findings have a major implication for the referral of patients for psychotherapy, which we draw from the combination of two of our observations. (1) Since the outcome of each patient's treatment is only modestly predicted by either pretreatment or during-treatment measures, the psychotherapy venture has to be viewed partly as an adventure. (2) At the same time, prediction about the outcome of psychotherapy for groups of patients can be made with considerable confidence: Treated groups of patients, like those in the Penn Psychotherapy Project, typically have the fortunate fate of benefiting from "moderate" to "much." By taking these two observations together, it follows that each patient who is motivated for psychotherapy and who seems at all suitable for it should be given an opportunity to try it.

APPLICATION OF FINDINGS IN THEORY BUILDING AND IN PRACTICE

The implications to be drawn from the best during-treatment predictors need to be incorporated into theory building about the psychotherapeutic process. A sketch of the construction of such a theory can be drawn from the eight curative factors (chapter 10) and most clearly from the operational measures reported in the second part of this book.

Curative Factor 1: Patient's Experience of a Helping Alliance

The outstanding area of successful prediction is located within the positive relationship qualities and, inside that area, for helping alliance measures. The following is a part of the theory that incorporates Curative Factor 1, i.e., the therapist's ability to allow to develop (or even at times to facilitate) the patient's experience of the helping alliance: When a helping alliance is present the therapist may be serving as a curative "transitional object" who through his or her supportive presence offers strength and understanding to the patient. The therapist who is experienced by the patient as supportive helps the patient to cope with thoughts and circumstances that might set off experiences of "expected or remembered helplessness" (Freud, 1926). Such experiences tend to center on the difficulties and dangers of getting certain crucial needs met, either through the patient's efforts or through the efforts of the therapist and others. This conceptual focus on the patient's needs and responses to getting needs met is part of the Core Conflictual Relationship Theme (CCRT) method (Luborsky, 1977b). Research with the CCRT method has shown that improved patients have an increased sense of mastery and lessened helplessness in dealing with their core relationship problems, as shown in the greater percentage of expectations of positive responses in their narratives about relationships in the later sessions of therapy (chapter 18).

Curative Factor 2: Therapist's Ability to Understand the Patient

A second facet of the theory of psychotherapeutic change is embodied in Curative Factor 2, i.e., the therapist's ability to understand and to manage the relationship problems in the transference. This curative factor involves the therapist's ability in helping the patient to be expressive and in using what is expressed to achieve understanding of the CCRT and the conflicts within it. The patient needs to persist in working problems through in the relationship with the therapist and at times to understand past relationships that are relevant to the current ones.

More research is very much needed on the curative power of the accuracy of the therapist's delineation of the transference pattern. For this research the CCRT method is of assistance for an objective procedure for determining the accuracy of the interpretation (Crits-Christoph & Luborsky, 1987). For practicing therapists the CCRT offers an objective way of deciding on the focus of interpretive work in psychotherapy (Luborsky, in preparation).

Curative Factor 3: Patient's Level of Self-understanding

A third curative factor is of cardinal importance for the theory of psychodynamic psychotherapeutic change: The patient's benefits are a function of increased self-understanding. The first level of self-understanding may be merely to get a grasp on the nature of the relationship pattern with others and with oneself. Even such an elementary increase in understanding can help the patient to overcome the symptoms and related relationship problems. Going beyond the learning of specific insights is a second level in which the patient obtains basic skills from the process of psychodynamic psychotherapy about how to acquire understanding and apply it to problem solving.

Curative Factor 4: Patient's Decrease in Pervasiveness of Conflicts

It clearly follows from the psychodynamic theory of symptom formation that pervasiveness of relationship conflicts should be associated with greater symptom severity and that a decrease in pervasiveness of these conflicts should lead to a lessening of the symptoms. Some of the results from our operationalized measure of pervasiveness of the conflicts clearly are consistent with this line of reasoning (chapter 18). Pervasiveness decreases from the beginning to the end of psychotherapy and the decrease is correlated with a decrease in the symptoms, as measured by the Health-Sickness Rating Scale and the Hopkins Symptom Checklist.

Curative Factor 5

A fifth facet of the theory of psychotherapeutic change has barely been touched on by operational measures and has been only briefly broached in this book. It can be defined as a two-sided factor: the therapist's ability to assist the patient in internalizing the gains and the patient's ability to internalize the gains. One of the main ways of accomplishing this is by working through the meanings of the eventual termination of the treatment. What the working through often achieves is a more internalized control-mastery system so that the gains persist after the treatment.

The field of curative factors in psychotherapy research is sustained by two distinct sources of understanding: the clinical and the quantitative. The clinical is represented by the recent torrent of treatment manuals, including a manual for psychoanalytic psychotherapy (Luborsky, 1984); the quantitative is represented by the steady flow of studies cited in the present work and by this work itself. The two sources do well presented side by side, as in the new guide to dynamic therapy research (Miller et al., in press), for they can inform each other. Inevitably, between these sources there must always be a gulf, but it is becoming less gaping.

APPENDIX

How to Use This Appendix

FINDINGS

Correlations are included when available; superscripts give the significance levels:

$$*p < .05$$
$$**p < .01$$
$$***p < .001$$

A plus sign (+) means a study's finding is significant and consistent with the main trend, and a minus sign (−) means the finding is significant but inconsistent with the main trend. A zero (0) indicates nonsignificance. The actual direction of the relation is always clear in the description of the study.

The lower limit defining a "main trend" is 2 or more significant correlations or findings in the same direction without contradiction. The trends in other combinations of findings are approximately consistent with this principle.

THE ENTRIES

Order of References

References are listed in order of date, so it can readily be seen which were available to us when we planned the study, i.e., 1970 and earlier versus after 1970.

Format

Before entering the data in the Appendix, for each study we prepared a detailed summary with columns for sample size, type of patients, treatment mode, and predictive and criterion measures. A precis of this was included in the Appendix entry: (1) The first part of the description gives the predictor measure. It is typically a before-treatment or early-in-treatment measure; if the assessment was at a different time, it is specified. (2) The second part of the description gives the outcome measure with which the predictor has been correlated or compared. "(T)" after the entry means that the outcome measure is the usual therapist rating of improvement; otherwise the measure is specified. The linking words between the predictor and the outcome measure are usually "related to" (which means significantly related to) or "unrelated to" (which means *not* significantly related to). Quotation marks in the description indicate terms used in the study itself. (3) The third part of the description is the correlation itself, if it was given by the study report or obtainable through conversions.

Number of Correlations

Each entry usually includes only one predictor versus one outcome measure. If there were more, the number and average of the correlations are noted.

"Penn Study" or "VA-Penn Study"

This note at the end of an entry means the study is part of the Penn Psychotherapy Project or VA-Penn study reported in this book.

CLASSIFICATION AND META-ANALYSIS

Classification Principle

Patient and therapist relationship factor entries are listed under the heading representing the target of the predictor measures, e.g., if patient reports that T has positive relationship qualities, entry is listed under T factors.

A Partial Meta-analysis

Within certain categories, where the measures were the same across the studies and where a correlation was available or obtainable through conversions, the *r*s were combined into a mean correlation coefficient. (Within a few studies, where the predictors had been correlated with several similar measures of outcome, a single mean *r* was first obtained.) At the end of the list of studies for these categories we have listed the mean *r* and the number of studies used to calculate it. Studies used as the basis for the mean *r* are identifiable through the presence of an *r* in the entries. Although no determination of the significance of the mean *r* is given, our aim was to provide an indication of the magnitude of effect a particular predictor variable has on psychotherapy outcome.

Patient Factors Pretreatment (and Apart from Sessions)

1. PSYCHOLOGICAL HEALTH-SICKNESS AND SIMILAR GLOBAL MEASURES

a. Global Measures of Health-Sickness and Adjustment

Main Trend. Better adjustment related to better outcome.

Adjustment unrelated to treatment success ($r = .08$) (T)	0	Seeman (1954)
Better psychological health on the Health-Sickness Rating Scale (HSRS) related to more improvement (rated by independent research team) ($r = .54^{**}$).	+	Luborsky (1962a)
Higher interviewer-diagnostician–rated Behavioral Adequacy composite related to T's higher posttreatment evaluation ($r = .24^*$ with residual gain) (T).	+	Fiske, Cartwright & Kirtner (1964)
Higher interviewer-diagnostician–rated Behavioral Adequacy composite related to better outcome ($r = .35^{***}$ with rated benefits; $r = .18$ with residual gain).	+	Fiske, Cartwright & Kirtner (1964); reanalyzed in Luborsky, Mintz, et al. (1980)
Greater felt disturbance (MMPI and Q Disturbance Scale) related to lower ratings of change.	+	Prager (1970)
Higher ego strength ratings related to better outcome ($r = .35^*$).	+	Kernberg et al. (1972)
Patient's (P) initial high disturbance as rated by T, T's supervisor, and independent assessor unrelated to P, T, and T's supervisor ratings of improvement. (0 of 9 correlations significant; mean $r = .03$.)	0	Prager & Garfield (1972)

Higher initial ego strength ratings unrelated to three outcome criteria (mean $r = .03$) (T).

0   Lerner & Fiske (1973)

Higher initial health-sickness (HSRS) related to better outcome ($r = .30^{**}$ with residual gain; $r = .25^*$ with rated benefits).

+   Luborsky, Mintz, et al. (1980)

Greater pretreatment psychiatric severity (on the Addiction Severity Index) related to poorer 6-month outcome (alcohol and drug dependent Ps) (9 of 14 outcomes at $p < .01$; mean $r = .31$).

+   McLellan et al. (1983)

P's higher ratings on "developmental level of the self-concept" by pretherapy clinician evaluation related to better outcome in work and interpersonal functioning ($r = .38^*$) but unrelated to symptomatic outcome ($r = .17$).

+   Horowitz, Marmar, Weiss, et al. (1984)

Addicted Ps with high levels of initial psychiatric symptoms had poorer outcomes 7 months after treatment started (1 month after termination) on seven outcome measures: drug use, employment, legal status, psychiatric functioning (mean $r = .37$) (VA-Penn study).

+   Woody et al. (1984)

P's high adaptive functioning pretherapy by DSM-III (Axis V) diagnosis related to better outcome on the HSRS ($r = -.30^*$), the interpersonal relationships subscale ($r = -.36^*$), and target symptoms ($r = .32^*$) (T).

+   Free et al. (1985)

P's initial disturbance (Eysenck) unrelated to outcome (four measures) (T).

0   Kolb et al. (1985)

Summary. Mean $r = .27$ (11); 10+, 0−, 4ns.

b. Severity of Diagnoses (Especially Presence versus Absence of Psychotic Trends)

Main Trend. Less severe diagnosis related to better outcome.

Absence of subclinical psychotic trends related to better outcome (inferred from MMPI and Rorschach).

+   Harris & Christiansen (1946)

Ps diagnosed as "psychoneurotic reaction" improved more than those with other diagnoses among the improved Ps.

+   Tolman & Mayer (1957)

Psychoneurotic and psychosomatic Ps improved more ($p < .01$) than psychotic or character-disordered Ps.

+   Katz, Lorr & Rubinstein (1958)

"Nonprocess" improved more than "process" schizophrenics.	+	Stephens & Astrup (1963)
Absence of social alienation/personal disorganization ("schizophrenic-like" phenomena) related to better outcome (T).	+	Gottschalk, Mayerson & Gottlieb (1967)
Absence of schizophrenia as presenting symptom: At end of *completed* treatments, fewer improved; anxiety group had more improved Ps.	+	Hamburg et al. (1967)
Schizophrenia or borderline-state diagnosis related negatively to symptomatic improvement.	+	Karush et al. (1968)
Ps with less severe DSM-II diagnoses (neuroses, transient situational disturbances) had better outcomes ($F = 4.78^{***}$, $r = .15^{***}$) than Ps with more severe diagnoses (psychoses) (T).	+	Pope, Geller & Wilkinson (1975)
Ps with more severe DSM-II diagnoses (personality disorders) had better outcomes than Ps with less severe diagnoses (neuroses, transient situational disturbances) or Ps without emotional disorders ($t = 2.20^*$; $r \approx .40^*$).	−	Nichols & Bierenbaum (1978)
Endogenous depressives required medication, whereas situational (exogenous) depressives improved with either medication or psychotherapy.	+	Prusoff et al. (1980)
Neurotics and personality trait disorders had significantly higher improvement scores than did borderline and psychotic Ps ($F = 17.88^{**}$, $r = .40^{**}$).	+	Jacobs & Warner (1981)
Sociopaths did not improve in psychotherapy; sociopaths with depression did improve, but depressives improved even more (drug addicted Ps) (VA-Penn study).	−	Woody et al. (1985)

Summary. 10+, 2−.

c. MMPI Severity Measures

Main Trend. Better initial adjustment on MMPI related to better outcome.

Less MMPI profile deviance related to improvement (neurotic Ps) (T).	+	Sullivan, Miller & Smelser (1958)
Greater maladjustment (MMPI) related to improvement ("discrepancies procedure") ($r = .50^{**}$ and $.45^{**}$) (T).	−	Apfelbaum (1958)

Less "psychological pathology" (MMPI, California   +   Hunt et al. (1959)
Personality Factor) related to improvement.

P's greater initial disturbance on MMPI and   +   Prager & Garfield
Q-Disturbance Scale related negatively to P's, T's,   (1972)
and T's supervisor assessments of good outcome (6
of 9 correlations significant with mean $r = -.36$).

Less disturbance (MMPI composite) related to   +   Sloane et al. (1975)
improvement in Target Complaints ($F = 5.19^*$).
    Summary. $4+, 1-$.

d. Barron Ego Strength Scale (from MMPI)

Main Trend. Greater initial ego strength related to better outcome.

Higher scores on the Barron Ego Strength Scale   +   Barron (1953a)
related to improvement (judge's ratings) in three
separate samples (mean $r = .36$).

Barron Ego Strength Scale scores unrelated to   0   Gallagher (1954)
outcome ($r = .08$) (T).

Barron Ego Strength Scale scores discriminated ($p <$ +   Wirt (1955)
.05) unimproved from improved groups (the
extremes of a hospitalized sample in psychotherapy)
(T).

Higher Barron Ego Strength Scale scores related (p +   Wirt (1956)
$< .001$) to improvement (supervisor ratings).

Barron Ego Strength Scale scores unrelated to   0   Sullivan, Miller &
outcome (T).   Smelser (1958)

Barron Ego Strength Scale scores unrelated ($r = .18$)   0   Getter & Sundland
to improvement (but related for females: $r = .23^*$,   (1962)
though not for males) (T).

Higher Barron Ego Strength Scale scores negatively   −   Distler, May &
related to one of three outcome measures for the   Tuma (1964)
total group of schizophrenics ($rs = -.17^*$, $.04$, and
$-.01$, mean $r = -.05$) (but positively related for
men [$r = .26^*$ with Symptom rating] and negatively
for women [$r = -.32^{***}$ with HSRS]).

Barron Ego Strength Scale scores unrelated ($r = .18$)   0   Endicott &
to outcome.   Endicott (1964)

Higher Barron Ego Strength Scale scores for   +   Young et al. (1980)
long-term treatment of nonschizophrenics related to
improvement on HSRS ($r = .56^{**}$) and the
Psychiatric Evaluation Form ($r = -.61^{**}$).
    Summary. Mean $r = .24$ (6); $4+, 1-$, 4ns.

e. TAT: Adequacy of Functioning

Main Trend. Greater initial TAT adequacy of functioning related to better outcome.

Greater TAT adequacy of functioning (ratings based on pretreatment TAT) related to better outcome (T).	+	Kirtner & Cartwright (1958a)
Greater initial TAT adequacy related to residual gain score showing decrease in MMPI Hs-Hy elevations ($r = .23^*$) (T).	+	Fiske, Cartwright & Kirtner (1964)

Summary. 2+, 0−.

f. Rorschach: Klopfer Rorschach Prognostic Rating Scale (RPRS)

Main Trend. Higher RPRS scores related to better outcome.

Higher RPRS scores related ($r = .66^{***}$) to better outcome (judges' ratings).	+	Mindess (1953)
Higher RPRS scores related ($r = .67^{**}$, pretherapy total weighted and a 2-point criterion) to better outcome.	+	Kirkner, Wisham & Giedt (1953)
RPRS scores discriminated between 19 most versus 16 least improved patients (with higher scores related to better outcome) ($t = 2.86^{**}, r = .56^{**}$) (T).	+	Sheehan et al. (1954)
RPRS scores unrelated to outcome (judges' ratings).	0	Filmer-Bennett (1955)
Higher RPRS scores related to better outcome for normally productive Ps ($p < .02$) (mean RPRS higher for improved Ps); unrelated to outcome for underproductive Ps.	+	Bloom (1956)
Higher RPRS scores (pretherapy weighted score related to T rating of P's success [but $n = 13$] (T).	+	Cartwright (1958)
Higher RPRS scores related to better outcome ($r = .54^*$ with improvement [$n = 21$]; $r = .48^*$ for 40 untreated Ps) (T).	+	Endicott & Endicott (1964)
RPRS scores unrelated to improvement in client-centered counseling (0 of 5 correlations significant; mean $r = -.14$) (T).	0	Fiske, Cartwright & Kirtner (1964)
RPRS scores unrelated to change and symptom improvement (T).	0	Whitely & Blaine (1967)

Summary. Mean $r = .49$ (5); 6+, 0−, 3ns.

g. Symptom Checklist (SCL) Severity

Main Trend. Greater initial SCL severity related to better outcome.

Number of complaints (SCL) related to improvement ($r = .67^{***}$).	+	Truax et al. (1966)
P's greater initial distress (on Symptom Inventory) related to improvement on Symptom Inventory ($r = .38^*$; one outcome).	+	Tollinton (1973)

Summary. Mean $r = .54$ (2); 2+, 0−.

h. Chronicity

Main Trend. Greater chronicity of illness negatively related to better outcome.

Duration of anxiety syndrome (examination of records) before hospitalization unrelated to outcome.	0	Miles, Barrabee & Finesinger (1951)
Overall posthospital adjustment best for "short-term psychotics," next best for nonpsychotics, and poorest for long-term psychotics (T).	+	Fairweather et al. (1960)
Greater "suddenness of onset" related to greater social recovery (posthospital adjustment) in psychotic mothers ($r = .77^{***}$).	+	Morrow & Robins (1964)
Degree of chronicity (examination of records) for 100 female inpatients unrelated to outcome.	0	Barry & Fulkerson (1966)
Greater chronicity of present illness (first 10 years of illness) negatively related to better outcome.	+	Uhlenhuth & Duncan (1968)
Presence of precipitating event related to better outcome in 8 of the 18 Ps reporting a definite external precipitating event prior to the onset of ulcerative colitis.	+	Karush et al. (1968)
Number of previous depressions unrelated to status at follow-up.	0	Weissman, Prusoff & Klerman (1978)

Summary. 4+, 0−, 3ns.

2. AFFECT

a. *Anxiety*

Main Trend. Greater initial anxiety related to better outcome.

Higher Taylor Manifest Anxiety related to better outcome ratings (i.e., distinguished between most and least successful groups, $t = 1.84^*$, $r = .41^*$) (multicriteria).

+ Gallagher (1954)

Taylor Manifest Anxiety unrelated to outcome (232 VA outpatients) (T).

0 Katz, Lorr & Rubinstein (1958)

Initial anxiety unrelated to outcome (T).

0 Roth et al. (1964)

Initial anxiety unrelated to three of three outcome measures ($rs = .16$, $-.09$, and .00). Higher Taylor Manifest Anxiety related to better outcome on the HSRS for schizophrenic women ($r = .39^{***}$); unrelated ($r = -.08$) for schizophrenic men.

0 Distler, May & Tuma (1964)

Greater anxiety (rated from tape recorded speech sample) related to better outcome ($r = -.54^{**}$) (T).

+ Gottschalk, Mayerson & Gottlieb (1967)

Anxiety as a presenting symptom (according to T): more of such Ps who complete treatment improve in character change than would be expected by chance (T).

+ Hamburg et al. (1967)

High P anxiety level as judged pretreatment from the MMPI related to better T-rated outcome ($p < .05$) (T).

+ Wogan (1970)

Greater initial anxiety related ($r = .52^{***}$) to global improvement. (Greater initial anxiety level related [$r = .66$] to better outcome for Ps whose initial HSRS was 50 or greater; $r = .11$ for ratings below .50.)

+ Kernberg et al. (1972)

Greater initial "experienced anxiety" (judged by T) related ($r = .33$) to 1 of 3 outcomes (mean $r = .14$) (T).

+ Lerner & Fiske (1973)

Initial anxiety on the Prognostic Index interview unrelated to outcome measures, residual gain ($r = -.16$) and rated benefits ($r = -.14$) (Penn study).

0 Luborsky, Mintz, et al. (1980)

Summary. Mean $r = .26$ (6); 6+, 0−, 4ns.

b. Depression

Main Trend. Greater initial depression related to better outcome.

Higher initial scores on MMPI Depression scale related to better outcome ($p < .05$) (T).	+	Gallagher (1954)
Higher scores on Gottschalk Hostility Inward Scale related to better outcome (T).	+	Gottschalk, Mayerson & Gottlieb (1967)
Higher scores on MMPI Depression Scale related to better outcome ($p < .001$).	+	Uhlenhuth & Duncan (1968)

Summary. 3+, 0−.

c. Other Affects

Main Trend. More affect related to better outcome.

Ps who began treatment with mobilized negative affect improved more ($p < .05$) (anxiety, fear, hostility, depression).	+	Conrad (1952)
Six measures based on a 60-adjective feeling and attitude scale unrelated to outcome (tension-anxiety, anger-hostility, depression, vigor, fatigue-inertia, thinking confusion) (T).	0	Roth et al. (1964)
Absence of flattening of affect, or emotional blunting (rated from case history; mainly schizophrenic Ps) related to better outcome.	+	Astrup & Noreik (1966)
Guilt on Buss-Durkee Guilt Scale unrelated to outcome.	0	Zuckerman et al. (1980)
Internalizing depressive Ps (diagnosed via MMPI) achieved more benefit from both analytic and experiential treatments than did externalizing impulsive Ps ($p < .05$).	+	Beutler & Mitchell (1981)

Summary. 3+, 0−, 2ns.

3. MOTIVATION AND/OR EXPECTATIONS

a. Motivation

Main Trend. Greater patient motivation for treatment related to better outcome.

Ps motivated by need to change were rated as more successful (T).	+	Conrad (1952)

High acceptance of responsibility related ($p < .05$) + Schroeder (1960)
to greater degree of improvement (T).

Motivation (clinical judgment by psychiatric team; 0 Siegal & Fink
from case record put in low versus high groups) (1962)
unrelated to outcome.

Greater motivation for treatment related ($r = .46^{**}$) + Strupp et al.
to better outcome (T). (1963)

Greater "need to change" (discrepancy score + Cartwright &
between P's self now, and as P would like to be) Lerner (1963)
related to four component improvement criteria ($p <$
.01) (T).

Higher initial "motivation for change" (judged by P) 0 Lerner & Fiske
unrelated to three outcome criteria (mean $r = .01$) (1973)
(T).

Higher ratings of P's motivation at intake related to + Keithly, Samples
both T's ($r = .65^*$) and independent clinician's ($r =$ & Strupp (1980)
$.66^*$) ratings of P's greater global change (two out of
four outcome criteria; mean $r = .60$) (T).

P's motivation for psychotherapy unrelated to two 0 Horowitz et al.
outcome measures ($rs = -.14$ and .30) judged by (1984)
independent clinicians.
   Summary. Mean $r = .31$ (4); 5+, 0−, 3ns.

b. Expectations

Main Trend. Higher patient expectations related to better outcome.

Greater P positive "anticipation of outcome" (one of + Lipkin (1954)
two measures) related to better outcome as assessed
by pre- to posttherapy change in TAT protocols (r
$= .76^{**}$ and $-.16$).

P's expectations (Picture Attitudes Test and Sentence 0 Brady, Reznikoff
Completion Attitudes Test) unrelated to & Zeller (1960)
improvement scores (chi squares $= .34$ and .12, rs
$= .05$ and .03) (T).

P's expectations of change unrelated to P perceived 0 Goldstein (1960)
personality change (Q-sort) (neither were T's nor
combined P's and T's expectations).

P's greater expectations of symptom reduction + Goldstein &
positively ($r = .41^*$) and curvilinearly related to Shipman (1961)
perceived symptom reduction.

Greater optimism about outcome related to better + Uhlenhuth &
outcome. Duncan (1968)

P's high Hope score (from pretreatment speech sample) related to improvement on Social Alienation-Personal Disorganization scale ($r = .42^*$).

+ Gottschalk, Fox & Bates (1973)

P's greater expectation of improvement related to improvement on Symptom Inventory ($r = .59^{**}$; one outcome criterion).

+ Tollinton (1973)

P's greater degree of change expected related to greater P-rated satisfaction ($r = .47^*$).

+ Richert (1976)

P's expectations of improvement pretreatment unrelated to 14 of 15 measures of improvement (P and independent clinician rated) (mean $r = .21$).

0 Martin & Sterne (1976)

P's expectations as to improvement unrelated to outcome (psychodynamic supportive therapy) by independent rater.

0 Persson & Nordlund (1983)

Summary. Mean $r = .36$ (7); 6+, 0−, 4ns.

d. Other Motivation Measures

Main Trend. Greater motivation unrelated to better outcome.

Self-referred versus court-referred Ps showed no difference in outcome.

0 Mindess (1953)

Ps with "congruent" (e.g., help with personal problems) versus "noncongruent" (e.g., somatic complaints) motivation showed no difference in outcome.

0 Gliedman et al. (1957)

Type of "transference expectations" unrelated to outcome (T).

0 Apfelbaum (1958)

No differences in outcome between research solicited and nonsolicited depressed female patients on seven measures of depression, assertiveness, and social adjustment.

0 Last et al. (1984)

Summary. 0+, 0−, 4ns.

4. POSITIVE ATTITUDES TOWARD SELF, THERAPIST, AND TREATMENT (BASED ON PRETREATMENT ASSESSMENTS)

Main Trend. More "positive" attitude toward self, therapist, and treatment related to better outcome.

Initial attitudes toward self rated from interview unrelated to outcome in 10 Ps (client-centered) (T).

0 Raskin (1949)

Ps who were more favorably oriented toward T (one of two measures) changed more (r = .61* and −.22).	+ Lipkin (1954)
Greater "favorableness of conscious attitudes" to psychiatric hospitals, psychiatrists, and treatment (on attitude tests) related to better outcome. On projective picture attitude tests, perception of treatment as neutral and hospital as supporting, and the P role as both active and passive related to better outcome (T).	+ Brady, Zeller & Reznikoff (1959)
Greater acceptance of responsibility (as assessed via content analysis of pretherapy interview) related to greater movement in treatment (chi square = 4.09*) (T).	+ Schroeder (1960)
Patient's greater positive attitude toward therapy assessed by the Sentence Completion Attitudes Test related to positive cognitive change by a modified Role Construct Repertory Test (r = .41*).	+ Richert (1976)

Summary. 4+, 0−, 1ns.

5. INTEREST IN AND CAPACITY FOR HUMAN RELATIONS

Main Trend. Greater interest in and capacity for human relations related to better outcome.

Greater ability to develop interpersonal relations related to better outcome (T).	+ Rosenbaum, Friedlander & Kaplan (1956)
Greater interest in human relations (in speech samples) related to better outcome (T).	+ Gottschalk, Mayerson & Gottlieb (1967)
More positive indicators of object relatedness by object relations technique related (p < .01) to better outcome (T).	+ Rayner & Hahn (1964)
Relatability (i.e., quality of object relationships in TAT) related to improvement (p < .05).	+ Isaacs & Haggard (1966)
Low "non-personal reference" related to improvement on composite of Rorschach, MMPI, and Q-sort battery, while high "non-personal reference" related to deterioration (t = 3.19**) (composite was one of three outcomes).	+ Truax & Wittmer (1971)

Greater pretherapy ratings of "P adequacy of interpersonal relations" by independent clinicians related to good outcome (residual change scores on the MMPI Depression subscale) ($r = -.42^{**}$).

+ Moras & Strupp (1982)

Drug-addicted sociopathic Ps (DSM-III) received no benefit from psychotherapy (VA-Penn study).

+ Woody et al. (1985)

Greater "quality of the P's important relationships" rated pretherapy by T and/or independent assessor related to better outcome (short-term psychoanalytic psychotherapy) as judged by P ($r = .72^{***}$) and T ($r = .53^*$). Stepwise multiple regression analyses combining the predictors produced parallel findings.

+ Piper, deCarufel & Szkrumelak (1985)

Summary. 8+, 0−.

6. INTELLECTUAL FUNCTIONING

a. IQ

Main Trend. Higher IQ scores related to better outcome.

IQ as measured by four subscales of the Wechsler-Bellevue Intelligence Scale was unrelated to outcome ($r = .30$).

0 Harris & Christiansen (1946)

Most successful of 100 VA outpatients scored higher on the Army Alpha.

+ Casner (1950)

"Definitely better" outcome group had higher ($p < .01$) Wechsler-Bellevue IQs than the "unchanged group" (IQ related [$r = .42^*$] to better outcome).

+ Miles, Barrabee & Finesinger (1951)

Higher scores on four Wechsler Adult Intelligence Scale (WAIS) subtests related ($r = .46^{**}$) to improvement.

+ Barron (1953b)

Full-scale WAIS score higher for improved versus unimproved Ps ($p < .01$) (T).

+ Rosenberg (1954)

Intelligence unrelated to outcome (T).

0 Rosenbaum, Friedlander & Kaplan (1956)

Higher Wechsler-Bellevue full-scale IQs related to better outcome; lower scores related to poorer outcome, but adequate performance was not discriminating ($r \approx .50$).

+ Rioch & Lubin (1959)

Four WAIS subtests related ($r = .36^*$) to TAT adequacy "residual gain" (one of five criteria; mean $r = .15$).

+ Fiske, Cartwright & Kirtner (1964)

Four WAIS subtests unrelated to outcome measures   0   Luborsky, Mintz,
($r = -.05$ with residual gain and $r = -.05$ with   et al. (1980)
rated benefits) (Penn study).

    Summary. Mean $r = .31$ (6); $6+$, $0-$, 3ns.

b. Intellectual Skills

    Main Trend. Higher estimates of intellectual skills related to better outcome.

Higher scores on Gough MMPI scale of intellectual   +   Sullivan, Miller &
efficiency related to better outcome.   Smelser (1958)

Good vocabulary and word fluency related to 3-year   +   McNair et al.
status of symptom reduction ($r = .42^*$); related to   (1964)
improvement rating ($r = .24^*$) (T); related to better
self-rating ($r = .29^*$).

Higher scores on abstract reasoning and other   +   Barry & Fulkerson
cognitive and perceptual tests related ($r \approx .30^*$) to   (1966)
better outcome.

    Summary. $3+$, $0-$.

c. Ability in Perceptual Tests

    Main Trend. Not enough studies to locate a trend.

General ability tests (including cube test, Stroop   0   Seeman (1962)
ratio, concealed figures, autokinetic effect,
flicker-fusion, mirror test) unrelated to outcome.

    Summary. $0+$, $0-$, 1ns.

7. AUTHORITARIANISM

    Main Trend. Not enough studies to locate a trend.

California F-scale unrelated to outcome (232 VA   0   Katz, Lorr &
outpatients) (T).   Rubinstein (1958)

    Summary. $0+$, $0-$, 1ns.

8. ETHNOCENTRISM

    Main Trend. Higher ethnocentrism related negatively to better outcome.

Higher Ethnocentrism scale scores related negatively   +   Barron (1953b)
($r = -.64$) to improvement (with intelligence
partialed out, the r remains significant: $-.34$).

Higher Ethnocentrism scale scores (as E-scores   +   Tougas (1954)
increase beyond the group mean, failure cases
increase) negatively related to good outcome (T).

Ethnocentrism scale unrelated to outcome (T).   0   Rosen (1954)
   Summary. 2+, 0−, 1ns.

9. SOMATIC CONCERN

Main Trend. Greater somatic concern related to better outcome.

Greater health concern rated in improved versus   +   Rosenberg (1954)
unimproved Ps related ($p < .05$) to better outcome
(T).

More somatic and psychological complaints during   +   Stone et al. (1961)
pretreatment period related to better outcome (T).

Greater degree of somatic complaints (judged by T)   0   Lerner & Fiske
unrelated to three outcomes (mean $r = .10$) (T).   (1973)
   Summary. 2+, 0−, 1ns.

10. SELF-UNDERSTANDING AND INSIGHT

Main Trend. Greater self-understanding and insight (pretherapy) related
to better outcome.

Initial understanding or insight (ratings of client   0   Raskin (1949)
statements) unrelated to outcome in 10 Ps
(client-centered psychotherapy) (T).

Ps with more insight (rated pretherapy) showed   +   Zolik & Hollon
more improvement (T).   (1960)

P's greater "externalizing of symptoms" pretreatment +   Stein & Beall
related negatively to outcome (T) (five outcomes,   (1971)
mean $r = -.32$). P's designation as "internalizer"
rather than "externalizer" related to positive overall
change rated by P and T ($r = .35^{**}$; $.54^{**}$ for
women, $-.03$ for men) (one outcome).
   Summary. 2+, 0−, 1ns.

11. "ATTRACTIVENESS," SUITABILITY, OR PROGNOSIS IN PSYCHOTHERAPY

Main Trend. Greater "attractiveness" as a suitable patient for psychotherapy or better prognosis related to better outcome.

Better prognosis related ($r = .48^{**}$) to "success" (T).   +   Strupp et al.
                                                          (1963)

Higher ratings of "attractiveness" for therapy (by   +   Nash et al. (1965)
independent interviewer) or "suitability" for therapy
based on age, education, occupation, ability to relate,
verbal facility, etc., related to better outcome ($p <$
.01). (These seem to comprise social class status and
achievements.)

Summary. 2+, 0−.

12. HEALTHY TRAITS AND COPING STYLES

Main Trend. "Healthier" personality traits and coping styles related to better outcomes.

Defensiveness unrelated to outcome for 10 Ps   0   Raskin (1949)
(client-centered psychotherapy) (T).

More negative and demanding attitude negatively   +   Conrad (1952)
related to better outcome (T).

Less rigidity and less stereotypy (improved versus   +   Rosenberg (1954)
unimproved) related to better outcome ($p <$ .01).

"Immediacy" of handling feelings in relationship   +   Kirtner &
problems differentiated the outcome groups (T).   Cartwright (1958b)

More defensiveness negatively related to   +   Zolik & Hollon
improvement.   (1960)

More defensiveness negatively related ($r = -.38^{**}$) +   Strupp et al.
to success (T).   (1963)

Ps with a more "refined and socially acceptable   +   Wogan (1970)
defensive style" assessed pretreatment from the
MMPI see themselves as progressing more rapidly in
therapy than Ps with low subtlety of defensive
pattern ($p <$ .05).

P's defensive style (obsessive versus hysterical)   0   Nichols &
unrelated to outcome.   Bierenbaum (1978)

P's belligerence pretreatment from T scores on   +   Armstrong, Rock
subscale of the Psychiatric Status Schedule   & Tracy (1981)
negatively related to P rated problem change ($r =
-.48^{**}$).

P's greater tendency to use these ego defenses   −   Buckley et al.
related to greater degree of improvement (T):   (1984)
reaction formation (self-report) ($r = .59^{**}$), undoing
(T) ($r = .57^{**}$), rationalization (T) ($r = .55^{**}$),
projection (self-report) ($r = .46^*$), coping style of
blame (self-report) ($r = .44^*$), and isolation (T) ($r =
.43^*$).

P's "excellence of defensive style" (rated   +   Piper, deCarufel &
pretreatment by T and/or assessor) related to better   Szkrumelak (1985)
outcome (short-term psychoanalytic psychotherapy)
as judged by P ($r = .47^*$) and T ($r = .50^*$).
Stepwise multiple regression analyses combining
predictors produced parallel findings.

P's initial coping style (extraversion/introversion)   0   Kolb et al. (1985)
unrelated to outcome (five outcome measures) (T).
    Summary. 8+, 1−, 3ns.

13. MASTERY VERSUS HELPLESSNESS AND PASSIVITY

Main Trend. Greater mastery related to better outcome.

Nonparticipation and passivity versus responsibility   +   Rayner & Hahn
and persistence of characters in TAT stories   (1964)
negatively related to good outcome ($p < .01$) (T).

Higher initial level of "learned resourcefulness" by   +   Simons et al.
the Self-Control Schedule related to reduction in   (1985)
depression (by BDI) (cognitive therapy) ($r = .53^{**}$)
    Summary. 2+, 0−.

14. MISCELLANEOUS TEST FINDINGS AND TRAITS

a. *MMPI Scales*

Main Trend. Some MMPI scale scores related to better outcome.

Pd, Pa, Sc, and Ma scales differentiated outcome   +   Harris &
groups' overall ratings by most experienced judges (p Christiansen (1946)
$< .02$).

Mf scale differentiated the most improved Ps in 100   +   Casner (1950)
VA outpatients.

Higher F, D, Pd, Pt, Sc, and Feldman Prognostic   +   Hunt et al. (1959)
Scale related negatively to improvement ($r = -.32^*$,
mean within-variable correlation) (T).

Higher F scale (test-taking attitude) related   +   Endicott &
negatively ($r = -.34^*$) to better outcome (judge's   Endicott (1964)
rating).

Higher K scale (test-taking attitude) related ($r =$ +   Endicott &
$.39^*$) to better outcome.   Endicott (1964)
    Summary. 5+, 0−.

b. Figure-Drawing Test

Main Trend. Not enough studies to locate a trend.

Greater primitivity of drawing of head related negatively to better outcome (12 of 19 unimproved Ps predicted by primitive drawing) ($p < .05$).	+	Fiedler & Siegal (1949)

Summary. 1+, 0−.

c. Rorschach: General Scores

Main Trend. Some aspect of Rorschach scoring related to better outcome.

Location determinants unrelated to outcome.	0	Harris & Christiansen (1946)
Subjective ratings of Rorschachs related to good outcome (supervisor's ratings).	+	Harris & Christiansen (1946)
10 of 11 Rorschach signs differentiated most and least improved among 36 women in "psychiatric treatment" (T).	+	Bradway, Lion & Corrigan (1946)
Specific scoring categories and overall clinical evaluations of Rorschach records differentiated improved and unimproved cases (T).	+	Siegel (1951)
Index based on nine Rorschach signs used in combination related ($r = .43$) to better outcome (follow-up social adjustment).	+	Filmer-Bennett (1952)
Rorschach (Harris-Christiansen Prognostic Index) unrelated to outcome (judges' ratings).	0	Barron (1953b)
Four Rorschach categories (M, FM, m, and shading) out of more than 15 related to good outcome (judges' ratings) (combined four measures $R = .70^{**}$).	+	Kirkner, Wisham & Giedt (1953)
Three separate methods of Rorschach analysis (also supervisors' ratings) unrelated to outcome.	0	Rogers & Hammond (1953)
Rated by general Rorschach analysis, a variety of personality factors related to good outcome (T).	+	Rosenberg (1954)
Sum of M, FM, and m responses differentiated most from least improved in 35 outpatients ($p < .01$) (T).	+	Sheehan et al. (1954)
Of 11 Rorschach scores, none related to outcome (judges' ratings) in 51 VA outpatients (T).	0	Roberts (1954)

More "inadequate" responses to Card IV on Rorschach (as a measure of attitudes toward authority) negatively related to better outcome.   + Dana (1954)

Global ratings based on Rorschach protocols unrelated to outcome (follow-up social adjustment).   0 Filmer-Bennett (1955)

Greater presence of "poor" Rorschach signs negatively related to better outcome.   + Rioch & Lubin (1959)

"Good" signs not found to be discriminating.   0 Rioch & Lubin (1959)

Three Rorschach scoring categories (R, Ch, C) out of 10 related ($r = .40^*$) to better outcome (T).   + Endicott & Endicott (1964)

M, Non F+%, EA, and other scores singly unrelated to outcome.   0 Gaylin (1966)

A discriminant function measure using total K, m, and R predicted change ($p < .05$) and symptomatic improvement ($p < .01$) (T).   + Whitely & Blaine (1967)

   Summary. 11+, 0−, 7ns.

d. Locus of Control

Main Trend. Not enough studies to locate a trend.

Greater P internality of locus of control related to better outcome (P and T ratings of therapeutic effectiveness) (T).   + Foon (1985)

P's locus of control unrelated to outcome (T).   0 Kolb et al. (1985)

   Summary. 1+, 0−, 1ns.

e. Other Psychological Tests and Ratings

Main Trend. Not enough studies of a similar kind to locate a trend.

Cultural as opposed to occupational interests (by Kuder Preference Exam) characterized most improved VA Ps.   + Casner (1950)

Greater Sensitivity (rated pretherapy in improved versus unimproved) related to better outcome ($p < .01$) (T).   + Rosenberg (1954)

Scores on the Behavioral Disturbance scale unrelated to improvement (T).   0 Katz, Lorr & Rubinstein (1958)

Scores on the Paranoid Schizothymia and Hysterical Unconcerned scales of Cattell's 16 Personality Factor Scale related ($p < .01$) to improvement (T).   + Hunt et al. (1959)

Scores on the Psychiatric Attitudes Test related to improvement (T).   + Brady, Zeller & Reznikoff (1959)

Greater difference in ascending and descending critical flicker-fusion measures related to better outcome ($r = -.30^{**}$) (multiple ratings).   + Barry (1962)

Gain scores in nine perceptual-motor and conceptual tests unrelated to improvement (T).   0 Fulkerson & Barry (1966)

Severe ego weakness and relative ego strength (extreme groups) judged prior to treatment related to outcome with greater ego strength related to better outcome.   + Karush et al. (1968)

Alcoholic P's categorization into subgroups via Eysenck Personality Inventory, Drinking Behavior Inventory, MacAndrew Alcoholism Scale, or Rohan's classification unrelated to outcome.   0 Gellens, Gottheil & Alterman (1976)

Depressed Ps with high extraversion and low neuroticism on Maudsley Personality Inventory related to good outcome at 1-year follow-up ($F = 5.85^*$) but not at termination, on Social Adjustment Scale Self-Report (four outcomes).   0 Zuckerman et al. (1980)

P's designation as alcoholic subtypes: obsessive-dependent, passive-dependent, or "no type" consumed less alcohol after treatment than those designated as aggressive-schizoid or mixed subtypes (binomial test $p < .03$). ("No type" improved most.)   + Zivich (1981)

P's greater hypnotizability pretherapy related to better outcome based on pre–post Symptom Checklist Intensity Score ($r = .38^*$) and to decrease in primary and total target symptoms ($rs = .35^*$ and $.48^{**}$, respectively) (six outcome criteria).   + Nace et al. (1982)

P's greater extraversion (Eysenck) combined with P's greater involvement in therapy (T) related to better outcome ($r = .65^{***}$)   + Kolb et al. (1985)

Summary. 9+, 0−, 4ns.

Patient Demographic and Life-Situation Factors

1. AGE

Main Trend. Age is mostly unrelated to outcome.

Ps under 30 years showed more improvement than did older Ps.	+	Casner (1950)
The 25 most improved Ps (in VA outpatients) were about 5 years older than the least improved Ps (mean 32 versus 27) (T).	—	Conrad (1952)
Age unrelated to outcome (23 Ps) (T).	0	Seeman (1954)
Age unrelated ($r = .16$) to outcome (T).	0	Cartwright (1955)
Age unrelated to outcome (T).	0	Bloom (1956)
Age related ($r = .47^*$) to better outcome, with older Ps improving more (but note narrow age range of 20–40).	—	Knapp et al. (1960)
Ps with successful outcome ratings tended to be younger ($p < .05$) (T).	+	Stone et al. (1961)
Age unrelated to outcome (also Q-sort) (T).	0	Gaylin (1966)
Age unrelated to improvement in brief treatment (T).	0	Gottschalk, Mayerson & Gottlieb (1967)
Age negatively related to good outcome (the 46+ age group improved less) (T).	+	Hamburg et al. (1967)
Age unrelated to status at follow-up.	0	Weissman, Prusoff & Klerman (1978)

Summary. 3+, 2−, 6ns.

2. SEX

Main Trend. Patient's sex mostly unrelated to outcome.

Females did better ($p < .05$) than males (T).	+	Seeman (1954)
P's sex unrelated ($r = -.03$) to outcome.	0	Cartwright (1955)
P's sex unrelated to outcome (27 analytic Ps).	0	Knapp et al. (1960)
P's sex unrelated to outcome (T).	0	Gaylin (1966)
P's sex unrelated to outcome (T).	0	Hamburg et al. (1967)

Ps' sex unrelated to outcome (T) (process schizophrenic).	0	May (1968)
Females did better than males ($r = .50^{**}$) (criterion: rating of success and satisfaction) (Penn pilot study) (T).	+	Mintz, Luborsky & Auerbach (1971)
P's sex unrelated to outcome.	0	Scher (1975)
P's sex unrelated to outcome.	0	Nichols & Bierenbaum (1978)
Female Ps did better than males on several self-report measures of improvement.	+	Kirschner, Genack & Hauser (1978)
P's sex unrelated to outcome (T).	0	Jones & Zoppel (1982)

Summary. 3+, 0−, 8ns.

3. RACE

Main Trend. Not enough studies to identify a clear trend.

P's race unrelated to status at follow-up.	0	Weissman, Prusoff & Klerman (1978)
White Ps were more satisfied with treatment overall than nonwhite Ps ($F = 8.06^*, r = .41^*$).	+	Neimeyer & Gonzales (1983)

Summary. 1+, 0−, 1ns.

4. RELIGION

Main Trend. Not enough studies to identify a clear trend.

Religious activities negatively related to good outcome (T).	−	Rosenbaum, Friedlander & Kaplan (1956)
Religion unrelated to status at follow-up.	0	Weissman, Prusoff & Klerman (1978)

Summary. 0+, 1−, 1ns.

5. SOCIAL ACHIEVEMENTS

a. Socioeconomic Status (SES)

Main Trend. Higher socioeconomic status related to better outcome.

High social status and financial success related to improvement (T).	+	Rosenbaum, Friedlander & Kaplan (1956)

Occupation level and annual earnings unrelated to improvement (232 VA outpatients) (T).	0	Katz, Lorr & Rubinstein (1958)
Higher social class related to better outcome (criteria at 3-year status, $r = .23^*$; symptom reduction, $r = .37^*$).	+	McNair et al. (1964)
Lower socioeconomic status (H-R scale Groups 4 and 5) related to greater improvement in brief psychotherapy ($t = 2.61^*$) ($r = -.55^*$) (T).	−	Gottschalk, Mayerson & Gottlieb (1967)
Higher socioeconomic status related to better outcome ($F = 1.83^*$) (T) (neurotic Ps). (For both neurotic and psychotic Ps [combined sample] SES unrelated to outcome.)	+	Pope, Geller & Wilkinson (1975)
Social class unrelated to status at follow-up.	0	Weissman, Prusoff & Klerman (1978)
P's higher socioeconomic status related to P-rated better outcome ($p < .05$). (Greater age fewer sessions and greater Eysenck Extraversion related to percent gain at follow-up but not at termination.)	+	Schramski et al. (1984)
Higher P social class related ($p < .05$) to better outcome assessed pre- versus posttreatment by an independent rater.	+	Persson, Alstrom, & Nordlund (1984a)

Summary. 5+, 1−, 2ns.

b. Occupational Adjustment

Main Trend. Better initial occupational adjustment related to better outcome.

Unemployment negatively related to good outcome.	+	Casner (1950)
Prior occupational adjustment unrelated to outcome.	0	Miles, Barrabee & Finesinger (1951)
Most improved of 50 VA Ps had been employed at beginning of treatment and had better occupational ratings.	+	Conrad (1952)
Work adjustment unrelated to outcome (T).	0	Rosenbaum, Friedlander & Kaplan (1956)
Initial employment status unrelated to outcome.	0	Tolman & Mayer (1957)
Higher occupational adjustment related to better outcome ($p < .01$) (T).	+	Sullivan, Miller & Smelser (1958)

Summary. 3+, 0−, 3ns.

c. Educational Level

Main Trend. Higher educational level related to better outcome.

Ps with 12 or more years of education improved more than less educated Ps.	+	Casner (1950)
Higher educational level related to better outcome (remission) in those patients with normally productive Rorschachs ($p < .01$).	+	Bloom (1956)
Education unrelated to outcome (T).	0	Rosenbaum, Friedlander & Kaplan (1956)
Higher educational achievement unrelated to outcome (T), but those Ps who "stay" in therapy are more ($p < .001$) educated than those who do not stay.	+	Sullivan, Miller & Smelser (1958)
Education unrelated to outcome for 27 analytic Ps.	0	Knapp et al. (1960)
Higher educational achievement related to better outcome ($r = .25^*$ with symptom reduction) (T).	+	McNair et al. (1964)
Higher educational level related to better outcome (T).	+	Hamburg et al. (1967)

Summary. 5+, 0−, 2ns.

d. Marital or Sexual Adjustment

Main Trend. No clear trend between marital or sexual adjustment and outcome.

No difference in prior marital adjustment of the three outcome groups.	0	Miles, Barrabee & Finesinger (1951)
Marital adjustment unrelated to outcome (T).	0	Rosenbaum, Friedlander & Kaplan (1956)
Marital status unrelated to outcome (T).	0	Tolman & Mayer (1957)
Ps with successful outcome had fewer signs of sexual maladjustment before treatment ($p < .05$) (T).	+	Stone et al. (1961)
Marital status unrelated to improvement in brief psychotherapy (T).	0	Gottschalk, Mayerson & Gottlieb (1967)
Marital status unrelated to status at follow-up.	0	Weissman, Prusoff & Klerman (1978)

Married and single Ps showed more improvement on   +   Free et al. (1985)
the HSRS than did Ps who were divorced or
separated (F = 4.28*) (T).
    Summary. 2+, 0−, 5ns.

e. Social Competence

Main Trend. Not enough studies to locate a trend.

Socially ineffective Ps improved more (T).   −   Stone et al. (1961)

Ps with high social competence had shorter   +   Zigler & Phillips
hospitalizations than Ps with low social competence   (1961)
(p < .001).
    Summary. 1+, 1−, 0ns.

6. STUDENT STATUS

Main Trend. Students have better outcomes than nonstudents.

Full-time college students improved more than   +   Casner (1950)
nonstudents.

Students improved more than nonstudents (T).   +   Rogers & Dymond
    (1954)

Students were more successful than nonstudents (r +   Cartwright (1955)
= .28*).

Students and nonstudents did not differ on outcome.   0   Gaylin (1966)
    Summary. 3+, 0−, 1ns.

7. EARLY HOME SITUATION

Main Trend. Not enough studies to locate a trend.

Ps in the two most improved groups did not differ   0   Miles, Barrabee &
on early home situation.   Finesinger (1951)

Ps who had more favorable early childhood   +   Rosenbaum,
environments were more likely to be seen as   Friedlander &
improved (T).   Kaplan (1956)
    Summary. 1+, 0−, 1ns.

8. PREVIOUS PSYCHOTHERAPY

Main Trend. Previous psychotherapy unrelated to outcome.

Presence, amount, duration of previous treatment   0   Klein (1960)
unrelated to outcome.

Previous therapy unrelated to improvement (T).	0	McNair et al. (1964)
Previous treatment made no difference in outcome (T).	0	Hamburg et al. (1967)

Summary. 0+, 0−, 3ns.

9. HEALTH INSURANCE

Main Trend. Not enough studies to identify a clear trend.

P having health insurance related to the number of treatment interviews ($F = 2.06^*$) and the length (in days) of treatment ($F = 2.22^*$).	+	Levitt & Fisher (1981)

Summary. 1+, 0−.

10. OTHER DEMOGRAPHIC

Main Trend. Not enough studies to identify a clear trend.

Demographic factors (unspecified) unrelated to outcome.	0	Bailey, Warshaw & Eichler (1959)

Summary. 0+, 0−, 1ns.

Patient Physiological Factors

Main Trend. Not enough studies to identify a clear trend.

Lower blood flow in calf in response to reassurance from T rather than psychiatrist related to better outcome ($p < .05$).	+	Clancy & Vanderhoof (1963)
Lower blood flow in calf of leg related to positive changes in Symptom Checklist ($p < .01$) before versus after psychotherapy.	+	Vanderhoof & Clancy (1964)

Summary. 2+, 0−.

Therapist Factors Assessed Apart from the Sessions

1. SKILL AS JUDGED BY OTHERS

Main Trend. Greater judged skill tends to be related to better outcome.

Greater therapist skill related to two of six change factors ($rs = .26^{**}$ and $.27^{**}$) rated at termination of therapy by T and P (mean $r = .14$) (T).	+	Nichols & Beck (1960)
Ps treated by more expert Ts (versus less expert Ts) gave higher scores to their Ts on rating level of regard of T, empathic understanding, and congruence (level of these variables related to change, and treatment by experts was longer) ($p < .01$) (T).	+	Barrett-Lennard (1962)
63% of Ps treated by psychoanalytic students of superior skills showed substantial change, with only 39% for the above average and 28% for the below average in psychoanalysis.	+	Klein (1965)
T's skills unrelated to outcome in 105 outpatients (T).	0	Muench (1965)

Summary. 3+, 0−, 1ns.

2. EXPERIENCE AND TRAINING

Main Trend. Greater therapist level of experience related to better outcome.

Greater degree of T's experience related to better outcome.	+	Miles, Barrabee & Finesinger (1951)
Nonsignificant trend for Ps of most experienced Ts to demonstrate greater improvement (Rorschach scores more accurately predicted P's final adjustment with the more experienced Ts).	0	Mindess (1953)
Ps treated by experienced staff improved more ($p < .05$) than Ps treated by residents (inexperienced staff) (T).	+	Myers & Auld (1955)
T's greater years of experience related to improvement ratings (Group A $r = .49^{**}$, Group B $r = .39^{**}$) (T) (mean $r = .44$).	+	Katz, Lorr & Rubinstein (1958)
Experience of T unrelated to outcome (T).	0	Sullivan, Miller & Smelser (1958)
Outcome less favorable in first than in subsequent analytic control Ps.	+	Knapp et al. (1960)

Ps of experienced Ts showed more improvement than Ps of inexperienced Ts (chi square = 7.245**, r = .50**).

+ Cartwright & Vogel (1960)

Degree of counselor experience (Ph.D., experienced trainee with 1 year internship, versus inexperienced trainees) unrelated to P reports of outcome (chi square = 3.21 ns, r = .12).

0 Grigg (1961)

T "experience" (square root of number of Ps treated by T) unrelated to outcome (none of seven correlations significant) (T).

0 Fiske, Cartwright & Kirtner (1964)

The same proportion (about 75%) of Ps reported considerable or greater improvement when treated by experienced or inexperienced Ts.

0 Strupp, Wallach & Wogan (1964)

Experience of T unrelated to outcome (T).

0 Gaylin (1966)

Schizophrenic Ps treated by experienced Ts were hospitalized for a shorter length of time ($p < .01$), showed less psychotic thought disorder on the Feldman-Drasgow Visual-Verbal Test ($p < .01$), and functioned at healthier levels (clinical status interview ratings) than control Ps treated by inexperienced Ts.

+ Karon & VandenBos (1970)

Experience of Ts unrelated to P improvement on Rorschach Psychological Functioning Scale.

0 Lerner (1972)

Ps of experienced Ts (Ph.D. or more than 2 years of experience) achieved more symptom relief as rated by P and T than those treated by inexperienced Ts.

+ Scher (1975)

Experience of Ts unrelated to P improvement.

0 Kirschner, Genack & Hauser (1978)

T experience unrelated to outcome.

0 Strupp & Hadley (1979)

Summary. Mean $r = .36$ (3); 7+, 0−, 9ns.

3. INTEREST PATTERNS (FROM STRONG VOCATIONAL INTEREST BLANK AND TYPE A VERSUS TYPE B)

Main Trend. Type A Ts are somewhat more often more effective with their Ps than Type B Ts.

Type A Ts (active, personality-oriented, problem-solving, expressive) are more effective in working with schizophrenic Ps than Type B Ts ($p < .05$) (T).

+ Whitehorn & Betz (1954)

Type A Ts much more effective than Type B Ts (regulative, mechanical interests) with schizophrenic Ps ($p < .001$) (T).	+	Betz & Whitehorn (1956)
Ps of Betz Type B Ts improved more than Ps of Type A Ts on four of eight P, T, and observer outcomes ($p < .05$). (Results differ from Betz and Whitehorn's, but were based upon different kinds of Ps.) (T).	−	McNair, Callahan & Lorr (1962)
Type A Ts were more effective in treating schizophrenic Ps than were Type B Ts ($p < .01$) (T).	+	Betz (1963)
No relationship between treatment by A or B Ts and discharge status (results depended on P's initial clinical status, not type of T) (T).	0	Stephens & Astrup (1963, 1965)
No relationship between treatment by A or B Ts and outcome.	0	Koegler & Brill (1967)
No relationship between treatment by A or B Ts and improvement of schizophrenics after 2 years of treatment.	0	Campbell et al. (1967)
Ts having interests similar to successful psychiatrists (Strong Vocational Interest Blank) related to better outcome.	+	Uhlenhuth & Duncan (1968)
Study 1: Type A Ts not more effective then Type B Ts (schizophrenic Ps).	0	Shader et al. (1971); also in Grinspoon et al. (1972)
Study 2: Type A Ts more effective.	+	Shader et al. (1971); also in Grinspoon et al. (1972)
No relationship between treatment by A or B Ts and improvement.	0	Bowden, Endicott & Spitzer (1972)
Type A Ts obtained better therapeutic results than Type B Ts ($F = 3.15^*$) (T).	+	Matthews & Burkhart (1977)

Summary. 6+, 1−, 5ns.

4. THERAPIST'S PERSONAL THERAPY

Main Trend. Amount of T's personal therapy unrelated to outcome.

Personal analysis of T unrelated to P outcome.	0	Katz, Lorr & Rubinstein (1958)
Months of personal analysis of T unrelated to outcome (T).	0	McNair et al. (1964)

Number of hours spent by T in analysis unrelated to outcome.	0	Bowden, Endicott & Spitzer (1972)
Satisfaction with T's own therapy unrelated to P's improvement on Rorschach Psychological Functioning Scale.	0	Lerner (1972)
Number of hours spent by T in personal therapy negatively related to P's change on the MMPI.	—	Garfield & Bergin (1971)

Summary. 0+, 1−, 4ns.

5. PERSONALITY QUALITIES OF THE THERAPIST

Main Trend. "Healthier" T personality qualities related to better P outcomes.

Personality characteristics of counselors rated by peers unrelated to outcome (T).	0	Aronson (1953)
Ts "Ability to enter the phenomenological field of another," "sympathetic interest," "acceptance of the value system of others," "social stimulus value to associates," "need to aggrandize self," and "aggressiveness" unrelated to changes in P's adjustment.	0	Ashby et al. (1957)
T's depression and anxiety (judged from MMPI) unrelated to outcome ($r = -.05$ and $.08$, respectively) (T).	0	Bergin & Jasper (1969)
T's greater "subtlety of defensive pattern" (i.e., social acceptability of defenses) as assessed pretreatment from the MMPI related to P-rated speed of progress ($p < .05$).	+	Wogan (1970)
Ts with "healthier" MMPI profiles had Ps who showed more positive change on MMPI.	+	Garfield & Bergin (1971)
Higher "pathogenesis" scores on TAT related negatively ($rs = -.73^{**}, -.71^{*}$, and $-.64^{*}$) to P's good functioning (errors on Visual-Verbal test, WAIS scores, and Porteus Maze scores) after 6 months of treatment.	+	VandenBos & Karon (1971)
T's greater "field differentiation" related to shorter duration of hospital stay, better ward performance, and lower readmission rate, the first two at chi square $p < .025$ (for an n of 10 Ts differentiated versus 17 Ts undifferentiated).	+	Pardes, Papernik & Winston (1974)

Summary. 4+, 0−, 3ns.

6. FAVORABLE THERAPIST'S ATTITUDE TOWARD TREATMENT

Main Trend. More "favorable" T attitude toward treatment related to better outcome.

More favorable T attitude toward psychiatry and treatment related ($r = .39^*$) to greater symptom reduction as reported by P.	+	Goldstein & Shipman (1961)
T's greater interest in psychotherapy related to better outcome (T).	+	McNair et al. (1964)
T's attitude toward treatment of process schizophrenic Ps unrelated to outcome (T).	0	May (1968)

Summary. 2+, 0−, 1ns.

7. THERAPIST'S PROGNOSTIC EXPECTATION OF PATIENT IMPROVEMENT

Main Trend. No consistent trend in the studies.

T's initial assessment of P's ranking of the importance of various topics for psychotherapy not different for one improved and one unimproved P (T).	0	Parloff, Iflund & Goldstein (1958)
T's greater expectation of improvement related negatively to better outcome on change in reality testing scale of the Psychiatric Status Schedule ($r = -.25^*$; three potential outcome measures with mean $r = -.11$).	−	Bowden, Endicott & Spitzer (1972)
T's expectation of improvement unrelated to P improvement on Rorschach Psychological Functioning Scale.	0	Lerner (1972)
T's greater expectations (early in treatment) of P improvement related to symptom reduction as measured by six of nine MMPI clinical scales and by two of three global measures of improvement (P and independent clinician rated) (mean of significant rs $= .39$) (mean $r = .31$).	+	Martin & Sterne (1975)
T's greater expectations of schizophrenic P improvement related to 12 of 15 independent observer and self-report measures of P adjustment at discharge (mean $r = .38$). T's greater expectations of schizophrenic P improvement related to all 15 independent observer and self-report measures of P adjustment at 9-month follow-up (mean $r = .29$).	+	Martin et al. (1977)

Summary. Mean $r = .17$ (3); 2+, 1−, 2ns.

8. THERAPIST DEMOGRAPHIC VARIABLES

Main Trend. Not enough studies with same predictor to identify a clear trend.

Sex of therapist unrelated to outcome (T).	0	Sullivan, Miller & Smelser (1958)
Professional discipline (psychiatrist, psychologist, social worker) unrelated to outcome (T).	0	Sullivan, Miller & Smelser (1958)
Most successful Ts were born to unusually young, or especially, to unusually old parents	+	Uhlenhuth & Duncan (1968)
Ps who saw female Ts rated themselves as more improved than Ps who saw male Ts (two of four outcomes significant).	+	Kirshner, Genack & Hauser (1978)
Women therapists rated their Ps as having greater overall treatment success ($F = 4.02^*$) (T).	+	Jones & Zoppel (1982)
T's race unrelated to P's overall satisfaction.	0	Neimeyer & Gonzales (1983)

Summary. 3+, 0−, 3ns.

9. AUTHORITARIAN

Main Trend. Not enough studies to identify a trend.

More nonauthoritarian Ts (Democratic Values Scale) tended to have better outcomes with their Ps (one of three outcomes significant).	+	Lerner (1973)

Summary. 1+, 0−.

Patient Factors as Judged from Sessions

1. PSYCHOLOGICAL HEALTH-SICKNESS

Main Trend. Greater psychological health related to better outcome.

Greater P health related to improvement ($r = .16$); success and satisfaction ($r = .56^{**}$) (Penn pilot study) (T).	+	Mintz, Luborsky & Auerbach (1971)

Summary. 1+, 0−.

2. AFFECT

Main Trend. No consistent trend.

Greater expression of feeling related to clinical rating of change on test battery (schizophrenic Ps) (r = .51*).	+	Van der Veen & Stoler (1965)
More hostile-competitive Ps during first three sessions (tape ratings) did better than less hostile-competitive Ps (Z = 2.84**).	+	Crowder (1972)
Amount of P emotional discharge (tape ratings) unrelated to outcome (mean r = .20).	0	Bierenbaum, Nichols & Schwartz (1976)
T rating of time spent by P expressing any unfavorable affect (anxiety, anger, or sadness) related to relapse (p < .05).	—	Jacobson, Deykin & Prusoff (1977)
P hostility to others related to outcome (.10 improvement; .40* success and satisfaction) (Penn pilot study).	+	Mintz, Luborsky & Auerbach (1971)
Greater P hostility (Vanderbilt PPS) negatively related to outcome (SADS-C Depression .03, Social Adj. −.09, P-rated change −.34*).	—	Rounsaville et al. (1987)

Summary. 3+, 2−, 1ns.

3. LIKABILITY

Main Trend. Greater P likability related to better outcome.

More successful Ps were more liked than the less successful Ps (p < .05); (10 raters of 2-minute tape segments).	+	Stoler (1963)
Greater likability related to higher percentage of time out of hospital and higher global ratings of change in the test battery (ratings on 28 schizophrenic Ps).	+	Stoler (1966)

Summary. 2+, 0−.

4. PROBLEM-SOLVING & SELF-EXPLORATION ATTITUDES

Main Trend. Better in-therapy problem-solving attitude related to better outcome.

How P conceptualizes and attempts to resolve problems related to better outcome (T).	+	Kirtner & Cartwright (1958b)

How P conceptualizes (Kirtner typology) and attempts to resolve problems (with residual gain score by interviewer-diagnostician, $r = .39^{**}$) related to better outcome (T).

+ Fiske, Cartwright & Kirtner (1964)

Time spent by P (depressed women) on "reflection" (problem solving) during first 2 months of therapy related to better outcome.

+ Jacobson, Deykin & Prusoff (1977)

More P (and T) exploration in therapy, as rated by clinical observer, related to T's global improvement ratings (T) ($r = .45^*$) ($F = 4.10^*$) (six outcome measures).

+ Gomes-Schwartz (1978)

Greater self-examination and exploration of feelings and experiences as judged by clinical observers of Session 3 taped segments related to better outcome (two of six outcomes) ($rs = .58^{**}$ and $.47^*$) (T).

+ O'Malley, Suh & Strupp (1983)

Summary. 5+, 0−.

5. THE PROCESS CONTINUUM OF PSYCHOTHERAPY

Main Trend. Greater Process development related to better outcome.

Higher scores on the Process scale related ($r = .89$) to better outcome (client-centered therapy).

+ Walker, Rablen & Rogers (1960)

Process scale distinguished most versus least successful cases ($p < .05$) and showed more successful begin and end therapy at higher levels of Process (client-centered therapy) (T).

+ Tomlinson & Hart (1962)

Change in Process ("personal constructs" and "relationships") is greater in 6 more successful versus 6 less successful Ps (client-centered therapy) (T).

+ Tomlinson (1967)

Ps improve most who start at a high level of Process (client-centered therapy) (T).

+ Gendlin, Jenney & Schlien (1960)

Summary. 4+, 0−.

6. EXPERIENCING

Main Trend. Greater experiencing related to better outcomes.

Successful Ps move from reporting feelings to expressing them directly (client-centered therapy) (T).

+ Gendlin, Beebe, Cassens et al. (1968)

Experiencing based on ratings of initial in-therapy behavior differentiated outcome groups (client-centered psychotherapy) (T).	+	Kirtner et al. (1961)
Greater level of experiencing in the second interview negatively related to better outcome. (Experiencing in the middle interview related positively to better outcome, while experiencing measured in next-to-last session unrelated to outcome.)	—	Ryan (1966)
P level of experiencing the first 5 therapy sessions unrelated to outcome.	0	Kiesler (1971)
Experiencing (psychodynamic therapy) early in treatment unrelated to P and T outcome measures. (Greater level of experiencing measured late in treatment related to better outcome.)	0	Fishman (1971)
Experiencing early in treatment unrelated to outcome by MMPI, TAT, and Butler-Haigh Q-Sort. (Greater level of experiencing measured late as well as change from early and middle to late in therapy were all related to better outcome.)	0	Custers (1973)
Greater P level of experiencing in high experiencers negatively related to P-rated satisfaction with therapy ($r = .72^*$).	—	Richert (1976)
Experiencing in second session unrelated to outcome by diagnostic evaluation and P-reported well-being and relaxation. (Greater level of experiencing measured from middle session related positively to all outcome measures. Experiencing measured from next-to-last session unrelated to diagnostic evaluation and P-reported relaxation but related to P-reported well-being.)	0	Bommert & Dahlkoff (1978)
Greater level of experiencing early and late in treatment related to better outcome by the Inner Support subscale of Personal Orientation Inventory (POI) (mean $r \approx .52$). (No relation between mean experiencing level and Post-Therapy Rating Scale or change on POI.)	+	Jennen, Lietaer & Rombauts (1978)
Greater experiencing (based on ratings by Marjorie Klein) of initial sessions unrelated to outcome (related to better outcome for males; unrelated for females) (Penn study).	0	Luborsky, Mintz, et al. (1980)

Greater level of experiencing in an initial interview + Nixon (1982)
prior to treatment related to better outcome by
Q-Sort Adjustment Score ($r = .53^{**}$), Q-Sort
Self-Ideal correlation ($r = .45^{**}$), and by Client
Global Rating ($r = .41^{**}$).

   Summary. Mean $r = .38$ (3); 4+, 2−, 5ns.

7. MOTIVATION

Main Trend. Not enough studies to locate a trend.

Greater P motivation (tape rated by judges) related + Keithly, Samples
to T's rating of improvement ($r = .65^*$) and P's   & Strupp (1980)
rating of improvement ($r = .66^*$) (four outcome
criteria).

   Summary. 1+, 0−.

8. THE ALLIANCE AND OTHER POSITIVE RELATIONSHIP QUALITIES

a. *Therapeutic or Helping Alliance*

Main Trend. Greater presence of alliance related to better outcome.

Greater "P contribution to the helping alliance scale" + Marziali, Marmar
discriminated good versus poor outcome ($r = 1.0^{**}$).   & Krupnick (1981)
"T contribution to the helping alliance" unrelated to
outcome ($r = .55$ns).

Greater helping alliance scores (Global Rating + Morgan et al.
Method) related to better outcome ($rs = .44^*$ and   (1982)
$.58^{**}$; two of two correlations significant) (T) (Penn
study).

Higher scores on helping alliance measures related + Hartley & Strupp
(slightly) to better outcome. At the 25% point in   (1983)
treatment, the Total scale and the P scale
discriminated high versus low outcome groups ($r =
.54^*$).

Greater helping alliance scores (Counting Signs + Luborsky et al.
Method) related to better outcome ($r = .57^*$ with   (1983)
rated benefits and $r = .58^{**}$ with residual gain).
Greater helping alliance scores (Global Rating
Method) related to better outcome ($r = .46^*$ with
rated benefits and $r = .44^*$ with residual gain)
(Penn study).

P, T, and judges' ratings of "P's positive
contribution to the therapeutic alliance" across six
sessions related to P, T, and judges' assessments of
good outcome (eight of nine correlations significant;
mean $r = .43$). "P's negative contributions" related
negatively to better outcome (seven of nine
correlations significant; mean $r = -.29$). "T's
positive contributions" related to good outcome (six
of nine correlations significant; mean $r = .28$), and
"T's negative contributions" unrelated to good
outcome (one of nine correlations significant; mean
$r = -.06$).

+ Marziali (1984b)

Greater "P's negative contribution to therapeutic
alliance" (using the Therapeutic Alliance Scale)
related to slower rate of decline in symptoms ($r = -.34^*$) (one of eight correlations significant).

+ Horowitz, Marmar,
Weiss, et al. (1984)

Higher scores on the Helping Alliance Questionnaire
rated by P (and by T) related to better outcome
(mean $r = .65$; all rs at $p < .01$) (VA-Penn study).

+ Luborsky,
McLellan, et al.
(1985)

Greater therapeutic alliance (California
Psychotherapy Alliance scales—T version and P
version) across early, middle, and late stages of
therapy and across three treatments (behavioral,
cognitive, and brief dynamic) related to better
outcome (20 of 50 correlations significant) (mean
$r = .23$).

+ Marmar, Gallagher
& Thompson (in
press)

Summary. **Mean** $r = .50$ (8); $8+$, $0-$.

b. Other Positive Relationship Qualities

Main Trend. **Greater positive relationship qualities related to better outcome.**

Predictive index (greater percentage of P statements
reflecting positive attitude toward self) during first
session related ($r = .90^{**}$) to better outcome (T).

+ Blau (1950)

Ps with early increases in reported positive actions
toward self and others and increases in their positive
evaluation of others were rated as more improved
(T).

+ Rosenman (1955)

More favorable P–T relationship related to more
favorable outcome on 3 of 14 scales for patient
comfort, effectiveness, and objectivity (significant rs
$= .67^{**}$, $.61^*$, and $.67^{**}$; mean of 14 $rs = .25$) (T).

+ Parloff (1961)

More positive relationship (Barrett-Lennard Relationship Inventory filled out by P and T) related to better outcome ($p < .001$).	+	Barrett-Lennard (1962)
Five measures of interview relationship labeled Rapport, Blocking, Hostile Resistance, Dependency, and Controlling Resistance unrelated to outcome (T).	0	Roth et al. (1964)
P self-rating of feeling understood by T related to improvement ($r = .59^*$) (T).	+	Feitel (1968)
Less passive-resistant Ps in first three sessions (tape ratings) did better than more passive-resistant Ps ($Z = -6.41^{***}$).	+	Crowder (1972)
Greater perceived mutual understanding of therapeutic relationship rated by P after third session related to P-rated improvement ($r = .26^*$) and T's assessment of greater degree of positive change and greater degree of problem resolution ($r = .39^{**}$ and $.33^{**}$).	+	Saltzman et al. (1976)
Six variables rated by P after third session on favorable feelings to T and satisfaction with therapy related to improvement (T) and degree of problem resolution (15 out of 22 correlations significant). Also, more negative P–T interaction as assessed by judges on a subscale of Vanderbilt Negative Indicators Scale related negatively to P's overall improvement on composite P, T, and clinician ratings ($r = -.49^*$).	+	Saltzman et al. (1976)
P's more positive experience of the conflict-centered beginning of supportive psychodynamic therapy as judged by questionnaire early in treatment related to better outcome (rated by independent observer).	+	Persson, Alstrom & Nordlund (1984b)

Summary. 9+, 0−, 1ns.

9. SELF-UNDERSTANDING AND INSIGHT

Main Trend. Self-understanding mostly unrelated to outcomes.

Insight (based on T's retrospective reports of their Ps) unrelated to outcome (T).	0	Rosenbaum, Friedlander & Kaplan (1956)
P's insight as rated by independent judges from Sessions 3 and 5 unrelated to outcome (Penn study).	0	Morgan et al. (1982)

Level of self-understanding (Session 3) related to outcome (r = .31* for understanding of relation to therapist with rated benefits; four other rs ns; .34* for understanding of relation to other people with residual gain; four other rs ns) (Penn study).	+	(Chapter 17, this book)

Change in level of self-understanding (from Sessions 3 and 5) unrelated to outcomes (5 rs with each criterion ns) (Penn study).	0	(Chapter 17, this book)

Summary. 1+, 0−, 3ns.

10. INVOLVEMENT

Main Trend. Greater P involvement in therapy related to better outcome.

Active involvement (T-judged from four sessions) related to T-judged satisfaction (r = .54) and improvement (r = .58) (mean r = .56).	+	Lorr & McNair (1964)

Greater P "involvement" in therapy (P participation and P hostility) as rated by clinical observer related to improvement on global ratings by T (r = .56**) (F = 7.46**) and clinician (r = .54**) (F = 6.73**) and change in Target Complaint ratings by T (r = .63***) (F = 10.8***) (six outcome measures) (mean r = .46) (T).	+	Gomes-Schwartz (1978)

Greater degree of P's involvement in therapy (i.e., active participant, uninhibited) as judged by independent clinicians (taped segments) of the third session related to better outcome (six of six potential T-, P-, and clinician-rated outcome measures) (mean r = .45).	+	O'Malley, Suh & Strupp (1983)

Greater P "involvement" in treatment (rated by T on Psychotherapy Process Inventory) related to better outcome (r = .81***) (T).	+	Kolb et al. (1985)

Summary. Mean r = .59 (4); 4+, 0−.

11. AMOUNT OF PATIENT TALKING

Main Trend. More patient talking related to better outcomes.

Amount of P's talking unrelated to P symptom relief and to T and P satisfaction.	0	Scher (1975)

Greater total speech time and average speech durations related to outcome (change in severity of target symptoms).	+	Sloane et al. (1975)

P talking in therapy related to overall improvement, rated by Ps, clinicians, and Ts ($rs = .51^{**}$, $.37^*$ and $.57^{**}$, respectively) (mean $r = .48$).

+ McDaniel, Stiles & McGaughey (1981)

Summary. 2+, 0−, 1ns.

12. OTHER PATIENT FACTORS

Main Trend. Not enough studies with the same predictor to identify a trend.

Maturity of behavior (reported during psychotherapy) is greater in more successful than less successful cases.

+ Hoffman (1949)

Discomfort-Relief quotient from casework records unrelated to outcome (criterion measures from social caseworker's judgment of movement) (T).

0 Mowrer, Hunt & Kogan (1953)

Discomfort-Relief quotient in several studies based on psychotherapeutic and counseling records showed high rs with T estimate of success and other measures of change—the quotient moved toward greater comfort (T).

+ Mowrer, Hunt & Kogan (1953)

Mean type-token ratio (ratio of number of different words to total words) increased for more successful versus less successful group—that is, the ratio moved toward greater diversity of words (T).

+ Roshal (1953)

"Complexity of language": Combination of number of syllables per word used by P and T related to T's success ratings ($r = .42^*$) and positive change in Q-adjustment ($r = .39^*$) (from 10-minute taped samples of first two interviews) (T).

+ Barrington (1961)

Ps who were more support-seeking (in first three sessions' tape ratings) did better than Ps who were less support-seeking ($Z = 7.08^{***}$).

+ Crowder (1972)

T ratings of time spent by the P discussing mental symptoms related to relapse for depressed patients ($p < .05$) (10 potential comparisons).

+ Jacobson, Deykin & Prusoff (1977)

P's resistance, as rated by independent judges from Sessions 3 and 5 unrelated to outcome (Penn study).

0 Morgan et al. (1982)

Summary. 6+, 0−, 2ns.

Therapist Factors as Judged from Sessions

1. SKILL

Main Trend. Greater therapist skill related to better outcome.

Ts with "best therapeutic behavior" (judged from taped sessions) had best outcomes (T).	+	Nash et al. (1965)
Greater T "expertness" (rated by P after first session) related to better outcome ($r = .56^{***}$).	+	LaCrosse (1980)
More errors in T's technique (on subscale of Vanderbilt Negative Indicators Scale) related negatively to P's overall improvement, a composite of P, T, and clinician ratings ($r = -.56^{**}$), T and clinician ratings ($rs = -.58^{**}$ and $-.51^{*}$, respectively) and T and clinician ratings of decrease in overall disturbance ($rs = -.59^{**}$ and $-.54^{**}$, respectively) (six potential outcome measures).	+	Sachs (1983)
Greater T "purity of technique" (in following a manual) related to better outcome (mean $r = .44$; seven of seven correlations significant). (The correlations are significant across Ts as well as within a T's caseload.) (VA-Penn study).	+	Luborsky, McLellan, et al. (1985)

Summary. 4+, 0−.

2. EMPATHY

Main Trend. More empathy related to better outcome.

a. Empathy as Judged by Ratings of Sessions

More "Accurate Empathy" (from tape segments) related to better outcome ($p < .01$).	+	Truax (1963)
More "Accurate Empathy" (from tape segments) related to better outcome (two of five potential outcome measures significant) (T).	+	Truax et al. (1966)
More "Accurate Empathy" related to a decrease in the MMPI Sc (schizophrenia) scale, but unrelated to other measures of change (Ward Behavior rating) (T).	+	Rogers et al. (1967)
Empathy related to outline (schizophrenic Ps) (clinician ratings of change, $r = .49^{*}$).	+	Van der Veen (1967)

"Accurate Empathy" (from tape segments) unrelated (r = .05) to outcome (T).

0 Bergin & Jasper (1969)

Empathy (tape segments) unrelated to four outcomes (mean r = .12).

0 Garfield & Bergin (1971)

Greater T empathy (tape rated by clinical observers) related to positive change on seven MMPI scales (r = .39* to .69**) (nine MMPI scales used as criteria) (mean r = .47).

+ Melnick & Pierce (1971)

T Empathy (judged from tape segments and entire sessions) unrelated to outcome (mean r = −.16; zero of two correlations significant) (T) (Penn pilot study).

0 Mintz, Luborsky & Auerbach (1971)

Higher "Accurate Empathy" (from tape segments) related (r = .41**) to change on MMPI.

+ Mullen & Abeles (1971)

T's greater empathy (tape rated by judges) related to improvement in self-esteem on Tennessee Self-Concept Scale (r = .42**; six potential outcome measures with mean r = .23).

+ Kurtz & Grummon (1972)

No differences in outcome were found for Ps treated by high versus low empathy Ts (t = .83, r = .12) (T).

0 Beutler, Johnson, Neville & Workman (1973)

Greater initial T "accurate empathy" related to P's continuing counseling beyond the initial interview (chi square = 9.37***, r = .57***).

+ Altmann (1973)

T empathy (P-perceived) unrelated to outcome.

0 Kalfas (1973)

Summary. Mean r = .26 (9); 8+, 0−, 5ns.

b. Empathy as Judged by Other Measures

Empathic Understanding Scale scores (rated by counselor and client) unrelated to counseling progress (mean r = −.29) (Q-Sort criterion).

0 Lesser (1961)

Relationship Inventory variables: T's regard for P (empathic understanding and congruence) rated by Ps after five sessions predicted change measures by T (p < .001) for low change versus high change Ps; same findings when rated by T, though not as strongly as when rated by P (T).

+ Barrett-Lennard (1962)

T's initial ability to understand the P's pretherapy self-image unrelated to outcome.

+ Cartwright & Lerner (1963)

Greater T "empathic understanding"   +   Feitel (1968)
(Barrett-Lennard Inventory) related to improvement
(r = .34*) (T).

Greater T empathy (P-perceived on Barrett-Lennard   +   Kurtz & Grummon
Relationship Inventory) related to improvement on   (1972)
the following: self-esteem on Tennessee
Self-Concept Scale (r = .44*), MMPI (r = .66**), T
global rating (r = .35*) and composite of outcome
criteria (r = .55**) (six potential outcome measures
with mean r = .45).

T empathy unrelated to outcome (by T and P).   0   Magnelli (1975)

T's greater "understanding" as rated by P related to +   Martin & Sterne
three of five measures of better posthospital   (1976)
adjustment (rs = −.31*, −.26*, and .22*; mean r
for five measures = .18).

Greater self-rated T empathy related to good   +   Jacobs & Warner
outcome with neurotics and personality trait   (1981)
disorders (r = .26**).

Summary. Mean r = .20 (5); 6+, 0−, 2ns.

3. ACCURACY OF INTERPRETATION

Main Trend. Not enough studies to establish a trend.

Greater accuracy of interpretation as judged by   +   Crits-Christoph et
degree the interpretations deal with independently   al. (in press)
established wish plus response from other
components of the Core Conflictual Relationship
Theme (Penn study).
   Summary. 1+, 0−.

4. FOCUS ON TRANSFERENCE

Main Trend. More transference interpretations related to better outcomes.

More T transference interpretations about T and   +   Malan (1976)
parents ("T-P" Link) related to outcome (Dynamic
Outcome Scale) (r = .43*).

More T transference interpretations about T and   +   Marziali (1984a)
parents in the same interpretation related to better
outcome (in brief therapy) by Dynamic Outcome
scale (r = .57**) (one of three measures).

More "transference-past" interpretations unrelated to outcome.   0   Piper et al. (1986)

Summary. Mean r = .50 (2); 2+, 0−, 1ns.

5. POSITIVE REGARD AND WARMTH

Main Trend. Greater T positive regard and warmth toward P related to better outcome.

Greater unconditional positive regard (by Barrett-Lennard Inventory) related to better outcome (r = .33*) (T).   +   Barrett-Lennard (1962)

More unconditional positive regard related to better outcome (p < .05).   +   Truax (1963)

Greater P perception of T "understanding" and "accepting" behavior related to better outcome from P and T ratings of improvement ("understanding" rs = .31* and .19*; "accepting" rs = .24* and .16*) (mean r = .23) (T).   +   Lorr (1965)

More nonpossessive warmth negatively related to global improvement (rated by P) (p < .05) (T).   −   Truax et al. (1966)

Positive regard unrelated to outcome with clinician's rating (r = .12).   0   Van der Veen (1967)

Greater T unconditional positive regard (Barrett-Lennard Inventory rated by P) related to better outcome (r = .77*) (T).   +   Feitel (1968)

T warmth unrelated to four of four outcome measures (mean r = −.14).   0   Garfield & Bergin (1971)

Greater T positive regard (tape rated by clinical observers) related to positive change on four MMPI scales (r = .39* to .60**) (nine MMPI scales used as criteria) (mean r = .39).   +   Melnick & Pierce (1971)

Nonpossessive warmth during early and middle stages of therapy unrelated (r = .26) to change on MMPI.   0   Mullen & Abeles (1971)

Greater T "facilitative skill" (sum of four Barrett-Lennard dimensions—regard, empathy, unconditionality, and congruence) unrelated to outcome (five outcome measures) (T).   0   Kolb et al. (1985)

T rated as "accepting" by Ps related to three of five measures of better posthospital adjustment (rs = −.28**, −.23*, and −.27**; mean r = .17).   +   Martin & Sterne (1976)

Greater T warmth and friendliness as rated by   +   Gomes-Schwartz
clinical observer, related to positive change in Target   (1978)
Complaint ratings by T ($r = .51^{**}$) ($F = 5.56^{**}$)
(six outcome measures, mean $r = .30$).

Greater "quality of the T-offered relationship" as   +   O'Malley, Suh &
judged by clinical observer from the third treatment   Strupp (1983)
session related to T's rating of improvement ($r =$
$.46^*$) (six potential outcome measures with mean
$r = .33$) (T).

Greater T warmth (Vanderbilt PPS) related to   +   Rounsaville et al.
outcomes (SADS-C Depression .30, Social   (1987)
Adjustment Scale $.40^*$, P-rated change $.60^{**}$).
   Summary. Mean $r = .32$ (11); 9+, 0−, 4ns.

6. GENUINENESS (OR CONGRUENCE)

Main Trend. More T genuineness related to better outcome.

Greater "self-congruence" (genuineness) related to   +   Truax (1963)
better outcome. Taped samples of T's improved Ps
rated higher ($p < .05$).

More T genuineness (rated from taped samples)   +   Truax et al. (1966)
related to better outcome (T).

Congruence (genuineness) unrelated to outcome   0   Van der Veen
($r = .19$ for clinician ratings of change).   (1967)

More T "genuineness" (tape rated by clinical   +   Melnick & Pierce
observers) related to positive change on five MMPI   (1971)
scales ($r = .40^*$ to $.61^{**}$) (nine MMPI scales used as
criteria) (mean $r = .40$).

More congruence unrelated to four of four outcome   0   Garfield & Bergin
measures (mean $r = -.03$).   (1971)
   Summary. Mean $r = .21$ (3); 3+, 0−, 2ns.

7. EMPATHY, WARMTH, POSITIVE REGARD AND GENUINENESS IN COMBINATION

Main Trend. Not enough studies to identify a trend.

Greater Accurate Empathy-Warmth-Genuineness   +   Truax et al. (1966)
combined related to better outcome (Ts providing
high conditions had 90% improvement but Ts
with lower conditions had only 50% improvement)
(T).

T's empathy, warmth, and genuineness combined (from tape segments) unrelated to outcome ($r = -.19$).

0   Beutler, Johnson, Neville, Workman & Elkins (1973)

Summary. 1+, 0−, 1ns.

8. LIKING THE PATIENT

Main Trend. T's liking for P moderately related to outcomes.

T's greater liking for P related ($r = .29^*$) to success in treatment (T).

+   Strupp et al. (1963)

T's liking for P unrelated to outcome ($rs = .11$, $-.02$) (schizophrenic Ps) (mean $r = .04$).

0   Van der Veen & Stoler (1965)

T's liking for P (by T's attitude inventory) unrelated to outcome.

0   Gottschalk, Mayerson & Gottlieb (1967)

T's liking for P related to outcomes for both experienced ($r = .25$) and inexperienced ($r = .20$) Ts, rs with three outcomes; all but one was significant (mean $r = .23$).

+   Brown (1970)

T's liking for P unrelated to outcome.

0   Bowden, Endicott & Spitzer (1972)

T's liking for P related to outcome.

+   Staples et al. (1976)

Summary. Mean $r = .19$ (3); 3+, 0−, 3ns.

9. HOSTILITY AND NEGATIVE ATTITUDE

Main Trend. Not enough studies to locate a trend.

Greater T hostility and criticism of Ps during therapy related to poorer posthospital adjustment (two of five outcomes) ($rs = .22^*$ and $.21^*$).

−   Martin & Sterne (1976)

Greater T Negative Attitude (Vanderbilt PPS) unrelated to outcomes (SADS-C Depression $-.12$, Social Adj. $-.14$, P-rated change $-.24$).

0   Rounsaville et al. (1987)

Summary. 1+, 0−, 1ns.

10. ENCOURAGING INDEPENDENCE

Main Trend. Encouraging independence moderately related to outcome.

Greater P-perceived "independence encouraging" by T related to better outcomes ($r = .13^*$ with P improvement).

+   Lorr (1965)

Greater T "encouragement of T independence"   +   Martin & Sterne
(P-rated) related to five of five measures of better   (1976)
posthospital adjustment (mean r = .28).

   Summary. Mean r = .21 (2); 2+, 0−.

11. DIRECTIVE AND ADVICE-GIVING

   Main Trend. Directive and advice-giving moderately negatively related
to outcome.

More evaluative comments (re goodness or badness)   +   Truax (1970a)
negatively related to outcome (one of three
correlations significant, mean r = .25).

Lower levels of T directiveness related to greater   +   Jacobs & Warner
improvement (F = 11.33**).   (1981)

Directive mode unrelated to outcome (improvement   0   Mintz, Luborsky &
r = −.04; success and satisfaction −.24) (mean r =   Auerbach (1971)
−.14) (Penn pilot study).

   Summary. Mean r = .06 (2); 2+, 0−, 1ns.

12. SUPPORTIVE

   Main Trend. Greater support related to better outcome.

More "T facilitation behaviors for the helping   +   Morgan et al.
alliance" (rated from Sessions 3 and 5) related to   (1982)
better outcome (r = .45* with rated benefits) (one
of two outcome measures) (Penn study).

Greater T support rather than interpretation or   +   Buckley et al.
insight (by averaging periodic T ratings) related to   (1984)
better outcome (r = .73***) (T).

   Summary. Mean r = .61 (2); 2+, 0−.

13. AMOUNT OF THERAPIST'S TALKING

   Main Trend. Amount of therapist's talking mostly unrelated to patient's
outcome.

Number of T words and number of words per T   0   Barrington (1961)
response unrelated to outcome.

Length of response related to outcomes (by P and T)   +   Truax (1970b)
(rs = .39, .34, 02, and −.09).

Percent time speaking unrelated to outcome.   0   DiLoreto (1971)

Verbal activity unrelated to outcome (P symptom   0   Scher (1975)
relief and P and T satisfaction).

Total-speech time, number of speech units unrelated   0   Staples & Sloane
to outcomes.   (1976)

Verbal productivity related to outcomes (by P and   +   Friedlander (1981)
T).
  Summary. 2+, 0−, 4ns.

14. THERAPIST'S PROGNOSTIC EXPECTATIONS

Main Trend. Not enough studies to locate a trend.

Initial T expectancy related to therapy outcome.   +   Berman (1979)

T early judgment of prognosis unrelated to outcome.   0   Prager (1970)

Better prognosis based on first interview related to   +   Brown (1970)
outcomes (.34*, .30*, .42*) (mean $r = .35$).

T's prognosis after third session (from Multiple   +   Saltzman et al.
Affect Adjective Checklist) related to P's and T's   (1976)
rating of problem resolution ($r = .26^*$; $.36^{**}$,
respectively) and T's rating of improvement ($r =
.32^{**}$) (four outcomes) (mean $r = .27$).
  Summary. Mean $r = .31$ (2); 3+, 0−, 1ns.

15. OTHER THERAPEUTIC PERFORMANCE FACTORS AND COMBINATIONS JUDGED FROM SESSIONS

Main Trend. Not enough studies with same predictor to identify a trend.

Greater "Type II" T behavior (taped sample from   +   Rice (1965)
second session) negatively related to T's ($r =
-.44^*$) ratings of better outcome (Type II =
distorted voice quality; language not fresh; mainly T
joins in self-observing the P; not exploring of inner
experience) (T).

Greater "Type III" T behavior (expressive style,   +   Rice (1965)
freshness of words, etc.) related to success in
client-centered therapy as judged by T ($r = .40^*$),
change in P's Q-adjustment score ($r = .42^*$), and
change in Taylor Manifest Anxiety scores ($r = .50^*$)
(five potential outcome criteria) (T).

Greater P perceived "authoritarian" behavior by T   +   Lorr (1965)
related negatively to better outcome ($r = -.19^*$)
(T).

Greater T "persuasive potency" related to better   +   Truax et al. (1968)
outcome as rated by T ($F = 10.28^{**}$) and by P ($F =
3.81^*$) (T).

High T empathy in context of low T directiveness,   +   Mintz, Luborsky &
or low T empathy in context of high T directiveness,   Auerbach (1971)
related to better outcome (judgment of P's success
and satisfaction) ($r = -.50^*$) (T) (Penn pilot study).

T's "strength" and "overall evaluation of T" (from   0   Melnick & Pierce
P's ratings on semantic differential) unrelated to   (1971)
outcome.

More supportive-interpretive Ts during first three   +   Crowder (1972)
sessions (tape ratings) did better with their Ps than
less supportive-interpretive Ts ($Z = -6.63^{***}$).

Greater T ability to recognize client personal   +   Magnelli (1975)
constructs related to outcome.

Greater P ratings of T's "trustworthiness" (after first   +   LaCrosse (1980)
session) related to better outcome ($r = .38^{**}$).

Greater P ratings of T's "attractiveness" (after first   +   LaCrosse (1980)
session) related to better outcome ($r = .45^{**}$).

Greater P ratings of T's "expertness, trustworthiness,   +   LaCrosse (1980)
and attractiveness" in combination related to better
outcome ($r = .53^{***}$).

Higher levels of T "uncovering technique" related to   +   Jacobs & Warner
poorer outcome with psychotics and borderlines and   (1981)
better outcome with neurotics and personality trait
disorders ($F = 4.19^*$).

Greater T resources to help P (P rating) related to   +   Rucker (1982)
outcome (by Goal Attainment Scale), especially
trustworthiness.

Greater efforts by T to "clarify the focus of   +   Horowitz et al.
treatment" (measured by T's report at fourth   (1984)
session) related to better outcome on Patterns of
Individual Change Scales (PICS) relationship
composite (by independent clinicians) ($r = .31^*$).

The Match (Similarity) Between Patient and Therapist

1. MMPI SIMILARITY

Main Trend. Patient–therapist similarity on the MMPI mostly unrelated
to outcome.

Similarity in MMPI profile shape between P and T: Relationship curvilinear with either extreme similarity or dissimilarity associated with lower success ratings.	0 Carson & Heine (1962)
Similarity in MMPI profile shape between P and T unrelated to outcome (T).	0 Carson & Llewellyn (1966)
Similarity in MMPI profile shape between P and T unrelated to outcome (an attempt to replicate Carson & Heine, 1962) (T).	0 Lichtenstein (1966)
Greater P–T similarity in "subtlety of defensive patterns" (i.e., social acceptability of defenses assessed pretreatment from MMPI) negatively related to P-rated speed of progress ($p < .05$).	− Wogan (1970)

Summary. 0+, 1−, 3ns.

2. RORSCHACH SIMILARITY

Main Trend. Greater patient–therapist similarity on Rorschach related to better outcome.

Ps rated as more successful showed more pre- to posttreatment shifts in Rorschach performance in direction of T's Rorschach than did less successful Ps ($p < .01$) (T).	+ Sheehan (1953)
After treatment, Ps showed significant changes in Rorschach M:C ratio in direction of their T (Ps whose T had an M:C ratio of 2:1 or better gave significantly more C after treatment).	+ Graham (1960)

Summary. 2+, 0−.

3. INTEREST AND VALUES TEST MEASURING P–T SIMILARITY

Main Trend. Greater patient–therapist similarity in interests and values related to better outcome.

Correct awareness of similarity ($r = .45^*$ with counseling progress) related to better outcome.	+ Lesser (1961)
Greater degree of P–T similarity (Strong Vocational Interest Blank and Ways to Live scale) related ($p < .05$) to improvement (T).	+ Welkowitz, Cohen, & Ortmeyer (1967)
Higher P–T congruence score (on appropriate therapeutic techniques) related to P rating of improvement ($r = .33^*$) (one of three correlations significant with mean $r = .16$) (T).	+ Schonfield et al. (1969)

Greater T "acceptance of P's values on premarital   +   Beutler, Pollack &
sex while rejecting the P's estimate of threat in the   Jobe (1978)
world" related to P rating of global improvement.
   Summary. Mean r = .31 (2); 4+, 0−.

4. SOCIAL CLASS SIMILARITY

Main Trend. Greater patient–therapist social class similarity related to better outcome.

Greater social class similarities of T and P related to   +   Hollingshead &
better outcome (T).   Redlich (1958)

Ps with professional occupations and Ps who are   +   Hamburg et al.
psychiatrists or analytic candidates are more likely to   (1967)
complete treatment than the general population (T).
   Summary. 2+, 0−.

5. RACIAL MATCH

Main Trend. Patient–therapist racial match unrelated to outcome.

P–T racial match unrelated to outcome.   0   Jones (1982)

P–T racial match unrelated to outcome.   0   Neimeyer &
                                               Gonzales (1983)

   Summary. 0+, 0−, 2ns.

6. OTHER SIMILARITIES

Main Trend. Greater patient–therapist similarity related to better outcome.

Similarity between T's description of P and ideal self   0   Hunt et al. (1959)
related to better outcome in only two of six cases
(T).

Similarity between P and T self-perceptions   0   Lesser (1961)
unrelated to progress in treatment (Q-sorts).

Assumed similarity: Same-sexed Ps who improved   +   Cartwright &
were early accepted by T as like self.   Lerner (1963)

Ps who improved most were in first session more   +   Landfield & Nawas
similar to their T on Kelly's Role Construct   (1964)
Repertory Test (p < .05) and changed toward T's
ideal.

P–T compatability: Greater similarity of scores on the Fundamental Interpersonal Relations Orientation Behavior (FIRO-B) related ($r = .45^*$) to supervisor's rating of P improvement (T).	+ Sapolsky (1965)
Greater P–T similarity on Interpersonal Discrimination Test related to improvement on P global ratings ($p < .01$) and P-rated symptom change ($t = 2.2^*$) (three potential outcome measures).	+ Carr (1970)
P's increasing similarity to T over time on semantic differential related to improvement on MMPI Dependency ($r = .49^*$) and Psychasthenia ($r = .44^*$) scales (of 10 scales used as criteria) as well as overall improvement on MMPI.	+ Melnick (1972)
Greater "P–T elicitation-response complementarity" (e.g., dominance followed by submission) tape rated by judges unrelated to outcome ($t = .716, r = .21$ns).	0 Dietzel & Abeles (1975)
Ps with similar perceptions (Q-sort) of their therapy to Ts related to greater improvement by T.	+ Astwood (1976)
Greater P–T match from scores on FIRO-F, FIRO-B, Omnibus Personality Inventory, and Differential Emotion related to T's rating of "satisfaction with progress of client" at termination ($t = 3.68^{**}$) (T).	+ Dougherty (1976)
P and T "mutuality of expectations" unrelated to outcome (P rates own expectations of T behavior, while T rates typical P expectations).	0 Martin, Sterne & Hunter (1976)
Greater P–T match on high personality integration (Tennessee Self-Concept Scale and Marcia Ego Identity Status Incomplete Sentences Blank) related to better outcome ($t = 3.04^{**}, r = .68^{**}$) (T).	+ Anchor (1977)
Level of congruence in selection of target problems unrelated to outcome measures.	0 Kreioberg (1977)
Sum of 10 mostly demographic similarities related to better outcome on residual gain ($r = .23^*$), rated benefits ($r = .24^*$) (marital status, match $r = .23^*$) (Penn study).	+ Luborsky, Mintz, et al. (1980)

The degree of P–T "interpersonal compatibility" as   +   Malloy (1981)
assessed by the FIRO-B related to improvement in
major financial living condition, employment, major
home and family problems as assessed by P pre-
versus posttreatment on the Mooney Problem Check
List ($p < .05$).

A "good match between the P's pretreatment   +   Persson &
attitude to the goal of treatment and how therapist   Nordlund (1983)
should function" related to better outcome.

P–T match on locus of control related to better   +   Foon (1985)
outcome (P and T ratings of therapeutic
effectiveness) (T).
  Summary. 12+, 0−, 5ns.

Treatment Factors

1. GENERAL CHARACTERISTICS OF PSYCHOTHERAPY

a. Number of Sessions and/or Duration of Treatment

Main Trend. Greater number of sessions and/or duration of treatment
related to better outcome.

Greater number of sessions related to improvement   +   Bartlett (1950)
($r = .31^{***}$).

Greater number of sessions related ($r = .34^{***}$) to +   Mensh & Golden
improvement (T).   (1951)

Curvilinear relationship with definitely better group   +   Miles, Barrabee &
receiving more treatment sessions than either the   Finesinger (1951)
markedly improved or the unchanged group.

The most improved Ps continued in treatment the   +   Conrad (1952)
longest (of 50 VA outpatients in short-term
treatment) (T).

More sessions related to better outcome (trend);   +   Seeman (1954)
more than 20 sessions (T).

For those Ps with greater than 14 sessions, greater   +   Cartwright (1955)
number of sessions related to higher success ratings
($r = .66^{**}$).

More sessions (a minimum number required for improvement) related to better outcome ($r = .61^{***}$) (T).	+	Myers & Auld (1955)
More sessions related to improvement (no data on treatment length or frequency). Better outcome related to greater length of treatment, with exception of a failure zone between the 13th and 21st interviews (T).	+	Taylor (1956)
Greater length of treatment related to better outcome ($r = 1.0^{***}$).	+	Tolman & Mayer (1957)
Log number of sessions related to T's higher rating of "movement in personal integration" ($r = .58^{***}$) (T).	+	Standal & van der Veen (1957)
Greater length of treatment related to success ($r = .32^{**}$) (T).	+	Sullivan, Miller & Smelser (1958)
More sessions related to improvement ($r = .36^{***}$) (self-rating; adult neurotics).	+	Graham (1958)
Greater duration of treatment related to improvement ($r = .34^{**}$) (T).	+	Bailey, Warshaw & Eichler (1959)
More sessions related to improvement ($r = .29^{**}$) (T).	+	Nichols & Beck (1960)
Log number of sessions related to T's rating of "movement on personal integration" ($r = .36^{*}$) and success ratings ($r = .49^{***}$) (T).	+	Cartwright et al. (1961)
Duration of treatment more influential on better outcome than sheer number of sessions (T).	+	Lorr (1962)
More sessions related to better outcome (at 1-year follow-up) (2 of 15 correlations significant with mean $r = .12$) (T).	+	Lorr et al. (1962)
More sessions related to greater social ($r = .22^{*}$) and psychological change, symptom reduction ($r = .32^{**}$), and greater insight ($r = .33^{**}$) at 3-year follow-up (mean $r = .29$) (T).	+	McNair et al. (1964)
Greater treatment length (log weeks, log interviews) related ($r = .36^{**}$) to higher success ratings (T).	+	Fiske, Cartwright & Kirtner (1964)
Length of treatment (6–10 versus 21+ sessions) unrelated to outcome as judged by the T ($r = .11$) and by independent judges ($r = .12$) (T).	0	Errera et al. (1967)
Greater length of treatment in months related to T ratings of outcome ($r = .46^{**}$) (one of three correlations significant, mean $r = .21$) (T).	+	Lerner (1972)

Greater length of treatment in sessions is unrelated to P, T, and behavioral ratings of outcome (mean r = .17) (T).	0 Lerner (1972)

Total number sessions unrelated to three criteria of change after 3 months (mean $r = -.04$).

0   Bowden, Endicott & Spitzer (1972)

More sessions related to improvement on five of six P-rated outcomes. (1) Decreased likelihood of suicide ($r = .25^{**}$), (2) improved grades ($r = .23^*$), (3) alleviation of specific problem ($r = .20^*$), (4) improved interpersonal relations ($r = .29^{**}$), and (5) enhanced self-respect ($r = .32^{**}$) (mean $r = .25$).

+   Weitz et al. (1975)

Greater length of treatment related to better outcome on rated benefits ($r = .27^*$) and residual gain ($r = .20$) (Penn study).

+   Luborsky, Mintz, et al. (1980)

As sessions continued P's symptoms were reduced, as rated by P ($R = 5.35^{**}$) and by T ($F = 5.52^{**}$) (T).

+   Bottari & Rappaport (1983)

Summary. Mean r = .46 (20); 23+, 0−, 3ns.

b. Frequency of Sessions per Week

Main Trend. Greater frequency of sessions sometimes related to better outcome.

Adult neurotics improved more (self-rating) when seen twice weekly versus once weekly.

+   Graham (1958)

Five-minutes daily Ps showed greater improvement than 25 minutes once a week (schizophrenic Ps).

+   Zirkle (1961)

Frequency (sessions per week) at 4-, 8-, and 12-month points unrelated to outcome.

0   Lorr et al. (1962)

Greater frequency of brief conversations (newly hospitalized Ps) related to reduction in anxiety and increase in self-esteem.

+   Dreiblatt & Weatherley (1965)

Frequency (once weekly, twice weekly, bi-monthly) unrelated to outcome.

0   Van Slambrouck (1972)

Frequency (one versus two sessions weekly) unrelated to outcome.

0   Caillier, P. (1980)

Summary. 3+, 0−, 3ns.

c. Fee Payment

Main Trend. Fee payment unrelated to outcome.

"Much improved" group contained more of fee paying Ps (T).

+ Rosenbaum, Friedlander & Kaplan (1956)

Fee-paying versus non-fee-paying Ps unrelated to outcome ($F = .62, r = .05$) (T) (controlling for diagnosis and socioeconomic status). (Fee related to better outcome [$F = 2.91^*$] when diagnosis and socioeconomic status uncontrolled.)

0 Pope, Geller & Wilkinson (1975)

Non–fee-paying Ps reported lower level of distress at outcome (one session treatment) on the Hopkins Symptom Checklist ($F = -3.81^*, r = -.28^*$) and a global rating of problem distress ($t = -2.54^{**}, r = -.35^{**}$) than fee-paying Ps. Differences in outcome were not significant for P ($t = -.70, r = -.10$) or T ($t = -.50, r = -.07$) ratings of improvement (two of four potential criteria significant, mean $r = -.20$) (T).

− Yoken & Berman (1984)

Fee payment unrelated to outcome (T).

0 Yoken & Berman (1987)

Summary. Mean $r = -.08$ (2); 1+, 1−, 2ns.

d. Waiting Interval between Application and Starting Psychotherapy

Main Trend. Greater length of wait before therapy negatively related to improvement.

Wait for 60 days before psychotherapy negatively related to improvement (T).

+ Gordon & Cartwright (1954)

Wait for 28 days before psychotherapy negatively related to improvement (T).

+ Roth et al. (1964)

Length of wait between evaluation and treatment negatively related to improvement.

+ Uhlenhuth & Duncan (1968)

Summary. 3+, 0−.

e. Role Preparation Provided to P

Main Trend. Preparation interview for psychotherapy related to outcome.

Preparation for treatment by role-induction   0   Hoehn-Saric et al.
interview related to better outcome on five of eight   (1964)
outcomes ($p < .05$). (Reanalyzed as nonsignificant
controlling for effects by Martindale, 1978.)

P given pretreatment information about   +   Truax et al. (1968)
psychotherapy related to better outcome ($F = 4.57^*$)
(one of two outcome criteria significant) (T).

P given pretherapy information about psychotherapy   0   Levitt & Fisher
unrelated to T ratings of improvement (T).   (1981)

Training of P in how to participate in therapy   +   Warren & Rice
related to greater involvement and personality   (1972)
change (T and P ratings for experimental group
significantly higher than for control group, $p < .05$).

Pretherapy training related to outcome.   +   Rich (1979)

Pretherapy training related to test outcome,   +   Eisenberg (1980)
unrelated to other outcomes. Midtherapy training
added benefits.

Summary. 4+, 0−, 2ns.

REFERENCES

Alexander, L., & Luborsky, L. (1986). The Penn Helping Alliance Scales. In L. Greenberg & W. Pinsof (Eds.), *The psychotherapeutic process: A research handbook* (pp. 325–366). New York: Guilford Press.

Alexander, L. B., Luborsky, L., Auerbach, A. H., Cohen, M., Ratner, H. K., & Schreiber, P. (1982, June). *The effect of the match between patient and therapist: Findings from the re-pairing study.* Paper presented at the annual meeting of the Society for Psychotherapy Research, Stowe, VT.

Altmann, H. A. (1973). Effects of empathy, warmth, and genuineness in the initial counseling interview. *Counselor Education and Supervision, 12,* 225–228.

Anchor, K. N. (1977). Personality integration and successful outcome in individual psychotherapy. *Journal of Clinical Psychology, 33,* 245–246.

Andrews, G., & Harvey, R. (1981). Does psychotherapy benefit neurotic patients? A reanalysis of the Smith, Glass, and Miller data. *Archives of General Psychiatry, 38,* 1203–1208.

Apfelbaum, B. (1958). *Dimensions of transference in psychotherapy.* Berkeley: University of California Press.

Appelbaum, S. (1977). *The anatomy of change.* New York: Plenum.

Armstrong, H. E., Jr., Rock, D. L., & Tracy, J. J. (1981). Relationship between belligerence and problem change: A replication. *Psychological Reports, 49,* 710.

Aronson, M. (1953). A study of the relationships between certain counselor and client characteristics in client-centered therapy. In W. U. Snyder (Ed.), *Group report of a program of research in psychotherapy* (pp. 39–54). State College: Pennsylvania State College Press.

Ashby, J. D., Ford, D. H., Guerney, B. G., Jr., & Guerney, L. F. (1957). Effects on clients of a reflective and a leading type of psychotherapy. *Psychological Monographs, 71* (24, Whole No. 453).

Astrup, C., & Noreik, K. (1966). *Functional psychoses: Diagnostic and prognostic models.* Springfield, IL: Charles C. Thomas.

Astwood, W. (1976). Congruence of patient and therapist understanding of psychotherapy and its effect on treatment outcome as perceived by the psychotherapist. Doctoral dissertation, New York University (Diss. 77-5286).

Atthowe, J. (1973). Behavior innovation and persistence. *American Psychologist, 28,* 34–41.

Auerbach, A. (1983). Assessment of psychotherapy outcome from the viewpoint of expert observers. In M. Lambert, E. Christensen, & S. DeJulio (Eds.), *The measurement of psychotherapy outcome.* New York: John Wiley & Sons.

Auerbach, A., & Johnson, M. (1977). Research on the therapist's level of experience. In A. Gurman & A. Razin (Eds.), *Effective psychotherapy* (pp. 84–102). Pergamon Press.

Auerbach, A. H., & Johnson, M. (1978). *Inventory of social and personality functioning (ISPF).* Unpublished manuscript.

Auerbach, A., & Luborsky, L. (1968a). Accuracy of judgments of psychotherapy and the nature of the "good hour." In J. Shlien, et al. (Eds.), *Research in psychotherapy* (Vol. 3, pp. 155–168). Washington, DC: American Psychological Association.

Auerbach, A., & Luborsky, L. (1968b). *The Prognostic Index Interview manual.* Unpublished manuscript.

Auerbach, A. H., & Luborsky, L. (1979). *The Prognostic Index Interview manual* (rev. ed.). Unpublished manuscript.

Auerbach, A. H., Luborsky, L., & Johnson, M. (1972). Clinicians' predictions of psychotherapy outcome: A trial of a prognostic index. *American Journal of Psychiatry, 128,* 830–835.

Auld, F., & Dollard, J. (1966). Measurement of motivational variables in psychotherapy. In L. Gottschalk & A. Auerbach (Eds.), *Methods of research in psychotherapy* (pp. 85–92). New York: Appleton-Century-Crofts.

Bachrach, H., & Leaff, L. (1978). "Analyzability": A systematic review of the clinical vs. quantitative literature. *Journal of the American Psychoanalytic Association, 26,* 881–920.

Bachrach, H., Luborsky, L., & Mechanich, P. G. (1974). The correspondence between judgments of empathy and other sensitivity measures. *British Journal of Medical Psychology, 47,* 337–340.

Baekeland, F., & Lundwall, L. (1975). Dropping out of treatment: A critical review. *Psychological Bulletin, 82*(5), 738–783.

Bailey, M. A., Warshaw, L., & Eichler, R. M. (1959). A study of factors related to length of stay in psychotherapy. *Journal of Clinical Psychology, 15,* 442–444.

Bandura, A. (1977). Self-efficacy: Toward a unifying theory of behavioral change. *Psychological Review, 84,* 191–215.

Barrett-Lennard, G. T. (1962). Dimensions of therapist response as causal factors in therapeutic change. *Psychological Monographs, 76*(43, Whole No. 562).

Barrington, B. (1961). Prediction from counselor behavior of client perception and of case outcome. *Journal of Counseling Psychology, 8,* 37–42.

Barron, F. (1953a). An ego-strength scale which predicts response to psychotherapy. *Journal of Consulting Psychology, 17,* 327–333.

Barron, F. (1953b). Some test correlates of response to psychotherapy. *Journal of Consulting Psychology, 17,* 235–241.

Barron, F., & Leary, T. (1955). Changes in psychoneurotic patients with and without psychotherapy. *Journal of Consulting Psychology, 19,* 239–245.

Barry, J. (1962). Prognosis and patient response to flickering light. *Journal of Clinical Psychology, 18,* 447–450.

Barry, J., & Fulkerson, S. (1966). Chronicity and the prediction of duration and outcome of hospitalization from capacity measures. *Psychiatric Quarterly, 40,* 104–121.

Bartlett, M. R. (1950). A six-month follow-up of the effects of personal adjustment counseling of veterans. *Journal of Consulting Psychology, 14,* 393–394.

Battle, C., Imber, S., Hoehn-Saric, R., Stone, A., Nash, E., & Frank, J. (1966). Target complaints as criteria of improvement. *American Journal of Psychotherapy, 20,* 184–192.

Beck, A. T. (1975). *Twisted thinking: A cognitive approach to psychopathology and psychotherapy.* New York: International Universities Press.

Beck, A., & Beck, A. N. (1972). Screening depressed patients in family practice. *Postgraduate Medicine, 52,* 81–85.

Beecher, H. K. (1959). *Measurement of subjective responses: Quantitative effects of drugs.* New York: Oxford University Press.

Bellak, L., & Smith, M. B. (1956). An experimental exploration of the psychoanalytic process. *Psychoanalytic Quarterly, 25,* 385–414.

Bergin, A. (1971). The evaluation of therapeutic outcomes. In A. Bergin & S. Garfield (Eds.), *Handbook of psychotherapy and behavior change: An empirical analysis* (pp. 217–270). New York: John Wiley & Sons.

Bergin, A., & Garfield, S. (Eds.). (1971). *Handbook of psychotherapy and behavior change: An empirical analysis.* New York: John Wiley & Sons.

Bergin, A. E., & Jasper, L. G. (1969). Correlates of empathy in psychotherapy: A replication. *Journal of Abnormal Psychology, 74,* 477–481.

Bergin, A. E., & Lambert, M. J. (1978). The evaluation of therapeutic outcomes. In S. L. Garfield & A. E. Bergin (Eds.), *Handbook of psychotherapy and behavior change: An empirical analysis* (2nd ed., pp. 139–190). New York: John Wiley & Sons.

Berman, J. (1979). Social bases of psychotherapy: Expectancy, attraction and the outcome of treatment. Doctoral dissertation, Harvard University (Diss. 80-13151).

Berzins, J., Bednar, R., & Severy, L. (1975). The problem of intersource consensus for measuring therapeutic outcomes: New data and multivariate perspectives. *Journal of Abnormal Psychology, 84,* 10–19.

Betz, B. J. (1963). Bases of therapeutic leadership in psychotherapy with the schizophrenic patient. *American Journal of Psychotherapy, 17,* 196–212.

Betz, B. J., & Whitehorn, J. C. (1956). The relationship of the therapist to the outcome of therapy in schizophrenia. *American Psychiatric Association Psychiatric Research Reports, 5,* 89–105.

Beutler, L. E., Arizmendi, T. G., Crago, M., Shanfield, S., & Hagaman, R. (1984). The effect of value similarity and client's persuadability on value convergence and psychotherapy improvement. *Journal of Social and Clinical Psychology, 1,* 231–245.

Beutler, L. E., Johnson, D. T., Neville, C. W., Jr., & Workman, S. N. (1973). "Accurate empathy" and the A-B dichotomy. *Journal of Consulting and Clinical Psychiatry, 38,* 372–375.

Beutler, L. E., Johnson, D. T., Neville, C. W., Jr., Workman, S. N., & Elkins, D. (1973). The A-B therapy-type distinction, accurate empathy, nonpossessive warmth, and therapist genuineness in psychotherapy. *Journal of Abnormal Psychology, 82,* 273–277.

Beutler, L. E., & Mitchell, R. (1981). Differential psychotherapy outcome among depressed and impulsive patients as a function of analytic and experiential treatment procedures. *Psychiatry, 44,* 297–306.

Beutler, L. E., Pollack, S., & Jobe, A. M. (1978). "Acceptance," values, and therapeutic change. *Journal of Consulting and Clinical Psychology, 46,* 198–199.

Bibring, E. (1954). Psychoanalysis and dynamic psychotherapies. *Journal of the American Psychoanalytical Association, 2,* 745–770.

Bierenbaum, H., Nichols, M. P., & Schwartz, A. J. (1976). Effects of varying session length and frequency in brief emotive psychotherapy. *Journal of Consulting and Clinical Psychology, 44,* 790–798.

Bloom, B. L. (1956). Prognostic significance of the underproductive Rorschach. *Journal of Projective Techniques, 20,* 366–371.

Bommert, H., & Dahlkoff, H. D. (1978). *Das Selbsterleben [Experiencing] in der Psychotherapie.* Munich: Urban and Schwarzenberg.

Bordin, E. S. (1959). Inside the therapeutic hour. In E. A. Rubinstein & M. B. Parloff (Eds.), *Research in psychotherapy* (Vol. 1, pp. 235–246). Washington, DC: American Psychological Association.

Bordin, E. (1975, June). *The generalizability of the psychoanalytic concept of the working alliance.* Paper presented to the annual meeting of the Society for Psychotherapy Research, Boston.

Bottari, M. A., & Rappaport, H. (1983). The relationship of patient and therapist-reported experiences of the initial session to outcome: An initial investigation. *Psychotherapy: Theory, Research and Practice, 20,* 355–358.

Bowden, C., Endicott, J., & Spitzer, R. (1972). A-B therapist variable and psychotherapeutic outcome. *Journal of Nervous and Mental Disease, 154,* 276–286.

Bradway, K. P., Lion, E. G., & Corrigan, H. G. (1946). The use of the Rorschach in a psychiatric study of promiscuous girls. *Rorschach Research Exchange, 10,* 105–110.

Brady, J. P., Reznikoff, M., & Zeller, W. (1960). The relationship of expectation of improvement to actual improvement of hospitalized psychiatric patients. *Journal of Nervous and Mental Disease, 130,* 41–43.

Brady, J. P., Zeller, W. W., & Reznikoff, M. (1959). Attitudinal factors influencing outcome of treatment of hospitalized psychiatric patients. *Journal of Clinical and Experimental Psychopathology, 20,* 326–334.

Brandt, L. W. (1964). Rejection of psychotherapy. *Archives of General Psychiatry, 10,* 310–313.

Brown, R. (1970). Experienced and inexperienced counselors' first impressions of clients and case outcomes: Are first impressions lasting? *Journal of Counseling Psychology, 17,* 550–558.

Buckley, P., Conte, H. R., Plutchik, R., Wild, K. V., & Karasu, T. B. (1984). Psychodynamic variables as predictors of psychotherapy outcome. *American Journal of Psychiatry, 14,* 742–748.

Butler, J. M., Rice, L. N., & Wagstaff, A. K. (1962). On the naturalistic definition of variables: An analogue of clinical analysis. In H. Strupp & L. Luborsky (Eds.), *Research in psychotherapy* (Vol. 2, pp. 178–205). Washington, DC: American Psychological Association.

Byrne, D. (1971). *The attraction paradigm.* New York: Academic Press.

Caillier, P. (1980). Effects of session frequency and session duration on process and outcome in short term time-limited psychotherapy. Doctoral dissertation, University of Manitoba, Canada.

Campbell, D., Stephens, J. H., Uhlenhuth, E., & Johansson, C. B. (1967). An extension of the Whitehorn-Betz A-B scale. *Journal of Nervous and Mental Disease, 144,* 45–54.

Carr, J. E. (1970). Differentiation similarity of patient and therapist and the outcome of psychotherapy. *Journal of Abnormal Psychology, 76,* 361–369.

Carson, R. C., & Heine, R. W. (1962). Similarity and success in therapeutic dyads. *Journal of Consulting Psychology, 26,* 38–43.

Carson, R. C., & Llewellyn, C. E. (1966). Similarity in therapeutic dyads. *Journal of Consulting Psychology, 30,* 458.

Cartwright, D. S. (1955). Success in psychotherapy as a function of certain actuarial variables. *Journal of Consulting Psychology, 19,* 357–363.

Cartwright, D. S., Kirtner, W. L., & Fiske, D. W. (1963). Method factors in changes associated with psychotherapy. *Journal of Abnormal and Social Psychology, 66,* 164–175.

Cartwright, D. S., Robertson, R. J., Fiske, D. W., & Kirtner, W. L. (1961). Length of therapy in relation to outcome and change in personal integration. *Journal of Consulting Psychology, 25,* 84–88.

Cartwright, D. S., & Roth, I. (1957). Success and satisfaction in psychotherapy. *Journal of Clinical Psychology, 13,* 20–26.

Cartwright, R. D. (1958). Predicting response to client-centered therapy with the Rorschach PR scale. *Journal of Counseling Psychology, 5,* 11–15.

Cartwright, R. D., & Lerner, B. (1963). Empathy, need to change, and improvement in psychotherapy. *Journal of Consulting Psychology, 27,* 138–144.

Cartwright, R. D., & Vogel, J. L. (1960). A comparison of changes in psychoneurotic patients during matched periods of therapy and no therapy. *Journal of Consulting Psychology, 24,* 121–127.

Casner, D. (1950). Certain factors associated with success and failure in personal-adjustment counseling (Abstract). *American Psychologist, 5,* 348.

Claghorn, J., Johnstone, E., Cook, T., & Itschner, L. (1974). Group therapy and maintenance treatment of schizophrenics. *Archives of General Psychiatry, 31,* 361–365.

Clancy, J., & Vanderhoof, E. (1963). Physiologic responses in therapeutic relationships. *Diseases of the Nervous System, 24*(8), 1–8.

Cohen, J. (1960). A coefficient of agreement for nominal scales. *Educational and Psychological Measurement, 20,* 37–46.

Cohen, J. (1962). The statistical power of abnormal-social psychological research: A review. *Journal of Abnormal and Social Psychology, 65,* 145–153.

Cohen, J. (1965). Some statistical issues in psychological research. In B. Wolman (Ed.), *Handbook of clinical psychology.* New York: McGraw-Hill.

Cohen, J. (1969). *Statistical power analysis for the behavioral sciences.* New York: Academic Press.

Cohen, J., & Cohen, P. (1975). *Applied multiple regression/correlational analysis for the behavioral sciences.* Hillsdale, NJ: Laurence Erlbaum.

Cohen, L., Sargent, M., & Sechrest, L. (1986). Use of psychotherapy research by professional psychologists. *American Psychologist, 41,* 198–206.

Colby, K. M. (1951). *A primer for psychotherapists.* New York: Ronald Press.

Conrad, D. C. (1952). An empirical study of the concept of psychotherapeutic success. *Journal of Consulting Psychology, 16,* 92–97.

Crits-Christoph, P., Cooper, A., & Luborsky, L. (in press). The accuracy of therapists' interpretations and the outcome of dynamic psychotherapy. *Journal of Consulting and Clinical Psychology.*

Crits-Christoph, P., & Luborsky, L. (1987, June). *How well does "accuracy of interpretation" predict the patient's benefits in psychotherapy?* Paper presented at the annual meeting of the Society for Psychotherapy Research, Ulm, West Germany.

Crits-Christoph, P., & Luborsky, L. (in press). The CCRT as a measure of outcome in psychoanalytic psychotherapy. In Jhannam, J. (Ed.), *Psychoanalytic Research Methods.* New York: Guilford Press.

Crits-Christoph, P., Luborsky, L., Popp, C., Mellon, J., Dahl, L., & Mark, D. (in press). Can clinicians agree in assessing relationship patterns in psychotherapy? The Core Conflictual Relationship Theme Method. *Archives of General Psychiatry.*

Cronbach, L. (1957). Two disciplines of scientific psychology. *American Psychologist,* *12,* 671–684.

Cronbach, L., & Furby, L. (1970). How we should measure "change"—or should we? *Psychological Bulletin, 74,* 68–80.

Cronbach, L., & Snow, R. (1977). *Aptitude and instructional methods: A handbook for research on interaction.* New York: Irvington.

Cross, D., Sheehan, P., & Khan, J. (1982). Short- and long-term follow-up of clients receiving insight-oriented therapy and behavior therapy. *Journal of Consulting and Clinical Psychology, 50,* 103–112.

Crowder, J. E. (1972). Relationship between therapist and client interpersonal behaviors and psychotherapy outcome. *Journal of Counseling Psychology, 19,* 68–75.

Cummings, N. A. (1975). The health model as entree to the human services model in psychotherapy. *Clinical Psychology, 29,* 19–21.

Cummings, N. A. (1977). The anatomy of psychotherapy under national health insurance. *American Psychologist, 32,* 711–718.

Cummings, N. A., & Follette, W. T. (1968). Brief psychotherapy and medical utilization in a prepaid health plan setting (Part 2). *Medical Care, 6,* 31–41.

Cummings, N. A., & Follette, W. T. (1976). Brief psychotherapy and medical utilization: An eight year follow-up. In H. Dorken et al. (Eds.), *The professional psychologist today: New developments in law, health insurance and health practice.* San Francisco: Jossey-Bass.

Curtis, H. (1973, May). *Toward a metapsychology of transference.* Paper presented to the annual meeting of the American Psychoanalytic Association, New York.

Custers, A. (1973). De manier van ervaren in het terapuitisch proces. *Psychologica Belgica, 13,* 125–138.

Dahl, H. (1972). A quantitative study of a psychoanalysis. In R. Holt & G. Peterfreund (Eds.), *Psychoanalysis and Contemporary Science* (Vol. 1). New York: Macmillan.

Dahl, H. (1983). Give choice a chance in psychotherapy research. *The Behavioral and Brain Sciences, 2,* 287.

Dana, R. H. (1954). The effects of attitudes towards authority on psychotherapy. *Journal of Clinical Psychology, 10,* 350–353.

Davanloo, H. (1980). A method of short-term dynamic psychotherapy. In H. Davanloo (Ed.), *Short-term dynamic psychotherapy.* New York: Jason Aronson.

Derogatis, L. R., Lipman, R. S., Covi, L., Rickels, K., & Uhlenhuth, E. H. (1970). Dimensions of outpatient neurotic pathology: Comparison of a clinical vs. an empirical assessment. *Journal of Consulting and Clinical Psychology, 34,* 164–171.

Derogatis, L., Lipman, R., & Rickels, K. (1974). The Hopkins Symptom Checklist (HSCL): A self-report symptom inventory. *Behavioral Science, 19,* 11–16.

Devine, D., & Fernald, P. (1973). Outcome effects of receiving a preferred randomly assigned, or non-preferred therapy. *Journal of Consulting and Clinical Psychology, 41,* 104–107.

DeWitt, K. N., Kaltreider, N., Weiss, D. S., & Horowitz, M. J. (1983). Judging change in psychotherapy: Reliability of clinical formulations. *Archives of General Psychiatry, 40,* 1121–1128.

Dietzel, C. S., & Abeles, N. (1975). Client-therapist complementarity and therapeutic outcome. *Journal of Counseling Psychology, 22,* 264–272.

DiLoreto, A. (1971). *Comparative psychotherapy: An experimental analysis.* Chicago: Aldine.

Distler, L. S., May, P. R., & Tuma, A. H. (1964). Anxiety and ego strength as predictors of response to treatment in schizophrenic patients. *Journal of Consulting Psychology, 28,* 170–177.

Dollard, J., & Mowrer, O. (1953). A method of measuring tension in written documents. In O. Mowrer (Ed.), *Psychotherapy: Theory and research.* New York: Ronald Press.

Dougherty, F. (1976). Patient–therapist matching for prediction of optimal and minimal therapeutic outcome. *Journal of Consulting and Clinical Psychology, 44,* 889–897.

Dreiblatt, I., & Weatherly, D. (1965). An evaluation of the efficacy of brief contact therapy with hospitalized psychiatric patients. *Journal of Consulting Psychology, 29,* 513–519.

Duhrssen, A., & Jorsweik, E. (1965). An empirical and statistical enquiry into the therapeutic potential of psychoanalytic treatment. *Der Nervenarzt, 36,* 166–169.

Duncan, S., Rice, L. N., & Butler, J. M. (1968). Paralinguistic features of peak and poor psychotherapy interviews. *Journal of Abnormal Psychology, 73,* 566–570.

Dyrud, J. E. (1975). The prescription of treatment for adults. In D. X. Freedman & J. E. Dyrud (Eds.), *American Handbook of Psychiatry: Vol. 5. Treatment* (2nd ed.). New York: Basic Books.

Eastwood, M. (1975). *The relation between physical and mental illness.* Toronto: University of Toronto Press.

Eisenberg, G. (1980). Midtherapy training: Extending the present system of pretherapy training. Doctoral dissertation, University of South Florida (Diss. 80-28932).

Ekstein, R. (1956). Psychoanalytic techniques. In D. Brower & L. Abt (Eds.), *Progress in Clinical Psychology* (Vol. 2, pp. 79–99). New York: Grune & Stratton.

Endicott, J., & Spitzer, R. (1972). Current and Past Psychopathology Scales (CAPPS), *Archives of General Psychiatry, 27,* 678–687.

Endicott, J., & Spitzer, R. (1978). A diagnostic interview: The Schedule for Affective Disorders and Schizophrenia. *Archives of General Psychiatry, 35,* 837–844.

Endicott, J., Spitzer, R. L., Fleiss, J. L., & Cohen, J. (1976). The Global Assessment Scale: A procedure for measuring overall severity of psychiatric disturbances. *Archives of General Psychiatry, 33,* 766–771.

Endicott, N., & Endicott, J. (1963). "Improvement" in untreated psychiatric patients. *Archives of General Psychiatry, 9,* 575–585.

Endicott, N. A., & Endicott, J. (1964). Prediction of improvement in treated and untreated patients using the Rorschach Prognostic Rating Scale. *Journal of Consulting Psychology, 28,* 342–348.

Engel, G., & Schmale, A. (1967). Psychoanalytic theory of somatic disorder: Conversion, specificity and the disease onset situation. *Journal of the American Psychoanalytic Association, 15,* 344–365.

Errera, P., McKee, B., Smith, D., & Gruber, R. (1967). Length of psychotherapy: Studies done in a university community psychiatric clinic. *Archives of General Psychiatry, 17,* 454–458.

Ersner-Hershfield, S., Abramowitz, S., & Barren, D. (1979). Incentive effects of choosing a therapist. *Journal of Consulting and Clinical Psychology, 35,* 404–406.

Eysenck, H. J. (1952). The effects of psychotherapy: An evaluation. *Journal of Consulting Psychology, 16,* 319–324.

Eysenck, H. J. (1959). *The manual of the Maudsley Personality Inventory.* London: University of London Press.

Fairweather, G., Simon, R., Gebhard, M., Weingarten, E., Holland, J., Sanders, R., Stone, G., & Reahl, J. (1960). Relative effectiveness of psychotherapeutic programs: A multicriteria comparison of four programs for three different patient groups. *Psychological Monographs, 74* (5, Whole No. 492).

Feitel, B. (1968). *Feeling understood as a function of a variety of therapist activity.* Unpublished doctoral dissertation, Teachers' College, Columbia University.

Feldman, R., Lorr, M., & Russell, S. B. (1958). A mental hygiene clinic case survey. *Journal of Clinical Psychology, 14,* 245–250.

Fenichel, O. (1941). *Problems of psychoanalytic technique.* Albany, NY: Psychoanalytic Quarterly.

Fiedler, F. E. (1950). The concept of an ideal relationship. *Journal of Consulting Psychology, 14,* 239–245.

Fiedler, F. E., & Siegel, S. M. (1949). The free-drawing test as a predictor of nonimprovement in psychotherapy. *Journal of Clinical Psychology, 4,* 386–389.

Filmer-Bennett, G. (1952). Prognostic indices in the Rorschach records of hospitalized patients. *Journal of Abnormal and Social Psychology, 47,* 502–506.

Filmer-Bennett, G. (1955). The Rorschach as a means of predicting treatment outcome. *Journal of Consulting Psychology, 19,* 331–334.

Fishman, D. (1971, August). *Empirical correlates of the Experiencing Scale.* Paper presented at the annual meeting of the American Psychological Association, Washington, DC.

Fiske, D. (1975). A source of data is not a measuring instrument. *Journal of Abnormal Psychology, 84,* 20–23.

Fiske, D. W., Cartwright, D. S., & Kirtner, W. L. (1964). Are psychotherapeutic changes predictable? *Journal of Abnormal and Social Psychology, 69,* 418–426.

Fiske, D., & Goodman, G. (1965). The post-therapy period. *Journal of Abnormal Psychology, 70,* 169–179.

Fiske, D., Hunt, H., Luborsky, L., Orne, M., Parloff, M., Reiser, M., & Tuma, A. (1970). The planning of research on effectiveness of psychotherapy. *American Psychologist, 25,* 727–737.

Fleiss, J. L., Spitzer, R. L., & Burdock, E. I. (1965). Estimating accuracy of judgment using recorded interviews. *Archives of General Psychiatry, 12,* 562.

Foon, A. E. (1985). Similarity between therapists' and clients' locus of control: Implications for therapeutic expectations and outcomes. *Psychotherapy: Theory, Research and Practice, 22,* 711–717.

Frank, J. (1971a). *Persuasion and healing* (2nd ed.). Baltimore: Johns Hopkins University Press.

Frank, J. (1971b). Therapeutic factors in psychotherapy. *American Journal of Psychotherapy, 25,* 350–361.

Frank, J. (1974). Psychotherapy: The restoration of morale. *American Journal of Psychiatry, 131,* 271–274.

Frank, J. (1975). Psychotherapy of bodily disease: An overview. *Psychotherapy and Psychosomatics, 26,* 193–202.

Frank, J. (1979). Present status of outcome studies. *Journal of Consulting and Clinical Psychology, 47,* 310–316.

Frank, J., Hoehn-Saric, R., Imber, S., Liberman, B., & Stone, A. (1978). *Effective ingredients of successful psychotherapy.* New York: Brunner-Mazel.

Free, N. K., Green, B. L., Grace, M. C., Chernus, L. A., & Whitman, R. M. (1985).

Empathy and outcome in brief focal dynamic therapy. *American Journal of Psychiatry, 142,* 917–921.

French, T., & Wheeler, D. R. (1963). Hope and repudiation of hope in psychoanalytic therapy. *International Journal of Psychoanalysis, 44,* 304–316.

Freud, S. (1912a). The dynamics of transference. In J. Strachey (Ed.), *The standard edition of the complete psychological works of Sigmund Freud* (Vol. 12, pp. 99–108). London: Hogarth Press.

Freud, S. (1912b). Recommendations to physicians practicing psychoanalysis. In J. Strachey (Ed.), *The standard edition of the complete psychological works of Sigmund Freud* (Vol. 12, pp. 111–120). London: Hogarth Press and Institute of Psychoanalysis.

Freud, S. (1913). On beginning the treatment. In J. Strachey (Ed.), *The standard edition of the complete psychological works of Sigmund Freud* (Vol. 12, pp. 121–144). London: Hogarth Press.

Freud, S. (1914). Remembering, repeating and working-through. In J. Strachey (Ed.), *The standard edition of the complete psychological works of Sigmund Freud* (Vol. 12, pp. 147–156). London: Hogarth Press.

Freud, S. (1920). Beyond the pleasure principle. In J. Strachey (Ed.), *The standard edition of the complete psychological works of Sigmund Freud* (Vol. 18, pp. 1–64). London: Hogarth Press.

Freud, S. (1926). Inhibitions, symptoms, and anxiety. In J. Strachey (Ed.), *The standard edition of the complete psychological works of Sigmund Freud* (Vol. 20, pp. 87–174). London: Hogarth Press.

Freud, S. (1937). Analysis terminable and interminable. In J. Strachey (Ed.), *The standard edition of the complete psychological works of Sigmund Freud* (Vol. 23, pp. 209–253). London: Hogarth Press.

Fried, D., Crits-Christoph, P., & Luborsky, L. (1987, June). *Does the relationship with the therapist become like a general relationship pattern?* Paper presented at annual meeting of the Society for Psychotherapy Research, Ulm, West Germany.

Friedlander, M. (1981). The effects of delayed role induction on counseling process and outcome. Doctoral dissertation, Ohio State University (Diss. 81-07322).

Fulkerson, S. C., & Barry, J. (1961). Methodology and research on the prognostic use of psychological tests. *Psychological Bulletin, 58,* 177–204.

Fulkerson, S. C., & Barry, J. (1966). Early test change as a predictor of duration and outcome of hospitalization. *Journal of Clinical Psychology, 22,* 268–270.

Gallagher, J. J. (1954). Test indicators for therapy prognosis. *Journal of Consulting Psychology, 18,* 409–413.

Garduk, E., & Haggard, E. (1972). Immediate effects on patients of psychoanalytic interpretations. *Psychological Issues, 7* (4, Monograph 28).

Garfield, S. L. (1977). Comments on "Dropping out of treatment": Reply to Baekeland and Lundwall. *Psychological Bulletin, 84,* 306–308.

Garfield, S. (1978). Research on client variables in psychotherapy. In S. Garfield & A. Bergin (Eds.), *Handbook of psychotherapy and behavior change: An empirical analysis* (2nd ed., pp. 191–232). New York: John Wiley & Sons.

Garfield, S. L., & Bergin, A. E. (1971). Personal therapy, outcome, and some therapist variables. *Psychotherapy: Theory, Research and Practice, 8,* 231.

Garfield, S. L., & Bergin, A. E. (Eds.). (1978). *Handbook of psychotherapy and behavior change: An empirical analysis* (2nd ed.). New York: John Wiley & Sons.

Garfield, S. L., & Bergin, A. E. (Eds.). (1986). *Handbook of psychotherapy and behavior change: An empirical analysis* (3rd ed.). New York: John Wiley & Sons.

Gaylin, N. (1966). Psychotherapy and psychological health: A Rorschach function and structure analysis. *Journal of Consulting Psychology, 30,* 494–500.

Gelder, M. G., Marks, I. M., & Wolff, H. H. (1967). Desensitization and psychotherapy in the treatment of phobic states: A controlled inquiry. *British Journal of Psychiatry, 113,* 53–73.

Gellens, H. K., Gottheil, E., & Alterman, A. I. (1976). Drinking outcome of specific alcohol subgroups. *Journal of Studies on Alcohol, 37*(7), 986–989.

Geller, J. (1986). The process of psychotherapy: Separation and the complex interplay among empathy, insight and internalization. In J. Bloom-Feshbach & S. Bloom-Feshbach (Eds.), *The psychology of separation through the life-span.* San Francisco: Jossey-Bass.

Gendlin, E. T., Beebe, J., Cassens, J., Klein, M., & Oberlander, M. (1968). Focusing ability in psychotherapy, personality, and creativity. In J. M. Shlien, H. F. Hunt, J. D. Matarazzo, & C. Savage (Eds.), *Research in psychotherapy* (Vol. 3). Washington, DC: American Psychological Association.

Gendlin, E. T., Jenney, R., & Shlien, J. (1960). Counselor ratings of process and outcome in client-centered therapy. *Journal of Clinical Psychology, 16,* 210–213.

Gerstley, L., McLellen, A. T., Alterman, A., Woody, G., Luborsky, L., & Prout, M. (in press). Interpersonal relationships in antisocial personality: A possible marker of therapeutic prognosis. *American Journal of Psychiatry.*

Getter, H., & Sundland, D. M. (1962). The Barron ego strength scale and psychotherapy outcome. *Journal of Consulting Psychology, 26,* 195.

Gill, M. (Ed.). (1967). *The collected papers of David Rapaport.* New York: Basic Books.

Gill, M., & Hoffman, I. (1982a). Analysis of transference: Studies of nine audio-recorded psychoanalytic sessions. *Psychological Issues* (Monograph No. 54).

Gill, M., & Hoffman, I. (1982b). A method for studying the analysis of aspects of the patient's experience of the relationship in psychoanalysis and psychotherapy. *Journal of the American Psychoanalytic Association, 30,* 137–167.

Glass, G. V., McGaw, B., & Smith, M. C. (1981). *Meta-analysis in social research.* Beverly Hills, CA: Sage.

Gliedman, L., Stone, A., Frank, J., Nash, E., & Imber, S. (1957). Incentives for treatment related to remaining or improving in psychotherapy. *American Journal of Psychotherapy, 11,* 589–598.

Goldstein, A. P. (1960). Therapist and client expectation of personality change in psychotherapy. *Journal of Counseling Psychology, 7,* 180–184.

Goldstein, A., & Kanfer, F. (Eds.). (1979). *Maximizing treatment gains: Transfer enhancement in psychotherapy.* New York: Academic Press.

Goldstein, A. P., & Shipman, W. G. (1961). Patient expectancies, symptom reduction, and aspects of the initial psychotherapeutic interview. *Journal of Clinical Psychology, 17,* 129–133.

Gomes-Schwartz, B. (1978). Effective ingredients in psychotherapy: Prediction of outcome from process variables. *Journal of Consulting and Clinical Psychology, 46,* 1023–1035.

Gordon, R. (1976). Effects of volunteering and responsibility on the perceived value and effectiveness of a clinical treatment. *Journal of Consulting and Clinical Psychology, 44,* 799–801.

Gordon, T., & Cartwright, D. S. (1954). The effect of psychotherapy on certain attitudes toward others. In C. Rogers & R. F. Dymond (Eds.), *Psychotherapy and personality change* (pp. 167–195). Chicago: University of Chicago Press.

Gottschalk, L. A., Fox, R. A., & Bates, D. E. (1973). A study of prediction and outcome in a mental health crisis clinic. *American Journal of Psychiatry, 130,* 1107–1111.

Gottschalk, L. A., & Gleser, G. C. (1969). *The measurement of psychological states through the content analysis of verbal behavior.* Berkeley: University of California Press.

Gottschalk, L. A., Mayerson, P., & Gottlieb, A. A. (1967). Prediction and evaluation of outcome in an emergency brief psychotherapy clinic. *Journal of Nervous and Mental Disease, 144,* 77–96.

Gottschalk, L. A., Springer, K. J., & Gleser, G. C. (1961). Experiments with a method of assessing the variations in intensity of certain psychological states occurring during two psychotherapeutic interviews. In L. A. Gottschalk (Ed.), *Comparative psycholinguistic analysis of two psychotherapeutic interviews.* New York: International Universities Press.

Graff, H., & Luborsky, L. (1977). Long-term trends in transference and resistance: A quantitative analytic method applied to four psychoanalyses. *Journal of the American Psychoanalytic Association, 25,* 471–490.

Graham, S. R. (1958). Patient evaluation of the effectiveness of limited psychoanalytically oriented psychotherapy. *Psychological Reports, 4,* 231–234.

Graham, S. R. (1960). The influence of therapist character structure upon Rorschach changes in the course of psychotherapy [Abstract]. *American Psychologist, 15,* 415.

Green, B. L., Gleser, G. C., Stone, W. N., & Seifert, R. F. (1975). Relationships among diverse measures of psychotherapy outcome. *Journal of Consulting and Clinical Psychology, 43,* 689–699.

Greenson, R. (1965). The working alliance and transference neurosis. *Psychoanalytic Quarterly, 34,* 158–181.

Greenspan, S., & Cullender, C. (1975). A systematic metapsychological assessment of the course of an analysis. *Journal of the American Psychoanalytic Association, 23,* 107–138.

Greenspan, S., & Wieder, S. (1984). Dimensions and levels of the therapeutic process. *Psychotherapy: Theory, Research and Practice, 21,* 5–23.

Grigg, A. E. (1961). Client response to counselors at different levels of experience. *Journal of Counseling Psychology, 8,* 217–225.

Grinspoon, L., Shader, R., & Ewalt, J. (1972). *Schizophrenia: Pharmacotherapy and psychotherapy.* Baltimore: Williams & Wilkins.

Gurman, A. S., & Razin, A. M. (Eds.). (1977). *Effective psychotherapy: A handbook of research.* New York: Pergamon Press.

Hamburg, D. A., Bibring, G. L., Fisher, C., Stanton, A. H., Wallerstein, R. S., Weinstock, H. I., & Haggard, E. (1967). Report of ad hoc committee on central fact-gathering data of the American Psychoanalytic Association. *Journal of the American Psychoanalytic Association, 15,* 841–861.

Hankin, J., & Oktay, J. (1979). *Mental disorders and primary medical care: An analytic review of the literature* (NIMH Series D, No. 5). Washington, DC: U.S. Government Printing Office.

Harris, R. E., & Christiansen, C. (1946). Prediction of response to brief psychotherapy. *Journal of Psychology, 21,* 269–284.

Hartley, D., & Strupp, H. (1983). The therapeutic alliance: Its relationship to outcome in brief psychotherapy. In J. Masling (Ed.), *Empirical studies of psychoanalytic theory* (Vol. 1). Hillsdale, NJ: Laurence Erlbaum.

Harway, N., Dittman, A., Raush, H., Bordin, E., & Rigler, D. (1955). The measurement of depth of interpretation. *Journal of Consulting Psychology, 19,* 247–253.

Hathaway, S. R., & Meehl, P. E. (1951). *An atlas for the clinical use of the MMPI.* Minneapolis: University of Minnesota Press.

Henry, W., Sims, J., & Spray, S. (1973). *Public and private lives of psychotherapies.* San Francisco: Jossey-Bass.

Hoehn-Saric, R., Frank, J., Imber, S., Nash, E., Stone, A., & Battle, C. (1964). Systematic preparation of patients for psychotherapy: 1. Effects on therapy behavior and outcome. *Journal of Psychiatric Research, 2,* 267–281

Hoffman, A. E. (1949). A study of reported behavior changes in counseling. *Journal of Clinical Psychology, 13,* 190–195.

Hollender, M. (1965). *The practice of psychoanalytic psychotherapy.* New York: Grune & Stratton.

Hollingshead, A. B., & Redlich, F. C. (1958). *Social class and mental illness.* New York: John Wiley & Sons.

Holmes, T. H., & Rahe, R. H. (1967). The social readjustment rating scale. *Journal of Psychosomatic Research, 11,* 213–218.

Holt, R. R. (1960). Recent developments in psychoanalytic ego psychology and their implications for diagnostic testing. *Journal of Projective Techniques, 24,* 254–266.

Holt, R. R. (1978). *Methods in clinical research: Vol. 2. Prediction and research.* New York: Plenum.

Holt, R. R., & Luborsky, L. B. (1958a). *Personality patterns of psychiatrists: A study in selection techniques* (Vol. 1). New York: Basic Books.

Holt, R. R., & Luborsky, L. B. (1958b). *Personality patterns of psychiatrists: A study in selection techniques* (Vol. 2). Topeka, KS: Menninger Foundation.

Holt, W. E. (1967). The concept of motivation for treatment. *American Journal of Psychiatry, 123,* 1388–1394.

Horowitz, L. M., Sampson, H., Siegelman, E., Wolfson, A., & Weiss, J. (1975). On the identification of warded off mental contents. *Journal of Abnormal Psychology, 84,* 545–558.

Horowitz, M. (1979). *States of mind.* New York: Plenum.

Horowitz, M. J., Marmar, C., Krupnick, J., Wilner, N., Kaltreider, N., & Wallerstein, R. (1984). *Personality styles and brief psychotherapy.* New York: Basic Books.

Horowitz, M. J., Marmar, C., Weiss, D. S., DeWitt, K. N., & Rosenbaum, R. (1984). Brief psychotherapy of bereavement reactions: The relationship of process to outcome. *Archives of General Psychiatry, 41,* 438–448.

Horwitz, L. (1974). *Clinical prediction in psychotherapy.* New York: Jason Aronson.

Howard, K., Kopta, S., Krause, M., & Orlinsky, D. The dose-effect relationship in psychotherapy. *American Psychologist, 41,* 159–164.

Hoyt, F., Marmar, C., & Horowitz, M. (in press). The Therapist Action Scale and the Patient Action Scale: Instruments for assessing activities during dynamic psychotherapy. *Psychotherapy: Theory, Research and Practice.*

Hoyt, M. (1980). Therapist and patient actions in "good" psychotherapy sessions. *Archives of General Psychiatry, 37,* 159–161.

Hunt, J. McV., Ewing, T., LaForge, R., & Gilbert, W. (1959). An integrated approach to research on therapeutic counseling with samples of results. *Journal of Counseling Psychology, 6,* 45–54.

Imber, S., Frank, J., Nash, E., Stone, A., & Gliedman, L. (1957). Improvement and amount of therapeutic contact: An alternative to the use of no-treatment controls in psychotherapy. *Journal of Consulting Psychology, 21,* 309–315.

Isaacs, K. S., & Haggard, E. A. (1966). Some methods used in the study of affect in psychotherapy. In L. A. Gottschalk & A. H. Auerbach (Eds.), *Methods of research in psychotherapy* (pp. 226–239). New York: Appleton-Century-Crofts.

Jacobs, M. A., & Warner, B. L. (1981). Interaction of therapeutic attitudes with severity of clinical diagnosis. *Journal of Clinical Psychology, 37*(1), 75–81.

Jacobson, S., Deykin, E., & Prusoff, B. (1977). Process and outcome of therapy with depressed women. *American Journal of Orthopsychiatry, 47,* 140–148.

Janis, I. (Ed.). (1982). *Counseling on personal decisions: Theory and research on short-term helping relationships.* New Haven: Yale University Press.

Jennen, M. G., Lietaer, G., & Rombauts, J. (1978). *Relationship and interaction between therapist conditions (as perceived by client, therapist and outside judges), client depth of experiencing during therapy and constructive personality change in individual psychotherapy.* Unpublished manuscript, University of Leuven, Belgium.

Johnston, M., & Holzman, P. (1979). *Assessing schizophrenic thinking.* San Francisco: Jossey-Bass.

Jones, E. (1982). Psychotherapist's impressions of treatment outcome as a function of race. *Journal of Clinical Psychology, 38,* 722–731.

Jones, E., & Zoppel, C. L. (1982). Impact of client and therapist gender on psychotherapy process and outcome. *Journal of Consulting and Clinical Psychology, 50,* 259–272.

Kalfas, N. (1973). Client-perceived therapist empathy as a correlate of outcome. Doctoral dissertation, University of Arizona (Diss. 74-7696).

Karasu, T. B., Stein, S. P., & Charles, E. S. (1979). Age factors in the patient–therapist relationship. *Journal of Nervous and Mental Disease, 167,* 100–104.

Karoly, P., & Steffen, K. (1980). *Improving the long term effects of psychotherapy.* New York: Gardner.

Karon, B. P., & VandenBos, G. R. (1970). Experience, medication, and the effectiveness of psychotherapy with schizophrenics. *British Journal of Psychiatry, 116,* 427–428.

Karon, B. P., & VandenBos, G. R. (1981). *Psychotherapy of schizophrenia: The treatment of choice.* New York: Jason Aronson.

Karush, A., Daniels, G., O'Connor, J., & Stern, L. (1968). The response to psychotherapy in chronic ulcerative colitis: Part 1. Pretreatment factors. *Psychosomatic Medicine, 30,* 255–276.

Katz, M. M., Lorr, M., & Rubinstein, E. A. (1958). Remainer patients' attributes and their relation to subsequent improvement in psychotherapy. *Journal of Consulting Psychology, 22,* 411–413.

Kazdin, A. (1986). The evaluation of psychotherapy: Research design and methodology. In S. Garfield & A. Bergin (Eds.), *Handbook of psychotherapy and behavior change* (pp. 23–68). New York: John Wiley & Sons.

Keithly, L. J., Samples, S. J., & Strupp, H. H. (1980). Patient motivation as a predictor of process and outcome in psychotherapy. *Psychotherapy and Psychosomatics, 33,* 87–97.

Kernberg, O., Burstein, E., Coyne, L., Applebaum, A., Horowitz, L., & Voth, H. (1972). Psychotherapy and psychoanalysis: Final report of the Menninger Foundation's psychotherapy research project. *Bulletin of the Menninger Clinic, 36,* 1–275.

Kiesler, D. J. (1971). Patient experiencing level and successful outcome in individual psychotherapy of schizophrenics and psychoneurotics. *Journal of Consulting and Clinical Psychology, 37,* 370–385.

Kiesler, D., Mathieu, P., & Klein, M. (1964). Sampling from the recorded therapy interview: A comparative study of different segment lengths. *Journal of Consulting Psychology, 28,* 329–357.

Kiresuk, T. (1973). Goal attainment scaling at a county mental health service. *Evaluation, 1,* 12–18.

Kirkner, F., Wisham, W., & Giedt, H. (1953). A report on the validity of the Rorschach prognosis rating scale. *Journal of Projective Techniques, 17,* 465–470.

Kirschner, L. A., Genack, A., & Hauser, S. T. (1978). Effects of gender on short-term psychotherapy. *Psychotherapy: Theory, Research and Practice, 15,* 158–167.

Kirtner, W. L., & Cartwright, D. S. (1958a). Success and failure in client-centered therapy as a function of client personality variables. *Journal of Consulting Psychology, 22,* 259–264.

Kirtner, W. L., & Cartwright, D. S. (1958b). Success and failure in client-centered therapy as a function of initial in-therapy behavior. *Journal of Consulting Psychology, 22,* 329–333.

Kirtner, W. L., Cartwright, D. S., Robertson, R. J., & Fiske, D. W. (1961). Length of therapy in relation to outcome and change in personal integration. *Journal of Consulting Psychology, 25,* 84–88.

Klein, H. A. (1960). A study of changes occurring in patients during and after psychoanalytic treatment. In P. Hoch & J. Zubin (Eds.), *Current approaches to psychoanalysis.* New York: Grune & Stratton.

Klein, H. (1965). *Psychoanalysts in training: Selection and evaluation.* New York: Columbia University Psychoanalytic Clinic for Training and Research.

Klein, M. H., Mathieu, P. L., Gendlin, E. T., & Kiesler, D. J. (1969). *The Experiencing Scale: A research and training manual* (Vol. 1). Madison: University of Wisconsin Extension Bureau of Audiovisual Instruction.

Klerman, G. (1986). Drugs and psychotherapy. In S. Garfield & A. Bergin (Eds.), *Handbook of psychotherapy and behavior change* (pp. 777–820). New York: John Wiley & Sons.

Klopfer, B., Ainsworth, M. D., Klopfer, W., & Holt, R. R. (1954). *Developments in the Rorschach technique.* New York: World.

Klopfer, B., Kirkner, F., Wisham, W., & Baker, G. (1951). Rorschach prognostic rating scale. *Journal of Projective Techniques, 15,* 425–428.

Knapp, P. (1972). *Segmentation and structure in psychoanalysis.* Unpublished manuscript.

Knapp, P. H., Levin, S., McCarter, R. H., Wermer, H., & Zetzel, E. (1960). Suitability for psychoanalysis: A review of 100 supervised analytic cases. *Psychoanalytic Quarterly, 29,* 459–477.

Koegler, R., & Brill, N. (1967). *Treatment of psychiatric outpatients.* New York: Appleton-Century-Crofts.

Kolb, D. L., Beutler, L. E., Davis, C. S., Crago, M., & Shanfield, S. (1985). Patient and therapist process variables relating to dropout and change in psychotherapy. *Psychotherapy: Theory, Research and Practice, 22,* 702–710.

Kreisberg, G. (1977). The relationship of the congruence of patient therapist goal expectancies to psychotherapy outcome and duration of treatment. Doctoral dissertation, Case Western Reserve University, Cleveland (Diss. 77-30997).

Kurtz, R., & Grummon, D. (1972). Different approaches to the measurement of therapist empathy and their relationship to therapy outcomes. *Journal of Consulting and Clinical Psychology, 39,* 106–115.

LaCrosse, M. B. (1980). Perceived counselor social influence and counseling outcomes: Validity of the counselor rating form. *Journal of Counseling Psychology, 27,* 320–327.

Lambert, M. J., Bergin, A. E., & Collins, J. C. (1977). Therapist-induced deterioration in psychotherapy. In A. S. Gurman & A. M. Razin (Eds.), *Effective psychotherapy: A handbook of research* (pp. 452–481). New York: Pergamon Press.

Lambert, M., Christensen, E., & DeJulio, S. (1983). *The assessment of psychotherapy outcome.* New York: John Wiley & Sons.

Lambert, M., Shapiro, D., & Bergin, A. (1986). The effectiveness of psychotherapy In S. Garfield & A. Bergin (Eds.), *Handbook of psychotherapy and behavior change: An empirical analysis* (pp. 157–212). New York: John Wiley & Sons.

Landfield, A. W., & Nawas, M. M. (1964). Psychotherapeutic improvement as a function of communication and adoption of therapist's values. *Journal of Counseling Psychology, 11,* 336–341.

Landman, J., & Dawes, R. (1982). Psychotherapy outcome: Smith and Glass conclusions stand up under scrutiny. *American Psychologist, 37,* 504–516.

Last, C. G., Thase, M. E., Hersen, M., Bellack, A. S., & Himmelhoch, J. M. (1984). Treatment outcome for solicited versus nonsolicited unipolar depressed female outpatients. *Journal of Consulting and Clinical Psychology, 52,* 134.

Lennard, H. L. (1962). Some aspects of the psychotherapeutic system. In H. Strupp & L. Luborsky (Eds.), *Research in psychotherapy* (Vol. 2, pp. 218–236). Washington, DC: American Psychological Association.

Lerner, B. (1972). *Therapy in the ghetto: Political impotence and personal disintegration.* Baltimore: Johns Hopkins University Press.

Lerner, B. (1973). Democratic values and therapeutic efficacy: A construct validity study. *Journal of Abnormal Psychology, 82*(3), 491–498.

Lerner, B., & Fiske, D. W. (1973). Client attributes and the eye of the beholder. *Journal of Consulting and Clinical Psychology, 40,* 272–277.

Lesser, W. M. (1961). The relationship between counseling progress and empathic understanding. *Journal of Counseling Psychology, 8,* 330–336.

Levinson, D. (1962). The psychotherapist's contribution to the patient's treatment career, pp. 13–24. In H. Strupp & L. Luborsky (Eds.), *Research in psychotherapy* (Vol. 2, pp. 13–24). Washington, DC: American Psychological Association.

Levitt, E. E., & Fisher, W. P. (1981). The effects of an expectancy state on the fate of applications and psychotherapy in an outpatient setting. *Journal of Clinical Psychiatry, 42,* 234–237.

Lewis, H. B. (1971). *Shame and guilt in neurosis.* New York: International Universities Press.

Liberman, B. (1978). The role of mastery in psychotherapy: Maintenance of improvement and prescriptive change. In Frank et al. (Eds.), *Effective ingredients of successful psychotherapy* (pp. 35–72). New York: Brunner-Mazel.

Lichtenstein, E. (1966). Personality similarity and therapeutic success: A failure to replicate. *Journal of Consulting Psychology, 30,* 282.

Lipkin, S. (1954). Clients' feelings and attitudes in relation to the outcome of client-centered therapy. *Psychological Monographs, 68* (1, Whole No. 372).

Locke, S. (1982). Stress, adaptation, and immunity: Studies in humans. *General Hospital Psychiatry, 4,* 49–58.

Lorr, M. (1962). Relation of treatment frequency and duration to psycho-therapeutic outcome. In H. Strupp & L. Luborsky (Eds.), *Research in psychotherapy* (Vol. 2, pp. 134–141). Washington, DC: American Psychological Association.

Lorr, M. (1965). Client perceptions of therapists: A study of therapeutic relation. *Journal of Consulting Psychology, 29,* 146–149.

Lorr, M., & McNair, D. M. (1964). The interview relationship in therapy. *Journal of Nervous and Mental Disease, 139,* 328–337.

Lorr, M., McNair, D., Michaux, W., & Raskin. A. (1962). Frequency of treatment and change in psychotherapy. *Journal of Abnormal and Social Psychology, 64,* 281–292.

Lower, R., Escoll, P., Little, R., & Ottenberg, P. (1973). An experimental examination of transference. *Archives of General Psychiatry, 29,* 738–741.

Luborsky, L. (1962a). Clinicians' judgments of mental health: A proposed scale. *Archives of General Psychiatry, 7,* 407–417.

Luborsky, L. (1962b). The patient's personality and psychotherapeutic change. In H. H. Strupp & L. Luborsky (Eds.), *Research in psychotherapy* (Vol. 2, pp. 115–133). Washington, DC: American Psychological Association.

Luborsky, L. (1969). Research cannot yet influence clinical practice. *International Journal of Psychiatry, 7,* 135–140.

Luborsky, L. (1971). Perennial mystery of poor agreement among criteria for psychotherapy outcome. *Journal of Consulting and Clinical Psychology, 37,* 316–319.

Luborsky, L. (1975a). Assessment of outcome of psychotherapy by independent clinical evaluators: A review of the most highly recommended research measures. In I. Waskow & M. Parloff (Eds.), *Psychotherapy change measures* (pp. 233–242). NIMH DHEW Publication No. (ADM) 74-120.

Luborsky, L. (1975b). Clinicians' judgments of mental health: Specimen case descriptions and forms for the Health-Sickness Rating Scale. *Bulletin of the Menninger Clinic, 35,* 448–480.

Luborsky, L. (1976a). Helping alliances in psychotherapy. In J. Claghorn (Ed.), *Successful psychotherapy* (pp. 92–116). New York: Brunner-Mazel.

Luborsky, L. (1976b). *The SE manual: A treatment manual for supportive-expressive psychoanalytically oriented psychotherapy.* Unpublished manuscript.

Luborsky, L. (1977a). Curative factors in psychoanalytic and psychodynamic psychotherapies. In J. P. Brady, et al. (Eds.), *Psychiatry: Areas of promise and advancement* (pp. 187–203). New York: Spectrum.

Luborsky, L. (1977b). Measuring a pervasive psychic structure in psychotherapy: The core conflictual relationship theme. In N. Freedman & S. Grand (Eds.), *Communicative structures and psychic structures* (pp. 367–395). New York: Plenum Press.

Luborsky, L. (1982). *Rating scales for therapist qualities: Adjustment, skill and interest in helping.* Unpublished manuscript.

Luborsky, L. (1984). *Principles of psychoanalytic psychotherapy: A manual for supportive-expressive treatment.* New York: Basic Books.

Luborsky, L. (1986a). *The core conflictual relationship theme method: Guide to scoring and rationale.* Unpublished manuscript.

Luborsky, L. (1986b). *A set of standard categories for the CCRT.* Unpublished manuscript.

Luborsky, L. (1987a). Research can now affect clinical practice—a happy turnaround [APA Award Presentation]. *The Clinical Psychologist, 40,* 56–60.

Luborsky, L. (1987b, December). Should analysts routinely do a follow-up? Implications of research studies. Paper presented at the annual meeting of the American Psychoanalytic Association, New York.

Luborsky, L. (in press). The application of psychotherapy manuals in research and practice. In N. Miller, J. Docherty, & L. Luborsky (Eds.), *A guide to doing psychodynamic treatment research.* New York: Basic Books.

Luborsky, L. (in preparation). *Finding a focus for brief psychodynamic psychotherapies—with help from transference measures.*

Luborsky, L., & Bachrach, H. M. (1974). Factors influencing clinicians' judgments of mental health: Experiences with the Health-Sickness Rating Scale. *Archives of General Psychiatry, 31,* 292–299.

Luborsky, L., Bachrach, H., Graff, H., Pulver, S., & Christoph, P. (1979). Preconditions and consequences of transference interpretations: A clinical-quantitative investigation. *Journal of Nervous and Mental Disease, 167,* 391–401.

Luborsky, L., Chandler, M., Auerbach, A., Cohen, J., & Bachrach, H. (1971). Factors influencing the outcome of psychotherapy: A review of quantitative research. *Psychological Bulletin, 75,* 145–185.

Luborsky, L., Crabtree, L., Curtis, H., Ruff, G., & Mintz, J. (1975). The concept "space" of transference for eight psychoanalysts. *British Journal of Medical Psychology, 48,* 1–6.

Luborsky, L., & Crits-Christoph, P. (in preparation). *The Relationship Anecdotes Paradigms (RAP) interview: A TAT-like method based on real events.*

Luborsky, L., Crits-Christoph, P., Alexander, L., Margolis, M., & Cohen, M. (1983). Two helping alliance methods for predicting outcomes of psychotherapy. *Journal of Nervous and Mental Disease, 17,* 480–491.

Luborsky, L., Crits-Christoph, P., Brady, J. P., Kron, R., Weiss, T., Cohen, M., & Levy, L. (1982). Behavioral versus pharmacological treatments for essential hypertension: A needed comparison. *Psychosomatic Medicine, 44,* 403–429.

Luborsky, L., Crits-Christoph, P., Brady, J. P., Kron, R. E., Weiss, T., & Engelman, K. (1980). Antihypertension effects of behavioral treatments and medications compared [Letter to the editor]. *New England Journal of Medicine, 303,* 586.

Luborsky, L., Crits-Christoph, P., McLellan, A. T., Woody, G., Piper, W., Liberman, B., Imber, S., & Pilkonis, P. (1986). Do therapists vary much in their success? Findings from four outcome studies. *American Journal of Orthopsychiatry, 56,* 501–512.

Luborsky, L., Crits-Christoph, P., & Mellon, J. (1986). The advent of objective measures of the transference concept. *Journal of Consulting and Clinical Psychology, 54,* 39–47.

Luborsky, L., & DeRubeis, R. (1984). The use of psychotherapy treatment manuals: A small revolution in psychotherapy research style. *Clinical Psychology Review, 4,* 5–14.

Luborsky, L., Graff, H., Pulver, S., & Curtis, H. (1973). A clinical-quantitative examination of consensus on the concept of transference. *Archives of General Psychiatry, 29,* 69–75.

Luborsky, L., & McLellan, A. T. (1978). Our surprising inability to predict the outcomes of psychological treatments—with special reference to treatments for drug abuse. *American Journal of Drug and Alcohol Abuse, 5,* 387–396.

Luborsky, L., & McLellan, A.T. (1980). A sound mind in a sound body: To what extent do they go together before and after psychotherapy? *International Journal of Psychiatry in Medicine, 10,* 121–131.

Luborsky, L., & McLellan, A. T. (1981). Optimal matching of patients with types of psychotherapy: What is known and some designs for knowing more. In E.

Gottheil, A. T. McLellan, & K. Druley (Eds.), *Matching patient needs and treatment methods for alcohol and drug abuse* (pp. 51–71). Chicago: Charles C. Thomas.

Luborsky, L., McLellan, A. T., Woody, G. E., O'Brien, C. P., & Auerbach, A. (1985). Therapist success and its determinants. *Archives of General Psychiatry, 42,* 602–611.

Luborsky, L., Mellon, J., Alexander, K., van Ravenswaay, P., Childress, A., Levine, F., Cohen, K. D., Hole, A. V., & Ming, S. (1985). A verification of Freud's grandest clinical hypothesis: The transference. *Clinical Psychology Review, 5,* 231–246.

Luborsky, L., Mintz, J., Auerbach, A., Christoph, P., Bachrach, H., Todd, T., Johnson, M., Cohen, M., & O'Brien, C. P. (1980). Predicting the outcome of psychotherapy: Findings of the Penn Psychotherapy Project. *Archives of General Psychiatry, 37,* 471–481.

Luborsky, L., Prystowsky, M., Levinson, A., Crits-Christoph, P., Cacciola, J., Stibbe, J., & Alexander, K. (in preparation). *Mood, stress and immunocompetence in humans.*

Luborsky, L., & Schimek, J. (1964). Psychoanalytic theories of therapeutic and developmental change: Implications for assessment. In P. Worchol & D. Byrne (Eds.), *Personality Change* (pp. 73–99). New York: John Wiley & Sons.

Luborsky, L., Singer, B., & Luborsky, L. (1975). Comparative studies of psychotherapy: Is it true that "Everybody has won and all must have prizes"? *Archives of General Psychiatry, 32,* 995–1008.

Luborsky, L., & Spence, D. (1978). Quantitative research on psychoanalytic therapy. In S. Garfield & A. Bergin (Eds.), *Handbook of psychotherapy and behavior change: An empirical analysis* (2nd ed., pp. 331–368). New York: John Wiley & Sons.

Luborsky, L., Todd, T. C., & Katcher, A. H. (1973). A self-administered social assets scale for predicting physical and psychological illness and health. *Journal of Psychosomatic Research, 17,* 109–120.

Luborsky, L., Woody, G. E., McLellan, A. T., O'Brien, C. P., & Rosenzweig, J. (1982). Can independent judges recognize different psychotherapies? An experience with manual-guided therapies. *Journal of Consulting and Clinical Psychology, 50,* 49–62.

Magnelli, R. (1975). An investigation of the role of personal construct systems and empathy in the psychotherapeutic relationship. Doctoral disseration, University of Nebraska (Diss. 76-13341).

Malan, D. (1963). *A study of brief psychotherapy.* New York: Plenum Press.

Malan, D. (1976). *The frontier of brief psychotherapy.* New York: Plenum Press.

Malloy, T. E. (1981). The relationship between therapist–client interpersonal compatibility, sex of therapist, and therapeutic outcome. *Journal of Clinical Psychology, 37,* 316–322.

Mann, H. (1973). *Time-limited psychotherapy.* Cambridge, MA: Harvard University Press.

Manning, W., & DuBois, P. (1962). Correlational methods in research on human learning. *Perceptual and Motor Skills, 15,* 288–321.

Marmar, C. R., Gallagher, D., & Thompson, L. W. (in press). The therapeutic alliance and the outcome of cognitive, behavioral, and dynamic psychotherapy for late-life depression. *Archives of General Psychiatry.*

Marmor, J. (1975). *Psychiatrists and their patients: A national study of private office practice.* Washington, DC: Joint Information Service of the American Psychiatric Association and the National Association for Mental Health.

Martin, P. J., Moore, J. E., Sterne, A. L., & McNairy, R. M. (1977). Therapists prophesy. *Journal of Clinical Psychology, 33,* 502–510.

Martin, P. J., & Sterne, A. L. (1975). Prognostic expectations and treatment outcome. *Journal of Consulting and Clinical Psychology, 43,* 572–576.

Martin, P. J., & Sterne, A. L. (1976). Post-hospital adjustment as related to therapists' in-therapy behavior. *Psychotherapy: Theory, Research and Practice, 13,* 267–273.

Martin, P. J., Sterne, A. L., & Hunter, M. L. (1976). Share and share alike: Mutuality of expectations and satisfaction with therapy. *Journal of Clinical Psychology, 32,* 677–683.

Martindale, C. (1978). The therapist-as-fixed-effect fallacy in psychotherapy research. *Journal of Consulting and Clinical Psychology, 46,* 1526–1530.

Marziali, E. A. (1984a). Prediction of outcome of brief psychotherapy from therapist interpretive interventions. *Archives of General Psychiatry, 41,* 301–304.

Marziali, E. (1984b). Three viewpoints on the therapeutic alliance: Similarities, differences, and associations with psychotherapy outcome. *Journal of Nervous and Mental Disease, 172,* 417–423.

Marziali, E., Marmar, C., & Krupnick, J. (1981). Therapeutic alliance scales: Their development and relationship to psychotherapy outcome. *American Journal of Psychiatry, 138,* 361–364.

Matthews, J. G., & Burkhart, B. R. (1977). A-B therapist status, patient diagnosis, and psychotherapy outcome in a psychiatric outpatient population. *Journal of Consulting and Clinical Psychology, 45,* 475–482.

May, P. (1968). *Treatment of schizophrenia.* New York: Science House.

Mayman, M. (1959). *Self-preservation, ego instincts, mastery and defense: A re-examination of Freud's "Beyond the pleasure principle."* Unpublished manuscript.

Mayman, M. (1960). *Form level scoring manual.* Topeka, KS: Menninger Foundation (Mimeographed).

McDaniel, S. H., Stiles, W. B., & McGaughey, K. J. (1981). Correlations of male college students verbal response mode use in psychotherapy with measures of psychological disturbance and psychotherapy outcome. *Journal of Consulting and Clinical Psychology, 49,* 571–582.

McLellan, A. T., Luborsky, L., Cacciola, J., Griffith, J., McGahan, P., & O'Brien, C. (1985). *Guide to the Addiction Severity Index: Background, administration and field testing results* (NIDA Treatment Report, Monograph 30, PHHS Publication N. (ADM) 85–1419). Washington, DC: U.S. Government Printing Office.

McLellan, A. T., Luborsky, L., Woody, G. E., O'Brien, C. P., & Druley, K. A. (1983). Predicting response to alcohol and drug abuse treatments: Role of psychiatric severity. *Archives of General Psychiatry, 40,* 620–625.

McNair, D. M., Callahan, D. M., & Lorr, M. (1962). Therapist "type" and patient response to psychotherapy. *Journal of Consulting Psychology, 26,* 425–429.

McNair, D. M., Lorr, M., Young, H. H., Roth, I., & Boyd, R. W. (1964). A three-year follow-up of psychotherapy patients. *Journal of Clinical Psychology, 20,* 258–264.

Mechanick, D. (1966). The sociology of medicine: Viewpoints and perspectives. *Journal of Health and Human Behavior, 7,* 237–240.

Meichenbaum, D., & Gilmore, J. B. (1984). The nature of unconscious processes: A cognitive-behavioral perspective. In K. Bowers & D. Meichenbaum (Eds.), *The unconscious reconsidered* (pp. 273–298). New York: John Wiley & Sons.

Melnick, B. (1972). Patient-therapist identification in relation to both patient and therapist variables and therapy outcome. *Journal of Consulting and Clinical Psychology, 38,* 97–104.

Melnick, B., & Pierce, R. M. (1971). Client evaluation of therapist strength and positive-negative evaluation as related to client dynamics, objective ratings of competence and outcome. *Journal of Clinical Psychology, 27,* 408–410.

Meltzoff, J., & Kornreich, M. (1970). *Research in psychotherapy.* New York: Atherton.

Mendelsohn, F. S. (1976). Long-term psychotherapy coverage under national health insurance. *The Bulletin, American Psychiatric Association, 18* (Area II District Branches), *18,* 8.

Menninger, K., & Holzman, P. S. (1973). *The theory of psychoanalytic technique* (2nd ed.). New York: Basic Books.

Menninger, K., Mayman, M., & Pruyser, P. (1963). *The vital balance.* New York: Viking.

Mensh, I., & Golden, J. (1951). Factors in psychotherapeutic success. *Journal of the Missouri State Medical Association, 48,* 180–184.

Miles, H. W., Barrabee, E. L., & Finesinger, J. E. (1951). Evaluations of psychotherapy, with a follow-up of 62 cases of anxiety neuroses. *Psychosomatic Medicine, 13,* 83–105.

Miller, N., Docherty, J., Luborsky, L. (Eds.). (in press). *A guide for doing psychodynamic treatment research.* New York: Basic Books.

Mindess, M. (1953). Predicting patient's response to psychotherapy: A preliminary study designed to investigate the validity of the Rorschach Prognostic Rating Scale. *Journal of Projective Techniques, 17,* 327–334.

Mintz, J. (1972). What is success in psychotherapy? *Journal of Abnormal Psychotherapy, 80,* 11–19.

Mintz, J. (1977). The role of the therapist in assessing psychotherapy outcome. In A. S. Gurman & A. M. Razin (Eds.), *Effective psychotherapy: A handbook of research* (pp. 590–602). New York: Pergamon Press.

Mintz, J. (1981). Measuring outcome in psychodynamic psychotherapy. *Archives of General Psychiatry, 38,* 503–506.

Mintz, J., & Kiesler, D. J. (1982). Individualized measures of psychotherapy outcome. In P. C. Kendall & J. N. Butcher (Eds.), *Handbook of research methods in clinical psychology* (pp. 491–534). New York: John Wiley & Sons.

Mintz, J., & Luborsky, L. (1970). P-technique factor analysis in psychotherapy research: An illustration of a method. *Psychotherapy, 7,* 13–18.

Mintz, J., & Luborsky, L. (1971). Segments versus whole sessions: Which is the better unit for psychotherapy process research? *Journal of Abnormal Psychology, 78,* 180–191.

Mintz, J., Luborsky, L., & Auerbach, A. (1971). Dimensions of psychotherapy: A factor-analytic study of ratings of psychotherapy sessions. *Journal of Consulting and Clinical Psychology, 36,* 106–120.

Mintz, J., Luborsky, L., & Christoph, P. (1979). Measuring the outcomes of psychotherapy: Findings of the Penn Psychotherapy Project. *Journal of Consulting and Clinical Psychology, 47,* 319–334.

Mitchell, K. M., Bozarth, J. D., & Krauft, C. C. (1977). A reappraisal of the therapeutic effectiveness of accurate empathy, nonpossessive warmth, and genuineness. In A. S. Gurman & A. M. Razin (Eds.), *Effective psychotherapy: A handbook of research* (pp. 482–502). New York: Pergamon Press.

Moras, K., & Strupp, H. (1982). Pretherapy interpersonal relations, patient's alliance, and outcome in brief therapy. *Archives of General Psychiatry, 39,* 405–409.

Morgan, R., Luborsky, L., Crits-Christoph, P., Curtis, H., & Solomon, J. (1982). Predicting the outcomes of psychotherapy by the Penn Helping Alliance Rating Method. *Archives of General Psychiatry, 39,* 397–402.

Morrow, W., & Robins, A. (1964). Family relations and social recovery of psychotic mothers. *Journal of Health and Human Behavior, 5,* 14–24.

Mowrer, O. H., Hunt, J. McV., & Kogan, L. (1953). Further studies utilizing the discomfort-relief quotient. In O. H. Mowrer (Ed.), *Psychotherapy: Theory and research.* New York: Ronald Press.

Muench, G. A. (1965). An investigation of the efficacy of time-limited psychotherapy. *Journal of Counseling Psychology, 12,* 294–298.

Mullen, J., & Abeles, N. (1971). Relationship of liking, empathy and therapist's experience to outcomes of psychotherapy. *Journal of Consulting Psychology, 18,* 39–43.

Mumford, E., & Schlesinger, H. (1987). Assessing consumer benefit: Cost offset as an incidental effect of psychotherapy. *General Hospital Psychiatry, 9,* 360–363.

Mumford, E., Schlesinger, H., Glass, G., Patrick, C., & Cuerdon, T. (1984). A new look at evidence of reduced cost of medical utilization following mental health treatment. *American Journal of Psychiatry, 141,* 1145–1158.

Murray, H. (1938). *Exploration in personality.* New York: Oxford University Press.

Myers, J. K., & Auld, F. (1955). Some variables related to outcome of psychotherapy. *Journal of Clinical Psychology, 11,* 51–54.

Nace, E. P., Warwick, A. M., Kelley, R. L., & Evans, F. J. (1982). Hypnotizability and outcome in brief psychotherapy. *Journal of Clinical Psychiatry, 43,* 129–133.

Nacev, V. (1980). Dependency and ego strength as indicators of patient attendance in psychotherapy. *Journal of Clinical Psychology, 36,* 691–695.

Nash, E., Hoehn-Saric, R., Battle, C., Stone, A., Imber, S., & Frank, J. (1965). Systematic preparation of patients for short-term psychotherapy: 2. Relation of characteristics of patient, therapist, and the psychotherapeutic process. *Journal of Nervous and Mental Disease, 140,* 374–383.

Neimeyer, G. J., & Gonzales, M. (1983). Duration, satisfaction, and perceived effectiveness of cross-cultural counseling. *Journal of Counseling Psychology, 30,* 91–95.

Nichols, M. P., & Bierenbaum, H. (1978). Success of cathartic therapy as a function of patient variables. *Journal of Clinical Psychology, 34,* 726–728.

Nichols, R. C., & Beck, K. W. (1960). Factors in psychotherapy change. *Journal of Consulting Psychology, 24,* 388–399.

Nicholson, R., & Berman, J. (1983). Is follow-up necessary in evaluating psychotherapy? *Psychological Bulletin, 93,* 261–278.

Nixon, D. (1982). *The relationships of primal therapy outcome with experiencing, voice quality and transference.* Unpublished doctoral dissertation, York University, Ontario.

Norcross, J., & Prochaska, J. (1982a). A national survey of clinical psychologists: Characteristics and activities. *The Clinical Psychologist, 35,* 1–8.

Norcross, J., & Prochaska, J. (1982b). A national survey of clinical psychologists: Affiliations and orientations. *The Clinical Psychologist, 35*(1), 4–6.

Norcross, J., Prochaska, J., & Gallagher, K. (1987, April). *Clinical psychologists in the 1980's.* Symposium presented at the annual meeting of the Eastern Psychological Association, Arlington, VA.

Nunnally, J. (1967). *Psychometric theory.* New York: McGraw-Hill.

O'Brien, C., Hamm, K., Ray, B., Pierce, J., Luborsky, L., & Mintz, J. (1972). Group versus individual psychotherapy with schizophrenics: A controlled outcome study. *Archives of General Psychiatry, 27,* 474–478.

Olbrisch, M. W. (1977). Psychotherapeutic interventions in physical health: Effectiveness and economic efficiency. *American Psychologist, 32,* 761–777.

Oltman, P. K. (1968). A portable rod-and-frame apparatus. *Perceptual Motor Skills, 26,* 503–506.

Oltman, P. K., Goodenough, D., Witkin, H. (1975). Psychological differentiation as a factor in conflict resolution. *Journal of Personality and Social Psychology, 32,* 730–736.

O'Malley, S. S., Suh, C. S., & Strupp, H. H. (1983). The Vanderbilt Psychotherapy Process Scale: A report on the scale development and a process-outcome study. *Journal of Consulting and Clinical Psychology, 51,* 581–586.

Orlinsky, D. E., & Howard, K. I. (1967). The good therapy hour: Experimental correlates of patients' and therapists' evaluations of therapy sessions. *Archives of General Psychiatry, 16,* 621.

Orlinsky, D., & Howard, K. (1975). *Varieties of psychotherapeutic experience.* New York: Teachers College Press.

Orlinsky, D., & Howard, K. (1978). The relation of process to outcome in psychotherapy. In S. Garfield & A. Bergin (Eds.), *Handbook of psychotherapy and behavior change: An empirical analysis* (2nd ed., pp. 283–329). New York: John Wiley & Sons.

Orlinsky, D., & Howard, K. (1986). Process and outcome of psychotherapy. In S. Garfield & A. Bergin, (Eds.), *Handbook of psychotherapy and behavior change: An empirical analysis* (3rd ed., pp. 311–384). New York: John Wiley & Sons.

Orne, M., & Wender, P. (1968). Anticipatory socialization for psychotherapy: Method and rationale. *American Journal of Psychiatry, 124,* 88–98.

Pardes, H., Papernik, D. S., & Winston, A. (1974). Field differentiation in inpatient psychotherapy. *Archives of General Psychiatry, 31,* 311–315.

Parloff, M. B. (1961). Therapist-patient relationships and outcome of psychotherapy. *Journal of Consulting Psychology, 25,* 29–38.

Parloff, M. (1986). Placebo controls in psychotherapy research: A sine qua non or a placebo for a research problem? *Journal of Consulting and Clinical Psychology, 54,* 79–87.

Parloff, M. B., & Dies, R. R. (1977). Group psychotherapy outcome research 1966–1975. *International Journal of Group Psychotherapy, 27,* 281–320.

Parloff, M. B., Iflund, B., & Goldstein, N. (1958). Communication of "therapy values" between therapist and schizophrenic patients. *Journal of Nervous and Mental Disease, 130,* 193–199.

Parloff, M. B., Waskow, I. E., & Wolfe, B. E. (1978). Research on therapist variables in relation to process and outcome. In S. Garfield & A. Bergin (Eds.), *Handbook of psychotherapy and behavior change: An empirical analysis* (2nd ed., pp. 233–282). New York: John Wiley & Sons.

Perry, J. C., Luborsky, L., Silberschatz, G., & Popp, C. (in preparation). *An examination of three methods of psychodynamic formulation based on the same videotaped interview.*

Persson, G., Alstrom, J. E., & Nordlund, C. L. (1984a). Prognostic factors with four treatment methods for phobic disorders. *Acta Psychiatrica Scandinavica, 69,* 307–318.

Persson, G., Alstrom, J. E., & Nordlund, C. L. (1984b). Relation between outcome and the patient's initial experience of the therapist and therapeutic conditions in four treatment methods for phobic disorders. *Acta Psychiatrica Scandinavica, 69,* 296–306.

Persson, G., & Nordlund, C. L. (1983). Expectations of improvement and attitudes to treatment processes in relation to outcome with four treatment methods for phobic disorders. *Acta Psychiatrica Scandinavica, 68,* 484–493.

Pfeffer, A. (1963). The meaning of the analyst after analysis: A contribution to the theory of therapeutic results. *Journal of the American Psychoanalytic Association, 11,* 229–244.

Pierloot, R., & Vinck, J. (1978). Differential outcome of short-term dynamic psychotherapy and systematic desensitization in the treatment of anxious outpatients. *Psychologica Belgica, 18,* 87–98.

Piper, W., Debbane, E., Bienvenu, J., de Carufel, F., & Garant, J. (1986). Relationships between the object focus of therapist interpretations and outcome in short term individual psychotherapy. *British Journal of Medical Psychology, 59,* 1–11.

Piper, W. E., de Carufel, F. L., & Szkrumelak, N. (1985). Patient predictors of process and outcome in short-term individual psychotherapy. *Journal of Nervous and Mental Disease, 173,* 726–733.

Pope, K. S., Geller, J. D., & Wilkinson, L. (1975). Fee assessment and outpatient psychotherapy. *Journal of Consulting and Clinical Psychology, 43,* 835–841.

Prager, R. A. (1970). The relationship of certain client characteristics to therapist-offered conditions and therapeutic outcome. Doctoral dissertation, Columbia University (Diss. 71-6108).

Prager, R. A., & Garfield, S. L. (1972). Client initial disturbance and outcome in psychotherapy. *Journal of Consulting and Clinical Psychology, 38,* 112–117.

Prusoff, B. A., Weissman, M. M., Klerman, G. L., & Rounsaville, B. J. (1980). Research Diagnostic Criteria subtypes of depression: Their role as predictors of differential response to psychotherapy and drug treatment. *Archives of General Psychiatry, 37,* 796–801.

Rapaport, D. (1946). *Diagnostic Psychological Testing* (Vols. 1 and 2). Chicago: Year Book.

Rapaport, D. (1958). The theory of ego autonomy. In M. M. Gill (Ed.), *The collected papers of David Rapaport* (pp. 722–744). New York: Basic Books, 1967.

Raskin, N. J. (1949). An analysis of six parallel studies of the therapeutic process. *Journal of Consulting Psychology, 13,* 206–221.

Raskin, N. (1965). The psychotherapy research project of the American Academy of Psychotherapists [Abstract]. *American Psychologist, 20,* 54.

Raskin, N. (1974). Studies of therapeutic orientation: Ideology and practice (Research Monograph No. 1). Orlando, FL: American Academy of Psychotherapists.

Rayner, E. H., & Hahn, H. (1964). Assessment for psychotherapy: A pilot study of psychological test indications of success and failure in treatment. *British Journal of Medical Psychology, 37,* 331–342.

Razin, A. M. (1977). The A-B variable: Still promising after twenty years? In A. S. Gurman & A. M. Razin (Eds.), *Effective psychotherapy: A handbook of research.* New York: Pergamon Press.

Reid, J., & Finesinger, J. (1951). Inference testing in psychotherapy. *American Journal of Psychiatry, 107,* 894–907.

Rice, L. N. (1965). Therapist's style of participation and case outcome. *Journal of Consulting Psychology, 29,* 155–160.

Rich, L. (1979). Effects of training clients to be ready for individual psychotherapy upon outcomes of psychotherapy. Doctoral dissertation, Michigan State University (Diss. 79-21188).

Richert, A. J. (1976). Expectations experiencing and change in psychotherapy. *Journal of Clinical Psychology, 32,* 438–444.

Rickels, K. (Ed.). (1968). *Nonspecific factors in drug therapy.* Springfield, IL: Charles C. Thomas.

Ricks, D. (1974). Supershrink: Methods of a therapist judged successful on the basis of adult outcome of adolescent patients. In D. Ricks, M. Roff, & A. Thomas (Eds.), *Life history research in psychopathology* (Vol. 3). Minneapolis: University of Minnesota Press.

Rioch, M. J., & Lubin, A. (1959). Prognosis of social adjustment for mental hospital patients under psychotherapy. *Journal of Consulting Psychology, 23,* 313–318.

Roberts, L. (1954). Failure of some Rorschach indices to predict the outcome of psychotherapy. *Journal of Consulting Psychology, 18,* 96–98.

Rogers, C. (1957). The necessary and sufficient conditions of therapeutic personality change. *Journal of Consulting Psychology, 21,* 95–103.

Rogers, C. (1959). A tentative scale for measurement of process in psychotherapy. In E. A. Rubinstein & M. B. Parloff (Eds.), *Research in psychotherapy* (Vol. 1, pp. 96–107). Washington, D.C.: American Psychological Association.

Rogers, C. R., & Dymond, R. F. (Eds.). (1954). *Psychotherapy and personality change.* Chicago: University of Chicago Press.

Rogers, C. R., Gendlin, E., Kiesler, D., & Truax, C. (Eds.). (1967). *The therapeutic relationship and its impact: A study of psychotherapy with schizophrenics.* Madison: University of Wisconsin Press.

Rogers, L. S., & Hammond, K. R. (1953). Prediction of the results of therapy by means of the Rorschach test. *Journal of Consulting Psychology, 17,* 8–15.

Rosen, E. (1954). Ethnocentric attitude changes and rated improvement in hospitalized psychiatric patients. *Journal of Clinical Psychology, 10,* 345–350.

Rosenbaum, M., Freidlander, J., & Kaplan, S. (1956). Evaluation of results of psychotherapy. *Psychosomatic Medicine, 18,* 113–132.

Rosenberg, S. (1954). The relationship of certain personality factors to prognosis in psychotherapy. *Journal of Clinical Psychology, 10,* 341–345.

Rosenberg, S. E., Silberschatz, G., Curtis, J. T., Sampson, H., & Weiss, J. (1986). A method for establishing reliability of statements from psychodynamic case formulations. *American Journal of Psychiatry, 143,* 1454–1456.

Rosenman, S. (1955). Changes in the representation of self, other and interrelationship in client-centered therapy. *Journal of Counseling Psychology, 2,* 271–278.

Rosenthal, R. (1979). The file drawer problem and tolerance for null results. *Psychological Bulletin, 86,* 638–641.

Rosenthal, R. I., & Jacobson, L. (1968). *Pygmalion in the classroom: Teacher expectations and pupils' intellectual development.* New York: Holt, Rinehart & Winston.

Rosenzweig, S. (1936). Some implicit common factors in diverse methods of psychotherapy. *American Journal of Orthopsychiatry, 6,* 412–415.

Roshal, J. G. (1953). The type-token ratio as a measure of changes in behavior variability during psychotherapy. In W. U. Snyder (Ed.), *Group report of a program of research in psychotherapy.* State College: Pennsylvania State College Press.

Roth, I., Rhudick, P. J., Shaskan, D. A., Slobin, M. S., Wilkinson, A. B., & Young, H. (1964). Long-term effects on psychotherapy of initial treatment conditions. *Journal of Psychiatric Research, 2,* 283–297.

Rounsaville, B., Chevron, E., Prusoff, B., Elkin, I., Imber, S., Stotsky, S., & Watkins, J. (1987). The relationship between specific and general dimensions of the psychotherapy process in interpersonal psychotherapy of depression. *Journal of Consulting and Clinical Psychology, 55,* 379–384.

Rounsaville, B., Weissman, M., & Prusoff, B. (1981). Psychotherapy with depressed outpatients. *British Journal of Psychiatry, 138,* 67–74.

Rucker, I. (1982). Counseling outcomes and perceived counselor social influence: Validity of the counselor rating form extended. Doctoral dissertation, North Texas State University (Diss. 82-28075).

Ryan, E. R. (1973). *The capacity of the patient to enter an elementary therapeutic relationship in the initial interview.* Unpublished doctoral dissertation, University of Michigan.

Ryan, R. P. (1966). *The role of the experiencing variable in the psychotherapeutic process.* Unpublished doctoral dissertation, University of Illinois.

Sachs, J. S. (1983). Negative factors in brief psychotherapy: An empirical assessment. *Journal of Consulting and Clinical Psychology, 51,* 557–564.

Saltzman, C., Luetgert, M., Roth, C., Creaser, J., & Howard, L. (1976). Formation of a therapeutic relationship: Experiences during the initial phase of psychotherapy as predictors of treatment duration and outcome. *Journal of Consulting and Clinical Psychology, 44,* 546–555.

Sampson, H. (1976). A critique of certain traditional concepts in the psychoanalytic theory of therapy. *Bulletin of the Menninger Clinic, 40,* 255–262.

Sanford, N. (1962). Discussion of papers on measuring personality change. In H. Strupp & L. Luborsky (Eds.), *Research in psychotherapy* (Vol. 2, pp. 155–163). Washington, DC: American Psychological Association.

Sapolsky, A. (1965). Relationship between patient–doctor compatibility, mutual perception, and outcome of treatment. *Journal of Abnormal Psychology, 70,* 70–76.

Sargent, H., Horowitz, L., Wallerstein, R., & Apfelbaum, A. (1968). Prediction in psychotherapy research [Monograph No. 21]. *Psychological Issues, 6.*

Schacht, T., Binder, J., & Strupp, H. (1984). The dynamic focus. In H. Strupp & J. Binder (Eds.), *Psychotherapy in a new key: A guide to time-limited dynamic psychotherapy* (pp. 65–109). New York: Basic Books.

Schachter, J. (1987, December). Introduction to the panel discussion on follow-up. Annual meeting of the American Psychoanalytic Association, New York.

Schaeffer, N. (1982). Multidimensional measures of therapist behavior as predictors of outcome. *Psychological Bulletin, 92,* 670–681.

Schaeffer, N. (1983). Methodological issues of measuring the skillfulness of therapeutic techniques. *Psychotherapy: Theory, Research and Practice, 20,* 486–493.

Schafer, R. (1948). *The clinical application of psychological tests.* New York: International Universities Press.

Schafer, R. (1958). On the psychoanalytic study of retest results. *Journal of Projective Techniques, 22,* 102–109.

Scher, M. (1975). Verbal activity, sex, counselor experience, and success in counseling. *Journal of Counseling Psychology, 22,* 97–101.

Schlesinger, H., Mumford, E., & Glass, G. (1980). Mental health services and medical utilization. In G. VandenBos (Ed.), *Psychotherapy: From practice to research to policy.* Beverly Hills, CA: Sage.

Schonfield, J., Stone, A., Hoehn-Saric, R., Imber, S., & Pande, S. (1969). Patient–therapist convergence and measures of improvement in short-term psychotherapy. *Psychotherapy: Theory, Research and Practice, 6,* 267–271.

Schramski, T. G., Beutler, L. E., Lauver, P. J., & Shanfield, S. B. (1984). Factors that contribute to post-therapy persistence of therapeutic change. *Journal of Clinical Psychology, 40,* 78–85.

Schroeder, P. (1960). Client acceptance of responsibility and difficulty of therapy. *Journal of Consulting Psychology, 24,* 467–471.

Seeman, J. (1954). Counselor judgments of therapeutic process and outcome. In C. Rogers & R. F. Dymond (Eds.), *Psychotherapy and personality change* (pp. 99–108). Chicago: University of Chicago Press.

Seeman, J. (1962). Psychotherapy and perceptual behavior. *Journal of Clinical Psychology, 18,* 34–37.

Seitz, P. F. D. (1966). The consensus problem in psychoanalytic research. In L. Gottschalk & A. Auerbach (Eds.), *Methods of research in psychotherapy* (pp. 209–225). New York: Appleton-Century-Crofts.

Seligman, M. E. P. (1975). *Helplessness: On depression, development and death.* San Francisco: Freeman.

Shader, R., Grinspoon, L., Harmatz, J., & Ewalt, J. (1971). The therapist variable. *American Journal of Psychiatry, 127,* 1009–1012.

Sheehan, J. G. (1953). Rorschach changes during psychotherapy in relation to the personality of the therapist [Abstract]. *American Psychologist, 8,* 434–435.

Sheehan, J. G., Frederick, C., Rosevear, W., & Spiegelman, M. (1954). A validity study of the Rorschach Prognostic Rating Scale. *Journal of Projective Techniques, 18,* 233–239.

Shlien, J., Mosak, H., & Dreikurs, R. (1962). Effect of time limits: A comparison of two psychotherapies. *Journal of Counseling Psychology, 9,* 31–34.

Siegel, N., & Fink, M. (1962). Motivation for psychotherapy. *Comprehensive Psychiatry, 3,* 170–173.

Siegel, S. M. (1951). Personality factors in psychotherapeutic improvement as identified by the Rorschach test [Abstract]. *American Psychologist, 6,* 341–342.

Sifneos, P. (1972). *Short-term psychotherapy and emotional crisis.* Cambridge, MA: Harvard University Press.

Silberschatz, G., Fretter, P., & Curtis, J. (1986). How do interpretations influence the process of psychotherapy? *Journal of Consulting and Clinical Psychology, 54,* 646–652.

Simons, A. D., Lustman, P. J., Wetzel, R. D., & Murphy, G. E. (1985). Predicting response to cognitive therapy of depression: The role of learned resourcefulness. *Cognitive Therapy and Research, 9,* 79–89.

Singer, B., & Luborsky, L. (1977). Countertransference: The status of clinical vs. quantitative research. In A. Gurman & A. Razin (Eds.), *The therapist's handbook for effective psychotherapy: An empirical assessment* (pp. 431–448). New York: Pergamon Press.

Sloane, R. B., Staples, F. R., Cristol, A. H., Yorkston, N. J., & Whipple, K. (1975). *Psychotherapy versus behavior therapy.* Cambridge, MA: Harvard University Press.

Smith, M. L., & Glass, G. V. (1977). Meta-analysis of psychotherapy outcome studies. *American Psychologist, 32,* 752–760.

Smith, M. L., Glass, G. V., & Miller, T. I. (1980). *The benefits of psychotherapy.* Baltimore: Johns Hopkins University Press.

Snyder, W. (1947). The present status of psychotherapeutic counseling. *Psychological Bulletin, 44,* 297–386.

Spence, D. (1966). *The Spence-Rubin Double Profile Procedure.* Unpublished manuscript.

Spitzer, R., & Endicott, J. (1975). Assessment of outcome by independent clinical evaluators. In I. Waskow & M. Parloff (Eds.), *Psychotherapy change measures* (DHEW Publication No. 74-120, pp. 222–232). Washington, DC: U.S. Government Printing Office.

Spitzer, R., Endicott, J., Fleiss, J., & Cohen, J. (1970). The Psychiatric status schedule. *Archives of General Psychiatry, 23,* 41–55.

Standal, S. W., & van der Veen, F. (1957). Length of therapy in relation to counselor estimates of personal integration and other case variables. *Journal of Consulting Psychology, 21,* 1–9.

Staples, F. R., & Sloane, R. B. (1976). Truax-factors, speech characteristics and therapeutic outcome. *Journal of Nervous and Mental Disease, 163,* 135–170.

Staples, F. R., Sloane, R. B., Whipple, K., Cristol, A. H., & Yorkston, N. (1976). Process and outcome in psychotherapy and behavior therapy. *Journal of Consulting and Clinical Psychology, 44,* 340–350.

Stein, K. B., & Beall, L. (1971). Externalizing-internalizing symptoms and psycho-therapeutic outcome. *Psychotherapy: Theory, Research and Practice, 8,* 269–272.

Stephens, J. H., & Astrup, C. (1963). Prognosis in "process" and "non-process" schizophrenia. *American Journal of Psychiatry, 119,* 945–953.

Stephens, J. H., & Astrup, C. (1965). Treatment outcome in "process" and "non-process" schizophrenics treated by "A" and "B" types of therapists. *Journal of Nervous and Mental Disease, 140,* 449–456.

Stoler, N. (1963). Client likability: A variable in the study of psychotherapy. *Journal of Consulting Psychology, 27,* 175–178.

Stoler, N. (1966). The relationship of patient-likability and the A-B psychiatric resident types. Doctoral dissertation, University of Michigan.

Stone, A., Frank, J. D., Nash E., & Imber, F. (1961). An intensive five-year follow-up study of treated psychiatric outpatients. *Journal of Nervous and Mental Disease, 133,* 410–422.

Stone, L. 1961. *The psychoanalytic situation.* New York: International Universities Press.

Strupp, H. (1964). *Fox-Strupp rating scales.* Unpublished manuscript.

Strupp, H. (1973a). On the basic ingredients of psychotherapy. *Journal of Consulting Clinical Psychology, 4,* 1–8.

Strupp, H. (1973b). Toward a reformulation of the psychotherapeutic influence. *International Journal of Psychiatry, 11,* 364–465.

Strupp, H. H., & Bergin, A. E. (1969). Some empirical and conceptual bases for coordinated research in psychotherapy: A critical review of issues, trends, and evidence. *International Journal of Psychiatry, 7,* 18–90.

Strupp, H. H., & Binder, J. L. (1984). *Psychotherapy in a new key: A guide to time-limited dynamic psychotherapy.* New York: Basic Books.

Strupp, H., Chassan, J. B., & Ewing, J. A. (1966). Toward the longitudinal study of the psychotherapeutic process. In L. Gottschalk & A. Auerbach (Eds.), *Methods of research in psychotherapy* (pp. 361–400). New York: Appleton-Century-Crofts.

Strupp, H. H., Fox, R. E., & Lessler, K. (1969). *Patients view their psychotherapy.* Baltimore: Johns Hopkins University Press.

Strupp, H. H., & Hadley, S. W. (1979). Specific versus non-specific factors in psychotherapy: A controlled study of outcome. *Archives of General Psychiatry, 36,* 1125–1136.

Strupp, H., Hadley, S., & Gomes-Schwartz, B. (1977). *Psychotherapy for better or worse.* New York: Jason Aronson.

Strupp, H., Moras, K., Sandell, J., Waterhouse, G., O'Malley, S., Keithly, L., & Gomes-Schwartz, B. (1981). *Vanderbilt Negative Indicators Scale: An instrument for identification of deterrents to progress in time-limited dynamic psychotherapy.* Unpublished manuscript, Vanderbilt University, Nashville, TN.

Strupp, H., & Wallach, M. (1964). Dimensions of psychotherapists' activity. *Journal of Consulting Psychology, 28,* 120–125.

Strupp, H. H., Wallach, M. S., & Wogan, M. (1964). Psychotherapy experience in retrospect: Questionnaire survey of former patients and their therapists. *Psychological Monographs, 78* (11, Whole No. 588).

Strupp, H. H., Wallach, M. S., Wogan, M., & Jenkins, J. W. (1963). Psychotherapists' assessments of former patients. *Journal of Nervous and Mental Disease, 137,* 222–230.

Sullivan, P. L., Miller, C., & Smelser, W. (1958). Factors in length of stay and progress in psychotherapy. *Journal of Consulting Psychology, 22,* 1–9.

Sundberg, N. (1964). A method for studying sensitivity to implied meanings. *American Psychologist 19,* 475.

Sundland, D., & Barker, E. (1962). The orientations of psychotherapists. *Journal of Consulting Psychology, 26,* 201–212.

Symonds, P. M. (1931). *Diagnosing personality and conduct.* New York: Appleton-Century.

Taylor, J. W. (1956). Relationship of success and length in psychotherapy. *Journal of Consulting Psychology, 20,* 332.

Teller, V., & Dahl, H. (1981). The framework for a model of psychoanalytic inference. *Proceedings of the Seventh International Joint Conference on Artificial Intelligence 1,* 394–400.

Tollinton, H. J. (1973). Initial expectations and outcome. *British Journal of Medical Psychology, 46,* 251.

Tolman, R. S., & Mayer, M. M. (1957). Who returns to the clinic for more therapy? *Mental Hygiene, 41,* 497–506.

Tomkins, S. (1979). Script theory: Differential magnification of affects. In H. Howe, Jr. & R. Dienstbier (Eds.), *Nebraska Symposium on Motivation* (Vol. 26, pp. 201–236). Lincoln: University of Nebraska Press.

Tomlinson, J. (1967). Situational and personality correlates of predictive accuracy. *Journal of Consulting Psychology, 31,* 19–22.

Tomlinson, T. M., & Hart, J. T. (1962). A validation of the process scale. *Journal of Consulting Psychology, 26,* 74–78.

Tougas, R. R. (1954). Ethnocentrism as a limiting factor in verbal therapy. In C. Rogers & R. Dymond (Eds.), *Psychotherapy and personality change* (pp. 194–214). Chicago: University of Chicago Press.

Truax, C. B. (1963). Effective ingredients in psychotherapy: An approach to unraveling the patient–therapist interaction. *Journal of Counseling Psychology, 10,* 256–263.

Truax, C. B. (1970a). Therapist's evaluative statements and patient outcome in psychotherapy. *Journal of Clinical Psychology, 26,* 536–538.

Truax, C. B. (1970b). Length of therapist response, accurate empathy and patient improvement. *Journal of Clinical Psychology, 26,* 539–541.

Truax, C. B., Fine, H., Moravec, J., & Millis, W. (1968). Effects of therapist persuasive potency in individual psychotherapy. *Journal of Clinical Psychology, 24,* 359–362.

Truax, C. B., Wargo, D. G., Frank, J. D., Imber, S. D., Battle, C. C., Hoehn-Saric, R., Nash, E., & Stone, A. (1966). Therapist empathy, genuineness, and warmth and patient therapeutic outcome. *Journal of Consulting Psychology, 30,* 395–401.

Truax, C. B., & Wittmer, J. (1971). Patient non-personal reference during psychotherapy and therapeutic outcome. *Journal of Clinical Psychology, 27,* 300–302.

Uhlenhuth, E., & Duncan, D. (1968). Subjective change in psychoneurotic outpatients with medical student therapists: 2. Some determinants of change. *Archives of General Psychiatry, 18,* 532–540.

Vaillant, G. (1964). Prospective prediction of schizophrenic remission. *Archives of General Psychiatry, 11,* 509–518.

VandenBos, G., & Karon, B. (1971). Pathogenesis: A new therapist personality dimension related to therapeutic effectiveness. *Journal of Personality Assessment, 35,* 252–260.

Vanderhoof, E., & Clancy, J. (1964). Physiological correlate of therapeutic change. *Archives of General Psychiatry, 11,* 145–150.

Van der Veen, F. (1967). Basic elements in the process of psychotherapy: A research study. *Journal of Consulting Psychology, 31,* 295–303.

Van der Veen, F., & Stoler, N. (1965). Therapist judgments, interview behavior and case outcome. *Psychotherapy: Theory, Research and Practice, 2,* 158–163.

Van Slambrouck, S. (1972). Relation of structural parameters to treatment outcome. Doctoral dissertation, Wayne State University, Detroit (Diss. 73-12613).

Wadden, T., Luborsky, L., Greer, S., & Crits-Christoph, P. (1984). The behavioral treatment of essential hypertension: An update and comparison with pharmacological treatment. *Clinical Psychology Review, 4,* 403–429.

Walker, A., Rablen, R. A., & Rogers, C. R. (1960). Development of a scale to measure process change in psychotherapy. *Journal of Clinical Psychology, 16,* 79–85.

Wallerstein, R. (1986). *Forty-two lives in treatment: A study of psychoanalysis and psychotherapy.* New York: Guilford.

Wallerstein, R., Robbins, L., Sargent, H., & Luborsky, L. (1956). The psychotherapy research project of the Menninger Foundation: Rationale, method, and sample use. *Bulletin of the Menninger Clinic, 20,* 221–280.

Warren, N. C., & Rice, L. N. (1972). Structuring and stabilizing psychotherapy for low-prognosis clients. *Journal of Consulting and Clinical Psychology, 39,* 173–181.

Waskow, I., & Parloff, M. (Eds.). (1975). *Psychotherapy change measures* (DHEW Publication No. 74-120). Washington, DC: U.S. Government Printing Office.

Wechsler, D. (1955). *Manual for Wechsler Adult Intelligence Scale.* New York: Psychological Corp.

Weiss, D. S., DeWitt, K. N., Kaltreider, N. B., & Horowitz, M. J. (1985). Proposed method for measuring change beyond symptoms. *Archives of General Psychiatry, 42,* 703–708.

Weiss, H., & Sampson, H. (1986). *The psychoanalytic process.* New York: Guilford Press.

Weissman, M. M., Prusoff, B. A., & Klerman, G. L. (1978). Personality and prediction of long-term outcome of depression. *American Journal of Psychiatry, 135,* 797–800.

Weitz, L., Abramawitz, S., Steger, J., Calabria, F., Conable, M., & Yorus, G. (1975). Number of sessions and client-judged outcome: The more the better? *Psychotherapy: Theory, Research and Practice, 12,* 337–340.

Welkowitz, J., Cohen, J., & Ortmeyer, D. (1967). Value system similarity: Investigation of patient-therapist dyads. *Journal of Consulting Psychology, 31,* 48–55.

Whitehorn, J., & Betz, B. A. (1954). A study of psychotherapeutic relationships between physicians and schizophrenic patients. *American Journal of Psychiatry, 111,* 526.

Whiteley, J., & Blaine, G. (1967). Rorschach in relation to outcome in psychotherapy with college students. *Journal of Consulting Psychology, 31,* 595–599.

Williams, H. V., Lipman, R. S., Rickels, K., Covi, L., Uhlenhuth, E. H., & Nattsson, N. B. (1968). Replication of symptom distress factors in anxious neurotic outpatients. *Multivariate Behavior Research, 3,* 199–212.

Winer, B. (1971). *Statistical principles in experimental design.* New York: McGraw-Hill.

Wirt, R. D. (1955). Further validation of the ego-strength scale. *Journal of Consulting Psychology, 19,* 444.

Wirt, R. D. (1956). Actuarial prediction. *Journal of Consulting Psychology, 20,* 123–124.

Witkin, H. A. (1949). Perception of body position and of the position of the visual field. *Psychological Monographs, 63* (Whole No. 302).

Witkin, H. A. (1950). Individual differences in ease of perception of embedded figures. *Journal of Personality, 19,* 1–15.

Witkin, H. A., Dyk, R., Faterson, H., Goodenough, D., & Karp, S. (1962). *Psychological differentiation.* New York: John Wiley & Sons.

Witkin, H. A., Lewis, H. B., & Weil, E. (1968). Affective reactions and patient–therapist interactions among more differentiated and less differentiated patients early in therapy. *Journal of Nervous and Mental Disorders, 146,* 193–208.

Witkin, H., Moore, C., Goodenough, D., & Cox, P. (1977). Field-dependent and field-independent cognitive styles and their educational implications. *Review of Educational Research, 47,* 1–64.

Wogan, M. (1970). Effects of therapist-patient personality variables on therapeutic outcome. *Journal of Consulting and Clinical Psychology, 35,* 356–361.

Wolberg, L. (1967). *The technique of psychotherapy.* New York: Grune & Stratton.

Woody, G., Luborsky, L., McLellan, A. T., O'Brien, C., Beck, A. T., Blaine, J., Herman, I., & Hole, A. V. (1983). Psychotherapy for opiate addicts: Does it help? *Archives of General Psychiatry, 40,* 639–645.

Woody, G. E., McLellan, A. T., Luborsky, L., & O'Brien, C. P. (1985). Sociopathy and psychotherapy. *Archives of General Psychiatry, 42,* 1081–1086.

Woody, G. E., McLellan, A. T., Luborsky, L., O'Brien, C. P., Blaine, J., Fox, S., Herman, I., & Beck, A. T. (1984). Severity of psychiatric symptoms as a predictor of benefits from psychotherapy: The Veterans Administration-Penn study. *American Journal of Psychiatry, 141,* 1172–1177.

Yeaton, W., & Sechrest, L. (1981). Meaningful measures of effect. *Journal of Consulting and Clinical Psychology, 49,* 766–767.

Yoken, C., & Berman, J. S. (1984). Does paying a fee for psychotherapy alter the effectiveness of treatment? *Journal of Consulting and Clinical Psychology, 52,* 254–260.

Yoken, C., & Berman, J. (1987). Third-party payments and the outcome of psychotherapy. *Journal of Consulting and Clinical Psychology, 55,* 571–576.

Young, R. C., Gould, E., Glick, J. D., & Horgreaves, W. (1980). Personality inventory correlates of outcome in a follow-up study of psychiatric hospitalization. *Psychological Reports, 46,* 903–906.

Zax, M., & Klein, A. (1960). Measurement of personality and behavior changes following psychotherapy. *Psychological Bulletin, 57,* 435–448.

Zetzel, E. (1958). Therapeutic alliance in the analysis of hysteria. In E. Zetzel (Ed.), *The capacity for emotional growth* (pp. 182–196). London: Hogarth Press.

Zigler, E., & Phillips, L. (1961). Social competence and outcome in psychiatric disorders. *Journal of Abnormal and Social Psychology, 63,* 264–271.

Zirkle, G. A. (1961). Five minute psychotherapy. *American Journal of Psychiatry, 118,* 544–546.

Zivich, J. M. (1981). Alcoholic subtypes and treatment effectiveness. *Journal of Consulting and Clinical Psychology, 49,* 72.

Zolik, E. S., & Hollon, T. N. (1960). Factors characteristic of patients responsive to brief psychotherapy [Abstract]. *American Psychologist, 15,* 287.

Zuckerman, D. M., Prusoff, B. A., Weissman, M. M., & Padian, N. S. (1980). Personality as a predictor of psychotherapy and pharmacotherapy outcome for depressed outpatients. *Journal of Consulting and Clinical Psychology, 48,* 730–735.

INDEX